ABOUT ISLAND PRESS

Island Press, a nonprofit organization, publishes, markets, and distributes the most advanced thinking on the conservation of our natural resources—books about soil, land, water, forests, wildlife, and hazardous and toxic wastes. These books are practical tools used by public officials, business and industry leaders, natural resource managers, and concerned citizens working to solve both local and global resource problems.

Founded in 1978, Island Press reorganized in 1984 to meet the increasing demand for substantive books on all resource-related issues. Island Press publishes and distributes under its own imprint and offers these services to other nonprofit organizations.

Support for Island Press is provided by The Geraldine R. Dodge Foundation, The Energy Foundation, The Charles Engelhard Foundation, The Ford Foundation, Glen Eagles Foundation, The George Gund Foundation, William and Flora Hewlett Foundation, The James Irvine Foundation, The John D. and Catherine T. MacArthur Foundation, The Andrew W. Mellon Foundation, The Joyce Mertz-Gilmore Foundation, The New-Land Foundation, The Pew Charitable Trusts, The Rockefeller Brothers Fund, The Tides Foundation, and individual donors.

ABOUT THE LINCOLN INSTITUTE OF LAND POLICY

The Lincoln Institute of Land Policy is a nonprofit and tax-exempt school established in 1974. Its specialized mission is to study and teach land policy, including economics and land taxation. The institute is supported by the Lincoln Foundation, established in 1947 by John C. Lincoln, a Cleveland industrialist. Mr. Lincoln drew inspiration from the ideas of Henry George, the nineteenth-century American political economist and social philosopher.

Land is a primary resource, and decisions about its use involve many areas of public policy. Patterns of land use and property taxation affect employment, housing, infrastructure, and the environment. Policies governing these areas, in turn, influence land use. The Lincoln Institute seeks to understand choices for land use and development, related regulatory and tax policies, effects on the environment and natural resources, and systems of governance by which land and tax policies can be implemented.

Integrating the theory and practice of land policy—and understanding forces that influence it—are the major goals of the Lincoln Institute. The institute brings together experts with different points of view in settings where they can study, reflect, exchange insights, and work toward consensus in creating more complete and systematic land policies. Through its courses and conferences, publications, and research activities, the institute seeks to advance and disseminate knowledge of critical land policy issues. The institute's objective is to have an impact on land policy—to make a difference today and to help policymakers plan for tomorrow.

LAND
CONSERVATION
THROUGH
PUBLIC / PRIVATE
PARTNERSHIPS

LAND CONSERVATION THROUGH PUBLIC / PRIVATE PARTNERSHIPS

Edited by Eve Endicott

LINCOLN INSTITUTE OF LAND POLICY

Foreword by U.S. SENATOR JOHN H. CHAFEE

ISLAND PRESS

Washington, D.C. ❑ *Covelo, California*

Library of Congress Cataloging-in-Publication Data

Land conservation through public/private partnerships / edited by Eve
Endicott ; foreword by Senator John H. Chafee.
p.   cm.
Includes bibliographical references and index.
ISBN 1-55963-177-5.—ISBN 1-55963-176-7 (pbk.)
1. Land use—Government policy—United States.   2. Conservation
Operations Program.   3. Land Trusts—United States.
4. Corporations, Nonprofit—United States.   5. Conservation of
natural resources—United States—Societies, etc.   I. Endicott,
Eve.
HD205.L336   1993
33.73'16'0973—dc20   92-35638
                                                        CIP

Printed on recycled, acid-free paper

Manufactured in the United States of America

10 9 8 7 6 5 4 3 2 1

*We dedicate this book to our children and all children
in the hope that it will inspire land conservation efforts
from which they will benefit and which they will carry on.*

Contents

Foreword
U.S. Senator John H. Chafee   xiii

Introduction   3

Why Government Turns to Nonprofit Organizations   4
Why Nonprofit Organizations Need Government   6
Issues in Land Conservation Partnerships   7
The Future   10

PART I
THREE NATIONAL NONPROFIT PARTNERS
AND HOW THEY WORK
13

1. Preserving Natural Areas: The Nature Conservancy
   and Its Partners   17
     Eve Endicott

Reasons for Preacquisition   18
Beyond Preacquisition   27
Lessons from the Past   35
Promise for the Future   40

2. Preserving Farmland: The American Farmland Trust
   and Its Partners   43
     Edward Thompson, Jr.

American Farmland Trust: Cultivating Partnerships   44
Partnerships in Practice   46
Lessons for the Future   58

3. Preserving Urban and Suburban Gardens and Parks: The Trust
   for Public Land and Its Partners   61
     William Poole for The Trust for Public Land

Local Governments' Need for Private Partners   62
Local Land Trusts in Public/Private Partnerships   69

Model Projects   72
Lessons from the Past   77
Promise for the Future   79

PART II
FEDERAL AGENCY PARTNERSHIPS
83

4. Preserving Wildlife Habitat: The U.S. Fish and
   Wildlife Service and the North American Waterfowl
   Management Plan   85
       Angela Graziano
       with contributions from Tom Massengale and Jerry Updike

   Need for Partnerships   87
   Partnerships in Practice: Two Model Projects   93
   Lessons from the Past   100
   Promise for the Future   102

5. Public/Private Land Conservation Partnerships in and
   Around National Parks   104
       Warren Brown

   The Need for Partnerships   105
   Partnerships for Additions to National Parks   107
   Partnerships with Park Neighbors to Protect Adjacent Lands   114
   Partnerships in Park Management and Operations   118
   Parks and Regional Partnerships   119
   Lessons from the Past   121
   Promise for the Future   126

6. National Park Service Partnerships Beyond the National Parks   129
       Christopher N. Brown

   Federal Assistance to Local Partnerships   131
   Lessons from the Past   140
   Promise for the Future   142

PART III
STATE AND LOCAL PARTNERSHIPS
147

7. State Partnerships to Preserve Open Space: Lessons from
   Rhode Island and New York   149
       Robert L. Bendick, Jr.

Evolution of State/Private Partnerships   150
Partnerships in Practice   153
Lessons from the Past   163
Promise for the Future   167

8. A State Program to Preserve Land and Provide Housing:
   Vermont's Housing and Conservation Trust Fund   172
   Pamela M. Dennis

   Guiding Principles of Vermont's Funding Program   173
   Funding and Staff   174
   Partnerships in Pursuit of Multiple Goals   175
   Promoting Speed and Flexibility   179
   Providing and Seeking Leverage of All Types   181
   Sharing and Expanding Protected Ownership   184
   Building Partnership Organizations   185
   Lessons from the Past   188
   Promise for the Future   192

9. Local Partnerships with Government   195
   Eve Endicott and Contributors

   Overcoming the Limitations of Size   196
   Capitalizingg on Local Strengths   205
   Lessons from the Past   213
   Promise for the Future   216

PART IV
FINANCING PARTNERSHIPS
219

10. Financing Open Space and Landscape Protection: A Sampler
    of State and Local Techniques   223
    Phyllis Myers for The Trust for Public Land

    New Commitment by State and Local Governments . 223
    Role of Nonprofit Organizations   226
    Long-Term Bonds   227
    Short-Term Debt Instruments   232
    Lease Purchases and Certificates of Participation   233
    Securitized Installment Sales   236
    Pay-as-You-Go Approach   238
    Special Taxes   240
    Trust Funds   244

Special Districts   246
Utilities   249
Development Exactions and Mitigation Banks   252

11. Direct Funding of Nonprofit Land Protection: A New Genre
    of State Land Conservation Programs   258
    Phyllis Myers for the Land Trust Alliance

    An Overview of Formal Partnership Arrangements   260
    The Programs' Structures: Two Models Emerge   270
    Accomplishments and Benefits of Direct Grant Programs   281
    Issues and Solutions   293
    Advocating, Designing, and Implementing a Direct Grant Program   302

    Appendix A: State Funding for Land Protection as of November 1992   315
    Appendix B: Selected Private Assistance Organizations   329
    Glossary   331
    Selected Readings   339
    Acknowledgments   343
    Index   345
    About the Contributors   359

Foreword

Open, undeveloped land and the freedom and possibilities it represents has always been an important part of the American identity. This nation's pioneering conservationists recognized the importance of preserving open space and natural resources for present and future generations. With the rapid development of the western frontier in the 1800s, came the realization that important natural resources were at risk of being destroyed. This lead to the establishment, in 1872, of our first national park (Yellowstone) and, in 1903, of our first national wildlife refuge (Pelican Island). The federal government has since protected over 89 million acres in national wildlife refuges and 80 million acres in national parks located in every state of the nation.

This is a tremendous accomplishment, but it falls short of the current imperative to protect natural areas from the rush of development, especially in vulnerable coastal regions. Unfortunately, as our need to protect undeveloped areas has increased, budget shortfalls have limited the federal and, in many cases, state, and local governments' ability to respond.

But as this book demonstrates, federal, state, and local governments have found able partners in national nonprofit organizations, and in public and private land trusts, to assist in land protection and acquisition. This book is a comprehensive guide to the complex world of protecting open spaces. It not only catalogues and describes the growing number of actors and methods involved in open space conservation, but it also sets forth useful case studies on how best to structure a wide range of land protection efforts. This book is an invaluable reference for those involved in land protection efforts across the nation.

As remaining open areas are lost, we are learning that protecting small or isolated islands of habitat is not enough to provide for healthy populations of wildlife and fish or to preserve biological diversity. Land conservation and management also is playing an increasingly important role in protecting drinking water supplies, controlling water pollution such as urban runoff, and reducing the impact of floods. Because the protection of larger land blocks and watersheds, as well as buffer areas and "green" corridors between parks and protected areas grows more costly and complicated, the partnerships and the creative land acquisition methods that are explored in this book are not only desirable, but essential.

As this book illustrates, innovative ways to protect and conserve undeveloped land are being used with increasing frequency. In order to stretch scarce resources, the federal government is placing more emphasis on partnerships and joint ventures. For example, the North American Wetlands Conservation Act authorizes the federal government to provide matching funds for joint ventures to protect waterfowl habitat in the United States and Canada, along with states and nonprofit organizations on both sides of the border. The Act, as described in Chapter 4, has been a tremendous success—financing projects in just two years to restore or protect over 600,000 acres of wetlands—and it is considered a model for far-reaching partnership efforts to protect international resources. Most important, states, national nonprofit organizations, and local groups play a vital role in this effort, and they consistently have exceeded the Act's requirements for nonfederal contributions to match the federal share of costs for conservation projects.

Another important topic highlighted in this book is the influence of the tax code when private property owners are trying to decide whether to preserve and protect open spaces and natural resources on their lands. Our tax policy should encourage the preservation of resources important to the public health and environment. To do this, Congress should enact introduced legislation to reduce the federal tax burden of private property owners who dedicate their property for conservation purposes.

Private groups, such as those featured in part 1 of this book—The Trust for Public Land, the American Farmland Trust and The Nature Conservancy—play a vital role in federal acquisition efforts by evaluating properties, negotiating with private landowners, and acquiring lands before federal funds are available. In some cases, landowners can take advantage of the tax code's charitable deductions by working with private, nonprofit groups to conserve open spaces.

I have had a long and productive history of working with The Nature Conservancy on land acquisition projects. Most recently, by working together, we were able to obtain funds to purchase coastal lands for addition to the Block Island National Wildlife Refuge. In fact, The Nature

Conservancy has protected over 7,000 acres of land in my state of Rhode Island alone and is a national leader in efforts to preserve biological diversity.

State government is another important partner in any land acquisition effort. But after years of picking up where the federal government left off, states are also facing daunting budget problems. In spite of these difficulties, their records are impressive. Bob Bendick, who worked with me on numerous land acquisition projects while he was the director of Rhode Island's Department of Environmental Management, has written an excellent chapter for this book on state land acquisition efforts. As Bob explains, states can play a crucial role in planning and coordinating land acquisition efforts involving a large number of partners, in addition to providing grants or matching funds for direct acquisition.

A number of states use land transfer taxes or bond measures to support acquisition efforts. These actions demonstrate a remarkable level of support for state efforts to preserve open space. The character and quality of life in many local communities depend upon the preservation of undeveloped areas—for wildlife, water protection, recreation, or farmland. Once lost, these resources cannot be replaced.

The tremendous growth in the number of local and regional land trusts across the nation, highlighted in chapter 9 of this book, demonstrates the level of public support for land conservation efforts. Now numbering close to 1,000, land trusts represent the fastest growing segment of the conservation community. These groups may soon form the backbone of the land conservation movement as they benefit from and build upon other land conservation efforts.

Land trusts and other local organizations also can play an important role in educating the public about the value of land conservation. When the financial impact of preserving open space is considered, the economic benefits are often overlooked. Protecting open space in a community can improve its quality of life, raise the property value of land located near natural areas, and increase opportunities for recreation and tourism.

This book describes, in detail, the nuts and bolts of the various approaches to land protection as well as the importance of building political support for each local venture. Such support is important to help raise necessary funds and to garner crucial local support for a project.

A renewed effort to protect natural areas could not come at a better time. The world is losing species at a rate quicker than any time in history since the dinosaurs became extinct 65 million years ago. The primary cause of an accelerating loss of biological diversity is the loss, degradation, and fragmentation of habitat. Although discussion of this problem often focuses on the loss of rainforests, the problem is not limited to the tropics. The loss of forests and other habitat areas is an equally serious problem in North America.

Between 1977 and 1987, the United States lost 3.95 million acres of forest. In addition, despite recent progress in slowing the loss of wetlands through regulatory and federal farm policy changes, we continue to lose about 290,000 acres of wetlands per year. Considering this level of habitat destruction, it is hardly surprising that there are now over 700 species listed as endangered or threatened in the United States. We must intensify our efforts to preserve valuable open space areas and the resources they contain. As this book makes clear, all of us have important roles to play in this critical effort.

U.S. Senator John H. Chafee

LAND
CONSERVATION
THROUGH
PUBLIC / PRIVATE
PARTNERSHIPS

Introduction

Subtly, without a lot of fanfare, the face of land conservation has been changing over the past two decades. Well before the rhetoric of public/private partnerships became commonplace, government agencies began working with private conservation organizations to preserve land—from natural areas for wildlife preservation and public recreation to prime farmland and community gardens. At first, in the 1970s, such partnerships were the exception. Pioneering state and federal agencies, looking to preserve more land more efficiently, turned to a few entrepreneurial nonprofit organizations that in turn wanted to enhance their land-saving abilities by tapping into the greater funding capacity of government. In the 1980s, this modest, piecemeal cooperative effort exploded into a nationwide movement involving every major federal landowning agency, every state, hundreds of localities, and a significant number of the nearly 1,000 private land protection organizations currently operating in states and communities across the country. Now it is almost the exception if significant land acquisition is accomplished without a partner from the private sector and one from the public sector, if not more than one from each side.

This book is an attempt to provide a detailed, inside look at this partnership movement as recorded by the individuals, private organizations, and government agencies that made the land-saving projects of the movement happen. It is designed to demonstrate the broad array of circumstances under which the public and private sectors can achieve more and better land conservation together than either one can alone. The authors hope that after the tour through the scores of actual land conservation projects that this book describes, the reader—be he or she a public official, land trust staffer, volunteer, citizen conservationist, or anyone else with the will to make a difference—will be newly inspired and better equipped to tackle the preservation of the land he or she holds most dear.

By any measure, the record of accomplishment is extraordinary once

3

one begins collecting the disparate pieces. Consider just the following achievements of private organizations, states, and government agencies:

• Three national land conservation organizations alone—The Nature Conservancy, Ducks Unlimited, and the Trust for Public Land—have actively assisted government in preserving more than 4 million acres.

• In the past ten years, thirteen states have adopted land conservation funding programs that encourage the involvement of private organizations. Altogether, more than 400,000 acres have been saved under these programs, at significant cost savings attributable to the nonprofit involvement. In just one representative program, in Vermont, close to 40,000 acres have been saved and more than $125 million worth of affordable housing and land conservation achieved for less than $35 million in public grants, thanks in large part to the private donations of land and cash leveraged by nonprofit organizations.

• In the six federal fiscal years from 1985 through 1991, the National Park Service and the U.S. Fish and Wildlife Service together completed 273 land acquisitions that were assisted by nonprofit organizations. According to Department of Interior figures, the federal government—and thus the nation's taxpayers—saved $32.3 million on these transactions through cost savings passed on by the private partners. A U.S. General Accounting Office report issued September 11, 1981, documented savings for fiscal years 1965–1980 of $50,837,939 for the National Park Service, the U.S. Fish and Wildlife Service, and the USDA Forest Service as the result of involvement of nonprofit organizations in land acquisitions.

WHY GOVERNMENT TURNS TO NONPROFIT ORGANIZATIONS

Little by little, project by project, even the most skeptical government bureaucrats have been won over to working with the private sector on land protection deals. Federal and state agency officials, local officeholders, planners, state legislators, and other public servants cite the following advantages to working with the private sector:

• *Nonprofit organizations bring agility to projects.* The term "agility" encompasses a wide variety of specific abilities and strengths that the private sector typically brings to a land acquisition transaction, attributes that almost invariably spell cost savings. These attributes include speed, the ability to bring money to the table and close quickly on a threatened parcel that might otherwise be lost or made more costly by bureaucratic delays; flexibility, the private sector's freedom from often constraining laws and regulations that make it impossible for most government agencies to bid at auctions, for example, or pay for land in installments; and creativity, the willingness of nonprofit staff members to master and use the complexities of the tax code and novel financing arrangements to get the deal done.

• *Nonprofit organizations create an "atmosphere of possibility."* Declawed by not having the power to condemn land and untainted by any history of unsuccessful negotiating with a particular landowner, the nonprofit representative can often, in the words of one land conservation organization, "create an atmosphere of possibility" around a stalled or seemingly impossible project and make it work. Landowners often prefer working with the private sector, and the nonprofit conservation community is becoming sufficiently widespread to provide a network of personal contacts with many landowners. An important component in creating the "atmosphere of possibility" may also be privately raised funds—or privately negotiated donations of land or interests in land—which may close a seemingly unclosable funding gap. Donors, whether foundations, corporations, or individuals, are usually more comfortable making gifts to a nonprofit organization, even if the donation eventually supports a government project.

• *Nonprofit organizations provide people.* Sometimes what the nonprofit organization has to offer is as simple—and as necessary—as an extra pair of hands. Legislatures are often more generous in appropriating large sums for land acquisition than they are in providing the staff to spend those funds effectively and expeditiously or to take care of the land once it is bought. Nonprofit staff members can provide invaluable negotiating help and then enlist volunteer land stewards. Usually the private sector is also closer to the people and thus better able to drum up the public support for getting the funds for land protection passed in the first place. In one state, New Hampshire, a coalition of conservation organizations did both, launching a successful campaign for a $50 million state land acquisition program and, in the process, raising enough money privately for new staff members to make the program work. Once public land-financing programs are in place, they are more likely to be continued if cost savings generated by nonprofit organizations demonstrate to legislators—and taxpayers—that they are getting more for their money than they are in other lines of the budget.

WHY NONPROFIT ORGANIZATIONS NEED GOVERNMENT

Many private land conservation organizations—especially the nearly 1,000 state, regional, and local groups usually called "land trusts"—were originally formed precisely to provide an alternative or supplement to public landownership. Yet from large national nonprofit organizations to land trusts serving a single town, many of these organizations have added work with government to their more traditional role of soliciting private donations of land or money to buy land. The reasons mostly concern the size of the conservation challenge:

• *More expensive land.* Although bake sales, or at least cocktail parties, still play a role in land protection, more and more land acquisition is simply too expensive for private charitable donations to fund.

• *A new emphasis on landscape-scale preservation.* Over the past decade, the private land conservation community has matured and raised its sights. While not abandoning the preservation of small but significant parcels with which the movement started, many organizations from the national to the local level have determined that their overall goals would be better achieved if they looked at larger landscapes. The Nature Conservancy's Bioreserve Program to protect entire threatened ecosystems, the American Farmland Trust's work on sustainable agriculture, the Trust for Public Land's work on watershed protection, and local land trusts' efforts to link existing public lands all reflect a new emphasis on preserving functioning ecosystems. The "greenways" movement to protect linear open space for scenic or recreational corridors has grown exponentially in recent years. The sheer scale of such efforts, combined with the fact that they often span multiple political jurisdictions, makes close cooperation with government essential. Landscapes are inherently expensive, time-consuming, and complicated to protect. The greater resources of the taxpayer are required, and long-term ownership is often too burdensome for even the best-funded private organizations.

• *A public move from pragmatic to programmatic protection.* Early cooperative efforts between government agencies were typically ad hoc and often were born of emergencies. A key addition to a state park was for sale, the market was strong, the bureaucracy was slow: enter the Trust for

Saving Land to the rescue. The Department of State Conservation would eventually find the money somewhere to pay back the trust. It was effective, but were the best parcels being saved, and were Band-Aids being used where comprehensive surgery was needed?

In more recent years, as private conservation organizations have started to focus on the bigger picture, so too have their agency brethren. Often at the urging of the private sector, the partners have cooperated on fighting for funding for and then implementing comprehensive land protection programs, most of them at the state level, and these programs have brought the two parties together as never before. Typically, the public programs provide a pot of money and solicit applications under strict eligibility criteria. Thus encouraged to come up with the best possible projects—and freed of the burden of finding all the money themselves—nonprofit organizations have been able to accomplish more than they might ever have believed possible. For most of them, there is no going back: cooperation with government is no longer an occasional diversion from their usual agenda; it is a necessity if the most important tasks are to be done.

• *A renewed interest in planning.* Such cooperation now involves more than just straightforward land acquisition. If larger—or, in the case of greenways, longer—landscapes are the order of the day, preservation must use tools that include working with human as well as wildlife habitats. The local land trust, which once formed because of a frustration with the ultimate impotence of regulation to save land, is now an eager participant in the town's comprehensive plan. Often, only by getting the planning and zoning process on its side can the private conservation organization aspire to more than a few disconnected holdings surrounded by hostile land uses. Land conservation partnerships are broadening to include everyone from the local planning board to the Army Corps of Engineers.

ISSUES IN LAND CONSERVATION PARTNERSHIPS

Both public and private sectors agree that there is great strength in the diversity they bring to projects. What one partner lacks in resources, authority, or expertise the other can often provide. With diversity, however, come differences too. When identifying the biggest problems associated with partnerships, the authors of this book almost unanimously pointed to lack of a clear consensus and turf consciousness. Some agencies worry that the nonprofit sector may try to set land acquisition agendas for them.

Career park personnel may bridle at new programs that enable nonprofit organizations to obtain funding for land stewardship when the park agency's own budget is being slashed.

Nonprofit organizations also may feel that the partnership process sometimes slights their reasonable needs. For example, private organizations may chafe at government agencies' asking for their help but then not being willing to pay the legitimate costs associated with rendering that help. Private organizations also point to the difficulty of relying on government agencies when businesslike dealings with landowners and private funding sources may sometimes be sabotaged by the political process. Tensions may arise when one nonprofit organization works hard to raise funds to match a government grant only to discover than another nonprofit organization has not been required to provide a match at all.

Universally, nonprofit organizations and their government partners point to better communication and consensus building as the best cure to these problems. On a day-to-day level, this means lots of communication, which in turn usually leads to trust and goodwill. In most cases, it is also best to establish formal understandings. The latter can range from written agreements that set forth the roles of the different partners in a particular transaction to "organizational protocols" that apply to all partnerships with a particular agency. Such protocols are illustrated by regulations of federal agencies like the National Park Service governing transactions with nonprofit organizations or state rules like those promulgated by New York's Department of Conservation.

Private partnership roles have been formalized in states that have adopted official partnership programs such as those described in the final chapter of this book. Such programs, with their application guidelines and other rules, have done a lot to clear up the confusion and solve the conflicts sometimes resulting from "opportunistic" partnerships. In many instances, formalized land acquisition programs have also helped overcome interagency turf issues. A natural resource protection agency may find itself working directly and harmoniously with an agricultural preservation agency when it becomes clear that by working on large, combined projects the two stand a better chance of success in competing for statewide bond funding. This spirit of interagency cooperation, in turn, makes it easier for nonprofit organizations to be of assistance. There is nothing harder for an outside organization than to try to steer a project through bureaucratic turf wars.

Indeed, the new generation of funding programs for land protection has institutionalized the other key ingredient of success: a common vision. It is much easier for the public and private sectors to communicate clearly and arrive at consensus when they are working toward a shared goal. Public/private partnership programs such as the U.S. Fish and Wildlife Service's North American Waterfowl Management Plan at the federal level and California's State Coastal Conservancy at the state level have succeeded in good measure because they set forth a clear, inspirational conservation vision for all to rally around. The most effective partnerships take place when the government officials who run such programs can rise above politics to inspire the entire land conservation community and citizenry to work in support of an ambitious vision.

Just as the ability of one person—whether the governor, the director of the land protection agency, or, in some cases, the head of a cooperating nonprofit organization—to communicate enthusiasm and high expectations for a partnership program is of tremendous importance, so too are the attitudes of the players in the individual transactions key to the success or failure of those projects. Government bureaucrats must overcome suspicions of "outside meddlers" and keep an open mind about unfamiliar techniques. Staffers of nonprofit organizations, and the donors who support them, must appreciate the importance of spending as much time and attention on consensus building as on "doing deals" to highlight in the next newsletter.

Yet important differences between the two sectors must also be maintained if both are to contribute complementary strengths to a program or transaction. A certain amount of bureaucratic uniformity is a necessary protection from a program made impossible to administer by unlimited variations in legal documents, funding arrangements, or management practices. Much of what the nonprofit sector has to contribute would be lost, too, if the rigor born of years of stretching to save as much land as possible for the least amount of money were lost in a flaccid reliance on too-easy government funding, be it for land purchases or day-to-day operations.

In the end, it is the personalities of the individuals involved in a partnership that make the difference. If the participants believe in doing everything possible to make a project work, it will work, and minor resentments about who got more press and who paid the interest costs will not get in the way. Ideally, there should be a good balance of temperaments and working styles. A charismatic government official who is impatient with details should be matched with a nonprofit staffer who is willing to slog away offstage. Too many generals spell disaster for partnerships: just one who can rally the troops is needed; after that, only foot soldiers need apply.

THE FUTURE

This book is intended to function as a carpenter's manual, listing and describing the use of the many tools for building and maintaining public/private partnerships. At the time of this writing, in many regions of the country real-life carpenters are out of work because the building boom is over—for the moment, at least—and the corresponding boom in government programs to protect special lands has slackened, too. Still, there is work for land conservation carpenters to do everywhere, whether it be honing their skills to prepare for the next boom, cultivating landowners whom they have not had time to get to know, or making the best use of the old programs that still exist and the new ones that are coming along despite harder times. Consider the following indications of continued vitality in the land conservation movement:

- Florida's record-setting 1990 $3 billion, ten-year land conservation bond was given a boost in 1991 with an increase in the documentary stamp tax that covers the debt service.
- Nevada voters approved a 1990 parks and wildlife bond act for $47.2 million.
- Arizona citizens voted in 1990 to dedicate $20 million in lottery proceeds each year to protect parks, wildlife and natural areas, and endangered species.
- Washington State appropriated $60 million in 1991 for a Washington Wildlife and Recreation Coalition to protect critical lands.
- Alabama voters in 1992 adopted a 30-year, approximately $200 million land acquisition and stewardship program called Alabama Forever Wild Land Trust. The revenue source is an existing oil and gas fund. Neighboring Georgia passed a $20 million bond for natural areas and wildlife habitat.
- A citizen initiative in 1992 in Colorado recaptured lottery proceeds originally destined for parks, open space, and wildlife, but siphoned off for other purposes. The new law will require that up to $35 million a year by 1998 of lottery monies go to the original intended purpose.
- In 1992, the Nebraska Environmental Trust Fund was established using a percentage of state lottery proceeds and creating a public/private partnership to complement existing protection efforts for the state's natural environment.

- The Virginia Park and Recreational Facilities Bond Act of 1992 is a $95 million general obligation bond for the acquisition of parks and natural areas.
- New Jersey's Green Acres, Clean Water, Farmland, and Historic Preservation Bond Act of 1992 designates $200 million for open space acquisition, $20 million of which is for matching grants for nonprofit organizations.

There is no question, however, that the 1990s will be different from the "bond and spend" 1980s and that the combination of greater economic concern and emphasis on protecting larger landscapes will require new sensitivities, new skills, and, perhaps most important of all, new education and consensus building in the communities where land preservation takes place. As one of the leading practitioners of partnerships, New York State's Bob Bendick, has urged in his contribution to this book, landowners and land users—from farmers and ranchers to timber companies and hunting and fishing enthusiasts—must be brought in more as partners in their own right. All involved must realize that land conservation works best when economic interests and ecological values are mutually supportive—and that both public and private sectors must work hard to ensure that this happens.

Finally, the federal government must again become fully active in promoting land conservation partnerships. Congress would do well to look at the success of state programs and the accomplishments of the U.S. Fish and Wildlife Service's North American Waterfowl Management Plan and the National Fish and Wildlife Foundation. If so much private land protection leverage can be achieved with the resources of some state and local governments and a few innovative federal programs, imagine how much more could be done if a revitalized Land and Water Conservation Fund challenged *every* state, every locality, and all the federal agencies to work creatively with the private sector.

☙

PART I

Three National Nonprofit Partners and How They Work

The nonprofit organizations that have pioneered work with government on land conservation are primarily national entities. The first one to get into the business of regularly teaming up with government to buy land was The Nature Conservancy (TNC), which embarked on a formal "government cooperative program" in the early 1970s.

Chapter 1 discusses the evolution of this Nature Conservancy program and gives an overview of why government so often needs the helping hand of a nonprofit organization to accomplish its land conservation agenda. Chapter 1 details the ways in which a nonprofit organization can lend the public sector the speed often needed to compete effectively in the marketplace, whether by optioning property or by preacquiring it through advancing funds. The chapter goes on to describe the flexibility that may be necessary to make a real estate deal work, whether it be the ability to bid at auctions, to sell off unneeded portions of property, or to pay in installments. Government agencies are typically barred by law or regulation from such "creative" activities, for reasons that may make sense on a broad scale but that can often stymie an individual deal.

Similarly, chapter 1 discusses tax-advantaged sales through bargain sales, tax-deferred exchanges, or sales under threat of condemnation that allow nonprofit organizations to work more effectively with private landowners in many instances. The chapter also illustrates how The Nature Conservancy, as an outside party with an abundance of innovative techniques at its disposal, can broker conservation solutions to seemingly intractable land disputes involving government agencies. Finally, chapter 1 shows how TNC's work with government, like that of many other land trusts, has evolved from emergency assistance to larger, preplanned assemblages and work on some of the most important ecosystem protection projects in the nation.

In chapter 2, Ed Thompson of the American Farmland Trust (AFT) describes the need for a private intermediary in government efforts to preserve farmland. Not only are farmers perhaps constitutionally more suspicious of government than other people, but also in most farmland preservation programs the whole point is to keep the landowner on the land. This circumstance makes it more imperative than in other land preservation situations that a necessarily broad, evenhanded public program be tailored to the individual circumstances of the farmer. As the chapter's case studies from Massachusetts, Maryland, and Nevada illustrate, AFT has become a skillful tailor, stitching together the needs of the landowner with those of multiple government agencies and other nonprofit organizations into an ultimately seamless creation. The chapter's final case study, from Illinois, describes AFT's efforts to go beyond preserving individual farms and to make farming as a whole more economically viable as well as ecologically sound. AFT's pilot sustainable agriculture program in Illinois illustrates how a nonprofit organization often can be more innovative and take more risks than government, testing and proving an approach that can then be disseminated by government on an appropriately larger scale.

The nonprofit organization profiled in chapter 3, the Trust for Public Land (TPL), was actually inspired by The Nature Conservancy's early government cooperative program. Unlike The Nature Conservancy, TPL carries out cooperative projects *only*; it does not own or manage land of its own. Although the reach of TPL's program is very broad—ranging from helping the National Park Service preserve historic buildings to assisting the USDA Forest Service in preserving forestland—chapter 3 focuses on TPL's land-saving activities in urban and suburban areas.

Many of the skills and abilities that TPL has honed are similar to those described in the chapter on The Nature Conservancy: the tools of flexibility; speed; knowledge of the tax code and of the public funding process, including innovative sources such as mitigation funding; and lots of experience in working with private landowners. Chapter 3 demonstrates how these skills can be put to work for government in urban and suburban communities anxious to set aside parkland or to preserve a bit of their cultural heritage. TPL has pioneered work with inner-city preservationists—many of them community gardeners—and added to its battery of skills those of community planning, organizing, and training. Chapter 3 provides myriad examples of TPL the enabler figuring out creative ways to make a deal work, and the chapter ends with an admonition to the nonprofit sector as a whole never to stop searching for better ways to help government and landowners get the conservation job done.

1

Preserving Natural Areas:
The Nature Conservancy
and Its Partners

Eve Endicott

The Nature Conservancy (TNC) is an international nonprofit organization dedicated to the preservation of the plants, animals, and natural communities that represent the diversity of life on earth by protecting the lands and water that they need to survive. Even though The Nature Conservancy has been given or has purchased many tracts of land on its own behalf and owns the largest system of nature preserves in the world—more than 1,300 as of 1992—its ambitious mission requires partners at all levels of government as well as in the private sector.

At one time or another, The Nature Conservancy has found itself in partnership with almost every federal landholding entity, including the Department of Defense; with all the states; and with hundreds of town and county governments and special districts across the country. (International government partnerships are beyond the scope of this book, but The Nature Conservancy is forging many.)

Of the 6.3 million acres in the United States protected by The Nature Conservancy in its four-decade history as a land-saving organization, roughly 3 million acres, representing more than 3,000 transactions, have been preserved in cooperation with government agencies—federal, state, and local. This gives The Nature Conservancy an unequaled breadth of experience in implementing land conservation partnerships.

How did this partnership business begin? Having started out in the

1950s as a "traditional" land preservation organization that busied itself with soliciting gifts of land and occasionally raising private funds to purchase choice parcels, in the early 1970s TNC found itself being called on more and more to add a third land-saving technique to its repertoire: assisting government agencies in purchasing land.

REASONS FOR PREACQUISITION

Most of The Nature Conservancy's early partnership projects with government—and a substantial number of its current projects as well—involve what is generically called preacquisition. The need for a private group to preacquire land for government agencies—that is, to buy land in advance of a government agency's ability to purchase it and then to resell it to that agency—arises for a number of reasons. Generally, those reasons fall within the categories of speed and flexibility.

SPEED

Desirable conservation land often comes on the market unexpectedly and, more often than not, might be sold before a government agency has the time to go through a typically lengthy review and purchasing process. Usually, a government agency has to put appraisals and sometimes survey work out to bid, meaning that months may pass before it can even make the landowner an offer. This process often makes sense from the standpoint of fairness and financial control. It works well in the many instances in which a government agency is working to buy a parcel of land that has not been—and often will not be—put on the open market. It is not well adapted, however, to the "emergency" situations that The Nature Conservancy has become experienced at handling.

The Nature Conservancy can obtain an appraisal from an appraiser on the government agency's approved list, sometimes within a matter of days. If necessary, it can often acquire the money to do this and other crucial preacquisition work from private sources. This kind of seed money is critical to TNC's work, enabling it to compete effectively in "hot" real estate markets or for particularly desirable parcels.

Advance Funding

In 1986, TNC preserved almost three times as much land as it did in 1985. Much of the increase reflected the impending hike in the federal capital gains tax. As landowners hurried to close by year's end, many government agencies realized that they could not act quickly enough and sought TNC's assistance. In several instances, TNC prepurchased property for government on as little as a few days' notice, using the revolving loan fund the organization had raised from private donors over the past four decades. Since the landowners would have increased their price to the government when the higher tax rate went into effect—and since TNC sells land to government agencies at its own cost—TNC's fast action saved state and federal taxpayers millions of dollars. The frequency with which TNC is asked to close deals on behalf of government in the December holidays has made many a TNC staffer wish that the Internal Revenue Service would change its tax year.

The Nature Conservancy can also act quickly to advance funds in instances in which government money to buy a particular piece of land is committed but not immediately available, as when bonds have been authorized but not yet sold or when a particular annual source of funding has not yet come through. Acting in these instances as "the First National Bank of Conservation," TNC, like any other bank, makes sure that the government agency is a good risk or that funds advanced—which are in effect a loan—are otherwise secured.

The sheer demand for financing from The Nature Conservancy in these situations holds a lesson for private funding sources, other land trusts, and government agencies setting up or evaluating land protection programs. As discussed in chapter 9, smaller land trusts are beginning to build revolving funds, and some government agencies are making low-cost loan funds available to nonprofit organizations.

Options

Of course, large or expensive parcels may require large revolving funds, which few small land trusts can aspire to have. It should be noted, however, that it is often enough for a private group to put a property "under option" rather than actually prepurchasing it or even entering into a purchase and sale contract that is binding on both buyer and seller. Options can buy critical time cheaply. An option is simply the landowner's agreement to give a conservation group the exclusive right to buy the property for x dollars paid over y period of time, typically six months to a year. The price to buy the option, known as the option consideration, is usually nominal but can vary from $10 to $10,000 or more. Since the option money is normally nonrefundable by the landowner if the conservation group fails to exercise the option (that is, to go ahead with the deal by the agreed deadline), it is good to keep the amount paid for an option as low as possible.

This option device often gives the government agency the time it needs to complete its paperwork and reviews or to obtain the money it needs. Then the private group can either exercise the option and resell the land to the public agency or assign the option to the public agency for closing. When the latter is done, the private group never actually has to put up the money or take ownership of the parcel. One small land trust that has used the assignment technique to good effect in government partnerships is Florida's Alachua Conservation Trust, discussed in chapter 9.

What would induce a landowner to give such an option? Why would he or she not just wait to see whether the government agency will or will not buy—and meanwhile keep the land on the market? The fact is that land-owners often would rather see their land preserved than developed and are willing to give conservation efforts time to work, especially if tax or other advantages are also involved. If the competing market is development, moreover, the landowner is probably being offered a purchase and sale contract with many time-consuming contingencies such as subdivision approval and financing. At the same time, the landowner wants to know that the conservationists are serious, that an agreeable price can be negoti-ated, and that the timing of such a purchase is not completely open-ended. In such circumstances, the option can be extremely helpful. A good example of this is the preservation of the historic Melrose estate in Natchez, Mississippi, by the National Park Service and the Trust for Public Land, discussed in chapter 5.

FLEXIBILITY

Other traditional reasons for preacquisition have to do with the flexibility of nonprofit organizations and the often paralyzing regulatory constraints on government. For example, many key tracts come up for sale at auction and may be most cheaply bought there, but government agencies generally are prohibited from bidding at auction. TNC is often asked to bid on the government's behalf, as in the following case.

Auctions: Florida's Enchanted Forest

The Enchanted Forest is a 235-acre remnant of old-growth oak woodland near Cape Canaveral, Florida, that harbors many rare birds and mammals.

Local environmentalists had tried for years to protect the property, slated to become an industrial park, but no one could pay the $10 million price.

By 1988, the developer/owners were in financial trouble. Still, they kept their price at $10 million. Brevard County, which wanted to preserve the land, really had no options: It could not pay the $10 million, more than the property appeared to be worth, but if it did nothing, the property was likely to be sold at auction to another developer.

Fortunately, The Nature Conservancy had established a good working relationship with the county, having helped it earlier to pass a bond issue to purchase environmentally sensitive lands. When the developers did default on their mortgage, TNC was able to step in and buy the property at auction, literally on the courthouse steps, for only $100 more than the mortgage, or $3.9 million. Not only did this use of a private intermediary reduce the purchase price to the county by more than half, but it also gave the county time to apply to the state for matching funds, further reducing its cost.

Installment Sales: Pennsylvania's Poconos Wetlands

Another limitation on government that often hampers its ability to purchase land is the typical legal prohibition on a public agency's giving a landowner a promissory note or mortgage and paying the landowner over time. Some landowners want to receive installment payments for tax or other reasons. The Nature Conservancy or another nonprofit organization can purchase the land, convey it to the government, deposit the government's repayment in the bank, and then make the payments on a note over whatever period of time the landowner wishes.

Conversely, a state or local agency may be interested in purchasing a large parcel of land but may not be able to accumulate all the money at once. The landowner, meanwhile, may insist on a lump-sum payment. If the eventual source for the government's repayment is secure, TNC may be able to use its loan funds to purchase the land in advance and then convey it to the agency in undivided fractional interests as the agency's installment payments are made.

Recently in Pennsylvania, The Nature Conservancy worked with a local land trust, the Wildlands Conservancy, to purchase a 3,835-acre pristine glacial bog as part of TNC's Poconos Wetlands preservation initiative. The Pennsylvania Game Commission was eager to own the property but needed to spread the project over two years to capture enough federal matching funds. Thanks in part to a loan guarantee from Ducks Unlimited, a national nonprofit organization specializing in waterfowl protection, The Nature Conservancy was able to advance the money for the acquisition. TNC then conveyed the land to the government agency in two separate installments as government funds became available. When government funds fell $50,000 short of the needed purchase price, TNC joined with the Wildlands Conservancy to raise the shortfall.

Dealing with Surplus Land

Because of statutory hurdles, one thing almost all government agencies have great difficulty doing is selling land once they own it. This is, of course, as it should be, for no one would advocate that land bought for a public purpose such as conservation be sold to the private sector without the strongest of reasons. Many states require a vote of the legislature before land bought for conservation can be sold.

Ironically, this otherwise most desirable of constraints may hamper public conservation efforts. Often, government agencies are unable to purchase desirable land from an owner of a large parcel that includes land not appropriate for conservation. Typically, the owner will not be willing to subdivide the parcel; it's all or nothing.

In the right circumstances, a nonprofit organization such as The Nature Conservancy can purchase the entire tract and then resell the unneeded or "surplus" parts, conveying to the public agency only the land it wants. Often, the land resold is important for agriculture, housing, economic development, or the like, and the local community would oppose its removal from such use and from the local tax rolls. Hence, TNC may be forestalling or solving a political problem as well.

LANDOWNERS' REASONS

Another set of reasons why private groups such as TNC have often ended up mediating government purchases centers on the needs and preferences of the landowner. The landowner, after all, must be happy, or the land will not be saved.

Preference for Dealing with the Private Sector

Many landowners simply prefer to deal with the private sector. It is often hard to differentiate between the people you pay your taxes to or the agency official who has just served you with a wetlands violation order and a new government representative who wants to help you protect your land.

Moreover, the landowner is unlikely to know anyone in the government agency personally, at least if it is a state or federal agency, whereas he or she may well know someone from the private organization's board or network of volunteer contacts. That is why it is critical for land trusts to include community leaders and representatives of the business community.

With volunteer structures and local staff in all fifty states, The Nature Conservancy can almost always find someone whom a landowner knows and trusts. And when the landowner has a good experience with a particular organization, he or she is more likely to be receptive to a later approach for another tract of land in another location, particularly if the attractiveness of the deal depends on tax advantages or good publicity that has benefited the landowner in the prior transaction.

As TNC has built a track record all over the country, it has turned that reputation to conservation's advantage with owners whose landholdings are far-flung, especially large corporations. Such corporate partnerships led to the donation by the Union Camp Corporation of 16,000 acres of the Okefenokee Swamp in Georgia in 1978; to the gift by the Prudential Insurance Company of North America of 118,000 acres along the Alligator River in North Carolina, worth $50 million, in 1984 (the largest known corporate conservation gift in history); and to the donation by General Motors of 4,000 acres at Bayou Cocodrie along the Mississippi delta in Louisiana in 1990. All of these lands are now owned by government. Many of TNC's corporate relationships have spawned multiple deals over the years.

The nationwide effects of good contacts are not confined to corporations. A good relationship with communications magnate Ted Turner led to his placing conservation easements on sensitive natural areas adjoining Yellowstone National Park, in the Red Hills Plantation area of northeastern Florida, and in the highly significant waterfowl habitat of South Carolina's ACE basin, a project described in detail in chapter 4. Overall, good relationships with landowners have helped The Nature Conservancy steer more than $120 million in outright gifts of land to the U.S. Department of the Interior's land acquisition program alone over the past two decades.

Tax Advantages

One of the most significant contributions The Nature Conservancy has brought to its government partners over time is tax expertise and the flexibility to engage in the acrobatics sometimes required to use the federal tax code's provisions to best advantage. In general, TNC can work with landowners either to save taxes or to defer taxes on a sale of land. In both cases, TNC makes it more attractive to sell the land at the lowest possible price—a savings it then passes on to the public.

Saving Taxes. Tax expertise has been of the greatest help in bridging the frequent gap between a government agency's appraisal or available funding and a landowner's sense of the property's worth. When the landowner's independent appraisal demonstrates a gap between the land's value and its selling price to The Nature Conservancy or to the government, the land-owner can claim a charitable deduction. That deduction can often, when combined with the other financial benefits of no brokerage fee and an all-cash sale, make up the difference between the landowner's expectations and the funds available. Sales to a charity for less than fair market value when the difference in value is claimed as a gift are called bargain sales; these make up a majority of The Nature Conservancy's purchases.

Bargain sales have proved particularly useful in the context of the "new generation" of state funding programs, many of which channel grants to local communities, and sometimes to nonprofit organizations, but which typically require a matching component of anywhere from 20 to 50 percent of the property's fair market value. (These programs are discussed in more detail later in this chapter and in chapter 11.) Often, such programs will treat the landowner's gift of value through a bargain sale as the match, enabling cash-poor communities or land trusts to undertake land-saving deals that they otherwise could not afford. The Vermont program described in chapters 8 and 11 has achieved more than $125 million worth of housing and conservation projects with only $35 million in state money. Much of the remaining value is represented by bargain sales negotiated by nonprofit organizations ranging from The Nature Conservancy to small land trusts. In theory, at least, a government agency can conduct a bargain sale on its own, since the charitable deduction is also available for sales to government agencies. The theory breaks down, however, because government agencies are typically re-quired to offer the landowner full fair market value but often cannot do so because they lack sufficient funds or do not have the required match. Also, there are situations in which a government appraisal is clearly too low and the landowner wishes to use a private intermediary to help seek a bargain-sale deduction.

Deferring Taxes. Techniques that help landowners postpone or defer taxes can often be as valuable financially as more immediate tax savings as well as being of interest to a potentially greater number of landowners. The most often used techniques for tax deferral are the tax-deferred exchange and the sale under threat of condemnation.

In a tax-deferred exchange, provided for under section 1031 of the Tax Code, the landowner "swaps" property held for a particular purpose (most often investment) for another piece of property, which he or she must use for the same purpose. (There can be no swapping of investment property for a second home.) The tax advantage is that the capital gain tax the landowner would have paid had he or she sold the first property is deferred until sale of the "swap" property (in the same way that an individual can reinvest the proceeds of a sale of his or her primary residence tax free).

Exchanges are always worth exploring for landowners who are hesitant to sell because of a large potential tax liability. This is usually the case when the owner has had the land for a long time, a situation that is especially problematic now that capital appreciation is taxed at the same rate as ordinary income. If the purchase of land is for a government agency, a nonprofit intermediary is required to perform the exchange, since government agencies have the same problems in swapping land that they often do in buying and selling surplus property.

At The Nature Conservancy's Limerock Preserve in Rhode Island—a lovely woodland oasis near Providence that boasts, thanks to its limestone outcroppings, more rare plants than any other place in the state—the owner of the last parcel necessary to complete the preserve was reluctant to join the three other landowners who had made bargain sales for conservation. She feared, rightly, that with her very low tax basis, or cost, in the property, which had been bought in the 1940s, much of her gain would be eaten up by taxes. She preferred to leave the property to her children to sell, giving them the benefit of the so-called stepped-up basis. (The children would pay taxes only on the difference between their selling price and the property's value at their mother's death.) TNC did not want to wait and thus jeopardize available state matching funds, which might not be available again.

The solution was to buy for the child with the fewest assets, in this case a son in Kansas, property that he wanted. TNC bought farmland in Kansas and swapped it with the mother for the Rhode Island natural area; now the son is leasing the farmland from his mother and will inherit it at her death. If the son later decides to sell, his gain will be determined by the value of the farmland in his mother's estate. As a result, the large capital gain in the

Rhode Island property will escape federal taxation, assuming that the mother's estate is below the estate tax threshold.

Landowners can also defer taxes through a sale under threat of condemnation, sanctioned by section 1033 of the Internal Revenue Code. In such cases, if a government agency is willing to take a parcel by eminent domain (also known as condemnation) and the landowner is willing to go along with such a taking, the landowner can reinvest the proceeds from the taking without first paying capital gains tax, just as he or she could if the taking were adversarial. Often, however, landowners and government agencies are reluctant to set the "taking" machinery in motion for fear that a friendly taking may turn out not to be so friendly after all or that the landowner may not be able to wait out the slow government process. If the government agency has the will and the wherewithal to go through with a taking, it can simply write a letter to that effect. Then the landowner can use a nonprofit organization as an intermediary buyer, taking advantage of all the reasons for dealing with the private sector enumerated earlier as well as receiving the advantage of tax deferral. The Nature Conservancy has facilitated several sales of important lands to state and federal agencies using this technique.

CONFLICT RESOLUTION: STILLWATER NATIONAL WILDLIFE REFUGE, NEVADA

Not all partnerships are born in harmony. Sometimes good land conservation efforts come out of conflict among government agencies, a local community, business interests, and conservationists. Look closely at any of these successfully resolved conflicts and you are likely to find a private organization that brokered the consensus. This is the case in an ongoing project in Nevada.

Where there is scarcity, there is usually conflict, and nowhere is this more true than in parts of our country where water is scarce. Nevada is not generally known for its wetlands. Yet the Stillwater National Wildlife Refuge, only 60 miles east of Reno, is a key stepping-stone for waterfowl and shorebirds on the Pacific flyway, ranking as one of only thirteen designated western hemispheric shorebird reserves.

Despite the fact that much of the area was owned by the U.S. Fish and Wildlife Service, the Stillwater wetlands were not really protected. They were threatened by a combination of drought, increased water diversions for agriculture, and litigation designed to preserve water flows within the ecologically and culturally significant Truckee River and Pyramid Lake ecosystems to the west. The Stillwater wetlands had shrunk from historical levels approaching 50,000 acres to fewer than 5,000 acres. There seemed to be no way for the federal government to increase water flows to Stillwater without running headlong into opposition from farmers or Indian tribes and without threatening another significant ecosystem.

Then, at the request of the manager of the local U.S. Fish and Wildlife Service refuge, The Nature Conservancy entered the decades-old fray. The Nature Conservancy came up with a new proposal: if total demand for water were reduced, both ecosystems could be protected. Specifically, TNC determined that the most effective way to reduce water demand was to purchase and retire marginal farmland within the area, then transport the resulting surplus water directly to the Stillwater wetlands.

Funds for the buyout are coming from the federal government and from a 1990 Nevada state parks and wildlife bond issue that The Nature Conservancy helped to get passed. To date, TNC has purchased more than $1.7 million worth of land and water rights from willing sellers for resale to the U.S. Fish and Wildlife Service and the Nevada Department of Wildlife at TNC's cost. Other partners in this project to achieve and maintain a delicate balance among all the water users in the area range from the Environmental Defense Fund to local farmers. Although Stillwater is still threatened by drought, all partners are cautiously optimistic at this point.

BEYOND PREACQUISITION

NEW REASONS FOR PARTNERSHIP

So far, most of the reasons described for government to work with The Nature Conservancy or other private partners have been technical requirements calling for an intermediary, not necessarily a partner, even though wonderful partnerships have often grown out of these projects. Historically, TNC used many of these "government cooperative" techniques for parcels that did not necessarily meet the organization's criteria for its own ownership. Meanwhile, TNC focused most of its private fund-raising efforts on buying parcels that met its stringent criteria for biological significance and retaining them under TNC stewardship.

In the past decade, however, much fuller partnerships have developed in which TNC and government agencies have joined to participate in projects of mutual conservation interest. In part, this is a reflection of the spread and growing maturity of the state Natural Heritage Programs—the computerized inventories and mapping of rare species habitat and unique natural areas that The Nature Conservancy has pioneered in all fifty states.

As these programs have, in almost all cases, become part of state government, that part of a state's land acquisition agenda that focuses on natural areas has come more to reflect the best available information on the state's most endangered ecosystems. This has resulted in much more investment by The Nature Conservancy in advancing individual states' priorities, from fund-raising to land stewardship.

Another component of this new era in partnerships for TNC and other land trusts is the new economic environment of the past decade. As the nation's most significant natural areas have become too costly to purchase with private donations alone, The Nature Conservancy has had to seek out government partners. At the same time, government too has often faced the need for supplemental funding, brought on partly by widespread increases in land prices and partly by the substantial reduction in federal funds allocated to land conservation (see chapter 10). Thus, what neither partner can now do alone both are endeavoring to do together. Although the increase in land prices has slowed and will presumably continue to fluctuate, it appears that few significant land conservation projects will be affordable in the future without government funding assistance.

Bold Fund-raising Partnerships across the Country

The need for public and private organizations to work together on shared priorities and to supplement each other's funds became so common in the mid- and late 1980s that certain TNC state programs took the initiative to seek legislation formalizing the partnership into an ongoing program. From Connecticut to Indiana, Iowa to Minnesota, Virginia to Wisconsin, The Nature Conservancy undertook to raise private dollars to match government expenditures on natural lands. Some of the earlier programs— which were necessarily relatively small because of the high ratio of private matching funds promised—have led to more ambitious public funding programs. Table 2 in chapter 11 affords a comprehensive look at state funding programs for acquisition of natural areas; what follows are descriptions of a few in which The Nature Conservancy played a particularly significant role.

In Indiana, the remnant prairies are remnant indeed (less than one-tenth of 1 percent of the original prairie still exists), but that does not stop the 33-acre Biesecker Tallgrass Prairie Preserve near Gary from sheltering rare plant and insect species that are critically endangered in the state. Because the land needed for the preserve was expensive green space at the junction of two highways, the cost was within the reach of conservation only because of a generous bargain-sale price negotiated by The Nature Conservancy. The Biesecker Prairie project was one of more than 130 successful land-saving efforts of the Indiana Natural Heritage Protection Campaign, a state-legislated effort launched in 1984 in which TNC agreed to raise $5 million to match the state's $5 million. Not only has TNC exceeded its private fund-raising goal and negotiated 95 percent of the deals for the state, but it has also placed $2 million of the private monies raised into a stewardship fund jointly administered by the state and TNC. That fund will ensure that the state-owned Biesecker Prairie is managed to protect the rare natural community.

Wisconsin was another of the first states to enact a public/private funding program with Nature Conservancy backing. The state's Natural Areas Match Grant Program, passed in 1985, stipulated that donations of privately raised funds or qualified natural land to the state for conservation purposes (including, interestingly, donations of restrictions on private lands and donations of management services) would trigger a dollar-for-dollar match of state funds for buying natural areas. The state's match was on top of a base acquisition budget and was capped at a total of $500,000 per year. As of mid-1991, private donations had totaled nearly $3 million, of which more than 90 percent was attributable to TNC efforts. There is little question that the taste of success provided by the match grant program in protecting more than 3,700 acres helped inspire Wisconsin's even more ambitious Stewardship Fund Program, now under way. The goal of this $250 million, ten-year bond program is to preserve 300,000 acres of key natural areas in a state that has already lost 99 percent of its native prairie and oak savannas and 60 percent of its southern hardwood forests.

Virginia is another state in which TNC helped introduce legislation to spur public fund-raising with the incentive of a private match. The Partners in Conservation Program is almost complete, with TNC's local Virginia program having raised $500,000 to match the state's $1.5 million. The tremendous media interest in this innovative program has stimulated gifts from unusual sources, including $30,000 from a law firm to help safeguard Poor Mountain, a 1,000-acre preserve that shelters what is believed to be the world's largest population of the globally rare piratebush, the oil of which has shown promise for retarding cancer.

Perhaps the greatest lesson for private land trusts to come out of these fund-raising partnership efforts is the importance of raising money and negotiating gifts to release government funds. Creative use of bargain-sale matches and private land donations, along with modest fund-raising, can bring many conservation players into these programs, as is well illustrated by Vermont's experience, described in chapters 8 and 11.

PACKAGING

As government entities and private organizations such as The Nature Conservancy have embarked on more joint ventures stemming from new economic realities, the fact that the different partners have different stakes in the project and different interests and strengths has led to the necessity of creatively "packaging" individual projects. Different ownership and management arrangements are being forged on a case-by-case basis to optimize partners' individual contributions and desires. A third party such as The Nature Conservancy is almost always required in order to bring multiple public partners (or a combination of public and private partners) to a project in which broad participation is needed.

Splitting Ownership Interests: Hither Woods State Park, Long Island

On Long Island, a novel arrangement was worked out to split ownership interests in the same piece of land in order to draw on as many sources of funds as possible. The 5,000-acre Hither Woods State Park on Long Island's eastern end is one of the last wilderness areas left there. In 1986, when a crucial 556-acre shorefront addition came up for sale, the state of New York asked for TNC's help. Given funding demands elsewhere in the state, the maximum amount the state parks department could put into the Hither Woods addition was $6 million, or two-thirds of the overall $9 million cost of the highly developable land.

Fortunately, Suffolk County, perhaps the leading county in the nation in appropriating money for open space, was willing to put $1.5 million into the deal. With so much leverage to be had, the town of East Hampton voted overwhelmingly in favor of supplying the remaining $1.5 million. Since the land adjoined a state park, it made sense for the state to have the majority ownership interest and overall management responsibility, but both the county and the town wanted a legal interest, as well as a say in management, to show for their large investments. TNC solved the dilemma by purchasing the land outright and then parceling out a two-thirds undivided interest to the state and a one-sixth undivided interest each to the county and the town. The property is leased to the state in accordance with a management agreement involving all the parties, including TNC, which will monitor the rare species.

Many of the state funding programs of the 1980s encouraged land acquisition by towns as well as state agencies. Often, however, towns do not have the matching monies to qualify for the state grants, and just as often they need help in negotiating and packaging the deal. Nonprofit organizations can use all the tools of traditional preacquisition and private fund-raising to help towns qualify for state funding, becoming fuller partners with public entities than ever before. National or statewide nonprofit organizations can contribute their familiarity with a state's often complex rules and procedures gained in previous partnerships. This new level of partnership is well illustrated by a Nature Conservancy project in Maine.

Putting Together an Affordable Deal: Maine's Kennebunk Plains

In 1987, The Nature Conservancy spearheaded a coalition of business, outdoors, and environmental groups that was successful in sponsoring a $35 million bond issue approved by 67 percent of Maine's electorate. The program provided for grants administered by the statewide Land for Maine's Future board, allowing many towns across the state to realize ambitious preservation dreams that had previously been unattainable. Under the terms of the program, priority was given to projects offering leverage and matching potential for the state money.

The 1,040-acre Kennebunk Plains tract, a remarkably large, undeveloped sand plain and forest in the expensive summer resort communities of Kennebunk and Wells, had been appraised to be worth more than $3 million. The landowner, a commercial blueberry operation, was willing to sell the land below fair market value if it could capture corporate tax savings that were slated to expire at the end of 1988. By acting as an intermediary for the towns, The Nature Conservancy was able to obtain the lower price and secure the property by year's end, several months before the state's funds could be made available.

In addition, The Nature Conservancy, working with a local land trust, conservation commission, and water district, raised $373,000 in cash contributions to stretch further the Land for Maine's Future funding. To sweeten the deal still more, TNC donated coastal waterfront land worth $540,000 to the state to establish a new state wildlife management area.

As is not uncommon, not all of the Kennebunk Plains tract was desirable for the state program. Although much of the plains comprised significant habitat for rare grassland plants and ground-nesting birds such as the grasshopper sparrow, a state-listed endangered species, one portion of the plains that was surrounded by a new subdivision was more appropriate for development. Since the Land for Maine's Future legislation prohibited resale of acquired property, the state would not have been able to carve out this piece easily. Therefore, The Nature Conservancy helped complete the deal by purchasing this small section and later reselling it to an abuttor, thereby reducing the state's overall purchase price even further.

When the complex Kennebunk Plains transaction was completed, not only had the statewide program obtained two outstanding wildlife and recreational properties for approximately fifty-nine cents on the dollar but also Kennebunk Plains was being managed through a cooperative effort of the state, The Nature Conservancy, and the local water district.

Perhaps the most common example of nonprofit packaging stems from the need to split development rights from fee interest to preserve farms, as discussed in the next chapter on the work of the American Farmland Trust. In addition, two complex and creative examples of Nature Conservancy packaging efforts to preserve ecological and recreational values along with working farms and forests are described in detail in Bob Bendick's chapter on state-level partnerships, chapter 7.

PATCHWORKS

The packaging efforts just described begin to hint at a longer-term role for private organizations such as The Nature Conservancy, typically a continuing role in land management. That more permanent role for nonprofit organizations in partnership projects is growing.

Instead of simply reacting to emergencies and forging divisions of cost and protective interests for particular pieces of land on an ad hoc basis, public and private partners are now working in concert to identify whole priority areas and to plan in advance who is best positioned to take what role in protecting individual tracts within those larger areas. "Patchworks," or "mosaics," of interlocking public and private ownership with

coordinated management policies are being created, covering entire wetlands systems, river corridors, prairies, and other ecosystems.

Many of the model projects in which The Nature Conservancy has
been involved fit this pattern. As discussed later in this chapter in the
context of TNC's Bioreserve Program, it is the wave of the future for
ecosystem preservation, in which no one private organization or government agency alone can tackle the mammoth job of protecting entire
biological systems.

An Ownership Patchwork: Cape May, New Jersey

Cape May, at the southern tip of New Jersey, has long been recognized by
birders as one of the largest staging areas for migratory shorebirds in North
America. In autumn, it also hosts one of the hemisphere's highest concen-
trations of birds of prey. Yet until recently, only a few isolated, disconnected parcels of land had been permanently protected there. TNC has
helped to organize an effort to connect and expand existing parcels protected by TNC, the state, and the federal government. After intensive
lobbying by TNC and others, including the local New Jersey Conservation
Foundation and the New Jersey Audubon Society, Congress established the
Cape May National Wildlife Refuge. The refuge will eventually take in
15,000 acres, but key parcels of land will continue to be owned by the state
and by the private conservation partners who lobbied for the refuge.

All partners in this effort agree that there is greater strength in
preserving and even expanding the existing diversity of ownership. Such an
approach takes advantage of the broad range of expertise available through
the private groups as well as their help with funding and management. For
example, the New Jersey Conservation Foundation's local landowning presence enables it to conduct an educational program sensitizing beach visitors to the birds' needs, an effort that benefits all landholding partners.
Meanwhile, The Nature Conservancy is acquiring land in an area where
complicated ownership arrangements make government action difficult.

Such mosaics of long-term public and private ownership coexisting as
part of a coordinated protection scheme are on the increase. They are being
encouraged by state government funding programs such as those discussed
in chapter 11, which may allow private organizations to hold fee title to
land purchased with government funds. On a federal level, ownership
patchworks have been promoted by the North American Waterfowl Management Plan's "joint venture" concept; two good examples, the Cache

River in Illinois and the Ace basin in South Carolina, are profiled in chapter 4, which discusses that program.

Stewardship Patchworks

Patchwork projects often involve cooperative management as well as ownership. Increasingly, one finds the private sector handling some aspect of managing a publicly owned preserve or, more rarely, the reverse. These arrangements make sense for a variety of different reasons. In one case, the private agency may have more expertise in the particular biological management issues involved or more access to volunteers. In another instance, a government agency and a conservation organization might split the burdens of management with the public agency, handling the tasks it can perform better than volunteers could, such as trash pickup and maintenance of structures, while the private group handles nature walks, shorebird protection, or fund-raising for maintenance through a "friends of the preserve" group.

Over the years, TNC has pioneered many variations on joint stewardship arrangements and is now embarked on new initiatives to restore altered habitat of rare species on public lands. Not surprisingly, given California's overall commitment to conservation and its reputation for innovation in all fields, that state is the site of many of The Nature Conservancy's more ambitious and unusual stewardship efforts on public lands.

Private Management on Public Lands: California's Nipomo Dunes. As part of a national agreement between The Nature Conservancy and the U.S. Department of Defense (DOD) to identify, monitor, and manage significant habitat on military bases, DOD is providing funding for TNC to study the ecology of the Nipomo Dune system found partly on Vandenburg Air Force Base. The DOD land is part of a patchwork of ownerships in this coastal dune and wetland system stretching seventy-five miles along the central California coast, home to sea otters, least terns, and more than eighteen rare or endangered plant species. The Nature Conservancy has agreements with DOD, Santa Barbara County, Pacific Gas and Electric, and even the state's Off-Highway Motor Vehicle Recreation Division to manage their lands under a coordinated scheme to protect—ultimately— more than 200,000 acres of this fragile habitat. In the case of Santa Barbara County, TNC purchased 567 acres of the dunes with a grant from the California Coastal Commission, conveyed the property to the county, then leased the property back under a twenty-five-year management lease.

The lease gives TNC the right to conduct research, revegetate with native vegetation, engage in prescribed burning, and limit public access to sensitive areas to protect habitat—all activities the county has neither the funds nor the in-house expertise to carry out.

Partnerships with Landowners: Sacramento River, California. Meanwhile, in California's interior, TNC is working with government and private landowners in a three-way management partnership. In 1989, The Nature Conservancy and the U.S. Fish and Wildlife Service (USFWS) entered into a partnership to preserve the vanishing riparian forests along California's Sacramento River. The orchard owners in the area were happy to sell the flood-prone land along the river but often wanted to sell larger parcels, including productive orchards. For its part, USFWS did not want to get into the fruit-growing business. To bridge the impasse, TNC proposed entering into a long-term (up to twenty years) management agreement with USFWS to manage the properties once the government bought them. To date, TNC has helped USFWS buy more than 13,000 acres in fee title and conservation easements in more than twenty-five separate transactions. The Nature Conservancy has subleased the orchard land back to farmers and uses the rent to help cover restoration costs along the river corridor, where TNC is replanting trees, controlling weeds, and monitoring the reforestation's success.

The foregoing examples only begin to illustrate the vast array of projects relying for their strength on a patchwork of different ownership, funding, and management arrangements. This trend within The Nature Conservancy will continue in ever more elaborate and creative ways as part of the maturation of TNC's new Bioreserve Program, discussed in more detail later in this chapter. Other excellent case illustrations of large areas with multiple ownership and management combinations can be found in the discussion of the North American Waterfowl Management Plan in chapter 4.

LESSONS FROM THE PAST

In some cases, partnerships between TNC and government entities and other similar public/private conservation efforts have resembled shotgun marriages more than well-planned relationships. The government party has come to the union somewhat resentful that a private partner is needed to make the deal work "right," and staff members of nonprofit organizations have complained that their time, energy, and donors are wanted but not fully appreciated.

As partnerships between TNC and individual federal, state, and sometimes local governments have matured, these tensions have eased and mutual understanding and respect have grown. Local land trusts and government bodies new to the partnership game would do well to heed some of The Nature Conservancy's and its partners' hard-earned lessons.

COMMUNICATION AND CLARITY

Not surprisingly, constant communication has been the key to smoothing out any rough spots that have emerged in these partnership relationships. In some cases, communication has been simply between two individuals— the head of the local TNC office and the government agency contact—but it has always been frequent and full enough for the individuals to know each other's needs and desires. For example, on Long Island, Nature Conservancy staff members meet with county administrators monthly to discuss ongoing projects.

One goal of such communication, besides simply to share information and ensure coordination, is to communicate the individual needs of the partners. Government agencies have particular needs in the partnership process, especially the need to protect the interests of the taxpayer. This and other government needs are spelled out by Bob Bendick at the end of chapter 7.

Along with the need for communication comes the need for clarity. What was clearly communicated, say, eighteen months ago, when a partnership project was entered into, may not be so clearly remembered now. The need for written documentation of consensus is especially important in long-term projects, when nonprofit and agency staff members as well as elected officials may well change. Even on Long Island, where The Nature Conservancy had carried out many partnership deals with Suffolk County, a number of misunderstandings cropped up at the last minute because crucial details had not been worked out in advance, so hurried and harried were the parties. Now, The Nature Conservancy and the county lay out all the details of costs, division of responsibilities, and so forth in a form letter *before* the wheeling and dealing starts.

RELIABILITY

For nonprofit organizations, the need for reliability stands above all others. As often as not, public/private partnerships involve a public agency asking a private land trust to go out on a limb to secure a threatened parcel, work with a difficult landowner, or the like. The Nature Conservancy has frequently performed such services on the basis of a simple "letter of intent" in which the government agency asks for TNC's assistance and states that it intends to repay its costs. In the vast majority of cases, these commitments have been lived up to. In the few cases in which the government agency has failed to reimburse The Nature Conservancy, usually because of a change in administration, the costs have been very obvious. Usually, after long negotiations, TNC has eventually been repaid but almost always at the cost of forgone interest, making The Nature Conservancy's revolving fund fall further behind rising land costs.

In those few instances in which government commitments have not been lived up to but The Nature Conservancy has not yet actually advanced money—or has had private funding to back the loan—it is not always clear that the government agency understands the full cost of its change of heart. This is a very serious matter because the effectiveness of The Nature Conservancy and other publicly supported charities is only as good as their reputation.

It means a lot to a landowner if The Nature Conservancy can say that it has never been let down by a particular agency or that it has never failed to exercise an option in similar circumstances. Moreover, TNC has a limited priority list, and if it disappoints a landowner once, it is unlikely to be able to work with him or her again.

The Nature Conservancy also has a much more personal relationship with its funding sources than a government agency does with its taxpayers or bondholders. If a private foundation's money goes into a deal on the promise that it will be repaid or matched by a government source, it is a real loss of credibility for the land-saving organization and a threat to future funding from that source if the government fails to follow through. Private donors are limited. The importance of credibility and reliability are even more important for small land trusts because they are working with a much smaller and more finite group of donors and landowners.

PUBLICITY

Hand in hand with the need for reliability during the acquisition process goes the need for credit and publicity once the deal is consummated. The Nature Conservancy, like many land trusts, is a membership organization that depends for its existence on the dues of satisfied members. To be satisfied, members need to see impartial evidence of accomplishment by and respect for "their" organization, which translates into good press. Similarly, if The Nature Conservancy or another nonprofit organization has played a role in protecting a public area, it makes an enormous difference to that organization to have its role acknowledged on the entrance sign that the government agency erects.

Of course, there is a delicate balance to be struck here, because the political representatives who approve the government agency's budget also want their constituents to see what a good job government is doing for them. Generally, there is enough room for everyone to get credit, and nonprofit organizations should make a point of highlighting the government's role in press releases (even though this is no guarantee of what will actually be printed). In the exhaustion of closing a deal it is difficult, but vital, for staffers to remember that likely as not, their organization will be looking for help from the involved agency or legislator in the future.

Perhaps one of the most crucial times for communication in a project is when the partners are about to go public. And since it is frequently not the particular government agency involved that is handling publicity but rather the governor's press office or equivalent, it is important for the nonprofit organization to establish an understanding of its needs at that level too. As suggested in chapter 7, joint ceremonies that also recognize the landowner's role are an ideal way to give everyone credit.

PERMANENCE

Finally, government agencies need to understand the nonprofit organization's need to assure itself and its cooperating landowners of the permanence of the protection of the land and the sensitive resources on it. Public officials often seem to take the approach that if the government owns it, it is safe for all time. Private landowners, especially those who elect to work through a nonprofit organization like The Nature Conservancy, may have a very different perspective. Often, the landowner will cite at least one example of a natural area's becoming a dump or being proposed as an oil storage terminal.

Although government agencies cannot always keep land from being converted to a different use or condemned by another government agency, it is clearly in their interest to work with their partners to erect hurdles to make that fate unlikely. Such hurdles at their simplest are deed restrictions limiting the use of the particular tract of land to open space, a wildlife refuge, or whatever is the intended purpose. At the very least, these restrictions establish a clear, indelible record of the intent of the parties at the time the parcel was purchased. More states are now willing to accept restrictions in deeds; examples include Connecticut, Virginia, and Pennsylvania.

In at least twelve states, many of them in the Midwest, a more systematic approach has developed through the enactment of so-called dedication programs. These are statewide systems of nature preserves administered by one state agency, with the properties accepted for dedication by that agency being statutorily protected from condemnation or conversion to a different use. Thus, in Illinois, which pioneered the dedication concept in 1963, a well-established nature preserve system includes state lands, private lands, and lands owned by nonprofit organizations ranging from universities to The Nature Conservancy and other land trusts. All are subject to "articles of dedication" recorded with the county clerk that protect the areas from development even by government condemnation. Recently, a number of counties have also enacted dedication systems, notably Suffolk County on Long Island. In Maryland, a publicly chartered statewide land trust, the Maryland Environmental Trust, holds conservation easements over locally owned parkland to ensure its perpetual conservation.

This is far from an exhaustive cataloging of the needs of the nonprofit organization, but subsequent chapters highlight other needs, from the perspective of other organizations. Meanwhile, a word should be said about the needs of the landowner in a public/private venture, in which, after all, the key private player is the seller or donor of land.

THE LANDOWNER'S NEEDS

First and foremost, the landowner needs honesty about how the transaction is going to unfold and who will own and manage the land. Although some developers and corporate landowners may not be concerned about who buys the land from them or from the land trust, most landowners do care, especially if they are going to continue to own some of the land or live nearby.

In most projects, the reason for government involvement can be easily stated to and understood by the landowner. Thus, if the landowner has ruled out a gift of the land or conservation easement, it can be clearly explained that the only source of funds to pay his or her price derives from the government and necessarily involves government ownership. If this raises concerns in the landowner's mind, the possibility of placing restrictions on the property prior to transfer should be fully explored. Where appropriate, it may help to have someone from the government agency who is experienced in discussing management issues with landowners meet with the owner on the land, along with a representative of the private organization.

Of course, there is nothing like the testimony of a previous satisfied customer, particularly one who had doubts at the beginning, and the nonprofit organization should seek to enlist such people to serve on its board and to visit landowners. It should be said, however, that some landowners simply will never accept government ownership of their land. This is one reason why the pioneering state funding programs allowing nonprofit ownership, profiled in chapter 11, are so important as models.

Also important is that the landowner understand the role of the nonprofit organization. This is especially true if the nonprofit organization's costs are to be reimbursed when the property is sold to the government agency, making it appear that the nonprofit organization is making money on the transaction. The costs involved must be clearly spelled out to the landowner.

Finally, as discussed in chapter 7, the landowner needs recognition too. Often, in the blaze of publicity surrounding the organization's and agency's triumphs, the landowner who made it all possible is forgotten. Although a landowner may do as well, if not better, financially through a conservation sale than in a market sale, even such a well-paid landowner, and certainly the majority who do make donations, typically will feel good about the deal only if he or she shares in the limelight. There is a measure of self-interest in this advice, since those landowners will be the organization's best ambassadors during the next diplomatic overture to an unknown landowner.

PROMISE FOR THE FUTURE

In the spring of 1991, The Nature Conservancy announced a new effort to preserve approximately seventy-five of the outstanding ecosystems of the world, or "last great places." In the United States, such identified ecosystems or bioreserves range from 6,460-acre Block Island off the coast of Rhode Island to 500-square-mile Gray Ranch in New Mexico. They include entire river watersheds, deserts, forests, and islands. Often, bio-reserve areas involve human settlements as well as pristine natural re-sources. Bioreserve conservation recognizes that economic health ultimately depends on ecological health. This large-scale effort brings a new dimension to Nature Conservancy protection techniques, requiring strategies to promote peaceful coexistence between man and nature. These strategies go far beyond traditional land acquisition and range from pro-moting sustainable development on the fringes of the Condor Reserve in Ecuador to establishing higher standards for on-site septic systems in the Florida Keys, where the fragile coral reef ecosystem is threatened by pollution.

Preservation efforts for such large areas will be based on alliances with private landowners and government, especially local government, far be-yond the partnerships required for land acquisition. It is impossible, for example, simply to buy all the ecologically sensitive land in a place like Virginia's 70-mile-long eastern shore, the large mainland ecosystem of which TNC's previously protected chain of fourteen barrier islands forms a part. Yet what happens to that shore's coastal bays and wetlands directly influences the water quality and consequently the food sources of the 250 species of waterfowl, shorebirds, and raptors that depend on the habitat of the Virginia Coast Reserve's barrier islands. In order to preserve the mainland "buffer area," The Nature Conservancy is working with local governments and landowners on everything from zoning that promotes farming (and therefore low-intensity development) to ecological perfor-mance standards to ensure that farming practices do not pollute the fragile wetlands.

In the Balcones canyon lands of the Texas hill country, an oasis of hills and streams near Austin, The Nature Conservancy's bioreserve effort is helping to resolve a development/conservation deadlock that had caused repeated clashes over land use. There, TNC helped organize and then chaired a planning committee of government officials, environmentalists, developers, and other business groups to develop a multipurpose resource protection and use plan.

The backdrop for the Balcones canyon lands conservation plan is the habitat conservation plan required under the Endangered Species Act for the area's federally listed endangered species. Instead of requiring devel-opers to fight for their projects one at a time and face costly individual federal reviews and possible litigation, the final conservation plan identifies whole areas appropriate for development. At the same time, the plan calls for a preserve system of about 65,000 acres, including several entire watersheds and large expanses of the oak/juniper habitat required by the critically endangered golden-cheeked warbler and black-capped vireo. These species are much more likely to survive in large preserves rather than in the disconnected protected parcels that would have resulted from piecemeal negotiations with developers.

Meanwhile, an unusual public/private partnership has already brought the plan a giant step down the road. In late 1990, TNC purchased 10,000 acres of core Balcones canyon land endangered species habitat from the Resolution Trust Company, the government receiver for property from failed savings and loan institutions. Because of the endangered species issue and The Nature Conservancy's ability to come up with cash, TNC paid a bargain price for the land. Meanwhile, preservation of this substantial habitat will allow the Resolution Trust Company to sell other lands it holds for development of needed housing. Thus, the Balcones Canyon Bioreserve can serve as a model for natural diversity issues being addressed on an ecosystem-wide basis rather than parcel-by-parcel.

Confronting broad land use issues is mostly untried ground for The Nature Conservancy, yet in most of the "last great places," incremental land acquisition alone will not be enough. In the years to come, TNC will be learning and applying important lessons about how to work with government on everything from local subdivision regulations, state-mandated comprehensive plans, and federally required endangered species recovery plans to promotion of compatible development, all in an effort to help humankind and nature coexist.

2

Preserving Farmland:
The American Farmland Trust
and Its Partners

Edward Thompson, Jr.

Agricultural land conservation is different from preservation of habitat, scenery, or open space. To be sure, open space is as essential to the practice of agriculture as it is for free-roaming wildlife or the relief of urban congestion, and much of the pastoral landscape is a scenic reminder of our agrarian heritage. But farmland is more than pretty countryside: it is actively and intensively used to produce food for a constantly growing population.

For this reason, it is not enough to preserve isolated pockets of farmland. If protecting discrete areas of endangered species habitat, unique landmarks, or special open spaces is a matter of safeguarding the "crown jewels," protecting land for agriculture is a matter of saving the entire kingdom. Nor can farmland simply be locked up or left in its original state if it is to fulfill the central purpose of agricultural conservation. Farmland is a *working* landscape in which production of crops and livestock requires human manipulation of the environment, driven by the profit motive, which has been the foundation of the American cornucopia. Ideally, the environmental manipulations used to grow our food will have a minimal impact on the natural ecosystems that sustain life in an even larger way.

These conditions—the indispensability of protecting wide expanses of land, keeping it in private hands, and permitting its free use for profit, while promoting its responsible use for the health of the environment—

distinguish agricultural conservation from other types of land preservation. They make partnerships indispensable to any meaningful effort to save farmland—and they mandate that one of the partners must always be the farmer.

AMERICAN FARMLAND TRUST: CULTIVATING PARTNERSHIPS

The American Farmland Trust (AFT) was founded in 1980 on the premise that the private sector, and agricultural producers in particular, could and must play a central role in conserving food-producing resources. AFT's mission is to stop the loss of productive farmland and to promote farming practices that lead to a healthy environment. It conducts policy-directed research and advises public agencies and officials who wish to adopt or refine conservation legislation. The landmark conservation provisions of three recent national farm bills were to a significant extent inspired and championed by the organization, as has been much of the state farmland protection legislation of the past decade.

One of the most useful ways of promoting policy reform, AFT has found, is to demonstrate the results one wants out in the field. Thus, from the beginning the organization has had a land trust arm that works with farmers and other institutional partners to show how farms and ranches can be saved in the same way they are lost: one at a time. Over the course of a decade, AFT has protected nearly 40,000 acres of important agricultural land from development and soil erosion and has helped hundreds of producers to save the environment from the impacts of farming. It could not have done so without the many local land trusts and other private sector institutions whose partnership it has cultivated.

ROLE OF GOVERNMENT

The scope of the challenge facing our agricultural resources—the nation is losing more than a million acres of farmland every year—effectively rules out the possibility that private institutions can meet it alone. Government must be an active participant. First, where necessary, it should use its police powers, through the exercise of planning and zoning, to regulate subdivision and thus stabilize rural land use. Otherwise, agriculture can be debilitated or put out of business by conflicts with neighboring residents.

Without the assurance that agriculture will continue to be a practical use of the land, it is too risky for most farmers to commit their land permanently and exclusively to agricultural use, one of the ultimate goals of agricultural conservation.

Although private covenants, like those embodied in conservation easements, might theoretically provide stability, the process of negotiating with individual landowners is just too slow to be practical in the real world. Indeed, one reason why easement negotiation is so slow is landowners' reluctance to commit their land in the face of uncertainty about what their neighbors will do.

Second, government must use its taxing and spending powers to compensate farmers for giving up the right to develop their land for houses, shopping centers, and the like. As necessary as it is to stabilize land uses in the short term, zoning alone is not the answer because it can be changed with the next election. Only by permanently retiring the development rights to farmland can true conservation be achieved. Remuneration of landowners—whether in cash or tax reductions or by some other means— is a necessary inducement to this kind of land use restriction. The private conservation community in America recognizes this principle but quite simply lacks the resources to carry it out on the scale necessary to protect a critical mass of farmland.

ROLE OF PRIVATE PARTNERS

If government is an essential participant in agricultural conservation, action by the private sector is also necessary. It is axiomatic that in acquiring land, private organizations are quicker to act, freer to structure creative conservation transactions, and in general more flexible and aggressive than government agencies. With enough expertise and venture capital, they can simply reach more landowners and nail down more deals than virtually any bureaucracy. These qualities are perhaps even more important in agricultural conservation than in the preservation of habitat and scenery.

To preserve the wide rural landscapes necessary to support agriculture, more landowners must be approached with conservation offers than is necessary when a limited number of scenic tracts are the target. An acquisition program must cater to many landowners in many different circumstances and enable them to compete fairly for limited funding. But typically, a government agricultural conservation program offers only one choice—for example, the purchase of conservation easements, generally referred to in this context as development rights. Such an offer will be of no interest to a landowner who, for instance, is seeking to sell an entire farm. In situations like this, private land trusts can supply the missing piece of the puzzle, matching the single government preservation offering with the diverse needs and circumstances of many individual landowners.

More critical, too, in agricultural conservation is the greater ability of private conservation organizations to establish relationships of trust with landowners who have an antipathy to government. This attitude is prevalent among commercial farmers, who have to contend with a bewildering array of government regulations. Yet, unlike the acquisition of, say, parkland, in which the landowner sells out and has nothing more to do with the land, agricultural conservation dictates that a farmer remain on the land. As we shall see, the farmer is the one indispensable partner in any farmland conservation initiative. Land without a farmer cannot be considered farmland.

PARTNERSHIPS IN PRACTICE

The American Farmland Trust has helped hundreds of farmers acquire or hold onto fertile land that otherwise was destined for development. As often as not, it has done so in partnership with government agencies and other private organizations. The following examples of such cooperative projects illustrate how many of the tools used in these projects, some discussed in other chapters, can be applied to protect farmland and— tackling what many consider to be the ultimate rural environmental challenge—to encourage ecologically friendly agricultural practices.

PRESERVING NEW ENGLAND'S FARMLAND: MASSACHUSETTS'S PIONEER VALLEY

In western Massachusetts, the Connecticut River meanders across a broad floodplain through Springfield, Hatfield, Greenfield, Deerfield, Northfield, and many other towns whose names evoke the rich agricultural heritage of the Pioneer Valley. Although vegetable growing is now the predominant farming activity, the distinguishing characteristic of this rural landscape is the scores of long, narrow barns once used to cure the cigar wrapper tobacco that was for generations the region's economic mainstay. Today, however, the deep, fertile valley soil is sprouting another crop: housing developments. Unless the land is protected from suburban sprawl, farming will not survive long in one of New England's premier agricultural regions.

A partnership between private land trusts and the Massachusetts Department of Food and Agriculture has been working to preserve this irreplaceable land. In 1979, Massachusetts committed $50 million to the purchase of agricultural preservation restrictions (essentially the same thing as conservation easements) from farmers all over the state. The American Farmland Trust convinced the agriculture department that purchases should be concentrated in the Pioneer Valley, matching AFT's own commitment to targeting its resources in exceptional farming areas.

Massachusetts has a strong tradition of private land conservation. The nation's first land trust, The Trustees of Reservations, was founded there a century ago. Thus, it did not take much to convince the state agriculture department that a partnership with land trusts could enable it to save more Pioneer Valley farms than could the government acting alone. The department encouraged AFT and other land trusts to acquire conservation easements over key parcels of valley farmland for subsequent resale to the state.

Helping a Farmer Meet a Deadline: Northwestern Massachusetts

Feeling pressure caused by several years of bad weather and low crop prices, Paul Webster, one of the largest potato growers in Massachusetts, decided that his farming operation needed an infusion of cash.[1] His original plan was to sell a portion of his land to a developer, who wanted to build forty houses on it. The local Franklin Land Trust heard of the pending sale and proposed an alternative: by selling only 35 acres of woodland for a few residential lots and selling a conservation easement over his remaining 220 acres of prime soils, Webster could satisfy his financial needs without having to give up his best land. The farmer and the developer were both willing to proceed, but Webster's financial difficulty was pressing, and the state agriculture department would not have funds to purchase the easement until the following fiscal year. Franklin also lacked the financial resources to preacquire the Webster easement, so the state turned to AFT.

The partners negotiated a complex deal for sharing the financial responsibility and risks of the purchase: AFT would put up the $230,000 easement purchase price at closing, and the developer would buy the woodland. Franklin, together with the towns of Ashfield and Hawley, whose boundary split the Webster property, agreed to place in escrow the estimated carrying costs that AFT's revolving fund would incur pending the state's repurchase of the easement. The state agriculture department committed itself to acquiring the Webster easement from AFT as a top priority. Eight months later, the sale was completed, and the better part of the Webster farm was permanently protected.

The Webster transaction, completed in 1988, is only one of more than a dozen easements AFT has preacquired for the Massachusetts Department of Food and Agriculture. The vicissitudes of the appropriations process have often left the agency short of cash at a time when farmers needed or wanted to sell conservation easements. And timing is usually critical to commercial farmers, whose operations are subject to so much uncertainty: commodity prices, government regulation, consumer preferences, and, of course, the ever-changing weather. As Paul Webster's situation illustrates, if the opportunity to sell a conservation easement is not there when the farmer needs it, the land is likely to be developed.

Making Preacquisitions Work

The problem of "too little, too late" is not uncommon among the states that purchase conservation easements, or development rights, to preserve farmland. (At this writing, states that purchase development rights include the New England states and Pennsylvania, New Jersey, and Maryland. A number of counties in California, New York, North Carolina, and Washington also have farmland preservation, or PDR, Purchase of Development Rights programs. Therefore, most of these states have sought the active cooperation of nonprofit land trusts as partners in the acquisition of farmland easements. Although their familiarity with local communities puts land trusts in a good position to learn when farmers may want to sell, many are not well funded and have turned to larger organizations such as AFT to help finance preacquisition of easements. Thus, a three-way partnership is formed.

In such partnerships, it is important that the relationships among the parties be defined carefully and, if possible, formally. "Handshake" financial commitments should be avoided, especially between friendly nonprofit organizations. Misunderstandings can result if things do not turn out as anticipated, possibly poisoning any future cooperation. A written agreement between the private partners is critical when both are to assume some financial risk.

AFT makes it a practice, as in the case of Webster, to ask for some financial participation by its local land trust partners. When the financial risk is shared, the risk borne by any one organization is reduced. The importance that the local group attaches to preserving that specific parcel of land is also put to the test, and the local group is given more incentive to do all that is necessary to consummate the transaction, including using its influence to ensure that the state agency fulfills its repurchasing commitment.

It is equally important that there be a clear understanding between the private land trusts and the public agency involved. The land trusts must thoroughly understand the criteria and process the state agency uses to acquire easements: purchase priorities, appraisals, payment of carrying and transaction costs, timing, availability of funds, and who ultimately makes the decision to disburse the funds. Ideally, the land trust should obtain a written purchase commitment from an official who has the authority to make it, though a pledge is usually the best that can be obtained. In deciding whether this pledge is adequate to make the risk acceptable, much depends on the track record of the purchasing agency and the personal relationships between land trust principals and responsible officials. There should be continuous communication between land trusts and the state at all phases of the transaction to ensure that expectations are fulfilled.

Finally, each partner's precise interest in the property to be acquired must be made absolutely clear. In the Webster transaction, AFT and Franklin simply adopted the easement instrument normally used by the state. This instrument forbids residential and nonfarm commercial uses but permits the practice of agriculture without restriction. Such flexibility is critical to agricultural conservation transactions in which the farmer is an active partner.

A MULTIPLE-OBJECTIVE PROJECT: MARYLAND'S SUGARLOAF FARM

From the observation windows at the top of the Washington Monument on a clear day, one can see Sugarloaf Mountain, a natural landmark rising out of Maryland's Piedmont Plateau, 40 miles as the crow flies northwest of the nation's capital. One can now hike there, too, entirely on public land. From the Watergate office complex in Washington, DC, the trail follows the Potomac River valley along the federally held Chesapeake and Ohio Canal towpath to a state park at the confluence of the canal and the Monocacy River and thence via a wooded path to Sugarloaf, the centerpiece of a

3,000-acre recreation area owned by Stronghold, Inc., a private foundation. If ever a stretch of land perfectly captured the idea of a greenway—a linear corridor of open space for recreational and related uses—this is it.

The crucial link in this spectacular greenway, the wooded path to Sugarloaf, could not have been acquired, however, without preserving the adjacent farmland, part of a single tract of land put up for sale by an investment partnership for subdivision into more than twenty expensive residential lots. Instead, the farm was purchased by the American Farmland Trust in partnership with two farmers, two state agencies, two counties, and a private foundation.

Sugarloaf Farm's 340 acres were approximately one-third forestland, which became the greenway, and two-thirds open cropland, some of the best in the region, carefully maintained with soil-conserving agricultural practices. The farmers, Bill Kies, a former county extension agent, and his partner, prominent local dairyman Alan Twaits, had leased the farm from the investors for more than twenty years, never dreaming that they would be able to purchase it. In 1990, when they did buy it from AFT, land prices averaged $7,000 per acre in the area, which was zoned to keep land open for agriculture by permitting only one house for each 25 acres. Obviously, keeping land open is not the same as keeping it affordable to commercial farmers—a much greater challenge now being faced in agricultural areas near cities. But in this case, thanks to the conservation partnership's ability to structure a multiple-objective project, the cost of the land was brought within the range that income from commercial farming could support.

The impending sale of Sugarloaf Farm came to AFT's attention through a local civic organization, the Sugarloaf Citizens Association, a defender of the environment of scenic western Montgomery County and southern Frederick County. A visit to the property confirmed the conservation possibilities of its strategic location and agricultural qualities. With a preliminary expression of interest from its potential state and county partners, AFT negotiated a six-month purchase option from the investor/owners to buy time to put the deal together.

The project's blueprint called for AFT to exercise the option to purchase the land, paying $2.4 million for the whole farm, and simultaneously to resell the wooded portion of the property in fee to the state natural resources agency, to resell the farmland to the farmers at an affordable price—as an organization devoted to agriculture, this was AFT's paramount objective—and to recover the balance of its investment by selling the development rights for the farmland to the state agriculture agency.

The Maryland Department of Natural Resources readily agreed to participate. Like the Massachusetts Department of Food and Agriculture, it fully appreciated the advantages of partnerships, was accustomed to working with land trusts, and had broad discretion in doing so. The strategic importance of the farm itself was also abundantly clear to the agency, which had recently persuaded Maryland governor William Donald Schaefer to create the nation's first Greenways Commission to promote this exciting new concept in conservation. What more spectacular way to do so than to link a well-known natural landmark with the landmarks of the nation's capital?

Expanding the Partnership; Covering Contingencies

The state agriculture department was another story, however. Its farmland easement acquisition program had elaborate procedures designed to give every farmer a more or less even chance of selling development rights. This constrained the agency from making an up-front commitment to purchase an easement on any particular property. The best the agriculture department could do was provide AFT with an official letter detailing its procedures, the current status of applications, and the range of prices paid for farmland easements. Although this information helped AFT assess its chances, it did not eliminate the potential risks of the organization's not being able to sell or of the closing being delayed. To share this risk, AFT's board of directors insisted that another partner be engaged.

Although Montgomery County is largely suburban, it has a very ambitious farmland protection program. In 1980, the western third of the county, 90,000 acres, was designated as an agricultural reserve and zoned to allow only one house per 25 acres of open space. At the same time, a transfer of development rights (TDR) program was established to enable farmers to earn compensation from developers who, by paying for development rights, could build at slightly higher densities in the urban area of the county. By 1990, when Sugarloaf Farm came up for sale, Montgomery County had put almost 30,000 acres under easement through TDRs and a county-financed farmland easement purchase program.

Montgomery officials were convinced that development of Sugarloaf Farm, even at a 25-acre density (but on 5- to 10-acre lots across the Frederick County line), would be inimical not only to agriculture but also to the scenic character of "an essentially undisturbed 19th Century agrarian landscape," according to its document nominating the land to the

National Register of Historic Places. But the TDR program was geared toward preserving land at the 25-acre density; thus, the price at which TDRs could be sold usually did not approach the value of easements restricting land to lower density. Thus, the sale of TDRs would not enable AFT to recoup the balance of its option price if it restricted Sugarloaf Farm exclusively to agricultural use.

To accomplish this critical conservation transaction, county officials agreed to an innovative plan. They voted to tap county farmland preserva-tion funds to lend AFT the balance of the purchase price, interest free for two years, to bridge the gap between the purchase price of the farm and the anticipated sale price of development rights to the Maryland Department of Agriculture.

Even this was not enough for AFT's board of directors, which was as concerned as the staff about a deteriorating real estate market. The board wanted a backup commitment in case the state agriculture department did not come through in time to repay the loan. Sale of an easement through the county's ordinary farmland easement purchase program, which could be guaranteed, would leave AFT a couple of hundred thousand dollars short. A timely grant from the Wallace Genetic Foundation made up part of the potential shortfall. But ultimately, the board was persuaded by a pledge from Maryland's secretary of natural resources to use his best efforts to find the balance in his department's budget. This was an extraordinary example of one government agency coming to the aid of another, in this case the state agriculture department, to achieve mutual conservation objectives.

As it turned out, the last partners to come on board were the farmers. Excited as they were at the prospect of owning this piece of prime farm-land, every acre of which they knew intimately, they of all parties could least afford to take a financial risk. Because of the soft real estate market and falling milk prices, the farmers were concerned that they might be paying more for the land than their farming operation could support. AFT itself was caught between a desire to do right by the farmers and the need to repay its loan. Even though an agreement in principle had been reached months before, it took long hours of hard negotiating to get everyone to sign the contract. Indeed, it was not until another farmer submitted a competitive bid to AFT that Kies and Twaits agreed to terms.

The terms of the contract called for AFT and the farmers to become joint owners of the land, but only until the development rights could be sold to the state agriculture department. The farmers' percentage of equity was equal to the agricultural value of the land, which was all they could afford. AFT's share was equal to the value of the easement, though it took an undivided interest in fee title. On the sale of development rights to the state agriculture department, AFT would repay the county's loan and deed its interest to the farmers.

Such shared equity agreements with land trusts are becoming increasingly popular. They make agricultural land near cities affordable to commercial farmers. Unlike standard mortgages, they typically give the land trust a share of any future appreciation in the land's value as well as the right to buy out the farmer if he or she decides to sell. This prevents the farmer from speculating and, theoretically, enables the land trust to control the price of land and make the same kind of offer to subsequent farmers.

The shared equity arrangement that AFT negotiated with Kies and Twaits was entered into only to bridge the gap until the development rights could be sold and AFT's share of the purchase price could be recovered. It was used in lieu of a standard mortgage to avoid the possibility of AFT's having to foreclose on the farmers—the last thing an organization that helps farmers wants to do. The arrangement also gave AFT the security of being able to buy out the farmers if for some reason the development rights could not be sold. This would allow AFT to negotiate some other kind of land-saving deal, including limited development, to repay the county's loan and prevent the possible loss of the land altogether. If terms such as this seem excessively cautious (not to mention hard to negotiate), remember that anything can happen, particularly in a weak economy. Indeed, as of this writing, it appears that budget cuts in Maryland will at the very least delay the development rights sale.

HELPING LANDOWNERS KEEP THEIR LAND: NEVADA'S RUBY VALLEY RANCH

Across the continent, in the Great Basin of Nevada, AFT had yet another opportunity to enter into a partnership to help protect both land resources and the livelihood of agricultural producers. In this case, the private party was a widow, representing the third generation of the Handley family to own and raise cattle on a 3,500-acre spread in Ruby Valley. She and her sons wanted to continue ranching but had been seriously hurt by low beef prices during the downturn in the farm economy in the mid-1980s. Extraordinarily high water levels in the extensive wetlands that comprised part of the ranch had also reduced the amount of forage available to their animals. The Federal Land Bank, from which the family had borrowed in better times, was about to foreclose. Both the ranching operation and the wildlife habitat on the ranch were in jeopardy. That was when AFT and The Nature Conservancy (TNC) stepped in.

Ruby Valley, 60 miles south of Elko in northeastern Nevada, is a scenic oasis in the high desert. Flanked by 11,000-foot mountains, the valley floor—a mosaic of meadows, hay fields, and seasonally flooded wetlands—supports both livestock and myriad migratory birds, including sandhill cranes, trumpeter swans, white-faced ibis, and dozens of species of ducks. One of the largest wetland complexes in the Great Basin, its value as habitat is enhanced by the farmland around it, particularly the hay meadows, which are excellent waterfowl staging areas. It is also one of the most endangered, for Ruby Valley is earning a reputation for its scenery and hunting. Thus, had the Handley Ranch been put on the auction block, purchase by a recreational developer would have been a distinct possibility.

To prevent this, AFT and TNC negotiated to purchase the Handley Ranch for $300,000 and to lease it back to the family, which could then rebuild its livestock operation without the burden of debt. Within four years, the ranchers could repurchase the land for the original price plus the sum of accumulated annual rent payments. Both lease and repurchase would be subject to a conservation easement, to be held jointly by AFT and TNC. A side agreement between the two conservation organizations spelled out their share of the purchase price, allocation of transaction expenses, and resale contingencies in case the Handleys did not exercise their option. It also called for them to enter into negotiation with the Handleys on the specific terms of the conservation easement.

The easement was the key to the project's success. It was the device by which ranching operations on the property would be balanced with protection of the critical wetlands habitat. This proved to be no mean feat, taking several months of intense but amicable discussions to accomplish. With AFT serving as interpreter and arbitrator, the TNC staff learned about the practical realities of raising livestock, and the Handleys gained a new appreciation of wetlands ecology. What emerged was a scientifically defensible, economically sound compromise that served the interests of both ranchers and wildlife.

A line was drawn to separate uplands from wetlands. Traditional ranching activities could continue on the uplands, where development was forbidden in order to preserve agricultural production capacity. Cattle could also be grazed, as they had historically been, on the seasonally flooded wetlands, subject to restrictions. Principal among these were the exclusion of livestock during the spring months, when waterfowl usage of the wetlands is greatest; an absolute ceiling on the amount of forage that could be removed through grazing; and limitations on the use of agrochemicals. All three provisions were the subject of considerable give and take. Of course, diking, draining, filling, and all development of the wetlands were also prohibited by the easement. The deal was closed, foreclosure on the ranch was averted, and another piece of the Ruby Valley wetlands puzzle was solved.

Balancing Agriculture and Ecology

The objective of the Ruby Valley project went a step beyond that of the Sugarloaf transaction. The conservation purpose being served was not simply preservation of open space, whether for agriculture or for recreation. It was protection of an entire functional ecosystem that could support both abundant wildlife and the production of food—a much more ambitious task, representing one of the central challenges facing industrial societies today. The course followed by the partnership of AFT, TNC, and the Handley family is a model for achieving harmony between agriculture and the environment.

Although The Nature Conservancy could have bought the Handley property itself, at auction if it came to that, it sought AFT as a partner because it recognized that keeping the ranch in business would help promote goodwill among neighboring cattle ranchers, whose lands include other portions of the wetlands complex TNC wanted to preserve. TNC staff members also realized that private stewardship of lands peripheral to critical wildlife habitat was a key to achieving a more holistic preservation, one that anticipated the bioreserve concept that is now the focus of the organization's mission. AFT agreed to participate in the venture because it was an excellent opportunity to demonstrate precisely the kind of cooperation between agriculture and environmentalism that could result in a sustainable food production system.

The Handleys, at first hesitant, joined the partnership because it gave them perhaps their last and best chance to hold onto the family farm. Even though the ranchers' operation was in extremis—or, more accurately, because of their predicament—the conservationists took great pains not to take advantage of them. This, one would like to think, is what kept the ranchers interested, even when some potentially divisive proposals concerning restrictions on their cattle operation were put on the table.

Openness and frankness characterized the negotiations over the all-important conservation easement. Lines of communication were kept open between Elko, Salt Lake City, San Francisco, Arlington, and Washington. (There was no choice but to ignore the mandate to keep supply lines short.) A neighboring rancher, an attorney and a friend of the Handley family, volunteered his services "to keep things aboveboard," making a valuable contribution toward mutual trust among the partners. Ultimately, the agreement reached by the partnership was a product of what former TNC president and current AFT board chairman Patrick F. Noonan described in AFT's *Tenth Annual Report* as essential to reconciling the need to grow food with the imperative of maintaining biodiversity: "The good faith of farmers in owning up to the impact of agriculture on the environment. And the good faith of conservationists in dealing fairly and squarely with the farming community."

FUTURE DIRECTIONS: SUSTAINABLE AGRICULTURE IN ILLINOIS

Corn and soybeans grow horizon to horizon in downstate Illinois, the heartland of middle America. At this writing, the closest green, open space in that state threatened by the bulldozer is the outfield turf at old Comiskey Park in Chicago. Nonetheless, it was in this region that the American Farmland Trust teamed up with local farmers, a foundation, and a state agency on a conservation project with even more far-reaching implications than those of the Handley project for achieving harmony between agriculture and its environment.

One partner, the Illinois Sustainable Agriculture Society (ISAS), is a group of farmers assembled by AFT in 1988 after a statewide search for operators willing to experiment with new farming methods. ISAS is dedicated to improving environmental quality and farm profits through the conservative use of expensive fertilizers and agrochemicals in crop production.

Variations on this kind of farming have gone by various names in the past—"organic," "alternative," "biological"—but sustainable agriculture is now the preferred term. Regardless of terminology, however, the emphasis today is on environmental *and* economic sustainability.

New Interest in Reducing Chemicals

Interest in sustainable agriculture has recently enjoyed a renaissance. Although partly the result of the increased attention being paid to environmental issues, including the contamination of groundwater in some agricultural areas, the revival of interest has also been motivated by declining profit margins in the farming business. Faced with declining commodity prices, farmers traditionally have been encouraged by government policy and by their creditors to increase production in order to maintain profits. Thus, they have taken on more debt and incurred greater production expenses in an effort to boost crop yields. Sadly, this strategy has bankrupted many farmers, has financially stressed many more, and, because increased chemical application has been the conventional way to improve yields, has contributed to pollution problems in America's heartland.

These drawbacks of traditional agriculture have also prompted interest in an alternative, environmentally beneficial path to profitability: reducing inputs rather than increasing output. Formal research on sustainable agriculture at educational institutions has mushroomed. But AFT wanted to demonstrate sustainable agriculture methods directly to farmers, using a proven educational method: the experience of the farmers themselves.

Teaming Up with Farmers

With a grant from the Ruth Mott Fund and cooperation of the Illinois Department of Energy and Natural Resources, AFT selected a group of farmers and helped them to incorporate ISAS. A dozen producers in as many different counties were chosen to conduct field trials of sustainable agriculture techniques during the 1989 growing season. Under contract with AFT, the cooperators marked out 5- to 20-acre test plots, where they reduced applications of fertilizer, herbicides, and insecticides. On adjacent control plots, they grew the same crops under identical conditions but using conventional chemical dosages.

In most cases, however, crop yields produced on the sustainable agriculture test plots were equal to or greater than those on the controls. This occurred despite very adverse weather conditions: a cold, wet spring and a hot, dry summer. In all cases, the farmers spent significantly less money on environmentally suspect chemical inputs.

The Illinois demonstration was so successful that AFT's public sector partner, the state natural resources agency, helped finance publication of the results in a booklet designed for farmers. (The agency is careful to stress that the demonstration was not the equivalent of academic research. But who can argue with success on the ground?) The state was also persuaded to come up with $180,000 to fund an expansion of the demonstrations, now under formal state auspices, to 100 farms in the following year. And AFT has expanded its own efforts to help establish sustainable agriculture organizations in Missouri and Indiana, with the prospect of adding several more states in the near future.

The roles of all three partners—a private land trust, a government agency, and the farmers themselves—were essential to the ultimate success of the ISAS project. AFT used its commitment, as well as its imagination and the freedom to exercise it, to become a catalyst for action that government and the farmers might otherwise have been reluctant, unmotivated, or unprepared to take.

But the truly indispensable partners were the farmers themselves. They demonstrated to a skeptical group of friends and neighbors that sustainable agriculture practices can work under field conditions. And they did it better, certainly, than any land trust or government agency ever could. Just as important, having been empowered by the organized framework and success of the ISAS project, the farmers have also become the nucleus of a growing constituency for sustainable agriculture within the farming community. This constituency was responsible for persuading the state of Illinois to expand the program to "critical mass" proportions so that it can truly begin to convert agriculture into a more sustainable industry.

LESSONS FOR THE FUTURE

From these case studies emerge a number of lessons that should be taken to heart by those contemplating agricultural land conservation partnerships. First and foremost, a successful partnership is more than just two organizations or agencies working on the same piece of property. True partners must have mutual conservation objectives for the ultimate use of the land. Which portions of a property are to be devoted to cultivation and grazing, which may be developed and to what extent, and which are to be left as natural habitat? What limitations, if any, are to be imposed on agricultural use? In many cases, as with the Sugarloaf Farm and Ruby Valley Ranch projects, the partners enter into a project assuming that their objectives are very similar, if not identical. This is especially likely to occur when the partners include agriculturally sympathetic conservationists and conservation-minded farmers. As in marriage, it is only as things progress that differences of opinion emerge. At some point a critical juncture is reached and differences must be resolved or the partnership is likely to dissolve.

A strong, shared commitment to achieving mutual objectives is another important, if not essential, ingredient of a successful conservation partnership. If one partner must do all the work or all the compromising, the arrangement will suffer from lack of mutuality and again is likely to break down. The Pioneer Valley and Sugarloaf Farm projects are both examples of partnerships in which all parties kept plugging away side by side to make the transaction work.

Open-mindedness by all partners to different approaches to problem solving is another critical element of successful partnerships. The Illinois sustainable agriculture demonstrations, for example, never would have got off the ground (or on it, as the case may be) if the farmers had not been willing to try new agricultural practices. And once a conservation project is initiated, the need for flexibility becomes even greater. Land-saving transactions almost never go the way they are initially structured, and the more complex the deal—the greater the number of partners involved—the more likely it is to depart from its original plan. The protection of Sugarloaf Farm was threatened several times by changing market conditions and the need to line up the many parties involved. The only thing that saved it was the willingness of all partners to consider new avenues to achieving their mutual objective.

It goes without saying that a conservation partnership must also collectively possess the technical expertise to complete the deal. This includes a familiarity with real estate structuring alternatives, which comes with experience, and the ability to apply the techniques creatively in negotiation. Land trusts and government agencies may be equally adept at this. Regardless of who the partners are, however, they should agree from the outset on who will do what, so as not to create confusion and dissension.

Financing, of course, is the sine qua non of a successful conservation project. The taxing power of government must usually be brought to bear to preserve large acreages of farmland, as in the case of the Pioneer Valley and other PDR programs. But bridge financing, often needed to secure the opportunity for permanent protection of the land, can often be raised more easily from private sources, as the Ruby Valley project tends to demonstrate. The point about agreeing on the roles of partners applies here in the extreme—few problems can break a partnership as easily as disagreements over money.

Finally, the trust of farmers is fundamental to the success of agricultural conservation partnerships. Particularly important is acceptance of the project's basic objectives and methods by farm leaders, who can make or break a transaction by supporting or opposing it. This is not confined to official support: a skeptical word uttered at the local coffee shop can ruin a deal. Some government agencies with strong local ties, such as the Soil Conservation Service, enjoy the trust of farmers, but most have a hard time of it just because they are government entities. Environmental agencies, those that acquire land for public uses, and the private organizations that assist them in this also are sometimes distrusted by farmers. The Nature Conservancy, to its great credit, showed awareness of this potential for conflict in approaching AFT to help put together the Ruby Valley project. Private groups, especially those like AFT and ISAS (there are many others—for example, the Marin Agricultural Land Trust and the Lancaster Farmland Trust) that have farmers on their staff or involved in their governance, generally have the easiest time gaining the confidence of local farmers. The farmers' support is the single most important ingredient in a successful partnership in which conservation of the land for agriculture is the ultimate goal.

NOTES

1. The names of the farmers mentioned in this chapter have been changed to protect their privacy.

3

Preserving Urban and Suburban Gardens and Parks: The Trust for Public Land and Its Partners

William Poole
for The Trust for Public Land

The Trust for Public Land (TPL) was founded in San Francisco in 1972 to acquire land for the public by using private business techniques. Over the years, TPL has expanded to nearly a dozen offices nationwide and has helped acquire and transfer to public ownership more than half a million acres of land.

Unlike some land conservation groups, TPL does not permanently own or manage land. TPL's role is that of an independent third party in public land negotiations. To landowners, land trusts, and acquiring public agencies, TPL offers supplemental expertise in tax planning, financial strategy, and real estate law.

About 66 percent of the support for TPL's overhead, staff time, and project costs is generated by the land transactions themselves. Often, a landowner will make a tax-deductible gift of land value to TPL by selling land to the Trust at a price below fair market value. TPL then recovers all or a portion of this gift when it resells the land to an acquiring agency. The balance of TPL's support is generated by contributions, grants, and low-interest loans from foundations, corporations, and individuals.

TPL is the only national land conservation organization founded specifically to save land for public use and appreciation and to help guide the growth of human communities. Although the Trust has helped to preserve a variety of wild and natural lands, a parcel need not be either large or environmentally pristine to warrant TPL's attention. TPL works to secure lands—and sometimes buildings—that serve a public benefit, such as lands of cultural, historical, recreational, environmental, or open space value.

Neighborhood parks and urban community gardens were among TPL's earliest projects, and much of the Trust's work continues to be focused in and around cities, where steady development and fluctuating land values create a demanding climate for public land acquisition. With its national scope and specialized staff, TPL has been able to innovate many urban land acquisition techniques and then pass these techniques on to local land trusts and other private partners.

LOCAL GOVERNMENTS' NEED FOR PRIVATE PARTNERS

The increasing development and urbanization of the past decades has prompted interest in reserving land for parks, gardens, nature reserves, and recreational open space. As more and more land is developed, communities increasingly move to secure open land before the opportunity is lost forever. In 1987, the President's Commission on Americans Outdoors reported that the greatest need for new open space existed in the nation's metropolitan areas, where most Americans live.

But despite this growing interest in community land conservation, the 1980s witnessed a significant drop in federal land acquisitions and in federal matching funds for state and local projects, as detailed in chapter 10. In response, state and local governments have passed open space bond acts or dedicated taxes to pay for local land acquisition. This trend has been most visible in heavily urbanized and fast-growing regions such as the Northeast, Florida, and the Pacific Coast states.

This surge of interest in acquiring public lands has brought new challenges for local land planners. Acquiring public agencies often lack the money, staff, agility, or expertise to compete effectively in the volatile urban land market. Urban land transactions often involve delicate timing, the splitting or combining of land parcels, or complex tax or legal circumstances.

Staffers in public agencies may find themselves constrained in fulfilling their open space agendas by political considerations or by mandated procedures and regulations. In the area of funding, appropriated monies may not cover a land transaction or may not be available when a desired parcel comes on the market. Sometimes landowners are distrustful of government, making negotiations difficult.

Rarely does exactly the right piece of land come on the market at exactly the right price and at exactly the right time. Much of TPL's work involves adjusting these variables—time, price, and land configuration—to meet the needs of both the landowner and the acquiring agency or land trust.

A private partner such as TPL can offer government and other partners flexibility in timing transactions; agility in assembling, splitting, and packaging parcels; expertise in negotiations, and in tax and other legal matters; assistance in acquiring easements; and skill at finding and maximizing public and/or private funding. By working with local land trusts and other community groups, a private partner can also help create an atmosphere for land preservation and a private alternative to government ownership of community land.

TIMING OF TRANSACTIONS

Acquiring agencies often ask a nonprofit partner for help in timing land transactions. A landowner may need to sell quickly to meet pressing obligations or may need to close a transaction within a certain calendar year. A government agency may anticipate authorization of funds or passage of a bond act or sale of bonds and may need to protect the land in the intervening period. (Many public agencies are enjoined by regulation from signing options based on anticipated funds.)

Sometimes an agency or advocacy group wants to create an "atmosphere for acquisition" by optioning a parcel in order to present a tangible choice for voters or legislative bodies. Once the land is optioned, planners and advocacy groups can say, "This land is available now if we want it."

TPL's most common method for protecting land for future acquisition is by purchasing a short-term option on the land. When necessary, TPL may purchase a property outright in anticipation of public acquisition.

An Option Pending a Bond: Salmon Creek, Washington

In the summer of 1989, a community group and county planners in rapidly developing King County, Washington, asked TPL to option 86 acres of wooded hillsides and ravines along Salmon Creek, about 20 miles south of downtown Seattle. A housing development was planned for the property. Acquisition of the property for public open space had been approved by the county, to be funded by a bond act on the November ballot. TPL's option protected the land until the bond act was passed and the bonds were sold. The option also helped pass the bond act because advocates could point to a tangible parcel that could be saved should the act be passed.

Options to Bring Out Votes: Boston's Mount Gilboa

In the Boston suburb of Arlington, TPL helped acquire for public open space the 3.5-acre summit of Mount Gilboa, the last large undeveloped parcel in town. Town planners and local activists asked TPL to option the land to present a clear choice to the town's representatives at the town meeting, who had to override a state tax-limiting initiative in order to acquire the land.

ASSEMBLING AND SPLITTING OF PARCELS

Sometimes an agency needs or can afford only a portion of an offered parcel. Or, alternately, an agency may need to acquire multiple parcels from different owners to accomplish a single project. Governments are often prevented by statute or regulation from assuming the risks of holding, splitting, combining, and reselling parcels on the open market. Private partners, on the other hand, can do this work—often in multiple transactions—and then transfer the land to the acquiring agency in the precise configuration required.

Sharing Costs among Multiple Agencies: Albuquerque, New Mexico

On the eastern border of the city of Albuquerque, TPL acquired for public ownership a narrow, 2-mile-long parcel sandwiched between a city open space and Cibola National Forest. Even though TPL negotiated a savings of more than $2 million on the $10 million price, neither the city nor the national forest could afford to purchase the entire parcel. So TPL acquired the land, split it into two parcels, and transferred a parcel to each agency.

Assembling a Critical Mass: Fairfield County, Connecticut

In rapidly developing Fairfield County, Connecticut, TPL purchased four-teen parcels in eight separate transactions to protect Weir Farm, the historic home of American impressionist painter J. Alden Weir. Connecticut's

Department of Environmental Protection wanted the land but could not proceed until enough parcels had been assembled to guarantee the creation of a significant open space.

HELP WITH NEGOTIATIONS

TPL is often asked to step in as an independent third party when negotiations have broken down between a landowner and a public agency. In other instances, an agency may be enjoined from entering into negotiations by procedural, legal, or regulatory encumbrances. Many agencies are not allowed to approach a landowner with an offer that is below fair market value. For their part, some landowners do not trust government agencies or become frustrated with protracted negotiations.

By maintaining an independent posture, representing neither the public agency nor the landowner, a private partner can often defuse a disagreement or break a deadlock. When an agency faces statutory or procedural barriers to negotiation, a private partner can often step in, construct a transaction, and then transfer the land to the agency.

Creating a Positive Atmosphere: Riverside, California

In Riverside, California, TPL stepped in to negotiate for a key parcel for a proposed park. City authorities were hesitant to negotiate because they could not afford the land's multimillion-dollar fair market cost, and the landowners had been frustrated by city regulations in their efforts to sell the land for development. By offering to close the transaction within six months, TPL created an atmosphere of possibility around the project. Thus encouraged, the landowner agreed to sell below market value, bringing the cost within the city's budget.

Serving as an Independent Party: San Bruno Mountain, California

In 1989, TPL negotiated the purchase of 93 acres of environmentally sensitive lands on San Bruno Mountain, south of San Francisco. These canyons were eligible for development under a preexisting habitat preservation agreement struck by public wildlife agencies, the county, developers, and local environmentalists. Wildlife agencies wanted to protect the habitat, but as signatories to the agreement they did not feel they could negotiate for the land. As an independent party, TPL negotiated a discounted sale with the landowner and transferred the land to the California Wildlife Conservation Board.

HELP WITH OWNERSHIP AND FINANCIAL PROBLEMS

Often, the key to placing land in public ownership is finding a sensitive solution to the financial and legal needs of landowners. A land trust or another private partner can counsel landowners on the tax benefits of bargain sales, showing them how deductions associated with charitable donations of land value may offset in some measure a lower selling price. At times, TPL has gone to great lengths to structure a transaction so that these savings can be realized.

Saving Taxes through Corporate Dissolution: Staten Island, New York

In 1986, TPL acquired for the New York State Department of Environmental Conservation a portion of Goethal's Bridge Pond, a critical wetland on Staten Island in New York City. The land was owned by a small private corporation. In order for the owners to benefit from the charitable deduction associated with the bargain sale, TPL had to acquire all of the corporation's stock by gift, then form a new board of directors to vote for dissolution of the corporation's assets.

THE ROLE OF EASEMENTS

Sometimes it is not necessary to purchase land outright to preserve it for public use. By selling or donating conservation easements, a landowner surrenders his or her rights to develop property but retains ownership of the land itself. Because this process involves a decrease in the value of the property, conservation easements also carry certain tax advantages for the landowner.

This technique is becoming particularly popular on the rapidly developing urban fringe, especially in cases in which a willing landowner donates an easement to a local land trust. But government agencies can also hold easements. TPL has used the technique many times to protect urban land without itself purchasing the land.

An Urban Garden through Easement: San Francisco's Telegraph Hill

On Telegraph Hill, a densely settled neighborhood of San Francisco, a parcel of land beneath a popular hillside garden had been scheduled for development. TPL bought the land and resold it to an adjacent landowner. The new owner did not need to use the land; under local zoning laws he needed only to own it, in order to make construction additions to his own property. TPL retained a conservation easement on the land and donated that easement to the city to protect the garden.

HELP IN FINDING AND MAXIMIZING FUNDS

Frequently, a problem with money prompts a government agency to call on a nonprofit partner for help. An agency may require a tax-deductible bargain sale to bring the price of a project within its budget, or it may desire nonprofit advocacy to encourage a legislative appropriation or passage of a public bond act.

Sometimes TPL is aware of special sources of public funds. The acquisition or optioning of a high-profile property by a private partner can also help generate significant donations from foundations, corporations, and individuals.

TPL maintains special revolving acquisition funds, which provide bridge financing until an agency or land trust can acquire a parcel. Once the land is secured through protective ownership of a public agency or land trust, the funds are returned to the revolving account to be used again. Such funds allow TPL to act quickly to leverage millions of dollars in potential acquisitions through relatively small option commitments.

With their inherent flexibility, nonprofit partners can often combine funds for an acquisition from two or more public or private sources— combining agency money, for example, with foundation grants, development mitigation funds, low-interest loans, or private gifts.

Leveraging Corporate and Foundation Funds: Cleveland, Ohio

In 1982, TPL helped the city of Cleveland and the state of Ohio acquire 18 acres of the former Euclid Beach Amusement Park on the shore of Lake

Erie east of downtown Cleveland. More than half of the funds for the high-profile project were donated by local businesses and foundations.

Creative Use of Toxic Cleanup Funds: Grand Junction, Colorado

In Grand Junction, Colorado, TPL helped the city assemble funding to reclaim a 50-acre junkyard along the Colorado River for a showpiece riverfront park. Some funding for the $2 million project came from a federal community block grant and a local charitable foundation. But it was the property's condition and former use as a uranium waste dump that suggested to TPL the largest source of funding. Nearly $1 million for the park will come from U.S. Department of Energy funds paid in lieu of the agency's having to replace dirt that will be removed during federal cleanup of the wastes.

Using Mitigation Funds: California's Blue Sky Ranch

In the city of Poway, California, TPL coordinated four sources of funding to secure Blue Sky Ranch, a scenic, 400-acre canyon in burgeoning San Diego County. Money for the $2.55 million project came from the city, the county, and the state's Wildlife Conservation Board. The most unusual source of funds was a local golf course developer, who donated $300,000 as an off-site mitigation payment for conversion of wildlife habitat elsewhere in the county. (Mitigation funds are discussed later in this chapter and again in chapter 10.)

A Lease Purchase Agreement: Brevard County, Florida

Sometimes a nonprofit partner can schedule payments on a transaction to fit the budget or timing of an acquiring agency. In Brevard County, Florida, TPL constructed a special lease purchase agreement for a new 24-acre park. The county had passed a tax to acquire such land but had not yet accumulated enough money to buy the parcel, which was scheduled for bankruptcy sale. TPL bought the land and leased it back to the county for immediate public use. The county is purchasing the land from TPL as tax funds accumulate.

In some instances, needed funds can be generated through a partial development transaction. This is done by splitting the parcel, selling a minor portion for development, and using the proceeds to help secure the major portion for public use.

Affordability through Limited Development: Mendham Township, New Jersey

In Mendham Township, New Jersey, TPL stepped in to help neighborhood residents preserve a 573-acre country estate that had long been used as if it was public land. To help generate the purchase price, TPL split off a portion of the land for development as clustered housing. TPL then helped establish a local land trust group to hold the open space for the community.

LOCAL LAND TRUSTS IN PUBLIC/PRIVATE PARTNERSHIPS

The swelling interest in preserving urban and suburban land is perhaps best reflected by the growth of local land trusts, as detailed in chapter 9. Private, legally incorporated nonprofit organizations, land trusts hold and manage community land and conservation easements, offering an alternative to government ownership.

TPL helped incorporate or train personnel for many of the nation's nearly 1,000 land trusts, and much of TPL's educational outreach is directed to these local groups. In addition, TPL often assists local land trusts with their first transactions and is available on an ongoing basis to help with complicated transactions and negotiations. In 1989, TPL organized its National Land Counselor Program to train local land trust staff members in the technical aspects of conservation real estate transactions.

JOINT LOCAL/NATIONAL PROJECTS

Local land trusts bring to transactions the same kind of flexibility that TPL does. Such groups are particularly active on the urban fringe, where communities strive to guide growth in the face of rapid development. By purchasing land or by holding donated properties or easements, land trusts can protect land that governments cannot. Working with a larger group like TPL can often enhance a local land trust's effectiveness.

Safeguarding an Urban Wildlife Sanctuary: New York City

In the Queens borough of New York City, TPL helped form the Douglas Manor Environmental Association, a local land trust, to protect land adjacent to a state-owned wildlife sanctuary. Using funds from a local foundation and a community group, TPL negotiated for purchase of a key property and combined it with conservation easements donated by owners of adjacent lands. The land trust subsequently transferred the land to the city for protection, but continues to hold easements on the adjacent properties.

Creating a Land Trust for a Building's Grounds: Manhattan's Tudor City

In 1987, TPL helped the residents of Tudor City, a historic residential complex in midtown Manhattan, establish a land trust to hold title to two 15,000-square-foot parks on the complex's grounds. Tudor City's owner wanted to build additional housing on the land, but the residents wanted the land preserved. When a new owner moved to resolve the conflict, TPL helped form Tudor City Greens, Inc., the land trust that subsequently received title to the land. TPL retained the conservation easements on the property, further guaranteeing that the parks will remain public resources in perpetuity.

Creating Parkland with Local Funding: Huntsville, Alabama

In the late 1970s, TPL helped organize the Huntsville Land Trust of Huntsville, Alabama. The group worked for ten years to protect the western slope of Monte Sano, which offered hiking and other recreational opportunities and provided a greenway extending to downtown Huntsville. In 1989, when a change in city administration promised a new opportunity to secure the land, TPL stepped in at the request of the mayor and the land trust to negotiate for the property. The city contributed two-thirds of the $5.1 million purchase price, and the land trust raised $1.7 million from private sources.

LAND TRUSTS FOR COMMUNITY GARDENS

Modern community gardens arose as part of the environmental and neighborhood self-help movements of the 1970s. Traditionally, these inner-city gardens were planted on land nobody wanted: abandoned lots, either private or city owned, available under informal, short-term leases for nominal fees.

More recently, as the value of such parcels has increased, threatening to displace urban gardeners, TPL and other nonprofit groups have moved to secure this land more permanently. Often, the first step is to incorporate the gardening group as a land trust, giving it legal status to negotiate long-term leases and to purchase and hold parcels. TPL then helps gardeners negotiate for long-term control of their sites.

Increasingly, TPL is also negotiating proactively with developers and local housing groups, urging inclusion of gardens and open space in new residential and commercial plans. Because local community feeling often runs strongly in favor of creating and preserving gardens and open space, developers encounter less public opposition to projects when such amenities are included in the plan.

Urban land trust work takes different shapes in different cities. In New York, for example, garden land trusts usually lease or purchase a single parcel. Other cities—Boston, for example—employ a neighborhood land trust model, and a few cities, notably Philadelphia, are experimenting with citywide land trusts for community gardens.

No matter what the model, community gardens are often found in a city's poorest neighborhoods. Gardeners frequently come from a variety of ethnic backgrounds and often do not even speak a common language. Inner-city residents have little experience with landownership and often lack the organizational skills and access to the legal services needed to secure a property for the long term. For all of these reasons, it is not enough for a nonprofit organization simply to help a group incorporate and then disappear.

The challenge to nonprofit organizations trying to help these groups is to find a way of providing ongoing support. Gardening groups need regular funding to meet minimum leasing fees and expenses, and they may require continuing organizational support to ensure long-term tenure on the land.

Working with Developers: Manhattan's Upper West Side

On the Upper West Side of Manhattan, TPL was asked to negotiate a specific strategy for saving a valued community garden after the land was slated for development. As part of the ensuing transaction, TPL took title to a half-acre garden site on the development parcel and transferred it to West Side Community Garden, Inc., the local land trust that will manage the land. The developer also agreed to pay half of the $335,000 cost of constructing the new garden.

Helping a City Work with the Community: Boston, Massachusetts

In the South End of Boston, TPL helped to organize a neighborhood land trust to own and manage a collection of vacant lots—many already planted as community gardens—owned by the Boston Redevelopment Authority (BRA). In 1986, as part of a long-term planning process, the BRA hired Boston Urban Gardeners (BUG), a community gardening group, to assess the neighborhood's open space requirements. Acting on BUG's recommendation, the BRA has decided to transfer some lots to the community for permanent protection and has asked TPL for help. A $100,000 mitigation grant from the Prudential Insurance Company will provide an ongoing endowment.

Providing Ongoing Support: New York City

Since 1987, TPL's Neighborhood Open Space Management Program has offered monetary grants and continuing assistance to community gardeners in New York City. Some grants help local gardens build and strengthen a core leadership group. Others help gardening groups organize educational programs and other outreach activities to their communities—particularly to children. It is hoped that children and young parents will become interested in the gardens and will go on to become the urban environmental leaders of tomorrow. The program is funded by the Mary Flagler Cary Charitable Trust.

With such support, urban land trusts represent one of the most promising new ways to create city parks, gardens, and open space. Additionally, such grass-roots projects recruit new—in this case, inner-city—citizens for the larger environmental movement. Building such environmental consensus is a parallel goal of all TPL projects.

MODEL PROJECTS

The brief project descriptions of the previous section only hint at the complexity and hard work typical of most of TPL's partnership projects.

The following four case studies illustrate in more detail the multitude of steps involved in this work.

PRESERVING LAND AMID RESIDENTIAL GROWTH: TUCSON, ARIZONA

In 1986, the city of Tucson set out to acquire seven contiguous parcels—three with homes and four building lots, 40 acres in all—in a booming residential area on the city's far eastern side. The city wanted the land for a park and had budgeted $1.1 million for the project. Officials at first announced that the city would pay market value for the land but had to backtrack when appraisals totaled $1.9 million, $800,000 beyond the city's means.

Tucson planners contacted TPL's southwestern office and asked whether a way could be found to acquire the land with the budgeted funds. TPL approached the understandably ruffled landowners to negotiate a bargain sale of each property. Staffers assessed the financial and tax position of each owner and worked out a discount figure that, when calculated with applicable tax advantages, would bring that owner's bottom line close to what it might have been at a nondiscounted price.

The key to the transaction was the discount offered by Leland and Joanne Case, whose 20-acre parcel was the largest in the proposed park. The Cases, in their nineties, were happy to sell their land at a substantial discount but did not want to leave their home. TPL split their property, leaving 5 acres and the house, to which the couple was granted lifelong tenancy. To honor the Cases' generosity, the new park was named in their honor.

TPL then bought the parcel of a second landowner and leased the house back for five years, in exchange for which the landowner agreed to serve as caretaker while the city completed plans for the park.

By similarly tailoring deals for each landowner and standing as a buffer between the landowners and the city, TPL was able to maximize potential tax advantages while avoiding conflicts between the city and the owners over the value of the land.

TPL bought and transferred three of these properties in 1986 and three more in 1987. One landowner refused to sell, but another contiguous property became available, and eventually TPL added that land to the new park. By combining the savings represented by the Cases' substantial gift of land value with the smaller gifts of the other landowners, TPL was able to transfer the property to the city at its budgeted $1.1 million. Part of the gifts also went to support TPL's work on this and other transactions.

SECURING AN URBAN WATERFRONT PARK: SEATTLE, WASHINGTON

In 1983, TPL pulled together funding from several disparate sources to secure a half-acre parcel on the southern shore of Lake Union, near downtown Seattle, Washington. The city had wanted to acquire the land, most recently owned by a Minnesota bank, and asked TPL to step in and secure the property when it came on the market.

The land—for years a littered parking lot—was needed to create a new waterfront park in a former industrial area along the heavily developed lakeshore. The park, it was hoped, would offer public access, recreation, and open space. One plan called for a maritime museum in the area—several historic ships were already moored nearby. Nearby also was the Center for Wooden Boats, a natural attraction for a public park.

TPL's entrance into the transaction created a sense that a maritime park on the waterfront was a real possibility. In assembling the funding, the trust eventually combined a state grant, a no-interest foundation loan, and a unique land-for-cash exchange.

The key element of the $445,000 transaction was a TPL-arranged agreement between the city and the private Seattle Yacht Club. The club maintained mooring facilities at nearby Lake Washington on submerged land that was scheduled to revert to city ownership in the year 2002. The club essentially agreed to exchange $300,000, to be used to purchase the Lake Union property, for undisputed ownership of the submerged moorage land.

TPL formed a legal partnership with the yacht club. The two parties then made a $50,000 down payment on the Lake Union property. The loan for the land spread payments over a year, giving the city time to apply for a $145,000 matching grant from the state Interagency Committee for Outdoor Recreation. In the meantime, a $100,000 payment came due, and the local Bullitt Foundation loaned TPL this money at no interest.

TPL officially transferred the property to the city in December 1984. Since acquiring this parcel, the city has gone on to purchase adjacent acreage on the southern shore of Lake Union. The city has considered several alternative plans for the new land, with many parties endorsing a maritime heritage park and museum.

MODELING CLINTON COMMUNITY GARDENS: NEW YORK CITY

In New York City, as in other major American cities, the 1970s witnessed a dramatic growth in local gardening groups. In New York, much of this gardening was accomplished on city-owned properties, vacant lots that had been repossessed for nonpayment of taxes over the preceding decade. By 1978, such land supported more than 200 community gardens, most operating under one-year agreements with the city's Operation Greenthumb.

In 1978, TPL began helping some of these gardening groups legally incorporate in order to negotiate more effectively the purchase or long-term control of city properties. TPL also began trying to influence municipal policy in favor of securing surplus city-owned land for local open space use.

Land values remained relatively stable over the next few years, during which period TPL helped a dozen local garden groups secure land from the city and private sources. Often, the city could be convinced to sell properties at public auction, or at special "restricted" sales, open only to nonprofit organizations with open space goals. Prices for these properties were typically between $1,000 and $5,000. TPL often helped fund such purchases by using money from local foundations.

But in the early 1980s, soaring land values pushed garden plots beyond the pocketbooks of inner-city groups. A crisis arrived in 1983, when the city consented to a restricted sale of Clinton Community Garden in the Hell's Kitchen neighborhood of Manhattan but set the minimum bid at $900,000.

The fight for Clinton Community Garden was a watershed for community gardens throughout New York City. In hopes of securing the land, TPL joined forces with two local groups, the Green Guerrillas and the Housing Conservation Coordinators, and the gardeners themselves to raise the purchase price by "selling" square-inch parcels for $5 each. The $125,000 raised fell well below the minimum bid, but the effort spotlighted the plight of the gardeners in the local media, and public sentiment to preserve the property grew.

Spurred by the community's support for the garden, the city agreed to preserve the lot by transferring it to the parks department, which signed a long-term management agreement with Clinton Community Garden, Inc., a TPL-organized land trust. Part of the $125,000 went into an endowment fund to meet future expenses and maintenance.

Using the Clinton arrangement as a model, TPL subsequently proposed an ongoing program to encourage New York to preserve more community gardens. If the city would work toward permanent or long-term protection for selected gardens, TPL would provide funding for those gardens from its newly established New York State Garden and Parks Preservation Fund.

A plan to this effect was announced in the spring of 1989. As of the early 1990s, three community gardening groups had signed ten-year leases with Operation Greenthumb. One garden, the Garden of Union in Brooklyn, has secured its land in perpetuity. The gardening groups use yearly grants from TPL—from $350 to $1,500—to offset maintenance expenses and fund special programs.

PURCHASING A HISTORIC LANDMARK: TAMPA, FLORIDA

In the fall of 1988, three public agencies—the National Trust for Historic Preservation, the Florida Department of Natural Resources, and the Tampa/Hillsborough County Historic Preservation Board—asked TPL to purchase and temporarily hold El Centro Español, a historic building in downtown Tampa, Florida.

An ornate two-story brick structure, El Centro was built in 1912 and once housed the oldest Latin social and mutual aid club in the South. For more than fifty years, it was the educational and cultural center of Ybor City, a neighborhood of Cuban immigrants who were workers in Tampa's famous cigar factories. At one time, the building contained a café, a theater, a ballroom, and community meeting rooms.

But El Centro had fallen into disrepair in recent years. The roof had caved in, and pigeons had invaded the once-exquisite interior. The most recent owners had been unable to afford repairs. One of the partners had declared bankruptcy, and the building was scheduled to be repossessed and sold at auction.

Everyone seemed to agree that El Centro was worth preserving. The U.S. Secretary of the Interior had designated El Centro Español as a national historic landmark, and the building's survival was seen as the key to revitalizing the surrounding historic district of Ybor City. The state was anxious to buy the structure for a museum and had listed it for purchase under Florida's Conservation and Recreation Lands Program.

But the state could not act quickly enough to prevent the foreclosure sale.

Moreover, the city of Tampa had placed a lien on the building pending repairs, and the state could not purchase the property until the title was clear.

TPL purchased the building, made the repairs, cleared the title, and held the property for resale to the state. The First Florida Bank loaned money to TPL to make the renovation. Other monies for the $2 million project came from a revolving fund set up for TPL by the Metropolitan Life Insurance Company. After the state reimbursed TPL for its costs, the money was returned to the revolving fund for use on other projects.

LESSONS FROM THE PAST

If TPL has learned one thing in nearly twenty years of urban land conservation, it is that every transaction is different, with its own unique set of challenges and opportunities. At the same time, most successful transactions have certain characteristics in common.

Government and agency officials need to feel that a transaction fits long-range goals and is supported by the voters. Landowners need to feel that they are getting helpful tax advice and a fair price in a confidential atmosphere. TPL's consistent role is to adjust every transaction with these ends in mind, rearranging variables until the transaction "clicks."

Crucial to this process is clear and consistent communication among all parties. With an assortment of private organizations active in the land acquisition arena, public agencies may sometimes be confused about an organization's goals and methods. TPL has found that it must frequently articulate its independent, third-party role as problem solver, negotiator, and facilitator rather than as a primary funding or land-banking agency.

ROLE OF LOCAL ENERGY

It is impossible to overrate the importance of local energy in preserving community land. Local land conservation groups identify land needs and educate their communities about projects as no outside nonprofit organization can. Many of the projects cited in this chapter were brought to TPL by local citizens and groups. Such community energy is particularly needed if a project requires lobbying for funds or private fund-raising efforts.

The importance of local energy is amply demonstrated by TPL's experience with community gardening groups. Early on, the Trust attempted to organize community gardeners at the same time as it was working to secure the land. The frequent failure of such groups led to the conclusion that the most effective groups are often those that coalesce out of neighborhood energy. In its work in preserving community gardens in New York City, TPL now works almost exclusively with up-and-running groups of community gardeners.

Grass-roots energy is also the driving force behind an ever-elaborating network of land trusts and environmental organizations. In many areas, local land trusts now work closely with regional affiliates and national groups like TPL, calling on such resources as required by the complexity of each transaction. By sharing its expertise with local groups, TPL hopes to seed new land-saving methods across the country. But it is grass-roots energy that will pay continuing dividends as local groups take on continuing projects, with and without TPL's help.

IMPORTANCE OF INFLUENCING URBAN POLICY

The past twenty years have also revealed that land preservation work in the nation's cities varies in several aspects from such work in rural or suburban areas.

City governments, faced with rising crime rates, crumbling school systems, a shrinking tax base, and dwindling federal dollars, often assign low priority to the acquisition of new public land. Urban land values are often high, and inner-city residents often wield little political influence in their quest for open land.

In many cities, the city itself is a principal landowner, and city officials often perceive community gardens and other open space as decorative but temporary uses for municipally owned land that may someday be sold for housing or business.

In such an atmosphere, influencing government policy can become an important element in creating new open space. The nonprofit partner must often be the partner out in front—developing an agenda for land protection, creating a consensus for public land, encouraging restricted sales for conservation use or community gardens, convincing authorities that open space ultimately pays big dividends for urban citizens.

TPL's New York Land Program has been particularly active in this area, developing alliances with local environmental groups to bring preservation needs to the attention of the public and city officials. For example, in 1986,

TPL, in cooperation with the New York City Audubon Society, released a Buffer the Bay plan to encourage protection of environmentally sensitive lands bordering Jamaica Bay, adjacent to the city's southern border. Some of this land was already protected in the Gateway National Recreation Area, but significant parcels remained exposed for development. Before release of the report, public agencies showed little interest in conserving the land. But after the report's release, targeted parcels in two shoreline locations were acquired by the city's parks and recreation department, which cited the TPL/Audubon plan when applying for state funds.

PROMISE FOR THE FUTURE

In the last two decades, methods for acquiring and securing land for the public have grown increasingly sophisticated and will undoubtedly continue to do so. Tight budgets, rising land values, and the public demand for more open land all suggest an increasing role for public/private partnerships.

GROWTH OF COOPERATIVE PLANNING

As private partners and government staffers work together on individual transactions, they often lay the groundwork for other joint ventures. In the future, the most effective partnerships will be long-term, as an agency learns a private partner's techniques and abilities and as the private partner comes to understand an agency's land acquisition goals.

In many areas of the country, local TPL offices have for some years enjoyed such ongoing relationships, working repeatedly with agencies as challenges arise. More and more, TPL also works proactively with agencies, community and economic development groups, and other nonprofit organizations to plan for open space components in long-range development plans.

A Long-Term Partnership: Bergen County, New Jersey

In 1989, densely populated Bergen County, New Jersey, announced a $40 million land acquisition program and asked TPL for technical advice and for ongoing help with many of the transactions. Included among these were four projects involving 1,260 acres in the Ramapo Mountains, among the few remaining large open tracts in the densely developed county. TPL helped negotiate each transaction and, as part of the trust's ongoing partnership with Bergen County planners, has moved on to negotiate the purchase of conservation easements over 1,200 acres of adjoining Ramapo Mountains land.

Urban Redevelopment through Private Land Banking: Washington, DC

In 1985, TPL stepped in at the request of local authorities to acquire a 26-acre parcel that was essential to the revitalization of an inner-city neighborhood in northeastern Washington, DC. A redevelopment plan for the parcel had foundered when a previous developer had gone into bankruptcy. TPL entered into a tripartite agreement with the District of Columbia and the insurance company that funded the purchase. By banking the land and helping plan the new development, TPL not only helped create new community open space but also helped add badly needed low-cost housing in a revitalized city neighborhood.

Helping a City Assess Its Open Space Needs: Baltimore, Maryland

In 1991, TPL joined park officials from Baltimore, Maryland, and researchers from the Yale University School of Forestry and Environmental Studies to conduct a comprehensive assessment of Baltimore's open space needs. The Open Space Opportunities Program compares the distribution of Baltimore's population with the distribution of its existing parks, playgrounds, and community gardens and will then catalog available land. TPL will recommend appropriate mechanisms for acquiring new parcels.

A Project Spurred by a Private Voter Survey: Austin, Texas

In Austin, Texas, a grant from the John and Florence Shumann Foundation helped TPL and Open Space Austin survey voters' attitudes toward preserving watershed land and other open space. Buoyed by the support shown in this survey, TPL joined city and county officials and other environmentalists to create an open space plan for Austin and to work toward passage of a bond act for new acquisitions.

RISE OF OPEN SPACE ASSEMBLAGES

Nowhere is the cooperative planning process more valuable than in helping to create new greenbelts, trailways, riverways, and other open space assemblages. In a tight economic environment, the linking of small, relatively inexpensive parcels can create long green corridors for wildlife and recreation, sometimes linking densely settled urban areas to larger blocks of rural open space.

Already existing rail corridors are increasingly being converted to recreational trail use. And in some of the nation's most densely settled areas, public agencies and private nonprofit groups are working to link green spaces along rivers, waterfronts, and other recreational and open spaces. Such linkages represent a great challenge and opportunity for the agencies and their nonprofit partners, calling on most of the techniques learned in twenty years of experience.

A Public/Private River Walkway: Hudson River, New Jersey

Since 1985, TPL has been working with state and county agencies to create a greenbelt walkway along 18 miles of the Hudson River in northern New Jersey. The walkway will be created through a combination of public land linkages and zoned open space on private lands. In 1988, TPL helped establish the Hudson River Waterfront Conservancy, a land trust that holds some of the land and assists in managing the walkway.

RISE OF MITIGATION FUNDING

Among the many new and promising sources of money for open space acquisition, mitigation funds deserve special mention. Such funds may be generated as part of development agreements or court settlements, or they may be mandated by legislation.

Nonprofit partners, with their inherent flexibility, may be able to combine, hold, and creatively disperse such funds in the most effective manner.

A Linear Park Funded by the Department of Transportation: Tampa, Florida

In Tampa, Florida, TPL is proposing to use mitigation funds from the Florida Department of Transportation to acquire land for a linear park to adjoin a roadway that will not be built for another decade. The monies, to mitigate for the altering of a historic neighborhood, are required by federal statute.

Wetlands Preservation Funded by an Oil Company: San Francisco Bay Area

Near San Francisco, TPL is purchasing wetlands and other habitat on San Francisco Bay with $2.7 in mitigation funds from a major oil company. These funds are part of a larger settlement between the oil company and the Sierra Club Legal Defense Fund to mitigate for the company's pollution of San Francisco Bay.

CONTINUING NEED FOR FLEXIBILITY

The growth of such new funding is only one indication of the continuing need for flexibility in preserving land for public use. Flexibility in the face of change may be the greatest single advantage private organizations have to offer their public sector partners. Each year, TPL structures projects using funds and techniques that were not even in the land-saving toolbox the year before. Nonprofit organizations and agency partners must never assume that they have learned it all, that the transaction toolbox is full. It may be that there are no impossible land acquisition projects, only projects that no one has yet thought of a way to complete.

PART II

꧁🙰꧂

Federal Agency Partnerships

Part I of this book described the three major national nonprofit organizations that engage in land acquisition partnerships with government. Here, in part II, two federal agencies that have pioneered in partnerships with the private sector describe the process from the government's point of view.

The first agency described, the U.S. Fish and Wildlife Service, is part of the U.S. Department of the Interior. Although the U.S. Fish and Wildlife Service has called on private organizations for help in a variety of circumstances, chapter 4 details one specific program of the agency, the North American Waterfowl Management Plan (NAWMP). The NAWMP focuses on preserving waterfowl habitat with myriad partners, from states, towns, corporations, and landowners to land trusts and volunteer land managers. That effort has resulted in a systematic and very successful series of partnerships all across the country, partnerships appropriately called "joint ventures" that stand out for being exhaustively planned rather than ad hoc.

In taking a habitat-wide, holistic view, the NAWMP's approach prefigured the new bioreserve strategy of The Nature Conservancy. NAWMP participants describe the many moving parts such a strategy entails and the close coordination necessary to make it a success. The NAWMP might also serve as a model for federal funding of other land preservation priorities, maximizing as it does the use of matching funds and the involvement of private landowners.

By contrast, chapter 5, the first of two chapters describing the partnership work of the National Park Service, looks more closely at the technical role private organizations can play in helping a federal land acquisition giant with the often daunting individual tasks of preserving important additions to national parks or, more rarely, creating new parks. Chapter 5 presents examples of situations in which the federal government's lengthy appraisal and appropriation process or other bureaucratic strictures made private sector involvement necessary to keep critical tracts from being converted to incompatible uses. Chapter 5 also stresses the important role of the private sector in preserving the surroundings of the national parks, land that often needs a lesser degree of protection than absolute federal ownership but that requires enough restrictions to preserve scenic views, animal wintering habitat, and the like.

The National Park Service's Warren Brown is quick to point out, however, that NPS itself must set its priorities and decide on the degree of protection suitable for any particular parcel of land. He warns against creativity for its own sake and a too-quick assumption that in every case conservation easements are less costly and more desirable than fee ownership.

Chapter 6 describes another aspect of the National Park Service's partnerships: their technical assistance program to local communities. This outreach effort recognizes the fact that there are many locally important places to preserve in the country, places that for one reason or another do not rise to the significance of national parks. Chris Brown of the National Park Service's Rivers, Trails, and Conservation Assistance Program describes the principles under which the program operates (multiple partners are required) and the wide variety of assistance it offers. Forms of help range from development of maps and inventories to coordination of public input and development of public relations tools such as posters. The kinds of projects given critical help through the program include revitalization of historic neighborhoods, development of trail corridors, and preservation of river valleys. This precariously funded program shows how a relatively small amount of federal resources—here, in the form of federal personnel—can leverage big results by energizing active private and public local support.

Although the focus here is on two federal agencies with a particularly long, rich history of partnership with the private sector, the USDA Forest Service, the Department of Agriculture, the Bureau of Land Reclamation, the Department of Defense, and others also are actively involved in such partnerships. Individual instances of private partnerships with these federal agencies can be found throughout the book.

4

Preserving Wildlife Habitat: The U.S. Fish and Wildlife Service and the North American Waterfowl Management Plan

Angela Graziano
with contributions from Tom Massengale and Jerry Updike

The U.S. Fish and Wildlife Service has long been in the forefront of public/ private partnership efforts. From the 1960s on, USFWS has asked for help from private sector partners when doing so would keep an essential property from being lost or make a property affordable through tax savings or private funding assistance. Many of these partnerships, however, have been of the ad hoc, opportunistic variety well described in earlier chapters.

More innovative, and with lessons to teach other government agencies at the federal and even state levels, is the systematic public/private partnership effort embodied in the North American Waterfowl Management Plan. This national—indeed, international—initiative to preserve wetlands habitat for waterfowl was designed from the ground up to make maximum use of partnerships.

By 1985, the prognosis for waterfowl was dim. Following periodic droughts and loss of habitat resulting from the conversion of wetlands for agriculture, industry, and urbanization, some North American duck species had declined to the lowest numbers ever recorded. In response, the United States and Canada developed an ambitious international plan for restoring duck populations to early 1970s levels and protecting and improving substantial acreage of wetlands and associated upland. In 1986, the

United States's secretary of the interior and Canada's minister of the environment signed the North American Waterfowl Management Plan (NAWMP). The plan establishes a fifteen-year framework for international cooperation in conservation of wetlands and restoration of waterfowl populations. Although the plan was designed primarily to benefit waterfowl, it also helps many other species by improving the wetlands that support them.

The NAWMP's overall objectives are to secure long-term protection for an additional 6 million acres of habitat in thirty-four geographic areas, which are the most important breeding, staging, and wintering areas for waterfowl; to restore duck populations to 62 million breeders that would produce a fall flight of 100 million birds, similar to the pre-1970s level; and to achieve cited population objectives for geese, swans, and ten principal species of ducks.

In 1988, the federal wildlife agencies of Canada, Mexico, and the United States signed a three-nation agreement, called the Tripartite Agreement, to improve the conservation of migratory birds and the wetlands habitats essential to their survival. This agreement linked the NAWMP to a continent-wide effort extending from the nesting grounds in arctic Canada to wintering areas that reach far into Mexico.

The NAWMP's emphasis on protecting and restoring wetlands is not only ambitious but also costly, with a projected price tag of $1.5 billion for the habitat protection components alone. To make this goal realistic, the NAWMP relies on a "joint venture" concept, fostering partnerships at all levels of government and with private organizations to carry out wetlands protection, restoration, and management practices. In essence, the NAWMP is a partnership of state, federal, provincial, tribal, territorial, and private organizations, all of which are dedicated to protecting and improving migratory bird habitat and restoring duck populations.

A twelve-member committee guides the implementation of the NAWMP. The director general of the Canadian Wildlife Service and the director of the U.S. Fish and Wildlife Service each appoints six members to serve three-year terms. Joint venture organizations in each target area establish management boards to seek out and commit resources from the private sector, states, territories, provinces, and federal agencies.

In the United States, a twenty-member implementation board composed of conservation groups and private foundations promotes legislation, fundraising, and communications support needed to implement the NAWMP and complete the joint venture projects. Currently, board membership includes representatives from the American Farmland Trust, the American Forest Foundation, the Berry B. Brooks Foundation, Ducks Unlimited, Inc., the Federation of State Waterfowl Associations, the International Association of Fish and Wildlife Agencies, the Izaak Walton League of America, the Land Trust Alliance, the National Association of Conservation Districts, the National Audubon Society, the National Fish and Wildlife Foundation, the National Rifle Association, The National Wildlife Federation, the Delta Waterfowl Foundation, the Sierra Club, The Nature Conservancy, the Wildlife Legislative Fund of America, the Wildlife Management Institute, The Wildlife Society, and the World Wildlife Fund. Canada and the United States each has a headquarters office to guide joint venture teams of federal, provincial, state, and private organizations in carrying out the program at the national and regional levels.

Since the implementation process began in 1987, twelve joint ventures for preserving habitat have begun operating in the United States and Canada. These are the U.S. Prairie Pothole; Central Valley Habitat; Lower Mississippi Valley; Gulf Coast; Atlantic Coast; Lower Great Lakes–St. Lawrence Basin; Playa Lakes; Upper Mississippi River–Great Lakes Region; Rainwater Basin, Pacific Coast; Canadian Prairie Habitat; and Eastern Habitat joint ventures. Additionally, two species-based joint ventures for the black duck and the arctic goose, both international in scope, are now fully organized.

NEED FOR PARTNERSHIPS

From an obscure and often misunderstood beginning, the North American Waterfowl Management Plan has gained prominence and become the leading international program in the preservation and conservation of wetlands and waterfowl. With a set of goals and objectives that many environmentally conscious entities can easily relate to, the NAWMP has brought together as partners federal agencies, states, and towns; more than 200 conservation groups; many corporations and businesses; and hundreds of private landowners for the benefit of waterfowl and wetlands conservation.

Clearly, the tremendous task of conserving wetlands resources is far too complex and costly for the U.S. Fish and Wildlife Service to accomplish alone. In designing and implementing the joint venture approach to help attain its ambitious goal of protecting more than 6 million acres of premier wetlands and restoring duck populations to their pre-1970s levels, the NAWMP recognized that partnerships are necessary (1) to fund this ambitious goal; (2) to bring in sufficient personnel and organizational capabilities to accomplish the complex and varied protection tasks implicit in the goal; (3) to include the largest number of wetlands areas—those owned by individuals; (4) to bring the best science possible to the task; and (5) to maximize the NAWMP's constituency through outreach and education. These varied aspects of the joint venture process are discussed and illustrated with case studies throughout this chapter.

COST-SHARING PARTNERSHIPS

There is no escaping the fact that the NAWMP is a costly endeavor. "We'll need to put in place more than $120 million annually during the remaining ten years to achieve the habitat objectives of the plan," says Robert G. Streeter, executive director of the program in the United States.

Boldly stated, then, the NAWMP needs partners to assist in the funding program as well as in delivering projects on the ground. The principle of cost sharing with nonfederal partners is built into the principal funding mechanism being used for the NAWMP, the North American Wetlands Conservation Act. Under that act, passed in 1989, each congressionally appropriated dollar must be matched by at least one nonfederal dollar. The result is more efficient use of federal funds for wetlands conservation.

Since initial funding in 1990, the North American Wetlands Conservation Council, established by the act to select the best projects, has approved more than $70 million in federal funding. Where has the $70 million dollars in matching funds come from? The largest part has come from the states. For example, California has contributed $3 million to the preservation of important wintering habitat in the Central Valley north of Sacramento. Missouri, as part of its Ten Mile Pond project in the Lower Mississippi Valley Joint Venture, has invested more than $2.5 million in acquiring and restoring diverse wetlands along the Mississippi flyway.

In many instances, private organizations, most prominently The Nature Conservancy (TNC) and Ducks Unlimited (DU), have also raised millions of dollars to leverage federal funds. Thus, in Illinois's Cache River project, TNC and DU together have raised approximately $5 million to match federal funds, and in the Ace Basin of South Carolina, part of the Atlantic Coast Joint Venture, the same organizations have raised more than $8 million in matching dollars. These projects are profiled in more detail later in this chapter.

Especially new and exciting about the NAWMP is the extent of its corporate funding. Leading the way with the largest corporate contribution to date, Dow Chemical Company is contributing $3 million over a four-year period to preserve and protect North America's wetlands through the NAWMP. This money will provide partial funding for projects at Mandalay Marsh in Louisiana, Parrot Ranch in California, Ace Basin in South Carolina, and Hillman Marsh in Ontario, Canada. Other private corporations have joined in the crusade for waterfowl and wetlands conservation.

One particularly innovative supporter of the NAWMP program is the National Fish and Wildlife Foundation. Created by Congress in 1984 as a unique, private nonprofit organization, the foundation uses federally appropriated funds as seed money to encourage private and state contributions through challenge grants. Foundation grants must be matched on at least a one-to-one basis, but more often than not foundation monies are matched at a much higher level. To date, the foundation has channeled more than $37 million into U.S./Canadian NAWMP projects, with $15 million coming from the foundation and $22 million coming from private and matching funds. Without this early help, it would have been very difficult to get the NAWMP started.

MULTIPLE STRENGTHS FROM PARTNERSHIPS

Partnerships are also essential to the success of the NAWMP because they provide diversity in expertise and capability not available in a single organization or agency. One organization may provide technical expertise in wetlands restoration, another in lobbying efforts, another in ability to deal creatively with landowners' tax and other needs, and yet another in implementing land management practices on public lands.

Preserving Wetlands: Consumnes River, California

Long hailed as an ideal wintering ground for pintails, tundra swans, wood ducks, cinnamon teals, and sandhill cranes, the Consumnes River valley in California's Central Valley provides a good illustration of the success made possible through cooperation of partners with diverse strengths. Over the years, the Consumnes's densely wooded riparian habitat has been cleared for dikes, permitting the conversion of nearby wetlands into dairy pastures and cropland. The resulting decrease in the number of waterfowl, accompanied by the diminishing numbers of shorebirds and marsh birds and several threatened or endangered species, prompted the NAWMP partners to act. Under the NAWMP banner, coordinated activities of The Nature Conservancy, Ducks Unlimited, and the Bureau of Land Management have established a 3,000-acre preserve along the river.

To aid in the complex and often ticklish process of converting pasturelands back into riparian wetlands, The Nature Conservancy has set up exchanges whereby farmers can swap their holdings in the floodplain for properties away from the river, in the foothills. To date, more than 1,500 acres have been secured in this way. Another partner, the Bureau of Land Management, has completed creative exchanges of surplus urban facilities for areas along the Consumnes that can be restored to productive wetlands.

Meanwhile, the tedious, time-consuming process of planting native hardwoods and shrubs to enlarge surviving riparian forests has been undertaken by scores of volunteers recruited by The Nature Conservancy. On "workdays," during which as many as 500 volunteers labor at one time, hundreds of acres have been planted, saving taxpayers thousands of dollars in land restoration costs. Here again, there is strength in diversity. While The Nature Conservancy specializes in forest restoration, Ducks Unlimited has taken on the job of wetlands restoration on land owned by USFWS, TNC, and the Bureau of Land Management.

Restoring Habitat: Quill Lakes, Saskatchewan, Canada

The Quill Lakes, Saskatchewan, project is another example of making the most of multiple strengths, this time in Canada. This prime prairie/parkland habitat provides wonderful opportunities to witness geese gathering to begin their seasonal migrations as well as to observe shorebirds, sandhill cranes, and many species of ducks. Unfortunately, farming practices have reduced the extent of wetlands and grassland cover in the area, thus reducing numbers of waterfowl and other wetlands wildlife. As a result, the Prairie Habitat Joint Venture—a prairiewide partnership, which in Saskatchewan includes the Canadian federal provincial departments of agriculture and wildlife and three nongovernment organizations, Wildlife Habitat Canada, Ducks Unlimited, and the Saskatchewan Wildlife Federation—developed a two-pronged approach to improve habitat conditions. Negotiations for conservation easements and fee title acquisitions of wildlife habitat and marginal farmlands by the Saskatchewan Wildlife Federation, and outreach programs with local farmers to adopt conservation farming by several joint venture partners, have enabled conservationists to begin regenerating quality nesting cover for waterfowl and other ground-nesting birds. To date, 16,340 acres have been secured at the Quill Lakes project. Nearly 22,000 acres have been improved through habitat restoration, development, and/or enhancement activities.

PARTNERSHIPS WITH INDIVIDUALS

Another major component of the U.S. Fish and Wildlife Service's habitat conservation activities under the NAWMP involves an increased emphasis on providing assistance in wetlands protection and restoration to private landowners. The private lands habitat assistance and restoration program—called Partners for Wildlife—emphasizes voluntary partnership involvement of the private landowner in habitat protection and restoration. The importance of this activity is underscored by the fact that 74 percent of the nation's wetlands are privately owned. Increasingly, private landowners are looking to the USFWS as a source of both technical and restoration assistance.

In Arkansas's Cache/Lower White Rivers Joint Venture, farmers in the Private Lands Program are finding that practices encouraged as helpful to wildlife by biologists from the U.S. Fish and Wildlife Service, the state, and Ducks Unlimited are good for farming, too. For example, leaving plant residue and shallow water on harvested cropland in winter contributes greatly to controlling weeds and soil erosion. This has the added benefit of keeping agricultural chemicals out of streams and, of course, providing winter feeding areas for ducks. A NAWMP-sponsored 4-H Club competition—Managing Harvested Rice Fields for Wintering Waterfowl—has helped stimulate participation and instill the conservation ethic in the farmers of the future.

PARTNERSHIPS IN RESEARCH AND MONITORING

Research and evaluation of accomplishments of existing projects under the NAWMP is also an important function that is made stronger through partnerships with private organizations and state government. To measure the effectiveness of the NAWMP's programs on wetlands and migratory bird resources, cooperators must monitor biological responses to habitat protection. A continent-wide evaluation team made up of representatives from the private and public sectors has developed an evaluation strategy to measure responses of migratory bird populations to the quality and quantity of wetland habitats and to policies and programs affecting wetlands. The partnership approach to monitoring and evaluation will help managers adjust the NAWMP programs to maximize wetlands benefits to wildlife over the fifteen-year plan and well beyond.

For example, many studies for the arctic goose and black duck joint ventures have been launched to examine the factors influencing annual recruitment on breeding grounds. Research information, generated by a variety of conservation-oriented agencies and private organizations, is necessary to guide management decisions for populations and wetlands practices. The conclusions reached as a result of these and other management studies help influence program planning and future policy-making decisions for the NAWMP. Success can be measured and communicated directly through these partnership arrangements. In another case, at the Cache River, Illinois, project, The Nature Conservancy is starting to study the success of its effort to regenerate bottomland hardwood forests. Tree planting was done very carefully, with the need to monitor success factored into the restoration design.

PARTNERSHIPS FOR EDUCATION

Partnerships with private conservation groups such as Ducks Unlimited and The Nature Conservancy not only have matched and secured funds for conservation projects and assisted with land acquisition and restoration but also have been of equal importance in outreach and education. Most of these national conservation groups have in-house communications teams and produce high-quality publications that are sent to supporters of the NAWMP in the United States, Canada, and Mexico. These publications boast a variety of success stories about the various joint venture projects and help to educate constituencies and gain support for the NAWMP. This access to multiple constituencies—between TNC, DU, the National Wildlife Federation, and the National Audubon Society alone, there are more than 7.5 million members—helps affect public opinion and government policy-making.

On the ground, staff members of private organizations have assisted the U.S. Fish and Wildlife Service and the NAWMP with education and constituency building by addressing rotary clubs and school groups and helping to secure publicity.

PARTNERSHIPS IN PRACTICE: TWO MODEL PROJECTS

Partnerships are essential to the NAWMP for all of the reasons just discussed. Perhaps most important, the partnerships increase the overall chance of success and stability for long-term undertakings because of redundancy in leadership and advocacy. In other words, the failure of one partner will not cause the project to fail; others will pick up the ball and run with it. The federal sponsors of the North American Waterfowl Management Plan are truly thankful to the partners (more than 250 to date) who have spent their time and effort on this very important international conservation plan. Unfortunately, not all of their individual contributions can be recognized here. The following illustrations of individual partnership projects can only begin to represent the efforts going on all across the country.

BUILDING ON SUCCESS: CACHE RIVER, ILLINOIS

Often, the strongest joint venture projects sponsored by the NAWMP build on earlier successful partnerships but raise them to a level of accomplishment and ambition that could not be attained by the smaller partners alone. The role of ordinary citizens as catalysts and the role of private organizations as partners in such efforts cannot be minimized, as well illustrated by the Cache River protection project in Illinois.

The Cache River wetlands project, located some 130 miles southeast of St. Louis, Missouri, now forms part of the New Madrid wetlands project of the Lower Mississippi Valley Joint Venture. This finger of bald cypress and tupelo swamp reaching into Illinois's southernmost tip looks more like a Louisiana bayou than midwestern farming country. In fact, farming in the area is often marginal and prone to severe flooding. The Cache River is seasonal home to a large segment of the Mississippi flyway's migratory waterfowl population and boasts at least thirty-six plant and animal species that are rare in the state, including the bald eagle.

In 1979, a local volunteer citizens' group, Citizens Committee to Save the Cache River (CCSCR), formed to try to halt destruction of the area's swamps and ancient bottomland hardwood forests—some bald cypress trees there are known to be more than 1,000 years old—and the tremendous wildlife habitat they provide. The CCSCR is an excellent example of the critical role ordinary citizens can play in laying the groundwork for a project, challenging professional organizations and government agencies to get involved, and then supporting the resulting partnerships with everything from citizen advice to volunteer tree planting to congressional lobbying.

The Illinois Department of Conservation and The Nature Conservancy had also become involved in protection efforts for the area by acquiring 200-acre Heron Pond in 1970. As the state and TNC got deeper into the project, however, largely at the urging of the citizens' group, they began to realize that the natural biological boundaries of the swampland required the safeguarding of a much larger area. Otherwise, the land protected through acquisition would ultimately be degraded through siltation from adjoining lands and uncontrolled water level fluctuations. Over the next eighteen years, The Nature Conservancy and the state of Illinois worked to protect about 8,000 acres in two separate areas along the Upper and Lower Cache River.

It was not until the coming of the larger planning vision mandated by the NAWMP, however, that the state and private partners could dream of looking at the Cache River wetlands system as a whole. In 1990, after two years of planning, the 35,000-acre Cypress Creek National Wildlife Refuge was established to link and expand existing preserved areas to their natural biological boundaries. As a result, Ducks Unlimited joined the partnership by buying land farther down the Cache River in an independent, privately funded effort.

Far from disappearing from view now that the federal government is committed to preservation and restoration along the Cache River, the nonprofit groups have redoubled their efforts. Two recent $100,000 challenge grants from the National Fish and Wildlife Foundation brought in $400,000 in matching funds from private donations solicited by TNC and DU for land acquisition and restoration. TNC recently received a separate million-dollar grant from the Spencer T. and Ann W. Olin Foundation to start addressing protection of the entire 60,000-acre Cache watershed as part of TNC's ecosystem protection program. (See chapter 1 for further details on this program.)

With the aggressive support of the Illinois congressional delegation—spurred by the lobbying of the citizens' group—Congress first appropriated funds in 1990 for refuge acquisition from willing sellers along the

Cache. These dollars also bring with them annual compensation for land taken off the local tax rolls, a key factor in winning community support for a venture of this size, and clearly something only the federal government can bring to the table.

Private organizations such as TNC have also worked to build support for the project through promoting publication of magazine articles and holding well-publicized events such as the dignitary-studded dedication of the new national refuge.

As acquisitions by the partners go forward, it is clear that land management will take on increasing importance and require active involvement by many private and public partners. Ducks Unlimited is restoring marginal farmland to its original wetlands state to create more feeding areas for waterfowl. The Nature Conservancy, using a combination of volunteers and paid staff members, is planting native bottomland hardwood species such as oaks and hickories in areas where indiscriminate clearing had devastated the forest and increased erosion and flooding. The Army Corps of Engineers has actively enforced wetlands regulations in the area and conducted hydrologic studies and may well participate in structural work to restore water levels in the river corridor, especially the summer flows necessary to sustain wetlands species through dry periods.

Meanwhile, the Soil Conservation Service and other agricultural agencies are working with local farmers to stem the influx of silt that threatens the wetlands. Finally, the Boy Scouts of America and the Illinois Department of Corrections have been particularly helpful in supporting reforestation efforts. Scouts and prison inmates annually collect two tons of acorns and other nuts for a major seeding effort. Truly, mighty oaks from little acorns grow.

THINKING BIG: SOUTH CAROLINA'S ACE BASIN

Meanwhile, in a very different part of the country, the coastal plantations of South Carolina, the North American Waterfowl Management Plan has united and elevated existing conservation efforts beyond what any of the individual partners could have hoped to achieve.

The ACE Basin is one of the largest undeveloped wetlands systems on the Atlantic seaboard. The area lies on South Carolina's coastal plain, about 45 miles south of Charleston, and is defined by the Ashepoo, Combahee, and Edisto river system (hence the acronym ACE) and St. Helena Sound, into which these rivers drain. The ACE Basin project boundary encompasses approximately 350,000 acres of diverse wetlands and upland habitats, providing an extensive and unique complex of fish and wildlife habitats.

The impressive array of biological values in the ACE Basin had not gone fully unnoticed by federal, state, and private conservation entities, but for the most part both public and private groups tended to look at the basin's biological wealth in a segmented and incremental fashion. For instance, some agency or group would note with interest the bald eagle, wood stork, American alligator, or loggerhead turtle nesting habitat in the basin; another would show interest in the great number of wood and dabbling ducks that wintered there; and still another would see important value in the extensive hardwood bottomlands, scattered rare plant species, or endangered shortnose sturgeon. Interestingly, as important as many of these incremental components were, none on its own made it to the top of the action list of any federal or state agency or any private conservation group. It was a classic case of not being able to see the forest for the trees.

The bigger picture, contained in a holistic ecosystem approach to the ACE Basin, was not perceived until the late 1980s. For the most part, the few conservation gains made in the preceding decade were initiated not by the actions of public or private conservation groups but by the actions of individual plantation owners within the area. In the mid-1980s, Gaylord and Dorothy Donnolley, acting on their own initiative, gave Sampson Island to the state through The Nature Conservancy. Several years later, Ted Turner gave TNC a conservation easement over a magnificent 5,000-acre former rice plantation on the Edisto River. Mr. and Mrs. Donnolley's leadership came to the fore again in 1987, when they offered three more ACE Basin islands to TNC and Ducks Unlimited, with the encouragement that the two organizations work together to seek protection of several other significant islands that were on the market.

Although the private gifts helped establish a record of conservation activity in the ACE Basin, the real catalyst for building a comprehensive public and private partnership to carry out an ecosystem-based conservation program for the area came from the Atlantic Coast Joint Venture of the North American Waterfowl Management Plan.

The NAWMP's partnership-building concept led to a meeting of representatives from USFWS, the South Carolina Wildlife and Marine Resources Department, The Nature Conservancy, and Ducks Unlimited in late 1987. This meeting accomplished several important steps. First, it led to consensus on the need for a major conservation effort in the ACE Basin; second, it resulted in the establishment of the ACE Basin Task Force to guide the process (the task force was made up of the four founding organizations plus a fifth private landowner representative); and third, it spawned a workshop of biologists knowledgeable about the basin to begin the process of synthesizing and expanding on existing information about the natural values of the area.

The scientific workshop proved to be an eye-opener as biologist after biologist marched to the podium to give information on important aspects of the ACE Basin. Suddenly, the fragments of information began to form a coherent picture. Everyone began to recognize that the entire system, not just the pieces, needed protection.

Elements of a Protection Strategy

With the necessity for an ecosystem approach firmly recognized, the ACE Basin Task Force proceeded to develop a comprehensive protection strategy. The task force's essential first steps included the following:

1. *Inventory and preserve design.* An initial "preserve design," or a boundary based on available biological data, was established, and an inventory process was developed that would allow adjustment of the preserve boundary as new knowledge was gained.

2. *Protection.* A protection strategy was developed that took advantage of existing public and private conservation programs and developed new protection mechanisms where no existing program fit the need. The protection strategy had to accommodate the realities of a public and private funding capacity that was far short of the acquisition and stewardship needs as well as the fortunate fact that much of the land within the preserve boundaries belonged to owners who, like the Donnolleys, had a substantial commitment to conservation and the means to achieve it.

The principal protection goals established by the task force, and corresponding achievements to date, are as follows:

- Establishing an approximately 18,000-acre refuge system within the basin through the U.S. Fish and Wildlife Service.
  Nearly 3,000 acres had been acquired as of the early 1990s.
- Establishing an approximately 16,000-acre national estuarine research reserve (NERR) through the National Oceanic and Atmospheric Administration.

Lands currently held pending NERR designation are 5,700 acres held by TNC and 1,700 acres held by DU.
- Expanding the boundaries of the state's Bear Island Wildlife Management Area.
  More than 3,000 acres were added; total acreage now exceeds 12,000 acres.
- Establishing a large private reserve and research center at Mary's Island in the heart of the basin.
  See the description of the Cheehaw-Combahee Reserve in the following section.
- Protecting significant private lands within the ACE Basin through conservation easements.
  Some 19,000 acres are currently protected by easements held by TNC and DU.
- Establishing a state wild and scenic river on portions of the Edisto River.
  Discussions are under way with the principal private landowner along the river.
- Establishing several South Carolina heritage trust reserves (areas owned by the state and given special state statutory protection) within the basin to protect endangered species and plant communities.
  A biological inventory is under way to identify and rank qualified areas.
- Establishing a program to protect the significant hardwood bottomlands within the ACE Basin by acquisition and easement.
  Biological inventory and preserve designs of hardwood bottomlands are under way.
- Establishing a "conservation brokerage" service that would either preacquire properties offered for sale within the preserve boundary for resale to private conservation buyers subject to conservation easements or, where preacquisition is unnecessary, steer conservation buyers to opportunities with the expectation of receiving easements in return.
  Approximately 13,000 acres in four separate transactions were protected through conservation brokerage, and an additional 4,000 acres are being held by DU for resale to conservation buyers.
- Establishing a formal working arrangement with Westvaco, the one large publicly held industrial timberland owner (17,000 acres) within the basin, to work cooperatively on "best management" forestry

practices and other conservation practices consistent with the protection goals of the ACE Basin project.

Westvaco and the task force signed a memorandum of understanding in 1991 and are working together to further the protection plan.

- Establishing a "private lands stewardship program" in the basin to provide technical wildlife and wetlands assistance and other biological management information to private landowners as a means to encourage excellent private management of lands within the basin.

A program is under way and is well received by private landowners; the South Carolina Waterfowl Association has also encouraged landowner participation through an extensive wood duck nesting box program.

3. *Public information.* A public information program was established to provide recognition for and education about the ACE Basin effort to ensure that both the biological values of the ACE Basin and the goals of the task force would be well articulated and disseminated to appropriate local, state, and national audiences. This endeavor has paid off immensely; the task force's efforts have had very little opposition and in fact have been enthusiastically embraced or formally endorsed by more than 100 local, state, and national organizations, ranging from the local shrimpers' association to the South Carolina Development Board.

In addition to obtaining endorsements and recognition by the broadest possible array of organizations, the basic objectives of the public information program include the following:

- Actively seeking attention for the ACE Basin in the media, with an emphasis on the print media. Toward this end, substantial coverage of the ACE Basin project has appeared in numerous national, state, and local magazines and newspapers. A high-quality photojournalistic book on the ACE Basin was scheduled for publication in 1992.
- Seeking to introduce specific audiences to the ACE Basin and educate them about it. Printed material, slide shows, and a video presentation were developed. Target groups ranged from the South Carolina congressional delegation to key staff members within federal agencies and congressional committees to local businesses. Government and civic groups were briefed on the project. Where possible, on-site tours of the basin were utilized as the primary educational format. Enormous time and effort have been given to "selling" the ACE Basin project,

and as a result a constituency for the project has been cultivated within targeted national, state, and local audiences.

The Plan in Action

Accomplishing each of these efforts has required a minipartnership tailored to the particular goals. In each of these subpartnerships, it is usually critical to have one agency assume a leading role. For example, one combined acquisition and conservation brokerage project within the ACE Basin project has been spearheaded by Ducks Unlimited while still involving the remaining major partners and four landowners.

This project, called the Cheehaw-Combahee Reserve, involves the protection of two plantations: Mary's Island Plantation and Cheehaw-Combahee Plantation, encompassing 21,524 acres located at the center of the ACE Basin. DU's work illustrates how important a private organization can be in accomplishing the NAWMP's objectives in a cost-effective manner.

Of the estimated $15 million cost of the project, only about one-third is being sought from public sources, which are the North American Wetland Conservation Council and the state of South Carolina. The balance of the cost will be contributed by Ducks Unlimited, The Nature Conservancy, and private landowners through gifts and sales at less than fair market value. Also contributing will be "conservation buyers," who will purchase buffer lands sold by Ducks Unlimited with tight conservation restrictions to protect the area's natural values.

In addition to providing privately raised funding, DU is playing a key role in the project by negotiating with the landowners, holding options and conservation easements, swapping property (something that a government organization cannot do), and committing funds to long-term management and a wetlands research facility on the plantation.

LESSONS FROM THE PAST

In assessing the reasons for the success to date of the two joint venture projects just described, Jerry Updike, the U.S. Fish and Wildlife Service's refuge manager for the Cache River project, and Tom Massengale, a key player for the private partners in the ACE Basin project, credit several factors:

- *Consensus on important goals.* Because all partners agree on goals set forth clearly in the joint venture planning documents and make a positive commitment to teamwork, they can work toward shared objectives instead of toward disparate, individual accomplishments.
- *Combined resources on a large scale.* Projects of this size require a major commitment of federal, state, and private resources. All involved must "think big."
- *Local authority.* In a partnership of this scale, agencies and organizations must provide support for their local managers and give them maximum flexibility, independence, and authority. The U.S. Fish and Wildlife Service is moving in this direction, serving as an example to other agencies, both federal and state. Given the myriad decisions required in such complex projects, partners cannot work together effectively if they have to go to multiple, distant levels for day-to-day authorizations.
- *Private organizations' flexibility and speed.* Whether in acquiring land or installing necessary structures, nonprofit organizations can usually act in a much more flexible and timely manner than can government. This ability is crucial in order to respond to real-world deadlines.
- *Diversity and redundancy of partners.* As Jerry Updike puts it, "With all the partners, there is always a way to solve a problem or resolve an issue. Someone can be called on to fill the gap and get the job done."
- *Day-to-day interaction of all the partners.* Updike affirms the importance of the people behind the partnerships knowing and trusting one another, something that can happen only if they communicate frequently. Massengale stresses that close coordination is essential to ensure both timely completion of tasks and no duplication of effort.
- *Credit.* Each participant must willingly share credit with all involved for the conservation victories achieved.

Needless to say, effective functioning of partnerships such as these does not occur by osmosis. A great deal of thought and effort must be given to building the team concept necessary to pursue such complex projects. In the end, perhaps the most important ingredients to success are a shared commitment to a common goal and a sense of respect and trust among the partners.

PROMISE FOR THE FUTURE

The North American Waterfowl Management Plan holds much promise for the future conservation of wetlands and associated habitats. Congressional recognition of the plan, through the North American Wetland Conservation (NAWC) Act and the Food, Agriculture, Conservation and Trade Act of 1990 (the Farm Bill), has boosted funding for conservation projects across the continent. The NAWC Act authorizes significant federal funding to stimulate public/private partnerships and broadens both the geographic and biological scope of the plan by authorizing a means of transferring U.S. funds to Canada and Mexico. The Farm Bill strengthens the wetlands provisions of the 1985 Food Security Act and increases the role of the U.S. Fish and Wildlife Service in wetlands protection and restoration.

The Farm Bill created a new umbrella Agricultural Resources Conservation Program to improve water quality and protect wetlands and other environmentally sensitive areas on farms through a variety of incentive programs. One such program, the Water Quality Incentive Program, will encourage farmers to adopt progressive agricultural practices such as using biological pest control agents and limiting fertilizer applications in areas prone to water quality problems. As support for sustainable agricultural practices grows along with its demonstrated profitability, wildlife and agriculture are becoming more compatible. For example, the winter flooding of rice fields described earlier in this chapter has been approved as a conservation practice eligible for Department of Agriculture cost sharing.

The progress of past joint ventures has catapulted the implementation of new partnership efforts across the continent. These projects include developing economic incentives for landowners to maintain wetlands and change land use practices; entering into long-term and sometimes permanent agreements with landowners to provide waterfowl habitat; improving water management; and sponsoring research to find new ways to aid the recovery of waterfowl populations. As of the early 1990s, four new five-year joint ventures were being established: the Pacific Coast, Rainwater Basin, Upper Mississippi River–Great Lakes Region, Great Plains, and Intermountain West joint ventures.

In Canada, the success of the first year's program has led to ambitious second- and third-year efforts. The partnership there includes the International Association of Fish and Wildlife Agencies, the National Fish and Wildlife Agencies, the National Fish and Wildlife Foundation, Ducks

Unlimited, the Canadian national government, provincial governments, neighboring states, and a half dozen or so private organizations—quite a partnership. The results have been amazing. In 1988 alone, $10 million was raised. A total of 17,755 acres of critical wetlands and upland habitat were protected, 8,371 acres of waterfowl habitat were developed, and many farm conservation programs were started.

Communications initiatives are also spreading the good news about the NAWMP to audiences throughout the continent. Newsletters, public service announcements, videotapes, posters, conservation education programs, and audiovisual material featuring several celebrities, such as Randy Travis, Jerry Clower, and Garfield the cat, have supported the plan and carried its message about the importance of conserving wetlands and their associated habitats. Enthusiasm and support for the plan continue to gain momentum at all levels, with public involvement increasing most dramatically at the project level.

In the final analysis, increased support for the NAWMP will be essential if the plan is to reach its objectives. More agencies and organizations must become involved to provide local support and funding and to use their communications capabilities to reach an even larger audience. The U.S. Fish and Wildlife Service is indeed involved in one of the greatest conservation challenges of the century, and becoming partners with a great diversity of conservation-minded individuals, agencies, and organizations is the only chance the NAWMP has to blossom to fruition.

5

Public/Private Land Conservation
Partnerships in and Around
National Parks

Warren Brown

One evening in 1870, several members of the Washburn expedition exploring the Wyoming Territory sat around a campfire near the Yellowstone River, debating what might be done with the scenic splendors before them. Some suggested forming a partnership to develop the land for hotels; others suggested that each individual stake a claim to what appeared to be the most advantageous spots for future development. A journal records that one member of the party, Cornelius Hedges, suggested that there ought to be no such private development and that the whole region should be set apart as a great national park. Others agreed, and in 1872 Congress withdrew 2 million acres of the public lands from settlement, occupancy, or sale and dedicated them as a "public pleasuring ground for the benefit and enjoyment of the people."

In a little more than a century, the National Park System has grown to include more than 360 units, encompassing 80 million acres (including about 54 million acres in Alaska). These areas are managed in accordance with the general mandate outlined in the National Park Service's 1916 Organic Act: "to conserve the scenery and the natural and historic objects and the wildlife . . . and to provide for the enjoyment of the same in such manner and by such means as will leave them unimpaired for future generations."

Creating a new national park, monument, historic site, battlefield, or recreation area ensures that land will be protected and conserved for present and future generations. However, not every site worth protecting is eligible to be a new unit of the National Park System. Units to be included in the system must meet stringent criteria for national significance, suitability, and feasibility. Even if a site meets those criteria, alternatives for protection outside of the National Park System may be more appropriate. Areas managed by the National Park Service (NPS) are a small but important part of the nationwide system of areas protected by other federal agencies, state and local governments, and the private sector.

This chapter discusses the National Park Service's experiences in working with private, nonprofit land conservation partners to protect park units—either within boundaries set by Congress or immediately adjacent to those boundaries. It also describes examples of partnerships with park neighbors, including broad strategies for protecting the general park setting rather than one or two specific parcels of land. The next chapter discusses partnerships to protect lands that are for the most part wholly unrelated to National Park System units, using NPS programs of technical and financial assistance to state and local governments and nonprofit organizations for conservation of open space and recreational resources, including important natural and cultural values.

The National Park Service has additional important roles and responsibilities in protecting historic resources in partnership with states, local governments, Indian tribes, and the private sector. These NPS cultural resources programs are concerned with much more than protection of historic structures and archaeological sites. They also address the conservation of historic landscapes, open space around historic sites, and a broad range of local preservation programs. These programs are discussed briefly in a few examples that relate to protection of existing park units, but they involve many other partnerships that are beyond the scope of this book.

THE NEED FOR PARTNERSHIPS

Until the early 1960s, parks were usually created by withdrawals of land already in the public domain or by donations of land assembled by state governments and private philanthropy. Starting with the Cape Cod National Seashore in 1961, the National Park Service began a systematic program of acquiring private lands with appropriated funds for park purposes. In the following four decades, an increasing number of new parks have been established east of the Mississippi in or near metropolitan areas and in other locations with a substantial amount of private land.

In 1965, Congress established the Land and Water Conservation Fund (LWCF) to support land acquisition with revenues from federal surplus property sales, motorboat fuel taxes, and federal recreation user fees. In 1968, the fund was expanded to include receipts from oil and gas lease revenues from the outer continental shelf, and since 1977 the fund has been authorized at an annual level of $900 million. However, monies actually appropriated from the fund and made available for land acquisition have fluctuated with cycles in federal budgets and administration policies, as described in chapter 10. NPS is not the only agency using the LWCF, which also supports land acquisition by the U.S. Fish and Wildlife Service, the Forest Service, and the Bureau of Land Management and provides matching grants to states for recreational facility development as well as land acquisition.

At the end of 1991, official estimates for NPS's land acquisition program showed more than 300,000 acres in 12,000 separate tracts, estimated to cost about $425 million, left to be acquired within currently authorized park boundaries. This does not count areas in Alaska, mineral interests, and needs in other park units that exceed current legislative ceilings. Leaving aside the official budgetary footnotes, this probably means that the National Park Service is looking at a backlog of land to be acquired that will cost more than $1 billion. Congress has been providing money to buy this land at a rate of $50 million to $100 million each year. But even at this rate, the job will not be done in ten or even twenty years because funding needs continue to grow when Congress authorizes new parks and boundary expansions for existing ones. Whatever help partners can give the National Park Service in finding and stretching funds will bring the NPS's goals that much closer.

A limited supply of federal acquisition dollars is not the only reason why the National Park Service is working with partners to help address land protection needs in and around park units. Partnerships with land trusts can also provide greater flexibility to respond quickly to opportunities, to meet landowners' objectives, and to make creative deals that might not be possible within the complex requirements of the federal acquisition process. Partnerships in land conservation also can be part of a broader strategy for building community support for protection of park resources and values.

PARTNERSHIPS FOR ADDITIONS TO NATIONAL PARKS

This section outlines how the private sector can help with immediate acquisition needs in parks and of necessity includes only a few illustrations of the many partnerships that are being formed to help protect units of the National Park System.

PRIVATE GIFTS

Private philanthropy was instrumental in establishing many of the nation's premier parks, including Acadia, Grand Teton, Virgin Islands, and Redwood national parks. Since 1965, the National Park Service's annual land acquisition budget has ranged from a high of $367 million to a low of less than $1 million. Private sector help is especially important during the low points in the cycle. Between 1985 and 1991, the average appropriation for NPS land acquisition was about $72 million, enough for an active program but far short of the level needed to complete acquisitions of many critical tracts. Even with administration support for recent increases in the federal acquisition budget, the need for private help continues as the gap between land needing protection and available federal funds grows with every new park, and every expansion of an existing unit, authorized by Congress.

Help from the private sector can take several forms. The most desirable from the National Park Service's standpoint is an outright gift of land or money. Some private organizations such as the Save the Redwoods League, profiled in this chapter, have been providing funds for land acquisition steadily over several decades. Large single gifts, such as the more than 35,000 acres assembled in the 1930s by John D. Rockefeller, Jr., for Grand Teton National Park, are rare but include some outstanding examples in recent years as well as in the past.

A Major Benefactor: R. K. Mellon Foundation

In 1990, the Richard King Mellon Foundation announced ten separate gifts of land valued at $21 million to the National Park Service and the U.S. Fish and Wildlife Service. This has been considered the largest single private gift of land ever given to the nation, encompassing more than 100,000 acres. The major portion of this gift comprised about 93,000 acres of wetlands for a wildlife refuge in North Carolina, but it included outstanding additions to National Park Service areas in New Mexico, Virginia, Colorado, Pennsylvania, and Maryland. The properties had been acquired over a period of years through The Conservation Fund, a private nonprofit organization based in Virginia, on behalf of Mellon. This remarkable gift reflected the Richard King Mellon Foundation's interest in land conservation in general and a special interest in Civil War battlefields, including important tracts at Gettysburg, Antietam, Fredericksburg, and Petersburg.

A Long-Term Fund-raising Campaign: California's Redwood Forests

In 1918, several prominent Californians, including Stephen Mather, first director of the National Park Service, organized the Save the Redwoods League with the express purpose to "rescue from destruction representative areas of primeval redwood forests and to cooperate with State and National Park Services in establishing redwood parks." Studies promoted by the league identified potential sites of national park quality in the 1920s, and the league launched a nationwide drive to collect funds for acquisition of privately owned timberlands. Funds raised by the league were matched by the state of California to create several outstanding state parks. The league also helped create the public support that led to the establishment of Redwood National Park in 1968 and its expansion ten years later. Since 1918, the league has raised more than $66 million from private donations. Although the National Park Service has paid more than $1.5 billion to acquire land for Redwood National Park, the league continues to raise private funds that supplement the federal and state shares of this partnership. This work continues in other areas, including Sequoia National Park, where in 1986 the league purchased a 422-acre inholding for $2.2 million and in 1987 sold it to the National Park Service for a bargain price of $1.1 million.

Small Gifts Count: Petrified Forest National Park, Arizona

On a scale somewhat more likely to be replicated by other land trusts, the Archaeological Conservancy, based in Santa Fe, New Mexico, donated an important Anasazi ruin for an addition to Arizona's Petrified Forest National Park. The ruin had been a subject of NPS interest for twenty years but was beyond the monument's boundary. Funds to purchase the 40-acre property were donated by a couple who were members of the Archaeological Conservancy and had worked as volunteers conducting archaeological site surveys in and around the park. Owners of the land were more than willing to sell—they had acquired it from a brochure and plat but had never visited the site, which lacked the utilities and good road access advertised. The Archaeological Conservancy purchased the land in 1985, resolved some outstanding mineral interest problems by an exchange, and then donated the tract to NPS.

BUYING TIME

Having money available to buy land is only one part of the equation that can lead to successful conservation. In the operations of the National Park Service and other government agencies, protection of sensitive or threatened lands is often a question of not only how much money there is but also when, where, and how that money will be available.

Before the National Park Service can begin serious negotiations to buy land, a parcel must be within a park boundary authorized by Congress and land protection plans must be approved, budget priorities established, and funds appropriated. Even under the best of circumstances, a new park authorization or expansion of an existing park is likely to take at least a year, with another year or two before acquisition funds appear in the budget.

Federal procedures for authorizing land acquisitions and appropriating funds usually move along at their own mysterious pace. That pace does not always match activity in the real estate market, where deals can be made or lost in a matter of hours or days rather than fiscal years. Private nonprofit organizations can be especially helpful in bridging this gap between federal intentions to protect land and the ability to buy it, due to lack of funds or the limited flexibility of the federal government to operate in the private real estate market.

Preserving a Historic Estate: Natchez National Historical Park, Mississippi

Melrose is one of more than thirty outstanding antebellum homes that attract visitors from around the nation to Natchez, Mississippi. When economic conditions forced the owner of Melrose to offer it for sale, local preservationists and others were concerned about the potential for subdivision of the grounds, which make an irreplaceable contribution to the site's significance.

The owner of Melrose wanted to see the property protected but could not afford to wait indefinitely for the National Park Service to complete studies of alternatives or for the legislative process to work its way through authorizations and appropriations. The Trust for Public Land stepped forward to bridge the gap between market pressures and government procedures. TPL paid for an option to buy the entire Melrose estate at a price somewhat less than fair market value. This option, which eventually extended over more than a year, provided the owners with the assurance they needed that real progress was being made toward a deal. The option also allowed TPL to begin serious negotiations with members of Congress and the National Park Service on the details of a park proposal and the future of Melrose. Most important, during the option period, when the owner had a limited amount of cash available, TPL was able to pay for appraisals, surveys, inventories, and other costs leading to a transaction.

Congress authorized the creation of Natchez National Historical Park in October 1988. The legislation specified that NPS could acquire Melrose only if 25 percent of the fair market value were donated to the federal government. TPL assigned its option to NPS in the spring of 1990 and the transaction was completed, with the bargain sale meeting the legislative requirements. Establishment of the park not only protected Melrose but also marked the beginning of a partnership to protect other historic sites in Natchez.

FLEXIBILITY

Getting funds for federal land acquisition authorized and appropriated is only part of the battle. Once funds are available, the National Park Service must obtain a preliminary title insurance policy to identify owners and encumbrances, then contract with appraisers and review the appraisals for consistency with federal standards. Additional studies are now required to ensure that properties to be acquired do not contain hazardous substances that would impose a liability on the federal government for cleanup. Like other federal agencies, NPS has other procedural requirements outlined in the Uniform Relocation Assistance and Real Property Acquisition Act of 1970, including the payment of sale expenses and, in some cases, moving costs. NPS also is bound by a variety of federal rules and regulations about disposing of property not needed for park purposes.

Private organizations often have the flexibility to overcome some of the legal and other constraints on NPS authority. Typical examples of partnerships to address this situation include cases in which NPS authority to buy land is confined by state lines or strictly limited by appraisal guidelines or cases in which the NPS is prohibited from bidding at tax sales or excluded from creative use of local regulatory programs. Illustrations of these limitations and nonprofit partnerships to overcome them are as diverse as the resources being protected.

Crossing State Lines and Administrative Boundaries: Vicksburg, Mississippi

The problems of addressing lands beyond current park boundaries are especially complicated when different states and different NPS regional offices are involved. For example, a canal in Louisiana across from Vicksburg National Military Park was part of Grant's strategy to control the Mississippi River and split the Confederacy. The owner of the last remaining portion of the canal (3 acres) offered to donate it, but NPS was unable to accept the offer because the property was outside of the park's authorized boundary. The land to be acquired also fell within the territory of the NPS's Southwest Regional Office in Santa Fe, whereas the park, in Mississippi, reported to the regional office in Atlanta. The Conservation Fund was able to accept the donation and coordinate negotiations involving the two NPS regional offices; now that legislation authorizing a boundary adjustment has been adopted by Congress, the organization will be donating the land to the park.

Competitive Bidding: Chaco Culture National Historical Park, New Mexico

Federal procedures for acquiring land based on appraised value and negotiated agreements with owners effectively prohibit the National Park Service from acquiring land at a county tax sale, auction, or similar forum involving open, competitive bids. Two 80-acre parcels of privately owned land within Chaco Culture National Historical Park in New Mexico went up for sale because of nonpayment of county property taxes. These parcels had been the subject of an archaeological survey and were known to contain features important to the park. Previous owners had died without wills, leaving title to the land unclear and taxes in default. The Archaeological Conservancy, based in Santa Fe, obtained a letter of credit from a bank and successfully bid at the tax sale. One tract has already been transferred to the National Park Service; another may require a suit to clear title before it can be added to the park.

Flexibility on Appraisals: Petersburg Battlefield, Virginia

NPS acquisition of a 2.3-acre tract at Petersburg Battlefield in Virginia was at a stalemate over a relatively small difference between appraisals. NPS and other federal agencies do not have the flexibility available in the private sector to buy land for more than the appraised value, even if there is a relatively small difference between the government's estimate and what the landowner requires for a negotiated settlement. Indeed, NPS must get approval from Congress for any purchase in excess of the approved government appraisal—an approval that takes many months, if it comes at all. When the corporate owner of this industrially zoned parcel would not agree to the government's offer, The Conservation Fund was able to purchase the land, absorb the few thousand dollars that had blocked an agreement, and sell it to NPS for the appraised value.

Using Local Regulatory Programs: California's Santa Monica Mountains

With a mandate to conserve resources "unimpaired," the National Park Service faces formidable obstacles in the arena of public opinion if it engages in deals that allow any development on vacant land. Effective participation in programs that involve transferable development rights or the like often requires an ability to sell land or rights in land. Although NPS has certain authorities to sell or exchange lands, its ability to participate in such programs is very limited.

The Santa Monica Mountains National Recreation Area has a boundary that looks like an exceptionally creative work of modern art. Within the "park" is a patchwork quilt of private, state, and local ownerships and jurisdictions. The original intent of the legislation establishing the national recreation area was to create a partnership as an alternative to direct federal purchase of all the land.

The nonprofit Mountains Restoration Trust works with the National Park Service in a number of ways to protect land within the national recreation area, including serving as the lead agency in mitigating new development in the Malibu Coastal Zone. This role implements a California Coastal Commission program that requires all new subdivisions to "retire" the development rights on a building site for each new one they create. The Malibu program is designed to avoid any net increase in the number of building sites and is implemented through a transfer of development credit (TDC) system.

The Mountains Restoration Trust has been responsible for 200 of the 500 TDCs transferred to date that have effectively moved development from important watersheds or other sensitive natural areas within the national recreation area to other places more suitable for new construction. For example, the trust acquired 200 acres that had been divided into ninety lots on steep slopes without adequate access for emergency vehicles. A loan (technically a revolving grant) of $750,000 from the California State Coastal Conservancy supported the acquisitions and the restoration of the subdivision to natural conditions. The trust is selling the TDCs from the lots to developers. Proceeds from the sales will allow the trust to return the loan to the State Coastal Conservancy, and the land will be donated to the National Park Service. The extremely high land values in the Santa Monica Mountains provide exceptional incentives for creativity in this and other types of strategies combining protection with development.

Limited Development: The Appalachian Trail

Land trusts also can become more active participants in the development game, subdividing and selling off portions of a tract that are not needed for park purposes. Examples of limited development projects involving park units are rare, but they have a notable record of success for the Appalachian Trail. In one case, the Trust for Public Land acquired a 170-acre farm near Garrison, New York, to protect the trail corridor. A limited development plan divided the farm into seven parcels that were sold subject to conservation easements. The Trust for Appalachian Trail Lands has agreed to monitor the easements that protect scenic values but allow for one building site on each parcel.

PARTNERSHIPS WITH PARK NEIGHBORS TO PROTECT ADJACENT LANDS

Most of the foregoing examples involve either a few tracts that present special opportunities for protection or potential threats to the park from a specific plan for private development. Each transaction has addressed an immediate problem. However, many parks are subject to adverse effects from adjacent land development on a continual basis. Since park boundaries cannot be expanded indefinitely, especially in view of funding shortages within existing parks, partnerships with the private sector can be the cornerstone of a long-range conservation strategy. To develop nonfederal solutions to land use issues, staff members from several different NPS programs may assist local communities or nonprofit organizations.

Nationwide publicity and concern about land use problems adjacent to parks reached a peak when a major regional shopping mall was planned next to Manassas National Battlefield Park in Virginia. In 1989, Congress passed legislation immediately taking title to about 560 acres where clearing and grading for the mall development were already in progress. This was a triumph for preservation forces but one that was reached at enormous cost, as subsequent court awards have already totaled more than $117 million. The Manassas experience has emphasized the need to anticipate adjacent land use problems and act early to avoid or mitigate them. At Manassas, efforts to work in cooperation with the private sector and local officials did not succeed. However, the experience has spawned partnership initiatives to avoid similar situations around other parks.

In 1990, the Department of the Interior announced an American Battlefield Protection Plan. The battlefield initiative envisions cooperative efforts by the National Park Service, state and local governments, and the private sector to protect battle sites both within and outside of the National Park System. The program, coordinated by a special staff within NPS, is working to develop partnerships focusing on imminently threatened properties. A priority list of sites has been developed where efforts will be made to explore all reasonable options for protection, including creative use of public and private tools such as zoning, designation of historic districts, technical assistance, and acquisition of land in fee and easement.

Historic sites in the East are often the most obviously affected by adjacent land developments. However, partnerships can also be used to help protect wildlife migration routes, scenic quality, recreational access, and other elements of the landscape that contribute to the quality of visitors' experiences.

Preserving a Park's Setting: Jackson Hole, Wyoming, and Acadia, Maine

Land around a park is often just as important to long-term resource protection and the quality of the visitor's experience as is land within the park's boundary. Adjacent lands often comprise critical habitat for park wildlife and are important parts of the scenic splendor of the park or its historic setting. Some partnerships might be in place to protect these lands even if the park were not there, whereas other parks have been the catalyst for conservation initiatives beyond park boundaries.

The Jackson Hole Land Trust operates on the borders of Grand Teton National Park in Wyoming. Since 1980, the trust has protected more than 5,300 acres of land, holding about 2,100 in fee and an additional 3,200 under easement. Although these protected lands contribute immensely to the quality of the setting for Grand Teton, the trust has typically operated without any direct involvement or financial support from the National Park Service. Acquisitions by the trust are usually undertaken with the assumption that the trust will provide continued stewardship through ownership or easement monitoring rather than by eventual transfer to the park.

By contrast, the Maine Coast Heritage Trust (MCHT) provides an example of much more direct cooperation with the National Park Service to protect land in and around a park. MCHT has assisted NPS by negotiating about 100 donations of fee and easement to protect Acadia National Park. MCHT has been especially successful in approaching landowners who are reluctant to deal directly with the federal government and has also helped NPS with easement monitoring, training on tax issues, and inventorying important lands outside the park boundary. This partnership is discussed in more detail in chapter 9.

Promoting Linkages: Cuyahoga Valley, Ohio

In some areas, partnerships are useful in encouraging the development of linkages between parks and other regional resources by trails or designated tour routes.

For example, in northeastern Ohio, an exciting greenway project is under way through the Cuyahoga Valley National Recreation Area. It follows the route of the historic Ohio and Erie Canal from Lake Erie at Cleveland to historic Zoar, Ohio. This 65-mile corridor is the focus of a new organization, the Ohio & Erie Canal Corridor Coalition (OECCC) organized with NPS assistance. The OECCC is a true partnership organization, with broad representation of user groups, municipalities, park districts, historic preservation interests, and environmental groups. The Ohio and Erie Canal corridor includes the Cuyahoga Valley National Recreation Area and encompasses 22 miles of the Cuyahoga River valley between the national recreation area and the urban areas of Cleveland, Akron, and Canton. The corridor project will expand the focus on recreation, historic preservation, and natural resources and will encourage appropriate economic development. A study is under way for possible designation of the area as a national heritage corridor. This would involve action by Congress to make the corridor an affiliated area of the National Park System where protection and management would be primarily the responsibility of state and local officials, with NPS providing technical and financial assistance. This role of the National Park Service is discussed fully in the next chapter.

Conserving Resources outside Park Limits: Richmond Battlefield, Virginia

Park boundaries or the limits of NPS ownership often do not encompass all of the resources that are important to a park. Partnerships can be especially important in protecting resources that are closely related to the park's purpose but are not within the practical limits of NPS's acquisition authority.

Richmond National Battlefield Park has a "boundary" encompassing everything within a 5-mile radius of the Richmond, Virginia, city limits. NPS owns about 730 acres in ten separate units. These NPS units are under continual pressures from subdivision and industrial development on adjacent lands. In 1987, a partnership was initiated among landowners, citizens, local governments, the commonwealth of Virginia, and the National Park Service to help conserve the significant historic values not only of the ten NPS units but also of the entire Richmond area. A memorandum of understanding was signed by the city, the surrounding counties, and NPS. Resources were inventoried, and a heritage initiative was agreed on to conserve important sites. In 1991, one county withdrew from the agreement, largely over concerns about "local control," but cooperative planning efforts have been continuing. The Natural Lands Trust, a private nonprofit organization based in Philadelphia, has served as a consultant in this initiative, helping to identify opportunities for limited development and mitigation strategies for specific projects.

The Garthright House is one example of the work being done to protect historic resources in and around the Richmond battlefields. This historic house and a few acres are owned by NPS, but the adjacent private lands were planned for subdivision and development. These adjacent lands included many burial sites of those killed in the battle of Cold Harbor. The Natural Lands Trust assisted the National Park Service in outlining alternatives for conservation, ranging from some development to public acquisition. This information was instrumental in the county government's decision to acquire 50 acres to protect the historic setting of the house and the grave sites.

PROTECTING SCENIC VIEWS AND PROMOTING COMPATIBLE USES: THE APPALACHIAN TRAIL

Sometimes lands outside the NPS acquisition boundary do not contain specific historic or natural resources directly related to the park but are an integral part of the park's scenic value or historic setting.

The Appalachian Trail is more than just a footpath. The trail offers views of the surrounding landscape that are often the critical element in the quality of experience for those using the trail. When the National Park Service began negotiations for land along the Housatonic River in Connecticut, the Stanley Works tool company was willing to sell a large tract of land that included much more than the 1,000-foot corridor needed for trail purposes. Local concerns about effects on the tax base were one factor that led to a partnership approach involving two land trusts: the Housatonic Valley Association and the Trust for Appalachian Trail Lands. The trusts helped develop a plan for the entire property defining the area needed to protect scenic values of the trail and other areas suitable for development. NPS acquired 1,276 acres in fee and easements on 504 acres, with the

Housatonic Valley Association acquiring the balance of the company's property for a limited development project.

PARTNERSHIPS IN PARK MANAGEMENT AND OPERATIONS

Acquisition of land by the National Park Service does not automatically ensure that it will be protected or managed for public enjoyment. Because funds and staff even at the federal level are limited, NPS also works with partners in the private sector in the management and operation of the National Park System. These partnerships most often take form through volunteers or concessionaires who help staff and maintain facilities. Partnerships in management and operation of land itself are less common but include some interesting cases in which land trusts have gone far beyond the role of serving as an intermediary in the acquisition process.

VOLUNTEER MANAGEMENT: THE APPALACHIAN TRAIL

In addition to providing some examples on the leading edge of creativity in land protection, the Appalachian Trail provides some of the more interesting examples of alternatives to federal ownership and management. Technically, the Appalachian Trail is a unit of the National Park System, and NPS maintains a trail project office in Harpers Ferry, West Virginia. However, management and maintenance of the trail are accomplished not by park rangers but by volunteer organizations through the private Appalachian Trail Conference. The National Park Service has delegated most of its management responsibilities to the conference, which in turn has delegated them to thirty-one member clubs. The trail clubs maintain both federally owned lands and lands that remain in private ownership subject to easements for trail purposes. In 1990, the Appalachian Trail Conference reported contributions of time and energy from more than 3,000 volunteers, who provided over 66,000 hours of labor valued at more than $500,000.

EASEMENTS FOR A NATIONAL HISTORIC SITE: HYDE PARK, NEW YORK

Easements held by private organizations can be another type of partnership supporting park operations by reducing NPS obligations for management and maintenance. At the Home of Franklin D. Roosevelt National Historic Site in Hyde Park, New York, NPS has authority to acquire any land within the original boundaries of the Roosevelt estate by donation. The Morgan property of 89 acres is an important part of the FDR home's historic setting. Mr. Morgan shared NPS's concern about protecting the open space and scenic qualities of this land and in the 1970s offered to donate his property to the park. Concerns about operating costs and effects on the local tax base were the most prominent reasons cited when NPS declined the offer.

Instead, Mr. Morgan donated an easement to Scenic Hudson, Inc., a land trust active in the entire Hudson River valley. The easement ensures that the open space character of the Morgan property will be protected and makes NPS acquisition of this land unnecessary.

Scenic Hudson, working with NPS's Rivers and Trails Conservation Assistance Program, has also helped the National Park Service complete a 3.5-mile trail linking the Home of FDR with Vanderbilt Mansion National Historic Site. The trail crosses the Morgan property and another private ownership. Establishing a trail that would be available for public use, even using an existing footpath, required that the parties overcome several legal hurdles related to liability and maintenance.

After considerable thought and negotiations, a memorandum of understanding was signed that explained the rights and responsibilities of each party: the National Park Service, the town of Hyde Park, Scenic Hudson, the Winakee Land Trust, and future cooperators, including the Boy Scouts and the Adirondack Mountain Club's local chapter, who together will be maintaining the trail. Liability insurance acquired by the land trusts through the national Land Trust Alliance was a key ingredient that allowed for the trail to cross private lands. The memorandum details each public agency's responsibility for maintaining the portion of the trail that crosses its property and for cooperating to make the project work across jurisdictional lines.

PARKS AND REGIONAL PARTNERSHIPS

Partnerships are also becoming more necessary to address broader issues than protection of a specific piece of real estate. Increasingly, the National Park Service is becoming involved as part of a coalition of interested organizations, agencies, and individuals seeking to protect resources in a

large and diverse geographic area where federal acquisition is neither necessary nor desirable. This type of partnership arrangement is most often used
to protect a combination of natural, cultural, and recreational values along
rivers, by creating trails or establishing heritage corridors or areas.

AMERICA'S INDUSTRIAL HERITAGE PROJECT: WESTERN PENNSYLVANIA

The National Park Service is working in partnership with the state of Pennsylvania, local governments, and the private sector in a nine-county area of
western Pennsylvania to inventory, plan, and protect historic, scenic, recreational, and other resources. Called America's Industrial Heritage Project,
the effort grew out of local interest in promoting tourism and economic
development. Although the project area includes four existing national park
units, it has focused other NPS programs, such as the Historic American
Building Survey/Historic American Engineering Record, the Historic Preservation Fund, and the National Register of Historic Places, on identifying
important resources and finding creative ways to protect them. An example
is the creation of a new $3 million visitor center for the Horseshoe Curve
National Historic Landmark, funded jointly by the state and NPS, which will
be managed through a cooperative agreement with a local nonprofit organization, the Altoona Railroaders Memorial Museum, Inc.

Similar partnership efforts are responsible for establishing regional historic tour routes, enhanced wayside exhibits, and economic revitalization
of downtown Altoona, as well as a State Heritage Park Program, which will
benefit existing NPS units and the entire region. Another part of this
project, the Allegheny Highlands Trail, is discussed in the next chapter.

America's Industrial Heritage Project was established primarily through
the efforts of Congressman John Murtha, who built a coalition of interested
individuals, organizations, and agencies and was instrumental in getting
both the authorizations and appropriations to implement specific action
plans. The project operates under the general direction of the Southwestern
Pennsylvania Heritage Preservation Commission, which was established
by Congress.

THE SALEM PROJECT: MASSACHUSETTS

A similar regional planning effort is under way in Salem, Massachusetts,
but it began with a partnership at the local level. The local partnership then

sought support from Congress for planning and development assistance, but there was no specific authorization by Congress, and there is no legislatively established commission. Instead, a regional planning effort is focusing on Salem Maritime National Historic Site, making its development a catalyst for economic revitalization, tourism, historic preservation, upgraded transportation systems, and a general improvement in the quality of life for the city of Salem and the surrounding county.

NPS is a member of the Salem Partnership, which includes representatives of the business community, nonprofit organizations, and the public seeking to revitalize Salem. Future plans for visitor use and interpretation at Salem Maritime National Historic Site will be coordinated with broader regional efforts to protect significant historic sites in private ownership. After only three years, results are reflected primarily in plans that chart a future direction for the community.

Funding from Congress has supported a comprehensive planning, design, and construction program for Salem, including land purchases for the historic site and planning assistance to the surrounding areas. Plans are being implemented to improve access, circulation, and parking in Salem; rehabilitate historic buildings and structures at the national historic site; increase the public's understanding and appreciation of Salem's importance to America's emergence as a nation; and provide a central visitors' center. Since 1987, efforts of the Salem Partnership and the Salem Project have been credited with encouraging nearly $60 million worth of private investment in downtown Salem. Other NPS efforts have focused on assisting citizens' groups in creating a system of walkways connecting important sites and features of the town.

LESSONS FROM THE PAST

The first national parks were established as a result of many people and organizations working together toward a common objective. The National Park System today is not just an assortment of places managed by another federal agency: Congress has declared that it is "a collective expression of a single National Heritage." Part of this heritage is a desire, in both business enterprise and government, to pool money, resources, skills, and expertise in common efforts to reach greater achievements. Partnerships seem to be the way of the future as federal, state, and local agencies seek help from one another and the private sector in managing resources and delivering services to the public. Such partnerships offer tremendous potential for accomplishment, but they also can generate disputes if one or more of the partners seeks to share profits without doing its share of the work. For partnerships to be successful, all of the partners should agree on goals and share equitably in both risks and rewards.

MAINTAINING A NATIONAL PERSPECTIVE

Because it is the *National* Park Service, NPS has a responsibility to maintain a national perspective on its acquisition program and priorities. This is not always consistent with the agendas of nonprofit partners, who may want to settle on a deal regardless of the implications for NPS priorities in other areas. Moreover, NPS must operate within the confines of the administration's budget requests, whereas other organizations may have more freedom to pursue additional appropriations from Congress or private donations. Watchdogs such as the General Accounting Office, the Department of the Interior's inspector general, and congressional oversight committees have expressed special concerns about this situation. These concerns revolve around who is in control of the budgetary process and how much a nonprofit organization may be adding to the cost of land to cover its overhead. This question of overhead is likely to get special attention when NPS is purchasing land that is under an option to a nonprofit organization but the nonprofit organization has not actually paid for the property and taken title.

To address these concerns, the Department of the Interior has adopted guidelines for transactions between nonprofit organizations and federal agencies using the Land and Water Conservation Fund.[1] These guidelines emphasize the independent role of the private partner, acceptance of the risk that appropriated funds may not be available, and the need for full disclosure of the terms of financial arrangements for the initial purchase. The guidelines also indicate that land acquired by a nonprofit organization for a federal agency should be within the boundaries of an authorized area and consistent with agency priorities. Nonprofit groups need to take special care in following the established rules and guidelines to avoid the appearance of impropriety in the eyes of the auditors.

The key to success in this type of partnership is for the federal agency and the nonprofit organization to understand thoroughly the pressures and constraints on their partners and to document those understandings in a formal letter of intent when a nonprofit group is acting as an intermediary for NPS. The excitement of seizing an opportunity must be balanced with the practicalities of the federal authorization and appropriation process.

Land trusts should also be careful about accepting the word at one level in the bureaucracy too readily. For example, a park superintendent or other staff member may privately agree that adding lands to the park would be desirable while an official agency position remains opposed to park expansion due to budgetary or other concerns. Of course, unless NPS and other federal agencies take their own initiatives in establishing priorities for land acquisition, boundary adjustments, and similar means of protection, other individuals and organizations are likely to take this leadership role.

ANTICIPATING PUBLIC CONCERNS

Equally important is the public's perception of the relationship between NPS and its nonprofit partners, regardless of the formal rules. Even if a transaction is undertaken entirely on the initiative of a nonprofit organization, it may be seen by the public as the first step in a plot to expand park boundaries and take additional private lands. Recent experiences at Antietam and Richmond national battlefields have been the subject of considerable press coverage focusing on the allegations of some property owners that nonprofit organizations are only a front for a federal land grab that will eventually force people out of their homes or off their farms.

Nonprofit organizations also should never underestimate the potential for loud opposition from a few people to any land acquisition for conservation purposes, especially when such acquisition may be linked to the federal government. Although confidentiality may be essential at some stages in negotiations, a strategy for communicating with the public and providing information about the purposes of a transaction should be developed before problems surface in the press. This strategy should include attention to the fact that property owners and local officials concerned about the tax base simply may not trust the public statements of a federal agency.

BALANCING CREATIVITY AND CRAFTSMANSHIP

For several decades, attention has been focused on opportunities for creative conservation by such means as cooperation with local zoning authorities, federal regulations, coordination with other agencies, easement

acquisition, and various methods of acquiring fee or easements by donation, exchange, or bargain sale. The search for ways to protect more land
with less federal money is not new. In the 1960s and 1970s, the emphasis
was on stretching federal funds because land prices were rapidly escalating; some of the initiatives in the 1980s also responded to fears of federal
land grabs and an ideology opposing federal ownership.

Partnerships with nonprofit organizations can be the foundation for a
creative conservation strategy. However, enthusiasm for creativity should
not overwhelm the need to focus on the target. For NPS, the target should
be a clear plan for resource management and public use. Then the interest
to be acquired should be carefully defined and methods of acquisition
explored. Problems arise when the first step is choosing a technique—
"Let's use easements" or "Let's try tax incentives"—before the purposes
of protection have been defined. Creativity is most valuable when it is
combined with craftsmanship—an ability to match the tools with the
objectives to be achieved.

Whether the interest to be acquired is in fee or easement, land trusts can
help in the acquisition process by providing the nongovernment presence,
perspective, or negotiating flexibility that may be the key to reaching an
agreement with a landowner. Land trusts can provide guidance on tax
issues, appeal for charitable contributions not likely to be directed toward
government agencies, and make creative arrangements for financing, limited development, or trades. Partnerships building on these strengths seem
to have a great deal of potential that has not been fully tapped. Land trusts
can often provide the missing ingredient in the recipe for successful conservation. They are especially important when NPS does not have adequate
funds available, and they should always be fully explored before NPS moves
forward with a purchase. Nevertheless, partnerships cannot be a complete
substitute for NPS's having adequate support for protecting land the old-
fashioned way: buying it for full market value with appropriated funds.

PARTNERSHIPS WITH INDIVIDUALS

The combination of limited funding and the feeling in some places that the
federal government already owns enough land has encouraged special
attention to the use of easements by both the National Park Service and its
land trust partners. Easements are in effect a partnership with the most
important part of the private sector: the landowners themselves. Since the

1930s, the National Park Service has acquired easements on more than 80,000 acres in at least eighty-six different park units.

Many NPS managers complain that easements are difficult to manage and enforce, although they do not usually explain how these difficulties compare with the problems of managing land owned in fee. In NPS's experience, there have been both substantial accomplishments and problems in protecting land with easements. The keys to success seem to be a precise definition of what uses are compatible with park purposes, an ability to translate these objectives into clear terms for the easement, and a strong program of monitoring the easement. The willingness of landowners to cooperate, ability of park managers to work with owners of land covered by easements, and stability of low market pressures for changes in land use also contribute to the success of an easement program within park boundaries. Land trusts can play an important role in ensuring an easement program's success by working with landowners and park managers to define the terms of an easement, providing advice on tax implications, and monitoring to ensure compliance with the easement.

Easements create a "permanent" partnership between an individual and the holder of the easement. NPS is also effectively in a partnership with individuals on a more temporary basis when it acquires land subject to reserved rights of use and occupancy. Reservations of use for life or for a specified term can facilitate acquisition at a time favorable for the owner and the government. However, reserved rights have also created some very awkward situations for both parties. Typical cases include those in which the seller elects, say, a twenty-year reservation, which seems like a good deal at the time but expires when the owner is elderly and unable to relocate easily, and NPS has limited authority to allow continued occupancy without charging a market rent that may be unaffordable. Similarly, as owners who sell easements age or are replaced by new owners, support for "partnership" may change and produce conflicts with park managers. Here again, land trusts can help by working with NPS and owners to explain the advantages and disadvantages of various acquisition strategies.

Units of the National Park System often require a different level of protection from that which may be adequate or appropriate for other organizations. Land within most NPS units needs to be available for public use and direct management of natural or cultural resources. Alternatives to fee ownership are most appropriate in those special situations in which traditional private uses (farming, ranching, or occupancy of historic homes) are part of the resource to be protected and are consistent with long-term park protection objectives. Partnership protection strategies using alternatives to fee purchase are also appropriate and are probably the only tools available for addressing uses of adjacent properties. But within park boundaries, fee ownership is usually necessary and provides the long-term assurance that land can be managed to meet changing demands of the visiting public and evolving understandings of how park systems operate.

PARTNERSHIPS FOR ECONOMIC DEVELOPMENT

Areas called "partnership parks" are becoming especially popular as communities learn of the experience in Lowell, Massachusetts, where federal funds for the Lowell National Historical Park have stimulated a remarkable economic revitalization. Unfortunately, the experience in Lowell is not likely to be repeated in every town with a declining industrial economy. Successful partnerships in park creation, protection, and management require a special combination of social and economic forces, along with local leadership. This leadership has to be backed with a commitment to action that will not fade in the face of slumps in the economy. Otherwise, the partnership is likely to be one-sided, with NPS providing money and the local partners spending it. For example, during the early 1990s several local economic development projects found their way into the NPS budget under the banner of partnerships that are little more than grants or gifts to local communities. Although these projects may have merit, they divert funds from existing park units and other priorities for resource protection.

These lessons should not discourage the pursuit of creative conservation strategies both inside and around parks. They should, however, encourage caution and formation of a clear plan for how these partnerships will be managed and maintained as they mature over time. With a mandate to protect resources unimpaired for future generations, NPS has less flexibility than many other organizations to break up a partnership if it is no longer working.

PROMISE FOR THE FUTURE

Public and congressional interest in protecting parks from adverse effects of adjacent land uses is expected to remain high. The symbolism of threatened parks is especially prominent in the news media, which has covered high-profile areas such as the Everglades, the Grand Canyon, Yosemite, and Yellowstone. Although partnerships with the private sector can play an important, but rather limited, role in protecting land within park boundaries, they are usually the only available methods for addressing the protection of adjacent lands.

People, as well as pressures for residential, commercial, and other types of development, are continuing to move closer to parks that were once remote. Similarly, newer park units or special projects to address heritage resources are increasingly located near major population centers. Park boundaries cannot expand indefinitely to prevent adverse effects of adjacent land uses. Partnerships with the private sector, using the full range of available creative conservation techniques, will be especially important in the years ahead. Land trusts can be partners in building constituencies and support in the community for park protection, especially by emphasizing the common interests of parks and their neighbors in enhancing the quality of life in a community.

Enthusiasm for partnerships involving the National Park Service is likely to continue and lead to the establishment of new parks or special projects as well as support for existing park units. Urban industrial areas and rural mining or agricultural areas experiencing a decline in traditional economic activities are increasingly looking toward tourism as their best hope for revitalization. The concept of a heritage corridor or partnership park is especially attractive to many areas seeking to duplicate the successes along the Illinois and Michigan Canal and along the Blackstone River in Massachusetts and Rhode Island. In these two projects affiliated with the National Park System, intergovernmental commissions are coordinating planning and protection of heritage resources encompassing rivers, canals, industrial sites, parks, and private lands. The NPS role is primarily to encourage and facilitate resource protection by local governments by providing national recognition and limited amounts of technical and financial assistance.

Congress is likely to continue to direct the National Park Service to become involved in managing or providing technical and financial assistance to these partnership parks. Such partnerships often present special opportunities for the National Park Service to encourage protection of important natural and cultural resources. They are especially exciting as opportunities to enhance the quality of life for more communities and to share with them part of the national park ethic. The challenge ahead is how to carry out these partnership programs in new areas without draining the funds needed to manage and maintain existing units of the National Park System. As the examples of the preceding pages illustrate, cooperation with land trusts and the private sector can help enhance the National Park Service's ability to deal with this challenge.

NOTES

1. See *Federal Register* 48, no. 155 (August 12, 1983): 36342–44.

6

National Park Service Partnerships Beyond the National Parks

Christopher N. Brown

The previous chapter described the array of partnerships forged in and around units of the National Park System. Another side to the National Park Service is its role in providing assistance to states and local governments outside the national parks. Since 1981, when programs from the Bureau of Outdoor Recreation and its successor, the Heritage Conservation and Recreation Service, were incorporated into the National Park Service, NPS has been in the technical assistance business. Under the Recreation Resources Assistance Division, the National Park Service operates the Rivers, Trails, and Conservation Assistance Program, actually a series of programs much broader in scope than the name implies.

These assistance programs help state agencies, communities, and non-profit organizations plan for open space needs such as river corridors, trail systems, greenways, long-distance trail connections, conversion of abandoned rail lines to recreational use, and statewide inventories of rivers and trails. Heritage corridors, which include cultural as well as natural resources, are also part of the menu. In all cases, these "river and trail" projects involve partnerships. Active for the past decade, the program annually assists approximately 100 projects around the nation, a few on the boundaries of NPS units but most independent of any federal area.

Opportunities for conservation of land without its designation as a national park abound. Creating a new national park is neither possible nor desirable as a solution to every land protection challenge. Units of the National Park System often get considerable attention for their symbolic importance, but they are only one part of the national system of areas being protected by states, local governments, other federal agencies, and the private sector.

As NPS assistant director William C. Walters has stated:

My view of a national system of parks includes everything from the corner tot lots to greenways and open space corridors. . . . Population trends indicate that our nation's population will grow by more than 40 million in the next 25 years, reaching 290 million by 2025. Without a national system of parks, our children and grandchildren will not have the open space and recreation opportunities necessary to improve the quality of life and provide for their individual health and well-being. The National Park Service has the opportunity *and* the responsibility to be on the cutting edge . . . in providing leadership to the local, county, regional, state, and private sectors in planning, acquiring, and developing that national system of parks.[1]

The National Park Service's capability to foster the creation of this national system of parks through partnerships is in its state and local Rivers, Trails, and Conservation Assistance Program. Working outside NPS units, this program does the following:

- Relies on partnerships with state and local governments and private nonprofit organizations to accomplish its objectives, which frequently include land protection.
- Provides a wide range of technical and resource assessment skills to its project cooperators.
- Provides staff rather than land acquisition or grants; it offers skilled planners—landscape architects, regional planners, and other resource professionals—to project cooperators. Together, they define issues and set goals, assess resources and develop options, and ultimately lay out a plan of action.

Unlike other programs of the NPS, the Rivers, Trails, and Conservation Assistance Program does not apply a test of national significance to projects it will work on. Although the great majority of its projects are in areas of national, statewide, or regional significance, the program's purpose is to assist local communities in protecting resources they deem important.

FEDERAL ASSISTANCE TO LOCAL PARTNERSHIPS

While a number of federal agencies provide technical assistance to state and local governments, the NPS has developed a unique approach.

PRINCIPLES OF FEDERAL TECHNICAL ASSISTANCE

According to the guiding principles of the National Park Service's Rivers, Trails, and Conservation Assistance Program, assistance must have the following characteristics:

- *Customer oriented.* NPS planners assist where help has been requested. The program is "client driven"; local project cooperators set their goals and agendas with NPS aid. With current limitations on funding, NPS can respond to about half of the requests it receives each year.
- *Cooperative and cost shared.* All projects are conducted cooperatively. NPS contributes staff time and expertise to match local sponsors' financial or in-kind contributions. Frequently, there are a number of partners and a memorandum of agreement that spells out each side's functional and financial responsibilities.
- *Short-term.* Almost never does the NPS have a continuing active role in these projects. After twelve to thirty months of assistance, the NPS moves on, invariably leaving behind a multijurisdictional arrangement (often incorporated) that will provide strong leadership in project implementation and management.
- *Results oriented.* The program stresses real, measurable conservation results: miles of river or trail designated or established, acres of land protected, stewardship organizations formed, dollars leveraged to support a project, or broad protection legislation passed as a result of NPS action. Even though land conservation is usually a major objective, the NPS does not itself purchase or protect land for its assistance projects; it frequently plays the role of midwife in the birth of a new project, however.

Within these principles, the National Park Service's Rivers, Trails, and Conservation Assistance Program offers assistance in public education, networking, building of public support, and planning and resource assessment as well as legislative assistance and training in promotion and fund-raising.

EDUCATION, NETWORKING, AND PUBLIC SUPPORT: ALLEGHENY HIGHLANDS TRAIL

The critical footing for a successful land conservation project is public support. None of the Rivers, Trails, and Conservation Assistance Program's projects can succeed without extensive public education and marketing; indeed, substantive public involvement is a cornerstone of the program.

For example, the Allegheny Highlands Trail project in northwestern Maryland and southwestern Pennsylvania has progressed largely because of its extensive, carefully thought-out public participation strategy. The trail follows a 57-mile-long abandoned rail line from Cumberland, Maryland, to Confluence, Pennsylvania, connecting the Chesapeake and Ohio Canal with the Youghiogheny River Trail and establishing a crucial link in a potential 315-mile trail from Washington, DC, to Pittsburgh. As good as the idea is, however, many local landowners and citizens were not enthusiastic about the trail.

The strategy to develop support for the trail included the following:

- Three public workshops to identify trail-related issues and alternatives and a workshop designed to address concerns of adjacent landowners in which an attorney, a real estate and insurance expert, a trail manager, and a representative from the national Rails to Trails Conservancy (which had adopted the project for sponsorship) formed a panel to respond to direct questions from workshop attendees.
- A four-color brochure that laid out the vision for the trail and, by listing cooperators, demonstrated the project's extensive support.
- A slide program prepared by the Somerset Conservation District to promote the trail concept.
- Extensive news coverage. NPS staffers went out of their way to keep the local press informed of the story. Efforts by the Somerset Conservation District and the Somerset County Rails-to-Trails Association, as well as the level of controversy the trail proposal had engendered, also kept the trail project in the news.
- An attractive, illustrated "Allegheny Highlands Trail Study Report" was produced by the NPS with its cooperators. This thoroughly

documented the resource opportunity, laid out potential actions, and underscored the breadth of support and depth of consultation occurring on the project.

Local, county, and state agencies and organizations, many individuals, and the NPS created a partnership to transform the Allegheny Highlands Trail plan into an on-the-ground success. The Somerset County Chamber of Commerce took the lead in marketing and promoting the trail in order to attract the funding to build the first 17 miles. The new Somerset County Rails-to-Trails Association reached agreement with CSX Corporation on a sale price for the first phase (17 miles) of the trail, and the association also received a $150,000 grant from the Richard King Mellon Foundation to help acquire the right-of-way. Construction of the trail began in 1991.

PLANNING ASSISTANCE AND RESOURCE ASSESSMENT

Because the NPS tries to provide the particular skills and expertise its local cooperator most needs, assistance from the NPS may take various forms.

Developing a Greenway and Trail System: Loudon County, Virginia

A thorough assessment of a project's natural and cultural resources is always an important building block in the National Park Service's trail corridor projects. Beginning in 1989, NPS's Mid-Atlantic Regional Office has assisted the town of Leesburg and Loudon County, Virginia, in developing an extensive greenway and trail system. The goal is to conserve open space and enhance the quality of life for local residents. Loudon County, located about 20 miles west of Washington, DC, faces development pressures from the expanding metropolitan area. NPS formed a partnership that included town, county, regional, and state planners as well as businesses, individual citizens, and private groups.

As a first step, key information about natural, cultural, and historical resources was gathered and incorporated into maps prepared by NPS and Loudon County. The commonwealth of Virginia and local partners contributed information through meetings, workshops, and questionnaires. Issues and goals were clarified through workshops, and the results were summarized in a newsletter compiled by NPS. Draft maps were presented to the public in workshops and mailings and were then revised for updated comprehensive plans for the town and county. A final report will include an action agenda for the county, town, and private sector. A greenways commission or a new land trust may be one instrument for implementation.

Developers already have offered new recreational corridors across proposed subdivisions, and Xerox Corporation, which has extensive landholdings along the Potomac River, has agreed to develop the Potomac Heritage Trail along its riverfront property, including construction of a bridge over Goose Creek. Unfortunately, a $5 million bond authorization to provide funds for land acquisition was defeated in March 1991; tightness of the county's budget (which required the layoff of 100 teachers during the same week the vote was held), more than objection to acquisition of public land, was the cause of the defeat.

Protecting a River Corridor: Wood-Pawcatuck River System, Rhode Island

Resource assessment and planning are equally important for river protection projects. For example, the Rivers and Trails Conservation Assistance Program was asked to come into rural Rhode Island to help nine towns, the state, and private citizens develop a coordinated strategy for protecting and enhancing the state's cleanest river system, consisting of the Wood and Pawcatuck rivers. The study area encompassed a quarter mile on each side of the rivers and extended to include wetlands, floodplains, and prime agricultural soils where these resources begin within the quarter mile and reach beyond it.

A Project Advisory Committee was formed to help direct the study. Working with the committee, NPS developed an innovative method for delineating and evaluating the qualities of the river landscape. Distinct resource areas and land use patterns of the river area were translated into seven planning unit types, some repeating along the corridor. Each unit type has its own character and is used to apply selected management recommendations. Results of the assessment not only documented the significance of various sites but also helped to develop appreciation for the values of the river corridor.

The newly formed Wood-Pawcatuck Watershed Association implemented the plan's recommendations by promoting public awareness through a wide range of activities, including establishment of a conservation easement program and promotion of river cleanups and information workshops.

The study also added impetus to the passage of a state bond issue that included $1 million to protect land along the rivers and begin additional planning in adjacent watersheds. Federal funds (through the Dingell-Johnson Program) and private foundation support have followed the state commitment. So far, more than 1,000 acres have been purchased, protecting both scenic and natural reaches of the river and access points at dams.

LEGISLATIVE ASSISTANCE: WILDCAT BROOK, NEW HAMPSHIRE

Sometimes NPS's role becomes one of facilitator in a longer-term legislative solution to resource protection. Such was the case on Wildcat Brook in New Hampshire. As a relatively pristine 14-mile stream coming out of the White Mountain National Forest and flowing through the town of Jackson, the Wildcat has outstanding scenic and recreational values, including a spectacular 165-foot cascade over granite ledges, which serves as the centerpiece of the town of Jackson. It was this waterfall that prompted developers to propose a small hydroelectric plant on the river in the early 1980s and that motivated local citizens to initiate a protection plan for the river.

The town of Jackson and NPS entered into a cooperative agreement in 1985 to develop a municipal conservation action plan for conserving the character and resource values of the Wildcat. A Wildcat Brook Advisory Committee was formed, and with strong participation from the state, local citizens, and private sector organizations, including the Appalachian Mountain Club, the plan was created. Key components of the planning process included a resident/landowner survey, results of which served to demonstrate the depth of support for conservation of the river corridor, and an evaluation of the effectiveness of existing conservation measures along the stream. The latter study demonstrated that further action was needed, and citizens of the town, along with the Society for the Protection of New Hampshire Forests, created a conservation easement program, which immediately began to receive donations. The town also passed a new town-wide zoning ordinance for minimum lot sizes based on soil characteristics. Further, a River Protection District with minimum 75-foot setbacks was established. Finally, a riverbank restoration and access plan was adopted and undertaken for the heavily affected area around the falls, using mostly volunteer and donated services.

As these conservation actions moved forward, Jackson citizens continued to worry about the hydropower proposal and, with a unanimous vote at the 1987 town meeting, decided to pursue the only sure means of prohibiting hydroelectric development: addition of the river to the national Wild and Scenic Rivers System. But Congress was reluctant to designate the river without a strong federal management role, a perceived intrusion that local citizens were unwilling to accept. As local conservation actions gathered steam, however, Congress was persuaded to break with tradition, and in 1988 Wildcat Brook became a federally designated wild and scenic river, with unprecedented reliance on local management and protection.

Congressional confidence in local action has been borne out. Ten easements covering 650 acres of riparian land have been obtained, and the new zoning ordinances give additional protection to other parts of the town. NPS, in partnership with the Forest Service, state and local residents, and nonprofit organizations, created a new national model for permanent river protection.

PROMOTIONAL AIDS

Many projects of the Rivers, Trails, and Conservation Assistance Program include production of promotional posters and brochures. Early on in the process of planning for resource protection, NPS and its local sponsors recognized that to inspire the public support needed for a conservation plan, education about an area's resources and public awareness of their values are critical. Thus, most projects include, near the outset, production of a brochure, poster, or other informational piece. The New Hampshire Heritage Trail project (a Massachusetts-to-Canada route following a major river valley), the Farmington River project in Connecticut (a multitown initiative to protect a unique river corridor), and the Ohio and Erie Canal project all used promotional posters or brochures. In two of the cases, the costs were underwritten by local businesses. Occasionally, with its local cooperators, NPS will also produce a videotape to support a project. This was done with the Wildcat Brook project in New Hampshire.

One promotional series produced by the National Park Service has proved especially effective: its Great Rivers of America posters. These 8½-by-11-inch posters, printed on both front and back, are produced in large quantities (5,000 or more). With a photograph, brief description, map, and sometimes more detailed resource information, each provides an attractive public relations piece that can be mailed out, distributed as a leaflet, or hung in store windows.

The National Park Service's designation of a local stream as one of the "Great Rivers of America" is a relatively inexpensive, effective way to bolster local pride and awareness and to provide the imprimatur of legitimacy that NPS involvement conveys.

FUND-RAISING ASSISTANCE: BEAR RIVER PROJECT, WYOMING

A hallmark of projects of the Rivers, Trails, and Conservation Assistance Program is that they leverage additional funding. NPS staff members may or may not play a direct role in helping to acquire funding, but the agency's involvement certainly helps to legitimize the significance of a local project and strengthen efforts to acquire financial support.

One example is the Bear River Project, an NPS-assisted effort in Evanston, Wyoming, to establish a 4-mile greenway along the Bear River as it passes through the town. Adjacent to the city is the recently improved Bear River State Park, but the river within the city has been badly degraded by years of neglect. After a two-year (1989–1990) cooperative planning effort, the city and a newly formed nonprofit organization, the BEAR Project, Inc., produced a comprehensive plan for the river corridor within the city limits. Federal, state, and local agencies have been eager to contribute to the project. Table 1 lists donations and in-kind contributions by various public agencies as of April 1991.

The total amount of NPS's contribution to the project is $42,000. In addition, NPS was directly involved with the BEAR Project, Inc., in arranging a $100,000 donation by the Chevron Corporation, which will be used to construct bridges and other greenway improvements. Chevron has also challenged other corporations in the region to participate in the project.

In addition to the corporate sponsorship led by Chevron, many individuals and businesses in the Evanston area have made small contributions to the project. The greenways effort has so far resulted in approximately 60 acres of river corridor land in Evanston being purchased and made available for public recreation and wildlife habitat.

TECHNICAL PAPERS

Often, NPS contributes to a project by producing a study or technical paper that assists a local group in its work. This paper may then be used on similar projects in other parts of the country. Such papers have consisted of the following:

- A review of model zoning and land use regulations from around the country designed to protect rivers.
- An analysis of twelve case studies of greenways.
- A handbook for establishing classification criteria and a nomination process for a state river protection program.
- A study of examples in which parks, recreation areas, and open space have contributed positively to land values and local economies.

TABLE 1

Public Agency Contributions to the Bear River Project

Contribution	Amount
U.S. Geological Survey—hydrologic studies	$150,000
U.S. Army Corps of Engineers—bridge and access design	$30,000
USDA Soil Conservation Service—diversion designs	—
Federal Land and Water Conservation Fund—locally matched recreational facilities	$25,000
Wyoming State Game and Fish Department—habitat improvement and bank stabilization	$73,500
Wyoming Recreation Commission (Phases I, II of state park)— park development	$1,372,000
Wyoming state government agencies (various agencies committed unspecified time and resources to the project)	—
Bridger Valley Conservation District—bank stabilization and a diversion structure to restore historic ice-making structures	$26,000
Uinta County Youth Services and state hospital adolescent treatment unit—2,000 hours' worth of labor at $5 per hour	$10,000
Uinta County—in-kind labor on stream bank stabilization	$13,000
City of Evanston—land purchases	$250,000
City of Evanston—in-kind labor on bank stabilization	$9,000
National Park Service (Rivers, Trails, and Conservation Assistance Program)—staff time, travel expenses	$42,000
Total documented funds committed to BEAR Project, Inc.	$2,000,500

PUTTING IT ALL TOGETHER: SNOHOMISH-ARLINGTON CENTENNIAL TRAIL, WASHINGTON

A good example of how all the elements described earlier can come together and create a broad ripple effect of protection is the Snohomish-Arlington Centennial Trail in Washington State. In 1989 and 1990, NPS and the Snohomish County Parks and Recreation Division, working with a newly formed citizens' organization, completed a concept plan for converting a 17.5-mile abandoned rail corridor into a trail linking Snohomish and Arlington, Washington, semirural communities on the northern edge of the burgeoning Seattle-Tacoma-Everett metropolitan area. NPS support (through two of its planners), in partnership with the county, local governments, and private citizens, took the following forms:

- Developing a vision, goals, and a strategy with the county and local citizens.
- Assisting the new citizens' support organization for the trail, the Snohomish-Arlington Trail Coalition, and networking with other national, state, and local entities.
- Writing draft and final planning documents.
- Developing a newsletter to disseminate information about and promote the trail.
- Assisting in a detailed resource inventory of cultural as well as natural features.
- Providing technical information on rail-to-trail conversions.
- Assisting in devising strategies to secure state and county funds for trail acquisition and development.
- Developing, with local partners, an implementation and action plan.

With the active support of the citizens' trail coalition (and a timely election in which the coalition was very active), the county seized an opportunity to protect open space and recreational potential before development and higher land prices made land acquisition all but impossible. The rail line follows the Pilchuck River for several miles and, from a ridge, has outstanding views of the Marysville valley.

This multipurpose trail is the first in Snohomish County and will form the backbone of a planned countywide trail system as well as a critical link in the regional trail system for the eastern Puget Sound area. NPS helped local citizens promote the project in its crucial early stages by developing solid resource information, a newsletter and other publicity, and press interest. The NPS also helped put a broader conservation emphasis on what initially was primarily a recreational pathway proposal.

A $1.1 million commitment from the state snowballed, with county and local support, into $4.2 million for trail acquisition and development of the initial 17.5 miles and extensions to the north and south. Most of the initial trail corridor purchased during 1990 is now open for public use.

Major trail construction began late in the spring of 1991. As a result of this trail/open space project, a "prairie fire" of success has spread throughout and beyond Snohomish County. Acquisition to complete the countywide, extended 44-mile trail is now under way, and the county will be pursuing rail banking of spur lines as they are abandoned and coordinating trail development with adjoining jurisdictions. Snohomish County is also working with state agencies and the Trust for Public Land to acquire nearly 300 acres of significant wetlands adjacent to the Snohomish-Arlington Centennial Trail.

LESSONS FROM THE PAST

The Rivers, Trails, and Conservation Assistance Program has developed a reputation for effectiveness based on the following principles.

MEANINGFUL PUBLIC INVOLVEMENT

Gone are the days when public involvement meant holding a public meeting to present a prepared plan and getting on with the implementation. In fact, agencies that continue to practice this form of citizen involvement find themselves time and again blocked in the actions they want to take. Even "scoping sessions" and mailed questionnaires have limited utility.

The Rivers, Trails, and Conservation Assistance Program has found that from the starting gun, a full range of its partners need to be involved—in charge, in many cases—with all aspects of a project. In fact, continuously expanding the list of active participants and partners is an expectation for all of the program's projects.

Preplanning, with all partners, lays out basic agreements and a course of action. Multiple working groups, research subcommittees, task forces, and advisory councils characterize most technical assistance projects. Volunteers put on their rubber boots and assess wildlife, water, and historic resources along a river shoreline. The importance of this meaningful involvement, with its implicit power sharing with and involvement of participants, cannot be overstated.

CLARITY

With the sheer number of local assistance projects NPS has undertaken in the past decade, it is not surprising that some have not met expectations on the public or the private side or both. One major ingredient of success seems to be a clear, well-defined understanding at the outset of each party's roles, responsibilities, and expectations.

Typically, the National Park Service establishes a memorandum of understanding or a cooperative agreement with all participants on a project to ensure that expectations are clear from the beginning.

TANGIBLE GOALS

With a program that relies so heavily on the often difficult to define concept of planning, it is equally important for the partners to define and achieve a tangible objective. For example, in Chattanooga, Tennessee, the North Chickamauga Creek Greenway became real in people's minds when the first mile and a half were on the ground and the city purchased a 180-acre farm to extend the greenway.

THE NPS IMPRIMATUR

Wearing of the federal badge—even the highly regarded badge of the National Park Service—does not portend an enthusiastic welcome in many communities, especially when the topic is land protection. Fears of a federal takeover are too great. Even though they are not usually dressed in the National Park Service uniform or wearing its badge, planners from the Rivers, Trails, and Conservation Assistance Program are sometimes met with suspicion when they begin projects: what are the "feds' " stated or hidden agendas? NPS planners virtually always are able to persuade local cooperators, however, that the agenda is theirs to be set and that NPS is available to help along the way.

At this point, National Park Service affiliation becomes a great asset. People are generally pleased (and foundations, state governments, and corporate funders take notice) when the National Park Service, the nation's premier conservation agency, is interested in *their* resource. The NPS's reputation for expertise in natural and cultural resources adds tremendous credibility to any study or recommendation. And the NPS "umbrella" provides a unique, safe, neutral meeting point for groups that have historically found it difficult to cooperate. The NPS's role becomes one of convener and facilitator as well as resource expert. Time and again, NPS is told, "We could not have begun working together without your help." In northwestern Colorado, two counties that had not cooperated on a project in eighty years have joined together on an NPS-assisted greenway for the Yampa River.

PROMISE FOR THE FUTURE

The historical seesaw between local initiative and federal activism in conservation has tilted for the moment toward state and local responsibility. That, added to the concern of most Americans for the environment, underlies the rising demand for technical assistance in planning, land protection, and management. NPS is experiencing a 20 to 30 percent increase in demand each year for its services under the Rivers, Trails, and Conservation Assistance Program. Unfortunately, the modest increases in funding that the program has sustained over the past decade do not begin to keep up with the demand.

However, a number of developments foretell the expanded availability of technical assistance of the type NPS offers.

COOPERATION WITH OTHER FEDERAL AGENCIES

The National Park Service is not the only federal agency providing assistance to state and local governments in land planning. Several federal agencies (the Soil Conservation Service, the Federal Emergency Management Agency, the U.S. Army Corps of Engineers, the Tennessee Valley Authority, the U.S. Fish and Wildlife Service, and the Environmental Protection Agency) provide various types of assistance to communities on flood-prone lands in river valleys. A new movement of cooperation among these agencies and the National Park Service is under way, called multiobjective management, or multiobjective river corridor planning (MORC) and multiobjective flood-plain management. This new cooperative effort promises, through better interagency coordination, to increase the attention given to natural and beneficial uses of floodway lands and to promote more conservation of the nation's floodplains.

INCREASING CAPABILITY OF THE PRIVATE SECTOR

Typically, the Park Service cooperates on local projects not only with local agencies and private sponsors but also with one or more national organizations. American Rivers, Inc., the Rails-to-Trails Conservancy, the American Hiking Society, the Land Trust Alliance, River Network, Inc., and the Association of State Floodplain Managers are all small nonprofit organizations that, despite staffs of fewer than thirty people, have an increasing capability to play intermediary roles in land protection. In fact, River Network, of Portland, Oregon, makes land protection a critical part of its funding schemes; the money it makes in land transactions between private and federal buyers plays a critical role in its operating budget.

The growing sophistication and capability of these nonprofit organizations will make public/private and national/local partnerships in land protection increasingly available around the country.

METROPOLITAN CORRIDOR PLANNING

The Rivers, Trails, and Conservation Assistance Program is going beyond planning for individual corridors to developing strategies for broader networks of open space. One current nationwide initiative is the Metropolitan Recreation Corridor Planning Project. With leadership coming from NPS's Washington, DC, office, the project's purpose is to assess valuable natural, cultural, and recreational resources comprehensively in a metropolitan area and to determine which of these resources should become components of a metropolitan-wide system of recreation corridors and how to achieve this. The term "recreation corridors" is a broad concept that includes rivers, trails, streams, bicycle lanes, floodplain lands, and walking tours. It emphasizes corridor protection and public access for recreation and for nonmotorized transportation.

These projects seek to develop a system of recreation corridors that revitalize abandoned or misused urban spaces and protect diminishing open space in surrounding suburban areas. They address the recreational needs of the inner-city dweller as well as the suburban resident. Pilot projects are under way in Richmond, Virginia, and Chattanooga, Tennessee.

URBAN RIVER RESTORATION

The nation has made tremendous investments in water quality improvement over the past twenty years. Now is the time to reap the benefits by making these rivers accessible for public outdoor recreation. Fifty percent of all Americans now live in the thirty-eight largest metropolitan areas, and almost all of these have rivers or streams. From the Charles and Potomac to the Chicago and South Platte to the Willamette and American and Los Angeles, rivers can be the recreational and aesthetic centerpieces of their cities. The National Park Service will be increasingly active in promoting partnerships to protect these river corridors.

REGIONAL TRAIL NETWORK PLANNING

The Rivers, Trails, and Conservation Assistance Program is actively engaged at the regional level in identifying and devising conservation schemes for interstate trail corridors. A pilot project that includes extensive public involvement has been under way in NPS's mid-Atlantic region for the past year, and states and nonprofit organizations there are taking increasing leadership in developing a land conservation agenda for such a trail.

SEED GRANTS AND CHALLENGE GRANT PROGRAMS

After a community has completed the planning process with NPS's assistance and has a strategy that has been accepted by the public and private partners, it often needs funds for development of a small organization (a land trust, watershed association, or task force) to coordinate implementation. A program that would provide matching seed grants for planning and implementation of river and trail projects has been discussed in many forms. There are two strong reasons for such a program: (1) NPS, having completed a multiyear technical assistance project, is in an excellent position to judge the potential effectiveness of small challenge grants, and (2) small amounts of federal funds (as much as $10,000) used as a challenge can leverage an equal or greater amount of public money, often twice the amount, in private funds. The National Park Service is currently developing and seeking authorization for this concept.

With their tie-ins to so many pressing issues of the 1990s—water supply, livability of cities, and the environment—the National Park

Service's technical assistance programs will undoubtedly continue to be in great demand. Expanding the range of tools available, as well as increasing funding, will allow these partnership programs to inspire state, local, and citizen-led land protection projects throughout the country.

ACKNOWLEDGMENTS

The author is indebted to the following individuals for their contributions to the chapter on partnerships beyond the national parks: Bill Spitzer, Sam Stokes, Paul Labovitz, Scott Hall, Sherry Peck, Christine Carlson, Charles Sundberg, Alicia Riddell, Phil Huffman, and Hugh Duffy.

NOTES

1. Walters, William C. "Local + Regional + State + National Parks = A National System of Parks." Washington, DC: U.S. Department of the Interior, National Park Service, *Courier*, September 1990, p. 52.

☙❧

PART III

State and Local
Partnerships

The following chapters first explore public/private partnerships from the standpoint of two public agency officials, both working at the state level. In chapter 7, Bob Bendick draws on years of experience in land protection work to illustrate and analyze what makes cooperative projects successful. He underlines the importance of priority setting and consensus building so that the political work can precede negotiation, which must often be confidential.

He reminds staffers of land protection agencies to cultivate their colleagues in other state agencies, who may be critical come check-writing or legal review time; he also adjures them to get out and meet with landowners in the evenings and on weekends—to act "unbureaucratically." Likewise, he cautions nonprofit workers not to underestimate the bureaucrats—and to give credit to all, especially landowners.

Bendick stresses that land saving must be put in a larger context if it is to continue to attract broad public support, especially in lean economic times. His Hodgkiss Farm case study illustrates the tie-in open space protection often has with agriculture and water quality protection, as well as the technique of a nonprofit group uniting divided interests in land, reshuffling them, and then spinning out new divided interests and parcels to conservation agencies and owners. In the Block Island case study, Bendick describes the development of a local partner who could make maximum use of state matching funds and, in the process, help preserve the beauty that is also the foundation of the island's economic well-being. Finally, Bendick's description of a partnership between a nonprofit organization and a private landowner—a timber company—in the Adirondacks suggests a promising direction for combining public recreational needs with the preservation of working landscapes.

In chapter 8, Pam Dennis describes another increasingly discussed, if still pioneering, effort to bring together human needs and environmental needs: the linking of open space protection and affordable housing. Dennis details the experience of the national leader in this effort, the Vermont Housing and Conservation Board. Many of the board's projects that she describes bring new meaning to the word "complex" with their often Byzantine financial and ownership arrangements, including the concept of shared equity in affordable housing. The board's strong policy of encouraging matching gifts—whether of funds, land, or services—also shows how ingenious and successful the private sector can be in obtaining such matches. Dennis shares some of the growing pains VHCB has experienced in its first years, especially in setting priorities and establishing appropriate methods of land valuation for farms. This glimpse into the day-to-day workings of the board by a front-line staffer should be of particular value to those contemplating similar programs, whether of direct grants to non-profit groups (a subject to be taken up in more detail in chapter 11) or of combined housing and land conservation programs.

Finally, chapter 9 looks at partnerships from the standpoint of local land trusts, relating the experiences of the national organizations profiled in part I to the state or local level. Particular attention is paid to ways in which private land trusts that lack substantial resources can buy expensive land and take on complicated, time-consuming deals. Financing methods and experiences in staff sharing are explored. Profiles of land trusts that have been particularly successful at building community support for government land protection programs and translating them for local landowners illustrate how often a local, private organization is crucial to effective public land conservation efforts. Chapter 9 also relates how local land trusts are being called on more often to play a role in day-to-day stewardship of public lands. Finally, the author takes the lessons of previous chapters and applies them to the local land trust situation, emphasizing the land trusts' need for professionalism and government partners' need to support land trusts' credibility in the community.

7

State Partnerships to Preserve Open Space: Lessons from Rhode Island and New York

Robert L. Bendick, Jr.

As the boat crossed the lake, I turned to look at a small island with a steep slope leading to a stone lean-to and a grove of pines. There was a moment of recognition, and then came the clear memory of trying to outpaddle a storm, then scrambling up the granite slope in the rain, enduring a brilliant flash of lightning and crash of thunder, and lying flat and tingling on a rock, watching as my untied canoe was blown from the landing by the squall.

The storm had been thirty years ago, but the island, the lake, and the lean-to were just the same—the same despite dizzying changes in the surrounding world, the same because this place had been protected from change by being part of Adirondack Park in northern New York State.

The Adirondack Park was created a hundred years ago when the New York State legislature realized what the U.S. Congress had realized at Yellowstone and Yosemite almost twenty years earlier—that left alone, the most beautiful and environmentally important places in America would be exploited for private use, thus destroying their unique public values.

In the 1880s, the role of government in America was vastly more constrained than it is today. Yet even then, before zoning, income taxes, and environmental laws, there was public acceptance that in some areas public ownership was needed to protect the wild forests, unspoiled lakes, and sources of rivers. In the West, much of such land was already publicly owned and could be conserved by designation as national parks or forests. In most of the rest of the country, the land was in private ownership and had to be purchased to be protected.

Whereas the setting aside of federal land continued through the turn of the nineteenth century, state parks grew more slowly. In no region of the country were all of the most important natural areas dedicated to public use. For a very long time, this was not apparent because farms and commercial forests provided open land and most people lived either in dense cities and towns or on farms. The working countryside extended to city boundaries.

After World War II, however, automobile use spread suburban growth outward from cities. With help from the federal Land and Water Conservation Fund, state park and forest systems grew steadily to keep up with the needs of growing populations. But in the late 1970s and the 1980s, the states' share of the fund declined at a time when second-home development along shorelines and mountains accelerated rapidly and suburban growth extended ever farther from older urban areas.

In response to the loss of landscapes long enjoyed by the public (even though they were privately owned), citizens worked through their state governments to raise more money to buy land to expand state holdings. As discussed in chapter 10, states and even localities passed bond issues, made special appropriations, and in a few cases, created dedicated funds to finance open space protection. Private land-saving organizations such as The Nature Conservancy, the Trust for Public Land, and local land trusts were created to protect open space when government could not or would not act to do so. At the same time, strategies to regulate land use were employed to conserve open space—or so people thought. Enacted at the local level, large lot zoning created the illusion of open space protection. A few states passed laws to protect wetlands and river corridors, and where they were strictly enforced, these laws did have a positive effect.

EVOLUTION OF STATE/PRIVATE PARTNERSHIPS

Until about 1980, most state public land conservation was straightforward. States raised money and negotiated to buy available land. When owners would not sell key parcels, many states used eminent domain proceedings to acquire what was needed.

After 1980, the pace quickened. Spurred by the environmental movement, citizen concern intensified, while property values, particularly in shoreline areas, escalated rapidly. There was public pressure to save a greater variety of land types. Land conserved by the state came to include endangered species habitat, river corridors, working farmland, aquifer recharge zones, long-distance trails, and urban shorelines. Saving land became a pressing political issue.

In response to all this, states looked for new ways to conserve land. As the pressure not to lose specific parcels to the bulldozers increased, states saw that their cumbersome financing and bureaucratic requirements could not move quickly enough to respond to development pressures. At the same time, creative conservationists in the private sector discovered that they could structure land purchases with property owners to take advantage of tax laws and specific family needs, thus reducing the cost of acquisition. This brought about the growth of simple partnerships between state governments and the private sector in which nonprofit land trusts acquired land from owners under payment terms fitted to that owner and then sold the land to state governments to become part of the state land system months or even years later, when state funds became available.

There are hundreds, if not thousands, of examples of such transactions. Many were coupled with bargain sales, donations of part of the value of the land to the nonprofit agency. (Landowners seem more willing to make such donations to private organizations than to the states themselves.) Some transactions also include private fund-raising—a source of money not usually available to state agencies acting alone. Two national organizations, The Nature Conservancy and the Trust for Public Land, gained the expertise and financial standing to participate in many such acquisitions for subsequent conveyance to states, but local and regional land trusts also played active roles. In New England, for example, the Maine Coast Heritage Trust, the Vermont Land Trust, the Society for the Protection of New Hampshire Forests, and the Trustees of Reservations (America's oldest land trust), among others, all participated in buying land that was later conveyed to states.

An example of a straightforward transaction of this type is the purchase of Patience Island in Narragansett Bay, Rhode Island. Patience, a 200-acre undeveloped island, had been earmarked to become part of the Narragansett Bay Islands Park System. The island was owned by a real estate partnership that had a number of other holdings. In 1980, as the northeastern real estate boom was escalating, the partnership that held Patience was experiencing financial difficulties and was threatened with litigation. It was feared that the island would be sold quickly to a more active real estate company that would soon subdivide it. Backed by a letter from the state expressing its interest to purchase the land, The Nature Conservancy stepped in ahead of court action and bought Patience Island for cash. The island was resold to the state a year later and eventually became part of the Bay Islands Park System and the Narragansett Bay National Estuarine Research Reserve.

It was not long, however, before state agencies and their nonprofit partners were driven by new trends and new pressures to pursue far more complex land-saving strategies. The most important of these new trends are outlined in the following sections.

A MORE SYSTEMATIC APPROACH TO SETTING PRIORITIES

The Nature Conservancy worked with states to create natural heritage inventories, which included systematic identification of habitats needed to protect rare and endangered plant and animal species. Some states conducted scenic or landscape inventories. As noted in the following section, others began looking at the preservation of larger natural and recreational systems. In each case, they identified priorities for land conservation in a more systematic way and began to direct land conservation efforts toward specific parcels or groups of parcels.

RECOGNITION OF THE NEED TO PROTECT LARGER SYSTEMS

The growing interest in ecosystems fostered by the environmental movement brought people to recognize that just saving individual parcels of land was not enough. People saw that river valleys, large wetlands, and entire coastlines needed attention to protect water and habitat quality. A parallel growth in linear recreation—hiking, bicycling, canoeing, cross-country skiing, and snowmobiling—reinforced this trend.

PURCHASES OF EASEMENTS AND DEVELOPMENT RIGHTS

Farms, ranches, and managed forests were recognized as critical elements of the landscape that were threatened by suburban and exurban growth. In Europe, preservation of rural (but not wilderness) landscapes had long been an objective of public policy, but land use laws in this country made such protection more difficult. In response to the need to save working landscapes and the need to find a more flexible approach to saving other lands, easements, deeded restrictions on the use of land, became an important tool of land protection. Easements can be very complex, however, and their use was not well suited to traditional state government approaches to buying and managing land.

DECLINE OF EMINENT DOMAIN

The trend toward assertion of personal rights and the accompanying resistance to government authority so prevalent in the 1980s brought resistance to the use of eminent domain to acquire land for conservation purposes. This required use of more flexible means for dealing with reluctant property owners.

AN UNPRECEDENTED BOOM IN REAL ESTATE DEVELOPMENT

During the 1980s, it became easy to obtain financing for real estate development regardless of whether there was a well-documented market for what was to be built. This accelerated development of recreational condominiums and second homes in the countryside. In response, state conservation departments had to find ways to move quickly and creatively to save land that otherwise might not have been threatened with development.

Together, these trends required state environmental agencies to join in more complex partnerships with the private sector and with other levels of government to save the public values of important open space.

PARTNERSHIPS IN PRACTICE

Those involved in land conservation can draw from the experiences of Rhode Island and New York State in carrying out three complex but successful land conservation projects. These projects—the conservation of Hodgkiss Farm in Dutch Harbor, Rhode Island; the cooperative effort to protect the landscape of Block Island, Rhode Island; and the protection of forestland by the Lyons Falls Pulp and Paper Company in the Adirondacks, New York—are described in detail in the following sections.

AN OLD FARM SERVES MANY PURPOSES: HODGKISS FARM, DUTCH HARBOR, RHODE ISLAND

Narragansett Bay extends about 40 miles southward from Providence, Rhode Island, at the head of the Providence River, to Newport and Point Judith on the Atlantic Ocean. Despite being adjacent to the metropolitan areas of Providence, Rhode Island, and Fall River, Massachusetts, and being just an hour's drive from Boston and three hours' drive from New York, Narragansett Bay has good (and improving) water quality and a pleasing coastal landscape.

Until the 1970s, the shoreline of the bay was spared from intensive urban development by the presence of the U.S. Navy and by Rhode Island's longtime economic malaise. Commercial fishing and shellfishing and tourism remained important industries. In 1973, however, the navy reduced its activities in Narragansett Bay and gave up important waterfront land. Later in the 1970s, and particularly in the 1980s, suburban growth around the bay accelerated rapidly.

During this time, the state of Rhode Island, which had a long tradition of public access to the shore and which over the years had acquired several metropolitan parks and beaches along the bay, faced important decisions about use of the surplus military land. Would the land become industrial sites or parks? Would the bay become an urban waterfront or retain its rural character? Although some former navy sites were dedicated to economic development uses, the state decided that a number of key island parcels should be incorporated into a Narragansett Bay Islands State Park. By 1987, that park consisted of nine sites on six islands. Of these, six had been acquired through the federal surplus land program and three had been acquired from private owners.

Two of the most spectacular of these sites were on Conanicut Island, located at the mouth of the bay. Despite being connected by bridges to the resort communities of Newport to the east and Narragansett to the west, Conanicut Island (the town of Jamestown, Rhode Island) was largely unspoiled. During the 1970s and 1980s, there had been some suburban development there, but the island still had active farming and other open land. Its two state parks—Beavertail Point and Fort Wetherill—were former military facilities featuring rocky cliffs plunging to the sea.

On the western side of the island was Dutch Harbor, a beautiful cove sheltered by Dutch Island, one of the park sites. At the northern end of the harbor was the 240-acre Watson Farm, donated years before to the Society for the Preservation of New England Antiquities and operated as a nineteenth-century farmstead. The rest of the harbor's shoreline remained in private ownership.

Just south of the Watson property was the 150-acre Hodgkiss Farm. The farm included several important natural and historic resources—a beautiful salt marsh fronting on a salt creek, two small barrier beaches, a freshwater marsh, active farm fields, and a nineteenth-century farmhouse. The property also surrounded a town drinking water reservoir. The farm provided exceptional wildlife habitat and was an important element in the scenic character of Dutch Harbor. Amid the development frenzy of the mid-1980s, however, Hodgkiss Farm was a prime target for subdivision for expensive single-family homes.

In 1987, development of the farm was imminent. The property had been willed to a brother and sister who had differing ideas about its future. The sister desperately wanted to keep the farm intact, to live there, and to provide a place for her daughter to grow crops for local consumption. The brother wanted to realize cash from a sale. The brother and sister had undivided interests in the land that would soon be divided through court action, thus forcing a sale of the entire property to developers waiting in the wings.

In 1982, the Rhode Island Department of Environmental Management had joined with several private land conservation groups, including The Nature Conservancy (TNC) and the Rhode Island Audubon Society, to adopt a formal list of natural areas in the state that should be protected from development. Following adoption of the list, these groups worked cooperatively to save the areas that had been given high-priority status for protection. In the mid-1980s, the Champlin Foundations, a private charitable trust in Rhode Island, began supporting these conservation efforts, first on a project-by-project basis and then with a large annual grant to The Nature Conservancy and the state for open space protection projects. This grant was used as a catalyst to draw out other funds. The 1980s development boom, the priority list, and the success of the cooperative effort supported by Champlin all had played important roles in inspiring the approval of state open space protection bonds in 1985, 1986, 1987, and 1989, thus giving the state funding to support a variety of open space protection projects. During this time, Jamestown had itself taken important steps to protect open land. Amazingly, this town of fewer than 4,000 people had approved $2.6 million in bonds to save what its citizens considered to be critical pieces of its landscape.

Thus, when the sister who owned a half interest in Hodgkiss Farm approached the Conanicut Island Land Trust for help in saving her family's land, and the land trust contacted the state and the town, an experienced and adequately financed team was able to respond.

First, the Dutch Harbor area was on the open space protection list that the state's environmental department had adopted years before. This meant that there had already been a public expression that the area of the farm was a valuable public resource. When state and Nature Conservancy officials visited the waterfront farm, they recognized its multiple values. Based on these values and on joint discussions with the property owner and the president of the local land trust, who was a friend of the owner, a strategy for saving the land was developed and, remarkably, was followed to a successful conclusion.

The strategy worked as follows. It was decided that The Nature Conservancy would attempt a cash purchase of the half share of the land owned by the brother who wanted to sell. Then, TNC would exchange its share of the title to the land with the sister for some cash and a variety of other rights in the land; the rights would then be sold to the state and to the town of Jamestown. The state and town, in turn, would then exchange rights to ensure public access.

The Nature Conservancy and the state participated in complex negotiations with the lawyers for the two owners. Ultimately, the following transactions were accomplished:

1. The Nature Conservancy bought the brother's share in a bargain sale, saving him taxes and a lengthy, expensive court battle.
2. The Nature Conservancy conveyed clear title to the sister for 75 acres of the farm and entered into an agreement allowing her to construct two houses in addition to the old farmhouse at designated locations. The locations were selected to retain the character of the landscape and to minimize environmental impacts.
3. In exchange, TNC received a cash payment from the sister, a development rights easement on the portion of the 75 acres that was being actively farmed, and outright title to the 75 acres along Dutch Harbor, Salt Creek, and the land surrounding the town reservoir.
4. The Nature Conservancy then sold the development rights for the farmland to the state Agricultural Lands Preservation Commission; gave easements protecting the historic character of the farmstead to

the local land trust; sold the entire shoreline and beach area to the state to be used as a nature preserve; and sold a buffer zone around the reservoir to the town. The state, the Champlin Foundations, the town, and the Agricultural Lands Preservation Commission all contributed money to the transaction, although the total cost was substantially below market value, thanks to the generosity of both landowners.

5. The state and the town then traded easements to provide a hiking trail and parking area on town property that would ensure convenient public access to the shore. The town council also assisted in approving the unusual subdivision of the land that was required in order to record the complex transaction.

Even though the 150 acres of the farm were legally divided into several pieces, the original physical appearance of this landscape was preserved forever. All of its wildlife and water supply values were protected. Active farming could continue, and public access was opened to the shore.

Despite their complexity, the negotiations were conducted without press coverage. When the transactions were complete, the governor held a ceremony on the land with a tearful and eloquent property owner and all the participants to announce the saving of the farm and the protection of two other exceptional parcels of land fronting on Dutch Harbor through the donation of development rights by their owners.

A COMMUNITY PROTECTS ITS FUTURE: BLOCK ISLAND, RHODE ISLAND

Block Island is an 11-square-mile remnant of the last glacier's terminal moraine located 12 miles off Rhode Island's southern shore. It has few trees, more than 300 freshwater ponds and wetlands, beautiful bluffs and beaches, and a large, protected harbor. There are several endangered plant and animal species on the island, and it is one of the most important migratory bird sites in the Northeast. There are 600 full-time residents, but private boats and public ferries may bring 10,000 people to the island on a summer weekend. During the summer and fall, Block Island is a remarkably pleasant place to be, but in the winter it is cold, isolated, exposed, and often lashed by hurricane-force gales.

Before 1975, there was little protected land on Block Island—just a state beach and a small wildlife refuge. After the island's big hotels fell into disrepair during the Great Depression, only a chronically depressed economy kept development away. Block Island was, as they say, undiscovered.

In the late 1970s, that began to change. More summer houses were built, and in the treeless landscape they did not go unnoticed. Neither the state nor outside conservation groups paid any attention to the place, but a few islanders became alarmed about the future of their landscape and created the Block Island Conservancy. The conservancy's leader was Rob Lewis, a retired sea captain who, in his cutoff pants and battered van, never tired of showing islanders and visitors the places that he thought should be saved.

Somebody listened, because in 1980 David and Elise Lapham, longtime summer residents of Block Island, approached The Nature Conservancy and the state about donating the development rights for 143 acres of shoreline cliffs on the island's northeast coast—an important migratory bird site. The Laphams eventually also agreed to donate a right of public access along a trail that ran across the top of the bluffs. The state, which at the time had almost no money of its own for open space acquisition, convinced the federal government to approve a Land and Water Conservation Fund project encompassing all of Block Island's coastline, using the high value of the Lapham easement donation as a match for federal grant money. This funding ultimately provided more than $2 million to begin the task of saving the island's landscape.

The state, again working with The Nature Conservancy, moved quickly to buy one property adjacent to the Lapham land to provide access to the trail, but then, in an action that would prove decisive to the island's future, paused to work with other organizations to establish a detailed list of priority sites for acquisition. The state Department of Environmental Management (DEM), the New Shoreham (Block Island) town council, The Nature Conservancy, the Block Island Conservancy, and the Rhode Island Audubon Society met and identified those places that had to be protected to retain the basic character of the island's landscape. DEM's planning section then produced a formal report that listed, in order of priority, the ten most important places to be saved. The report also explored the positive and negative effects of land preservation, including effects on the tax base. By the end of the process, there was a clear consensus on what had to be done.

Backed by federal funds (kept in place with the help of Senator John Chafee) and private contributions, the state, The Nature Conservancy, and the town of New Shoreham contacted property owners to begin negotiations. Ultimately, all of the projects on the original priority list were acquired in fee or through easement, almost all at well below market value. During this process, the Champlin Foundations took a special interest in several Block Island projects, including the Lewis-Dickens Farm on the island's southwest corner.

The state/TNC coalition progressed with exceptional help from Nature Conservancy negotiators, but in the early 1980s, development pressure increased rapidly and became a growing concern of the town government. With the leadership of two first wardens (Block Island's title for mayor), Jack Gray, who was also a real estate agent, and Edie Blaine, a descendant of one of the island's oldest families, this tiny community approved a $1 million bond issue for open space acquisition and worked with the state to buy critical beach properties and easements over upland tracts.

With the rapid expenditure of their own bond funds and seeing the availability of state grants, the town determined to do more. Rob Lewis's son Keith, also a merchant seaman, who had become involved in open space issues through a substantial donation of the bulk of his own property, stayed home from sea for a year to lead the open space preservation effort. Working against the backdrop of the mid-1980s real estate boom, Keith and other islanders created a remarkable coalition of environmentalists, the island's real estate agents, and the chamber of commerce to lobby the state legislature to enable Block Island to establish a town land trust funded by a 2 percent tax on real estate transfers (later raised to 3 percent). Despite opposition from mainland real estate interests, the legislature could not say no to the islanders. The first board of the land trust was elected by the voters in 1986. Board members immediately surveyed all of the island's residents for their opinions on the next set of priority acquisitions and then began an additional series of successful negotiations with their friends and neighbors.

Having learned of the unusual level of cooperation and success in saving Block Island's landscape, two more national organizations, the Conservation Foundation and The Conservation Fund, joined the effort. The Conservation Foundation (now merged with World Wildlife Fund, U.S.) brought land use planning expertise and a focus on efforts to solve problems related to land preservation efforts, such as providing affordable housing for island families.

The Conservation Fund reinforced a long-standing theme of land acquisition on the island: the connection of individual parcels through greenways and pathways. That effort took a major step forward in the summer of 1991 with the dedication of an extremely complex greenway project linking many of the previously protected open spaces.

What was accomplished in all of this? Over the past ten years, every major landmark on the island has been saved. Public or conservation ownership has risen to almost 20 percent of total land area. Not a single critical undeveloped parcel was lost. Eminent domain was threatened by the state but never used, probably because of the overwhelming pressure exerted by residents and other property owners not to allow exploitation of their land. There was one notable failure: the conversion of a cottage colony into an out-of-place condominium complex. The state's Coastal Council failed to be sufficiently protective, and developers found a zoning loophole. Islanders picketed the work site, but the building went ahead. In an ironic outcome, the complex was eventually auctioned off to pay the developer's debts.

There is now every expectation that the land saving will continue until the landscape as a whole, and underground water supplies as well, are saved by a connected series of protected parcels of land, most of which are accessible and usable by the public. The continuing preservation effort on Block Island has been given an enormous boost by The Nature Conservancy's inclusion of the island in its Bioreserve Program, described in chapter 1.

One might suggest that what is described here is in large measure the successful effort of a few people to save a beautiful place for their exclusive use. It is not so. Block Island's saved land serves a diversity of interests. On warm days, ferry loads of day-trippers come from the mainland (the round-trip costs about $8), ride their bicycles, go to the beaches, and walk the nature trails. Access is free; all kinds of people come. In many ways, the island functions as a state park under many ownerships. Sometimes it is crowded, but when the ferries leave, everything is pretty much the same.

The chamber of commerce has backed land conservation because it has saved the island's primary economic assets—its beauty and free public access to the shore. With those assets protected, people will always come to the hotels, restaurants, and shops and buy the homes that come up for sale. Owners of seasonal homes are content because the character of the island and the value of their investments are protected. Environmentalists are pleased because the places they care about, including habitat for endangered and threatened species, have been saved from development and because visitor use is managed in a way that has little permanent effect on land.

PROTECTING A WORKING FOREST: THE ADIRONDACKS, NEW YORK

The Adirondacks is a region of mountains, forests, lakes, and rivers extending westward from Lake George and Lake Champlain in northern New York State. The Adirondack Forest Preserve was created in 1885 and Adirondack Park was formed in 1892 to protect the exceptional natural resource and scenic values of this large region. The park is about the size of Massachusetts.

Adirondack Park is not typical of American parks in that less than half of the park's land area is in public ownership. The remaining land is held by private owners, many of whom own only camps or summer homes around lakes and ponds. There are, however, hundreds of thousands of acres in the Adirondacks owned by the forest products industry, private clubs, and large individual landowners. Although these lands are managed for timber production and recreation, they also include important wildlife habitat and scenic and water resources. The commercial forestlands have traditionally been leased for hunting and fishing.

In recent years, several long-standing timber holdings in New York State and throughout the Northeast have been threatened with subdivision and development for second homes because of changes in the economics of the forest products industry and as a result of corporate mergers and takeovers. After passage of New York State's 1986 Environmental Quality Bond Act and, that same year, of a law standardizing the acquisition of conservation easements, the state Department of Environmental Conservation (DEC) began, for the first time, actively seeking easement purchases. This resulted in an agreement for acquisition of the 40,000-acre Henry Lassiter easement in 1989, land formerly owned by Diamond International.

The Lyons Falls Pulp and Paper Company owns substantial amounts of forestland in the western Adirondacks. In 1988, this company made it known that it would consider the sale of recreational and development rights easements over parts of its land as part of an effort to expand its overall timber holdings. At the same time, two large tracts of forestland came on the market in the company's area—the 10,800-acre J. P. Lewis tract and the 3,200-acre Three Lakes tract, owned by Patten Corporation. Patten was known for subdividing large tracts for development of second homes.

DEC had appraised these tracts for outright purchase but then entered into discussions with The Nature Conservancy's Adirondack office about a possible land exchange with Lyons Falls. George Davis, a longtime Adirondack naturalist, planner, and activist, had similar discussions with Lyons Falls. Having just completed the Lassiter purchase, DEC was enthusiastic about the possibility of easements.

Ultimately, all of these parties worked with the progressive-minded Lyons Falls executives to work out the following arrangement:

1. DEC released its appraisals and negotiations for the J. P. Lewis and Three Lakes tracts to The Nature Conservancy, which purchased these lands outright.
2. The Nature Conservancy then conveyed the underlying titles to both tracts, including timber rights but subject to recreational and development rights easements, to Lyons Falls in exchange for development rights and recreational easements over an additional 3,000 acres of Lyons Falls land along the Moose River.
3. The Nature Conservancy then sold all 17,000 acres of development rights and recreational easements to the state to preserve the entire area from incompatible development and to recover its costs.

Together, these transactions set aside for public purposes four ponds; 5 miles of undeveloped shoreline on North Lake; miles of streams, including the middle and north branches of the Black River; all of Gull Lake; and frontage on the Moose River. However, though the project was reasonably simple in concept, it proved difficult to complete. Obstacles included the varying needs and timetables of the landowners, the problems of gaining approval of such a multifaceted arrangement within New York State's complex land acquisition process, and, finally, problems with protecting the fee title owner from liability for a range of recreational uses. Resolution of this last concern required extraordinary efforts by DEC's senior management, the New York State attorney general's office, Lyons Falls executives, and The Nature Conservancy.

Even though it was difficult to complete, the Lyons Falls project can serve as a model for other efforts to protect open space for recreational and environmental purposes while retaining a working forest. It adds the natural resource industry to the public/private partnership and suggests the possibility of large-scale exchanges of development and access rights across the forests of the Northeast and elsewhere in the country.

LESSONS FROM THE PAST

The examples described in this chapter and other open space protection efforts suggest several lessons for making cooperative efforts to save open land successful.

BUILDING A CONSENSUS FOR ACTION

State governments today—indeed, all levels of government—operate under conditions of intense public scrutiny. Public and press evaluate and reevaluate their actions and decisions on a weekly basis. Additionally, there is often suspicion among different levels of government. All of this contributes to rapid changes in policy and direction in response to public opinion.

For state government to pursue the consistent long-term policies essential to creating strong partnerships with nonprofit organizations and other levels of government, it is essential to establish a firm base of consensus on the need for open space protection and on the priorities for such protection. At the height of the mid-1980s development boom, creating a consensus for saving individual parcels of land from development was not difficult. But separate reactions to specific development threats will not save those parts of the landscape needed to provide a permanent framework of protected natural areas around which we can build our lives.

Block Island's efforts to save open space have succeeded because the state and all of the other groups involved took the time to agree on a clear, public list of priorities for what needed to be saved. As land on this list was protected, the people involved have continued to seek public opinion on the next set of priorities. This approach recognizes that not every parcel of land can or should be set aside from development. When priorities are adopted openly and clearly, individual partnership transactions are not then disrupted by public questioning of why government is pursuing a specific effort. This allows the state government to engage in complex individual negotiations on a confidential basis with the assurance that the necessity for a project will not be reevaluated later. Thus, the Hodgkiss Farm transaction could be negotiated entirely in private because the town and state had already agreed on the need to save the farm and because they communicated frequently during the negotiation process.

Similarly, state government must be as open as possible in working with organizations and individuals to plan for protecting open land. Ideally, as was the case on Block Island, there should be consensus among all those involved. From the state perspective, this is not always possible. Sometimes there are natural areas of statewide or national importance that may need to be protected even over the objections of local residents. Inclusion of Patience Island and large parts of Prudence Island as part of the Narragansett Bay Islands Park was not supported by everyone in the town of Portsmouth, where the islands are located, but at least the park proposal was discussed thoroughly with the town and was understood and supported on a statewide basis. The state and its nonprofit partners could then proceed with individual transactions without fear of the purchases being rejected as part of a larger political process. Even in the intense ongoing discussions over the future of state land acquisition in the Adirondack Park, there is general agreement that a public list of land acquisition priorities would benefit both local and state interests.

CREATING RELATIONSHIPS WITH THE PRIVATE SECTOR

State government, particularly in larger states, does not relate easily to outside partners. State agency officials often feel that they are on the front lines, encumbered by bureaucracy, politics, the press, and insufficient resources. It is difficult to take risks in such an environment, whether real or perceived. Working cooperatively with private sector organizations is a risk outside of normal government operations. However, several things can be done to make such risk taking easier.

The kind of public priority setting mentioned earlier is important. In addition, environmental officials need to cultivate those in other state agencies with care and respect. The budgeting, fiscal control, and legal agencies within state government can have a profound effect on the success of often unorthodox partnership transactions. These agencies must not be seen as obstacles to creative land purchases but must be made part of the partnership. For example, the New York State attorney general's office ultimately played an essential role in making the Lyons Falls acquisition work. It is important that environmental agency officials be able to deal with their private partners with the confidence that their negotiations will not be subverted by other agencies.

There has been an alarming turnover in senior state environmental officials in recent years. Personal relationships are critical to the success of partnerships. Both on Block Island and in Jamestown, the key people involved on the public and nonprofit sides worked together closely for ten years. The familiarity and trust that developed over time made it easy to move quickly and efficiently. Land transactions are visible and often popular activities, so appointed officials are themselves often actively involved. It is important that agency workers at the civil service level be brought into this process so that as agency heads change, the partnership relationships can continue.

In recent years, much improvement has been made in nonprofit environmental groups' attitudes toward state officials. Nothing is more likely to sour a partnership relationship than people from the private sector treating state officials as less than competent and as less dedicated than they are to the cause of land conservation.

It is also important to recognize local as well as regional and national nonprofit groups in building partnerships. The Nature Conservancy and the Trust for Public Land have systematized their relationships with state government, but a local land trust is often the key to a successful land-saving effort. In Jamestown, the president of the local land trust supported the landowner's confidence in the progress of difficult negotiations and helped bring the town and the state together. On Block Island, Captain Rob Lewis, the president of the Block Island Conservancy, and his son Keith, founder of the town land trust, helped interest people from off the island in its unique quality and problems and gave islanders confidence that state and off-island conservationists could be trusted. More on Keith Lewis's local perspective on land-saving partnerships can be found in chapter 9.

MAKING RELATIONSHIPS WORK IN THE LONG RUN

In land conservation as in other pursuits, a promising partnership can easily founder in the heat of both failure and success. This can usually be avoided by caring for the bonds that keep partners together. The importance of communication cannot be overemphasized. With multiple parties involved, landowners can become confused and misunderstandings can develop over timing, funding, and who said what. From the state perspective, communication cannot be a nine-to-five effort. When there is potential for misunderstanding, responsible state officials need to call people in the evenings and on weekends or whenever necessary. Visits to landowners on their property, at their convenience, are particularly important to dispel distrust of bureaucracy.

Publicity and public announcements are difficult to manage but are critical to leaving all the parties to an effort with a good feeling. State agency personnel must balance their obligation to give elected officials the opportunity to make announcements and receive credit for important accomplishments with recognition for their partners and for landowners, who have often donated part of the value of their land. Announcement ceremonies are a good way to fulfill these obligations, particularly if the governor is willing to attend and to thank the participants personally. Great care is needed in the preparation of guest lists and speaking programs for such ceremonies and in the drafting and timing of press releases to announce accomplishments. Agency officials should try to put themselves and the agency in the background. Properly designed ceremonies on Block Island and Conanicut Island were emotional events and encouraged other property owners to participate. When press coverage is favorable, others want to become part of the team.

Things do not always go well. Public conflicts over land conservation are inevitable. In such cases, communication is essential to ensure constant, organized responses to the press. Patience is also important. A situation is rarely as bad as it may seem to be when it first hits the newspapers. For example, a controversy over a very complex effort to protect a barrier beach and adjoining upland in Little Compton, Rhode Island, placed the state and conservation groups in opposition to the town government, yet it appears that after almost four years of difficult press coverage the project will succeed and the partnership will remain intact.

A consistent source of nongovernment money can be extraordinarily helpful in sustaining successful long-term conservation efforts. The Champlin Foundation's donation of $2 million per year for six years for the partnership of The Nature Conservancy and the Rhode Island Department of Environmental Management allowed for rapid, flexible responses to land conservation opportunities without the strain of constant searches for funds. Such funding should be used as a catalyst for drawing out public and other private sources of money. Another example is the Trust for New Hampshire Lands, created by a coalition of private organizations interested in land conservation that was spearheaded by the Society for the Protection of New Hampshire Forests. The local coalition raised $2 million in private funds to pay for the program's administrative costs and has successfully challenged the state legislature to appropriate $45 million to date in acquisition funds.

State officials need to be aware of the needs and roles of different private sector land conservation organizations. There are territories that must be respected. The Nature Conservancy and the Trust for Public Land, organizations with differing strengths and interests, have both been very active in New York State and elsewhere. State agencies can get the most out of working with each by ensuring that there is no competition for the same land and that both national groups respect the interests of and work with local land trusts.

PROMISE FOR THE FUTURE

During the national real estate boom years of the 1980s, which coincided with years of state fiscal strength, the ability of state governments to pursue successful land conservation efforts grew rapidly. Complex partnerships with private sector land conservationists were part of this growth. Much of this success, however, addressed the saving of individual parcels of land. Efforts to save a larger framework of open space have really just begun.

The challenge of the 1990s will be, during a time of severe fiscal constraints in state government, to try to protect whole pieces of landscape to serve multiple uses. Block Island continues to be in the forefront of such an effort with The Nature Conservancy's expanded bioreserve partnership there. Proposals by the Hudson Greenway Council to save the landscapes of the Hudson Valley and by The Nature Conservancy to save key parts of the Connecticut Valley ecosystem are large-scale efforts just under way. In the world of the 1990s, however, protection does not necessarily mean acquisition. It means working in a variety of ways to conserve the public and private values of open land.

Larger greenway and ecosystem projects require that we build on the experience of the 1980s by focusing on the following areas:

- Finding ways of protecting the working landscapes of farms and forests while respecting the traditional ways of life and economic concerns of farmers and forest managers.
- Recognizing that land conservation is an important tool for overall environmental protection.
- Understanding that waterways, reservoirs, lakes, bays, and sounds are public open spaces and that their protection must be connected to conservation of adjacent land.

- Bringing together policies for development, transportation, and open space management at the state level as a template for establishing patterns of growth.
- Restoring a federal/state relationship in land conservation.

Each of these directions can be supported by new kinds of public/private partnerships, as explored in the remainder of this chapter.

PRESERVATION OF WORKING LANDSCAPES

Privately owned farmlands and forestlands are important open space resources. They have traditionally provided wildlife habitat, access for fishing and hunting, scenery, and particularly, in the case of forestland, protection of water resources, all at no cost to the public.

But in many parts of the country, making a living from farming and keeping forest products companies profitable have become difficult. Over the past ten years, the use of easements, or the purchase of development rights, has been successful in conserving farmland and ranchland. In Massachusetts, 28,000 acres of farmland development rights are owned by the state, and the Lyons Falls case illustrates how easements are now being used to protect forestland.

If state government can better recognize the difficulties faced by the natural resource industry and can use a variety of means to address these difficulties, open space can be protected while rural economies are sustained and public stewardship costs are minimized. As was the case with the Lyons Falls project, nonprofit conservation organizations should play a role in this effort.

The simplest approach is continuation of programs for state purchase of development rights, combined with improved farm and forest taxation laws. In the Adirondacks and elsewhere, however, there is now discussion of creating private nonprofit natural resource trusts designed to support long-term protection of working forests. Such trusts could buy titles to forestland from willing sellers from the forest products industry, sell development rights to state agencies, and hold the titles and timber rights either for later sale to other forest products companies or for long-term management. Leasing of recreational rights could also provide income to such trusts. Critical areas such as river corridors could be sold outright to states for protection of ecological features and recreational access or could be reserved by easement for these purposes.

Land Conservation as Environmental Protection

Even in comprehensive state environmental agencies such as those in New York, Rhode Island, Vermont, and Massachusetts, there has continued to be a separation between land conservation and environmental protection. Yet we realize more and more that patterns of land use and the presence or absence of open space, including forests and wetlands, have a direct effect on water and air quality. The Adirondack Forest Preserve was created originally to protect sources of clean water. We are only now recognizing the remarkable intuition of the early conservationists.

Protection of watersheds and aquifers for drinking water supplies, of the shorelines of rivers and estuaries for water quality, and of forests for fixation of atmospheric carbon have now been recognized as important reasons for saving open land. By adding additional public values to the balance sheet for land conservation, the need for environmental protection brings new sources of popular and fiscal support to open space coalitions. Hodgkiss Farm contained a critical link in the town's water supply; protection of the Catskill region of New York is closely tied to preserving New York City's water supply. In each case, municipal funds have enhanced, or can enhance, state/private partnerships.

Protection of Land and Water Together

Water-based recreation has become increasingly important over the years, yet both freshwater and saltwater shorelines are the focus of private development. Lakes, rivers, bays, and sounds are themselves public open spaces, but these places become inaccessible when their shorelines are intensely developed. Waterfront land is expensive, but its potential for long-term public use, as well as for habitat protection, warrants emphasis in protection. Land and water together can create a natural framework around which other land uses can be structured.

New Directions in Transportation and Land Use Policy

Land conservation depends not only on avoiding growth where it is not wanted but also on encouraging it where it is wanted. Transportation policy, the location of parks and greenways as amenities, and private investment strategies can all focus development within existing communities or in new communities in ways that protect the character of adjacent land. Partnerships among land conservationists, municipal governments, and private developers could produce exciting alternatives to urban sprawl in the 1990s.

POTENTIAL FOR NEW FEDERAL/STATE FUNDING PARTNERSHIPS

For almost twenty-five years, the Land and Water Conservation Fund made grants to the states to support natural resource planning, land acquisition, park development, and historic preservation. As was the case on Block Island, these grants fostered cooperation among federal, state, and local agencies and contributed to the creation of a nationwide system of parks and open spaces. The near loss of this state grant system during the Reagan years was a serious setback to state land conservation efforts, although it was buffered in part by state budget surpluses in the late 1980s. Those surpluses have now turned to deficits, and it has become extremely difficult for states to obtain money for land conservation. A renewed state focus of the Land and Water Conservation Fund or, even better, passage of an endowed trust for open space, parks, and historic preservation could restore the federal government as a partner in creating a coherent system of parkland and open space in this country.

A restored state grant program could be enhanced by expansion of the excellent technical assistance efforts of the National Park Service and by more systematic encouragement by NPS of partnership park efforts such as the national heritage corridors in Rhode Island, Massachusetts, Pennsylvania, and Illinois. (See chapters 5 and 6 for more information on these National Park Service programs.)

COOPERATIVE STEWARDSHIP EFFORTS

Acquiring open space to conserve public values does not guarantee that those values will be protected in the long run. The land must be cared for in ways that respect its natural character and use. Stewardship by state agencies is suffering from budget cutting and work force reduction. This encourages the complaint against additional land acquisition: "How can you think about buying more land if you can't take care of what you already have?"

States must find ways to meet their basic stewardship obligations, but the partnership approach applies here too. Land protected through easements and managed through joint public/private efforts requires fewer state dollars for stewardship than traditional state parks. The idea of natural resource management trusts might be particularly useful here, and consideration should also be given to the connection between social programs and conservation. The Civilian Conservation Corps remains a very successful model for accomplishing multiple public objectives.

State government today is beset by fiscal and economic problems. The need for land conservation and for other forms of environmental protection is being measured against needs for education, law enforcement, health care, and housing. There is every indication that citizens still care about land, nature, clean water, and the outdoors, but tests of efficiency, cost-effectiveness, and practicality will be applied for every government action.

Two things can enhance the ability of land conservation to compete with other state government interests in these difficult times:

- Effective partnerships with the private sector and among government agencies.
- A recognition in these partnerships of the multiple public values of open space protection.

If we pursue these goals as effectively as we have begun to do over the past ten years, we can ensure that the outdoor places and experiences our children enjoy today will be intact for their children to enjoy thirty years from now.

8

A State Program to Preserve Land and Provide Housing: Vermont's Housing and Conservation Trust Fund

Pamela M. Dennis

In the 1980s, accelerated residential and commercial development in Vermont was forcing housing beyond the reach of many Vermonters and was causing the disappearance of significant agricultural and natural lands. Recognizing that the same development pressure was responsible for both of these losses, conservationists and proponents of affordable housing felt a strong need to work together to create a solution. In 1986, these nonprofit advocates formed the Vermont Housing and Conservation Coalition to lobby for a state trust fund that would assist in the protection of Vermont's agricultural and natural lands and that would also help finance affordable housing projects.

The coalition, composed of nonprofit housing and conservation organizations, directors of Community Action Project agencies, representatives from smaller coalitions of housing and environmental advocates, and members of planning districts, envisioned a nonregulatory program that would provide funds to fill the gap left after all available public and private resources had been allocated. The coalition's legislative proposal emphasized the role that nonprofit organizations could play in leveraging public funding with private funds and donations of land. The proposed legislation also provided a framework whereby nonprofit housing and conservation organizations could serve as local contacts in an area, do the legwork associated with putting a project together, and, where appropriate, own an interest in the property being preserved.

In May 1987, after strong lobbying by the coalition during the entire legislative session, the Vermont legislature established the Vermont Housing and Conservation Board (VHCB), assigning it the responsibility of "creating affordable housing for Vermonters, and conserving and protecting Vermont's agricultural land, historic properties, important natural areas and recreation lands."[1] The enabling legislation incorporated many of the recommendations of the coalition.

The Vermont Housing and Conservation Board is made up of nine members, including the commissioner of agriculture, the secretary of development and community affairs, the secretary of natural resources, the executive director of the Vermont housing finance agency, and five public members, one of whom must represent lower-income Vermonters and one of whom must be a farmer. VHCB is not a full-fledged state agency but rather is a public instrumentality of the state, responsible for meeting the goals enumerated in its enabling statute. This difference allows the board more flexibility, enabling it to act quickly and function differently from a state agency.

VHCB's primary responsibility is to provide funds in the form of grants or loans to eligible applicants for projects that will meet the goals of the statute. Eligible applicants include municipalities, certain state agencies, nonprofit organizations, and cooperative housing organizations whose purpose is the creation or retention of permanently affordable housing for lower-income Vermonters.

GUIDING PRINCIPLES OF VERMONT'S FUNDING PROGRAM

The Vermont Housing and Conservation Board will consider funding any activity "which will carry out either or both of the dual purposes of creating affordable housing and conserving and protecting important Vermont lands, including activities which will encourage or assist" the following:

- the preservation, rehabilitation, or development of residential dwelling units which are affordable to lower income Vermonters;
- the retention of agricultural land for agricultural use;
- the protection of important wildlife habitat and important natural areas;
- the protection of historic properties or resources;
- the protection of areas suited for outdoor public recreational activity;
- the development of capacity of an eligible applicant to engage in an eligible activity.[2]

The statute directs VHCB to give priority to projects that combine the dual goals of affordable housing and conservation of Vermont's agricultural land, historic properties, important natural areas, or recreation lands. When considering which projects to fund, VHCB must consider the need to maintain balance between the dual goals, the need for a timely response, the level of participation or funding of other groups, what will be needed to sustain the project in the future, the need to complete projects without displacing lower-income Vermonters, and the long-term effect of the proposed project.

FUNDING AND STAFF

The initial appropriation in 1987 to the trust fund was $3 million. In 1988, the legislature provided an additional $20 million and, importantly, an annual commitment of a portion of the state's property transfer tax. In 1989, the state budget was tighter, and after a difficult fight for funds, the legislature eventually committed $7.25 million in state bonds to the fund. The state allocated a total of $28.4 million to the trust fund in fiscal year 1991. In 1992, the state committed $11.65 million in state bonds and $1.45 million in property transfer tax to the trust fund. VHCB receives approximately 18 percent of the total property transfer tax received by the state each year.

To assist with implementation of VHCB's goals, the board employs a staff of nine. The staff consists of an executive director, a project development director, three project development specialists, a general counsel, an administrative officer, a grants administrator, and an office manager. When technical assistance is required that cannot be provided by staff members, other individuals are employed on a contract basis.

PARTNERSHIPS IN PURSUIT OF MULTIPLE GOALS

The establishment of the Vermont Housing and Conservation Board created the capacity for public and private organizations to work together in an effort to provide affordable housing and land conservation. The program creates a synergistic relationship that capitalizes on the strengths of each partner, allowing the accomplishment of projects that neither partner could complete alone. Nowhere is this more evident than in projects that combine multiple goals.

SAVING LAND AND PROMOTING AFFORDABLE HOUSING

The Vermont Housing and Conservation Board works to maintain an overall balance between funds allocated to affordable housing projects and to conservation projects. At the same time, the board recognizes the need to take advantage of opportunities when they arise and thus does not deny funds to a good project merely because it will temporarily upset the distribution of allocations. When commitments begin to tilt toward one goal or the other, the board and staff work to bring the balance back to a fifty-fifty distribution by encouraging applicants to bring in the needed projects.

Conservation and housing projects do not usually overlap; the very nature of one endeavor frequently excludes the other. Some situations arise, however, in which land identified as significant for protection includes sites suitable for affordable housing. Because the board does not encourage conservation groups to develop affordable housing and vice versa, applicants from the two sectors must work together when a project has the potential for meeting both goals. In this way, the board encourages the creation of partnerships. The following case study illustrates such a partnership between two private organizations and the board itself.

Saving a Farm and Building New Housing: Farrell Farm

In 1989, the 150-acre Farrell Farm was the last remaining commercial dairy farm in the town of Norwich, located along the Connecticut River in the Upper Valley region of Vermont. Faced with foreclosure, the landowner chose to work with the Upper Valley Land Trust (UVLT) to sell development rights on the farm. The two partners decided to consider the possibility of funding part of the purchase price by developing affordable housing on a portion of the farm.

A feasibility study and appraisal of the property funded by VHCB indicated that the development rights for the 110 acres of prime farmland were worth $2,000 per acre, or $220,000; that a maximum of fourteen units of affordable housing could be constructed on the northern end of the farm at a land value of $100,000; and that the balance of the $460,000 in costs could be recouped by selling one 20-acre residential lot on the southern end of the farm. Housing Vermont, Inc., a statewide nonprofit real estate development firm, expressed strong interest in developing affordable housing on the northern parcel.

Based on this information, UVLT applied for and received a VHCB grant of $250,000 and a zero-interest loan of $210,000. At the time of this request, UVLT had raised $17,000 from Norwich residents and had received a commitment of $5,000 from the Norwich Conservation Commission and pledges from charitable creditors to back the loan request.

Charitable credit is a tool sometimes used by land trust organizations to help in financing a project. The land trust solicits donors who are willing to lend their credit to a project, with the creditors guaranteeing that if there is a shortfall, they will pay a portion (up to their entire commitment) of the project's cost. This is a valuable tool that enables nonprofit organizations to secure loans that they otherwise could not obtain to complete projects with potential to generate a return on the investment. In this project, UVLT anticipated that profits from the sale of the two housing sites would allow repayment of the loan.

With the VHCB funds in hand, UVLT closed on the property, restricting the farmland with conservation easements, and began marketing the northern and southern parcels. Plans for affordable housing development on the northern parcel progressed, with the Upper Valley's nonprofit Twin Pines Housing Trust taking the lead on marketing and developing the affordable housing units and Housing Vermont providing substantial support as development consultant. Fourteen Cape Cod–style houses will be clustered on approximately 5 acres of the parcel, with the remaining acreage available as common space to be used for a community garden and a recreational area.

The houses will remain perpetually affordable through a ground lease mechanism whereby the Twin Pines Housing Trust will retain ownership of the land and the buyer of each house will own the improvements and agree to share with Twin Pines in any gain from appreciation of the house. Any capital gain received by Twin Pines from the sale of a house will be applied to the resale price, lowering the effective resale price and allowing new eligible buyers to buy the house for less than full market value.

Plans for the southern parcel did not progress as quickly. Due to the slumping real estate market, UVLT was unable to locate a buyer willing to pay the listed price of $100,000 for the parcel. It then developed that the owner of the adjacent farm wished to acquire the property for market garden uses.

UVLT returned to VHCB with a request that the board forgive part of the loan in order to allow UVLT to sell the southern parcel to the neighbor, subject to a conservation easement. VHCB agreed to some, but not all, of the reduction, forcing UVLT to ask its charitable creditors to assist with repaying the remaining portion of the loan.

This project illustrates the incredible effort required to complete a project with dual goals and the fact that ambitious plans do not always work out as originally envisioned. Such projects require an enormous amount of time and energy, to say nothing of money. It was only through a partnership effort that the Farrell Farm project was successfully completed.

One Farmer's Vision for Helping Others: Smith Farm

Another example of a combined housing and land conservation project provides an even more striking illustration of how large a role the individual partner—the landowner—often plays in such projects. The board cannot provide funds directly to individuals, but it can respond to initiatives brought forth by individuals and developed with the assistance of a nonprofit organization, town, or state agency.

Occasionally, in Vermont and elsewhere, there exist individuals who epitomize generosity and love of the land. Walter Smith is such a person. Having farmed his 470 acres for forty-nine years, Mr. Smith reached the point at which he could no longer farm the land on his own. Rather than sell his land and live on the proceeds for retirement, he worked with the nonprofit, statewide Vermont Land Trust, the Central Vermont Community Land Trust (CVCLT), and Shared Housing for Rural Elders (SHARE) to create a unique project funded by VHCB.

In order to protect his farm, in perpetuity, Mr. Smith first donated conservation easements on the bulk of his 320-acre parcel. He then sold the two land trusts a "remainder interest" in the farm, which allows him to remain there until his death, at which time the land and farm buildings will pass to the land trusts for resale to another farmer. Mr. Smith retained two residential lots, which he can sell or develop for housing whenever he chooses should he need additional income or face a financial emergency.

To increase the availability of affordable housing in the area, CVCLT purchased two lots on the farm for development of such housing. Moreover, if Mr. Smith does not develop the lots he retained, they too will be developed into affordable housing after his death. Funding from VHCB covered the purchase of both the remainder interest and the affordable housing sites.

In addition to protecting his farm for future generations, Walter Smith chose to share the farm with others during his lifetime. With the assistance of SHARE, a statewide organization dedicated to helping elderly people remain in their homes, he shares his house with four other people who sought to live in a rural extended family setting. Rent payments help Mr. Smith meet homeowner expenses, and the other house members receive affordable housing in a farm setting.

SAVING OTHER RESOURCES

Not only does VHCB encourage housing and land conservation groups to work together, it also encourages all groups to look at resources that might be beyond their usual field of vision. The board's funding application requires, for example, that the applicant determine whether a project contains resources of interest to the Division for Historic Preservation and the state Nongame and Natural Heritage Program.

Preserving a Historic Farmhouse: McManaman Farm

McManaman farm, located in northeastern Vermont but owned by a resident of California, was rented to a young farm family that could not afford to buy it. The purchase of development rights for the farm by the nonprofit Vermont Land Trust, funded by a grant from VHCB, reduced the price to a level the farm family could afford.

The VHCB grant application requires that applicants determine whether a project contains any historically significant resources. After being asked by the Vermont Land Trust to review the project, the Vermont Division for Historic Preservation identified the farmhouse as a structure of statewide historical significance and recommended its protection. Accordingly, the board's grant conditions included a requirement that a historic facade easement be placed on the farmhouse, stipulating that any changes to the facade be approved by the Division for Historic Preservation. Through this project, the Vermont Land Trust and VHCB were able to preserve a historic structure in addition to protecting 146 acres of agricultural land.

PROMOTING SPEED AND FLEXIBILITY

The Vermont Housing and Conservation Board is an example of an instrumentality of the state designed specifically to avoid some of the problems of previous public land acquisition programs. Indeed, VHCB's unique structure complements and encourages the speed and flexibility of its nonprofit partners. Monthly meetings by the board and immediate responses at the meetings to applications create an environment in which nonprofit organizations can act quickly to obtain control of a property. Applicants gain funding from the board without the delay typically found in other programs, during which time the costs of partnership projects often escalate. The alacrity with which the board can provide funds is important in the volatile real estate market, in which land can be lost to development for failure to acquire it promptly when it becomes available.

VHCB also works with nonprofit organizations to design flexible financing plans ranging from outright grants or grants combined with long-term, low-interest loans to loans with creative financing terms, such as no payments for the first ten years, with payments beginning as other debt is retired. This ability of the board's to address diverse funding needs has encouraged smaller nonprofit groups to put together land-saving projects that previously only larger organizations could afford. Farrell Farm, discussed earlier in this chapter, offers a good example of flexible financing through loans and grants provided to a nonprofit organization. The following example illustrates how the board's promptness in committing funds can complement a nonprofit organization's ability to act quickly to secure an important property.

REDUCING COSTS THROUGH A SPEEDY RESPONSE: KNIGHT ISLAND

In June 1989, The Nature Conservancy (TNC), in conjunction with the Vermont Department of Forests, Parks, and Recreation and the Lake

Champlain Islands Trust, requested a grant to assist with the acquisition of Knight Island, the last large, unaltered island in Lake Champlain still in private ownership. The 180-acre island provides habitat for eight rare and endangered plant species and was a high-priority acquisition for the state. The owner planned to offer the island to a global market for $750,000 through the local Sotheby's affiliate but agreed to sell it to TNC for $600,000 in a bargain sale. To discount the price so significantly, the owner wanted to sign a purchase and sale contract as soon as possible.

In order to sign a purchase and sale agreement, TNC needed a commitment from VHCB for a portion of the cost of the project, because it could not assume the entire cost itself. The board awarded The Nature Conservancy, the Lake Champlain Islands Trust, and the Department of Forests, Parks, and Recreation an immediate grant of $380,000 for the project and a one-to-one matching grant of $110,000, with the board matching every dollar raised by the organizations for the project up to a limit of $110,000. Through its own fund-raising efforts and those of its partners, The Nature Conservancy was able to acquire the island. TNC transferred ownership of the island to the state after developing a management plan and placing conservation restrictions in the deed.

SAVING MONEY AT AN AUCTION: HARDWICK FARM

Auctions provide another means by which nonprofit organizations can preserve significant parcels at reasonable prices. VHCB's ability to commit funds in advance of an auction is another example of its capacity to make the most of private sector and conservation opportunities.

The Venezuelan owners of the 310-acre Hardwick dairy farm in Vermont's Northeast Kingdom had listed the farm with an auctioneer. When approached by the nonprofit Vermont Land Trust, the auctioneer agreed to call off the auction if the land trust could come up with the asking price. The land trust sought a loan from VHCB to acquire the property, but VHCB determined that the asking price might be above the appraised value of the farm. The board wanted to avoid using public funds to distort the market by paying too much for a property. Some board members felt that going to auction would be the best way to see what the market would bear.

After reviewing information on the farm's value, the board authorized a loan to the Vermont Land Trust of as much as $400,000 for purchase of the farm at auction. The last bid prior to the Vermont Land Trust's offer was made by a developer, but the trust was able to acquire the farm for $400,000. As a result of VHCB's timely backing, Hardwick Farm is now subject to permanent conservation restrictions, and a farm family is leasing the property with an option to buy.

PROVIDING AND SEEKING LEVERAGE OF ALL TYPES

The Vermont Housing and Conservation Board has also been creative in maximizing the leverage of its funds, whether by providing small grants at opportune times or by requiring applicants to seek out every possible matching dollar and donation of land or services. The following are just a few of the different ways in which VHCB, in its first three and a half years, achieved more than $125 million worth of housing and conservation for an investment of only $35 million.

ENCOURAGING APPLICANTS TO NEGOTIATE BARGAIN SALES

Bargain sales, sales by the owner of a property for less than fair market value, which make the owner eligible for a charitable deduction from federal income taxes, significantly reduce the cost of projects in areas of a state where development value is high. Nonprofit organizations provide most of the "people power" in negotiating these sales.

Saving Estate Taxes and Income Taxes: Brookside Farm

The owner of the 174-acre Brookside Farm in Hartford, Vermont, wished to sell development rights to keep the farm from being divided after her death to pay estate taxes. After the sale of development rights, she wanted to give the property to her two sons, who planned to continue farming the land.

The project included a proposed trail system to cross the farm, linking a nearby village, a local science museum, and a picnic area. VHCB favors projects such as this, which provide additional public benefits that meet its goals.

The development rights on the farm were appraised at $353,000, much more than the board could spend on this one project. The Upper Valley

Land Trust was able to negotiate a bargain sale for $180,000, with the landowner donating $173,000 in value. In addition, UVLT committed itself to raising $20,000 locally for the project. A volunteer trail crew from the town conservation commission contributed the design and construction of the trail. Thus, a VHCB grant of $169,725 to the project leveraged $194,575 to complete a project with a total value of $364,300.

ENCOURAGING DONATIONS OF LAND OR INTEREST IN LAND

Donations of land or conservation easements also help increase the amount of resources protected for the board's investment. Nonprofit organizations often work with landowners to encourage donation of fee title to land or conservation easements on certain portions of a project's land.

Seeking Donations to Make a Project Affordable: Green Acres Farm

Ruth Shumway, owner and operator of the 290-acre Green Acres dairy farm bordering the Connecticut River in the Upper Valley region of Vermont, wanted to protect her farm so that it would remain a farm after she could no longer operate it. She was motivated both by her care for the land and by her need to realize some of the value of the property immediately. The Upper Valley Land Trust's original protection proposal was for a grant to acquire development rights on 100 acres of cropland and 150 acres of upland forest and the fee to a narrow mile-long strip on the Connecticut River containing an important floodplain forest.

At the urging of the board's staff, eager as always to reduce costs, UVLT instead negotiated the purchase of restrictions on the critical agricultural land only, with a donation of a conservation easement on the less threatened upland forest. The owner also agreed to donate the floodplain forest in fee to The Nature Conservancy and to provide public access to the Connecticut River. With contributions of $10,000 in private funds and $5,000 in town monies, a project worth $187,305 was accomplished with a VHCB grant of $142,155.

Leverage in the form of donated value does not have to come from the landowner whose land or development rights are being purchased. A project's value can be enhanced by neighboring landowners as well, as illustrated in the Huntington Farm example. A nonprofit organization's contacts in the project's area can be particularly helpful in acquiring this leverage.

LEVERAGING FUND-RAISING AND VOLUNTEER EFFORTS

In addition to leveraging funds through private negotiations of bargain sales and land gifts, many VHCB projects include leveraging of funds through both private and public fund-raising. Money can be provided by towns, private donors, foundations, or other public funds available through state or federal programs. For example, all projects submitted to the Vermont Housing and Conservation Board by The Nature Conservancy contain some form of leverage, often representing 50 percent of the total cost of the project. This leverage may consist of matching funds from foundations or the federal government, donation of overhead costs by The Nature Conservancy, local or regional fund-raising, or donations of time and services such as donated appraisals or surveys. Sometimes, the board needs to provide very little leverage. By providing money to pay for an option, for example, the board can buy the time to allow a nonprofit organization to do the rest. The best projects combine a variety of kinds of donations to stretch state funds and at the same time build a broad-based constituency for conservation that will support future efforts.

Spurring Private Fund-raising: Jewett Pond

In one example, The Nature Conservancy submitted a request to the board for a grant of $5,000 to secure a six-month option to purchase 148 acres of land bordering the Roy Mountain Wildlife Management Area in Barnet, Vermont. The parcel included the shoreline of the unprotected half of unspoiled Jewett Pond. The owners of the parcel agreed to sell a six-month option on the parcel for a nonrefundable price of $5,000, to be applied against the $100,000 purchase price. Since the option money was nonrefundable, it would have been hard to raise privately.

Armed with VHCB's grant of $5,000, a local group formed Friends of Jewett Pond to organize fund-raising for the project. Funds were sought from the Vermont Department of Fish and Wildlife, the town of Barnet, and local contributors. In all, TNC and the Friends of Jewett Pond raised more than $40,000 in private donations to match public funds for the project.

Combining Multiple Donations: Huntington Farm

The Upper Valley Land Trust negotiated leverage at every stage of the project to save Huntington Farm, a horse farm located in Strafford, Vermont. First, UVLT, working with the Working Land Fund, another nonprofit organization, obtained a donation of in-kind services to leverage a project feasibility grant. A landscape architect donated time in the preparation of site planning and a resource inventory of the area. The Service Corps of Retired Executives (SCORE) donated time and expertise to develop a business plan for the farm by analyzing the farm's current financial situation, developing an accounting system, and making recommendations to increase the farm's profitability. In addition, UVLT made a direct mail appeal to leverage the project's cost and raised nearly $40,000 from 227 donors. The land trust also obtained donations of conservation easements from five landowners for more than 400 acres of surrounding land. One donated easement includes the land surrounding the historic Strafford meeting house and contains the birthplace of Justin Morrill, founder of the Land Grant College System. This project provides a superior example of how a local land trust can work with a community to generate support and funding for land conservation.

SHARING AND EXPANDING PROTECTED OWNERSHIP

Just as the Vermont Housing and Conservation Board's policies and procedures promote multiple sources of funding for projects, so too do they recognize the legitimate desire of the funding partners to share in ownership or to place restrictions on the land. Some projects are acquired by a private nonprofit organization and then transferred to the state, subject to conservation restrictions held by the nonprofit group and VHCB. This format allows a state agency to protect a property that it otherwise might be unable, for lack of money or staff, to acquire and at the same time allows the group to safeguard the resources it values by means of the conservation restrictions. Both the Knight Island and Jewett Pond projects discussed earlier in this chapter are examples of projects that The Nature Conservancy acquired but eventually transferred to state ownership subject to restrictions.

In combined farmland and housing projects, ownership interests typically look like this: VHCB, the Vermont Department of Agriculture, and the applicant land trust co-hold the development rights; the farmer owns the restricted farmland; and the nonprofit housing organization owns the affordable housing site. Although the number of different parties involved may seem complex, VHCB feels that there is strength in numbers.

In protecting land resources, the board also seeks to promote the assemblage of a "critical mass" of land. Under its guidelines for evaluating farm projects, VHCB considers whether the farm is "geographically located in a farming area or farming community," whether it is "part of a critical mass of farms or farmland," and whether it is "in proximity to other productive agricultural areas."

The board also encourages natural area projects that will link or expand on already protected lands as well as acquisitions that mark the beginning of a planned preserve. Thus, The Nature Conservancy has already brought two projects successfully before the board for acquisition in the planned 1,300-acre East Creek Preserve along Lake Champlain. The projects included transfer of an Indian and Revolutionary War archaeological site to the Division for Historic Preservation, resale of farmland subject to conservation restrictions to a farmer, and retention of ownership of the important natural areas, with public access provided. The Nature Conservancy will continue its efforts to protect and raise private funds for this preserve, seeking funds from VHCB to fill funding gaps on particular parcels.

BUILDING PARTNERSHIP ORGANIZATIONS

The Vermont Housing and Conservation Board assists its grantees in many ways beyond providing funding for land acquisition. In a program similar to the California State Coastal Conservancy's program described in chapter 11 but otherwise quite unusual, the board provides funding to increase organizational strength through capacity grants and covers planning and other ancillary costs. The board also develops or improves capacity through its monitoring program and through workshops and technical assistance.

FUNDING OPERATIONS

The broad-based capacity grant program is a semiannual competition for organizational development funds to help nonprofit organizations develop

or maintain the staff and expertise needed to generate high-quality projects. Established organizations can apply for as much as $40,000, and
new groups can apply for as much as $15,000 each year. Because funding
is limited, the applicant must generally serve an entire county or a
geographic region encompassing several towns. The applicant is required
to provide an in-kind or cash match of at least 25 percent of the funds
requested from VHCB.

Helping to Staff the Green Mountain Club

The Green Mountain Club (GMC) is a nonprofit organization recognized
by the Vermont General Assembly as "founder, sponsor, defender and
protector of the Long Trail." The Long Trail extends the length of Vermont,
north to south, and served as the inspiration for the Appalachian Trail. In
1987, in partnership with The Nature Conservancy, the Green Mountain
Club began a land acquisition campaign to protect the Long Trail permanently. In 1989, GMC requested capacity funds from VHCB to help cover
the costs of hiring a land acquisition coordinator, who would plan and
negotiate acquisitions of parcels along the Long Trail projects on its own.

Promoting Independence; Recognizing Need

Although VHCB's goal is for all of its applicants eventually to become self-
sustaining, the board is committed to supporting organizations over time
provided that they demonstrate the effectiveness of their organization
through development of successful projects. Applicants frequently return
to the board for further funding after receiving an initial capacity grant.
Thus, the Green Mountain Club requested half of the cost of continuing the
position of land acquisition coordinator following funding of the position in
the previous year. The organization raised funds to support the other half of
the position.

Without nonprofit organizations to generate projects, VHCB would have
a reduced ability to protect land resources. The board has worked to foster
capacity in areas of the state where it does not exist and to support existing
organizations so that they can remain healthy. In lean financial times, as in
the early 1990s, the board has chosen to allocate more funds to its capacity
grant program, recognizing that with nonprofit organizations completing
fewer projects, they will need more organizational funding in order to
maintain themselves.

FUNDING PROJECT COSTS

VHCB also assists its grantees in developing projects through project-related capacity grants, through its project feasibility fund, and through grants to specific projects. Project-related capacity grants are usually provided to assist with the formulation of a project. The board will provide a grant to plan, develop, or organize a project when there is reasonable likelihood that these activities will result in a viable project consistent with the board's goals. Funds are typically used to study whether a project will succeed, to obtain technical assistance to help develop a project, or to assist with the planning of a large project containing more than one parcel.

The board's project feasibility funds provide similar support of costs for single projects. Grants have an $8,000 ceiling and can be used only for contracted services, not for staff time. Applicants frequently request funds for appraisals, soil testing, market studies, or financial planning and evaluation. Funding decisions are made by VHCB staff members rather than its board of directors. Before receiving funds, the applicant must provide adequate assurance that the property will not be sold for at least four months after the disbursal of feasibility funds. Such "site control," typically in the form of an option to purchase, helps protect the board from investing in a potential project only to lose the property before a project can be developed. The feasibility fund has resulted in increased capacity for generating projects because it allows the applicant organization to share the risks and costs of projects that may not prove to be successful.

Finally, applicants may also request funding from the board to help cover the actual costs incurred by the organization in assembling a successful project and monitoring the project on completion. These costs may include staff time, legal costs, mapping and documentation, and stewardship costs.

MONITORING AND TRAINING PARTNERS

The Vermont Housing and Conservation Board does not simply provide funds for projects and hope that they achieve the board's goals. Grant agreements for the projects have specific conditions that must be met and reporting requirements that the grantee must follow. VHCB staff members review project reports to ensure that conditions are met and that the projects are achieving their goals. Staff members also monitor the organizations to see how they are doing. The board has a vested interest in its grantees and wants to ensure that they remain strong and capable of both stewarding the projects they have completed and continuing to bring in new projects.

To strengthen its nonprofit partners as a group, the board sponsors workshops on such topics as business plan development and fund-raising to guide organizations in their development. When an organization needs individual assistance, the board sometimes funds consultants to work with it. For example, after the Regional Affordable Housing Corporation, a newly formed housing group in southern Vermont, completed its first project, VHCB sponsored a consultant to help the organization develop a long-range plan. The board hoped that the plan could enable the housing group to develop a sound financial base from which to begin new projects.

LESSONS FROM THE PAST

In the four years since it was formed, the Vermont Housing and Conservation Board has encountered a wide range of problems inherent in protecting the state's rural resources and expanding the supply of affordable housing. The board has solved a great many problems and is continuing to develop solutions for others. The following sections summarize the most significant issues faced by VHCB.

SETTING PRIORITIES

Land conservation systems with limited funding need to be proactive rather than reactive to crises. Organizations must articulate general land protection goals and then demonstrate how acquisition of particular parcels will contribute to those goals. For example, The Nature Conservancy has well-established priorities for land protection and has a list of the most important parcels to acquire.

Newer organizations do not always have specific protection priorities, and VHCB is no exception. Recently, VHCB has begun attempting to determine its priorities for funding, focusing first on farm projects. Working with its primary farm project applicants (the Vermont Department of Agriculture, the Vermont Land Trust, and the Upper Valley Land Trust), VHCB staff members tried to develop priorities for funding farm projects. This was an extremely difficult task because staffers had no clear-cut criteria for determining "a good farm." Should it be based on soils or on good management? Should VHCB spend money on projects in areas where the development pressure is now or in areas where there may be development pressure in the future and today's prices are low? These and other questions were discussed before the board adopted minimum criteria for considering funding requests.

The board also developed an application process for farm projects in which grants are issued twice per year instead of on a rolling basis. The farms in each round are evaluated only against each other, and each round consists of two steps. Initial decisions on the projects are made by a statewide agricultural advisory committee made up of farmers, extension agents, and staff members of the Soil Conservation Service, the Vermont Department of Agriculture, the USDA Agriculture Stabilization and Conservation Service, and VHCB members. The committee evaluates the farms based on a short application form, and decisions are made using the board's new farmland preservation criteria. Only farms that pass the first evaluation are asked to submit a full application, which is evaluated by the entire board.

VHCB chose this approach to funding farm projects because the limited amount of money currently available and the large number of farmers interested in the program mean that the board will be unable to fund many of the projects submitted. This approach seemed to be the fair way to make difficult decisions on allocating limited farmland protection dollars. For farm projects, the board has sacrificed some of its ability to respond quickly in order to ensure that it is funding the best projects.

VALUING DEVELOPMENT RIGHTS OF FARMS

In addition to establishing a new system for selecting the best farms, the board has been wrestling with the issue of how much to pay to protect farms. In the past, VHCB has relied on appraisers to determine the value of a farm's development rights. In order to arrive at this value, an appraiser measures the fair market value of the property before conservation restrictions are imposed; this number is known as the "before" value. The appraiser then determines the value of the property subject to the proposed conservation restrictions; this is the "after" value and generally reflects the value of the land for farming and open space. The difference between the two values is the value of the development rights. Since appraisals can measure only present value, properties located in areas of current high development pressure have a high development rights value, while properties in areas with little or no current development pressure have a correspondingly low development rights value—or none at all.

As more farmers in areas with little or no development pressure have sought to sell their development rights, more nonprofit groups have brought projects before the board that show little or no value for these rights. In such cases, although the board recognizes the conservation value in the development rights even when the appraisals do not indicate any market value, the board has no method of determining this intrinsic value. The McManaman Farm project discussed earlier in this chapter exemplified this dilemma. Acquisition of the historic facade easement on the farmhouse was one means by which the board could contribute more funds to the project and make the sale financially attractive to the farmer. Unfortunately, this method is not available in most projects.

Dissatisfied with the constraints of using conventional appraisals and its inability to recognize value in areas with no current development pressure, VHCB staff members developed a proposed system modeled after the system created for the Montgomery County, Maryland, Purchase of Development Rights Program. Maryland values easements according to the significance of the easement to the organization purchasing it. For example, the greater the land resource, such as high soil quality, and the greater the public benefit, such as access to trails or water, the greater the amount the landowner would be paid for the easement.

The system does not involve an estimate of a property's development rights value. In fact, with this formula, farmers located in an area subject to development pressure might receive a price that is far below the development rights value. Such farmers would have the option of paying for an appraisal of the property by an appraiser approved by VHCB's staff. If the appraisal were to come in at a higher value than the formula yields, the landowner could request that the board pay the higher amount.

This proposed system would allow the board to invest in projects in areas where there is little current development pressure but where long-term preservation of productive land and, thus, preservation of functioning agricultural communities are priorities.

THE LEVERAGE ISSUE

Another issue that the Vermont Housing and Conservation Board is beginning to address is the policy question of how much leverage to require in conservation projects. Without some form of leverage, the nonprofit applicant method of land conservation may not be cost-effective. In other states, straight purchase of development rights or acquisition projects without leverage do not usually require nonprofit "middlemen." When the Vermont Housing and Conservation Coalition first began working to create the trust fund, they assumed that every project would be leveraged. The nonprofit organization not only would develop the project and secure the involvement of the local community but also would gain financial support for the project.

Leverage in Farmland Projects

Although the idea of leveraged projects has worked for many of the board's projects, farm projects often lack outside sources of funding. Currently, in addition to funding acquisition of a farm's rights, the board frequently pays for costs associated with assembling the project and provides support for the nonprofit organization's salaries through capacity grants. Unless the nonprofit organizations can bring something to the projects that state specialists cannot, it is arguable that it would be better simply to hire several state workers to put together farm projects.

There are, however, other benefits that local nonprofit organizations can bring to a project. Locally based organizations can generate support for specific projects and for land conservation in general, and this support can be influential in the funding of a program such as VHCB. Often, it may be the nonprofit organization's local contacts that persuade the owner of a particularly valuable property to participate in the program. Once enthusiasm is generated for a project, local individuals are more likely to become informal stewards, keeping an eye on properties and reporting any problems such as illegal dumping or vandalism. These benefits of a local nonprofit organization are much more difficult to achieve for a statewide organization, which does not have the same contact with the community.

Although there are other benefits to a local nonprofit organization developing projects besides the ability to leverage projects, if the nonprofit group truly has the support of the community, there should be some local funds or donations in the projects it brings to the board. And as funds for the state program decline, locally leveraged projects will become increasingly necessary.

Gifts as Leverage

Even though leverage should be considered an important part of a partnership project, there is also a risk involved in being too rigid about requiring it, particularly in the case of land donations. In one case, an applicant organization anticipated a donation of an easement to provide leverage and the board conditioned its grant on that donation, but the donation was not received. Without the board's grant, the nonprofit organization could not acquire the property, and the property was lost.

Another point to consider in requiring receipt of donations prior to disbursement of funds for a project is that the Internal Revenue Service will not permit these donations to be used for tax write-offs if there is any condition requiring the donation. If the donation will benefit the donor (for example, if it leverages the protection of land adjacent to the donor's property), the IRS may not perceive the donation to be a tax-deductible gift. The fact that a donor cannot benefit from tax deductions if the donation is a condition of the board's grant provides further incentive for the applicant to obtain the donation prior to requesting funds from the board.

PROMISE FOR THE FUTURE

The greatest challenge facing the Vermont Housing and Conservation Board is to meet the ever-growing needs of its constituents. To carry its vital efforts into the future, the board will need to expand its sources of funding and deal with the growing issue of land stewardship.

FUNDING FROM THE FEDERAL GOVERNMENT

One of the problems of the past also holds the seeds of promise for the future: the sheer popularity of the program among landowners and VHCB's inability to keep up with demand. When word of a successful project spreads through a community, VHCB staff members frequently receive a flood of requests for information about the board and the possibility of obtaining funds. In some cases, nonprofit groups have also been overwhelmed by requests to initiate projects. This situation highlights the problems of starting an ambitious program, creating a great demand, and then not having the funds to meet all deserving needs.

As state funds available for land conservation in Vermont become scarce, two federal sources of money may serve to stretch the ever-shrinking state dollar. The 1990 Farm Bill creates a five-year program known as Farms for the Future, by which eligible states can obtain federally guaranteed and subsidized loans of as much as $10 million per year as a two-to-one match of state dollars to be used for farmland conservation. To date, $920,000 per year for five years has been committed to be put toward the Vermont farmland conservation program. In addition, the Forest Stewardship Act of 1990 establishes the Forest Legacy Program, through which the Forest Service can acquire conservation easements on important forest-land threatened by conversion to nonforest uses. The federal share of the total program costs can be as high as 75 percent. These two federal programs—although still in the development stage, with many issues unresolved at this writing—should expand the ability of the states to protect important lands and forge new partnerships in land conservation.

STEWARDSHIP

As VHCB partnerships prove successful, nonprofit organizations are finding themselves responsible for protecting a large amount of property. Careful stewardship of these projects—whether through actual management or through monitoring of easements—is rapidly becoming a full-time job for many organizations. The Vermont Land Trust has chosen a creative way to resolve the stewardship issue: It is establishing a separate title-holding subsidiary organization, Vermont Conservation Lands, Inc., to handle the stewardship of its properties. This organization may eventually serve as the holder of conservation restrictions negotiated by other organizations, ensuring that even if a group is not incorporated or does not have the financial base necessary for long-term sustainability, the lands on which it negotiates conservation easements will be protected.

COMMUNICATION

Public/private partnerships such as the Vermont Housing and Conservation Board offer the opportunity to consolidate resources throughout the state. Although the focus of this book is public/private partnerships, existing public entities should not be overlooked as a significant resource. VHCB has benefited from the skills and knowledge found in many state agencies and municipalities and has worked in partnership with these government

entities to protect many land resources. All levels, from private to municipal to federal, need to converge to protect significant land resources.

And, of course, the overriding principles of partnerships apply in Vermont as elsewhere: the need for communication, to keep everyone involved
and informed from the beginning, and the need for consideration, to share
credit and glory.

Although coalitions for the sake of coalitions are to be avoided, organizations that foster the same goals should gather on a regular basis for
enlightenment, encouragement, and planning. Frequently, open discussion
helps to avoid conflict and minimize overlap. It can also increase the
productivity of each group through the sharing of ideas and efforts. Vermont has a strong affordable housing coalition that regularly meets to
discuss issues and works together to find ways to meet Vermont's need for
affordable housing. A formal coalition for land protection has yet to
develop, but there is informal communication among land conservation
groups. Development of ongoing communication will only enhance the
Vermont program.

NOTES

1. VT. STAT. ANN. tit. 10, § 302 (1987).
2. Ibid., § 303 (3).

9

Local Partnerships
with Government

Eve Endicott and Contributors

Formal cooperation between government agencies and private land conservation groups at the state or local level—the organizations typically described as land trusts—has grown tremendously over the past decade. This growth has coincided with the meteoric growth in the number and size of such land trusts. According to statistics compiled by the Land Trust Alliance, a coordinating group and advocate for the nation's land trusts based in Washington, DC, there are now nearly 1,000 land trusts in America, more than double the number of ten years ago. Although many land trusts are headquartered in New England, they are multiplying rapidly, especially on the West Coast and in the mid-Atlantic region.

In all, land trusts have helped to protect an area about twice the size of Delaware, or nearly 3 million acres. In 1989 and 1990 alone, land trusts helped to protect more than 630,000 acres. Behind these impressive numbers is a total membership of close to 800,000 people. Significantly, approximately 70 percent of land trusts' funds for land acquisition come from individuals, with only 10 percent coming from government.

As land trusts have become more numerous and more sophisticated, they, like their sister national organizations before them, have progressed from the passive acceptance of gifts of land (still an important role, of course) to the more complex business of preidentifying key parcels or even whole ecosystems or greenways and forging partnerships with governments to get the protection job done.

Local land trusts (the term "local" is used here to describe statewide land trusts as well as those with smaller geographic spans) can enjoy all the same advantages in working with public agencies as do the pioneering national organizations profiled in part I of this book. Illustrations of such local public/private partnerships abound in the previous chapters: from community gardening groups in New York putting city-owned vacant lots to productive use (chapter 3) to the innovative limited development work of the Housatonic Valley Association in Connecticut in helping the National Park Service protect lands adjacent to the Appalachian Trail (chapter 5) to the critical preacquisition and packaging role played by the Vermont Land Trust in Vermont's agricultural preservation program (chapter 8).

It would be impossible to profile all of the successful partnerships between government agencies and local land trusts across the country. It seems more realistic and useful to focus on those areas of partnership endeavor that may be hardest for a small land trust to achieve and to suggest ways of overcoming the limitations of size. Equally important is to highlight those aspects of being small and local that give land trusts a positive advantage in working with government and that make them increasingly critical partners in virtually every land conservation project. After all, since every parcel of land is situated in one particular locale, ultimately all land protection is local.

OVERCOMING THE LIMITATIONS OF SIZE

The primary handicaps local land trusts suffer by virtue of their typically smaller size are, not surprisingly, financial: lack of capital to purchase land and inadequate operating resources to pay staff.

PROTECTING EXPENSIVE LAND

Authors of previous chapters have stressed the advantages of speed and flexibility that private organizations bring to the business of land protection with government. Many of the transactions described to illustrate these advantages involved the private sector putting up millions of dollars either in loans or in outright grants. With the high cost of much of the important land remaining to be saved, how can a relatively small private organization such as a local land trust hope to play a meaningful role?

Land trusts are nothing if not ingenious, and examples abound of local land trusts making projects happen that otherwise would not, sometimes with creativity bordering on smoke and mirrors. This ingenuity has enabled land trusts to take on the important task of optioning and even preacquiring land for government, whether to provide the speed or certainty that the landowner requires or to tailor the parcel's size to the government agency's interests.

One especially innovative land trust in Florida shows how the obstacle of an inadequate or nonexistent revolving loan fund can be gotten around, to the benefit of government. Meanwhile, in the West, two well-established land trusts have proved that deals that initially seemed beyond the government's reach, let alone the local land trust's, can be put together with a little ingenuity, a lot of staff time, and liberal help from foundations and conservation buyers. Finally, in states with government loan funds, local land trusts are showing how the leverage of public funding can stimulate private giving in the public interest.

Packaging a Deal for Government: Gainesville, Florida

Sometimes a government agency needs a land trust simply to provide the staff to negotiate an acquisition; to advance the money for an option, appraisal, and survey; and then to arrange the closing. This familiar role, first played by The Nature Conservancy and later the Trust for Public Land, has recently been taken on by a number of land trusts. One notable example is the Alachua Conservation Trust in Gainesville, Florida. The Alachua Conservation Trust (ACT) was formed in 1988 with the help of the Trust for Public Land, with an initial goal of filling an empty niche in the community by helping public agencies—ranging from the city to the state to the regional water management district—to buy land. All levels of government had monies to spend on land acquisition, but only the water district had a staff to negotiate the acquisitions.

ACT solved the "liquidity" problem by the skilled use of options and so-called simultaneous (or, more accurately, back-to-back) closings. ACT obtains the appraisal for a property and, working in close cooperation with the government agency, negotiates an option with the landowner, typically for six months. Once the government funds are available, ACT either assigns the option to the government agency for a predetermined fee or acquires the property and then immediately sells it to the agency, using the government check to pay the landowner.

The assignment fee negotiated by ACT and the government agency is based on the theory of "shared savings." The less the total deal costs the government, the higher will be the fee to ACT to support its overall work. This arrangement, pioneered by ACT and adopted by other land trusts in Florida, provides an incentive to the land trusts to negotiate the best prices possible and to minimize transaction costs, all to the taxpayers' benefit. The landowners, who are helping to provide these savings, are content with the arrangement because of the combination of tax savings from the bargain sale and the fast action and responsiveness that ACT provides.

Creative Negotiating and Conservation Brokerage: Wyoming's Hatchet Ranch

Just as national groups have taken on ever more creative and complex projects, so have some of the better-established local land trusts. This is not a searching out of complexity for complexity's sake; it is the inevitable outcome of higher land prices and other realities of the 1980s and 1990s, including new elements to contend with such as hazardous waste. The Hatchet Ranch project of the Jackson Hole Land Trust (JHLT) well illustrates how important staff time is to negotiating these complex deals, especially if conservation brokerage is also involved. Fortunately, time is a commodity that a local land trust may well have in greater abundance than money.

Hatchet Ranch, at 760 acres, is the largest ranch in Wyoming's Buffalo Valley, an enclave of ranchland within the Bridger-Teton National Forest at the eastern gateway to Grand Teton National Park. In 1989, the threat of development to the scenery, wildlife, and traditional ranching of the valley prompted Congress to appropriate $2.8 million to the Forest Service to begin protection of the valley. Unfortunately, Hatchet Ranch alone had an asking price of $4.5 million—and a developer willing to pay close to that amount.

The Jackson Hole Land Trust immediately recognized that it needed another partner if it was to make the deal work within the Forest Service's budget. From its extensive contacts built up over ten years of working in the community, JHLT identified several potential conservation buyers— individuals who were interested in buying the land as ranchland, subject to conservation easements to be held by the federal government and JHLT. That enabled JHLT to scale the Forest Service's purchase down to a package that it could afford: the eighty most critical acres in fee and a strict conservation easement over the 680-acre balance.

When the four-party closing between the seller, the Forest Service, the land trust, and the conservation buyer finally took place, the twenty-one documents on the table and the fifteen people around it only hinted at the complexity of the transaction. The land trust played a critical role by accomplishing the following:

1. Negotiating a considerable reduction in the overall purchase price.
2. Putting up forfeitable "earnest money" to satisfy the sellers that the conservationists were serious.
3. Tracking down and contacting fourteen separate owners of mineral rights and two owners of rights-of-way to clarify the title.
4. Dealing with the unexpected legalities and costs resulting from hazardous materials being found on the property.
5. Negotiating new conservation easement language with three levels of the Forest Service and two levels of the Office of the General Counsel of the U.S. Department of Agriculture.
6. Working with three different potential conservation buyers.
7. Working with the U.S. congressional delegation to obtain a special waiver to expedite congressional oversight.

The project's director, Story Clark, estimates that the project took 3,000 person-hours (50 percent of two people's time for a year), much of this time spent dealing with emergencies: a problematic appraisal, problems with the title, and hazardous waste problems. Local land trusts often excel at this kind of labor-intensive crisis resolution, whereas government officials with more rigid job definitions simply may not be able to spare the time. Echoing the advice of others in this book, Clark also credits part of the success of the Hatchet Ranch project to an early memorandum of understanding with the Forest Service formalizing the land trust's role and providing a solid basis for the later, protracted team effort. She also credits a conservation buyer who was willing to be part of a lengthy, complex, and often frustrating, but ultimately successful, project.

Stretching Funds with Outside Help

Although avoiding actual outlays of purchase money is usually preferable for land trusts—and possible, as illustrated above—it is sometimes necessary or desirable to put up cash. The following are examples of ways that land trusts have been helped to assemble capital for land purchases.

Using a Small Revolving Fund and Foundation Loans: Gallatin National Forest, Montana. As local land trusts mature, several of them are beginning to build small revolving funds of their own, freeing themselves from dependence on borrowing from large organizations, whose loan funds are often tied up, or from banks, which charge high interest rates if they will make a loan at all. Typically, however, such revolving funds are still too small for a substantial land acquisition. The Montana Land Reliance, a statewide land trust formed in 1978, offers a good example of how a relatively small revolving fund can be used in combination with other loans from foundations to buy a large and important parcel.

The 6,000-acre tract involved adjoins the Gallatin National Forest, just north of Yellowstone National Park, and provides critical habitat for winter elk. Together, the Montana Land Reliance and three separate foundations put up the purchase price, taking back mortgages on separate parcels as security. Repayment for the loan is expected to come from resale of the property to the Forest Service and a sale to one conservation buyer, subject to an easement. Although the Montana Land Reliance and the foundations hope to recoup the foregone interest on their funds, they do not have to do so, nor do they have an absolute deadline, factors that allow them the freedom to put together the best conservation deal possible.

Using Government Loan Funds: Maryland and Rhode Island. Public/ private partnerships can, of course, work both ways. Increasingly, government is facilitating private conservation efforts, especially at the local level. Thus, in a growing number of states, nonprofit conservation groups of all sizes have access to loan funds set up specifically to make private land conservation efforts possible. One example is the Maryland Environmental Trust (MET), a state-funded land trust established to protect scenic, environmental, and cultural sites in Maryland. MET recently made a loan to the fledgling Central Maryland Heritage League for a down payment on the purchase of a 25-acre Civil War battlefield site. The balance of the purchase price came from the most traditional source of loan funding, a purchase money mortgage given by the landowner. MET's $50,000, zero-interest loan must be paid back in three years. The local group is raising the funds to repay MET and the landowner through a nationwide campaign using the technique of selling honorary deeds to a square foot of battlefield for $25 apiece.

Rhode Island has a similar program that offers interest-free loans for as long as five years. The Barrington Conservation Land Trust, near Providence, Rhode Island, successfully applied for a $59,000 loan to supplement state grants, providing protection to one of the last working farms in the town of Barrington. The trust's president is very pleased with how the fund-raising project has increased the trust's overall visibility and support as well as swelling its volunteer ranks. So far, $25,000 has been raised, mostly through small gifts. Having a long period over which to raise the money has allowed the trust to encourage multiyear pledges, which are helpful to donors at both ends of the income spectrum, from those who can use multiyear charitable deductions to those on fixed incomes. Although it may take several years to repay the loan, the land trust is confident that it will be done, with the help of planned events ranging from a walkathon to a "roast" for a popular volunteer to an exhibit in the public library. Land trusts in states without such public loan funds should make obtaining one a legislative priority; they are a low-cost way for government to leverage land protection through private action.

MAKING EFFICIENT USE OF STAFF

Lack of capital to pursue significant land protection projects may not be the only financial limitation on a small land trust. Finding money to hire staff members to do the negotiating is typically also a problem. Although some land trusts may find that a volunteer work force is sufficient for their needs, it has been the experience of most land trusts that volunteers simply cannot give the long-term continuity of effort required by a sustained program of complex partnership projects. Each project is a learning experience, and it is important to have staffers who will be around long enough to apply the lessons they have learned.

Seeking Government Support for Operations

Once the decision is made to hire a staff, the problem is how to pay the staff's wages. The Trust for Public Land and land trusts it has helped to set up, such as the Alachua Conservation Trust, have pioneered the concept of "increments." The nonprofit organization negotiates a bargain sale price with the landowner on behalf of a government agency, allowing the nonprofit organization to charge the transferee public agency the land cost plus staff and other costs while still selling the land for no more than fair market value, and often less. Faced with an inability to negotiate a bargain sale itself, a shortage of staff members, and often the need to seize the opportunity of working with a sympathetic or pressed seller, the government agency will often find this service a bargain, even with the nonprofit group's costs added in.

In states fortunate enough to have grant programs that include seed grants to land trusts, these will be a critical source of funding, especially in an organization's early years. Here again, government is often getting a good deal. Relatively small operating grants to the Green Mountain Club by the Vermont Housing and Conservation Board, profiled in chapter 8, have resulted in several acquisitions on behalf of the state as well as more than $850,000 in private funds raised for protection of land along a statewide asset of great public value, Vermont's section of the Appalachian Trail.

Although government funds may allow land trusts to take on projects they would never have dreamed of before, it is important for them to plan for the day when government support may no longer be available. From that perspective, it seems as if the regional land trusts, such as the Upper Valley Land Trust in Vermont and New Hampshire, the Maine Coast Heritage Trust, and the Montana Land Reliance, have the best chance of success over the long haul, since their support base should be large enough to ride out rough times.

Whatever the size of the land trust, there is no question that it is easier for it to raise operating money on a sustained annual basis in a community once it has a successful record of tangible success—acres saved—to point to; cooperative ventures with government can give an organization this track record and then help it broaden its sights to include more private land conservation, education, and fund-raising.

Sharing Resources

In the absence of special government funding, a smaller land trust may find it difficult to support a staff person to conduct partnership projects. But it may be able to gain access to such expertise by forming partnerships with larger land trusts or by pooling resources with other, similar organizations.

Arrangements among private land trusts to share staff or resources are relatively recent but are growing, and different models are being explored throughout the country. What they have in common is the ability to combine the strengths that local land trusts (or chapters or committees) provide— familiarity with the land and people in the community, ability to generate local enthusiasm and support, volunteer assistance—with the expertise, coordination, and financial backing that a larger organization can offer.

Teaming Up to Share Staff. On Cape Cod, for example, sixteen land trusts gain professional assistance through the Compact of Cape Cod Conservation Trusts. The compact is staffed by an experienced land conservationist who provides various types of technical assistance to member land trusts, including staffing for specific conservation projects. The participating land trusts pay dues ranging from $1,000 to $4,500, depending on the level of assistance desired, plus a share of the compact's administrative costs. The compact also provides a regional voice and perspective for the participating land trusts, which are town based.

The compact's arrangement—in effect a pooling of resources among Cape Cod land trusts to fund a shared staff person—has served the region well and has been instrumental in the extraordinary successes of public/ private partnerships there in the 1980s. From 1985 to 1988, Cape Cod towns, urged on by the land trust community, put up a total of $114 million to save sensitive lands from an avalanche of development.

Tapping into Larger Organizations. Often, regions with small land trusts already have a larger conservation organization serving the area to which the land trusts can look for assistance. In Michigan, for example, the Grand Traverse Regional Conservancy and the more local Old Mission Conservancy have joined in a mutually beneficial partnership in which Grand Traverse professionals perform the staff work on conservation projects within the territory covered by the Old Mission Conservancy. Old Mission, with connections in the community and a locally respected name, raises funds for the projects and pays for Grand Traverse's staff time and related expenses.

In Berkshire County, Massachusetts, eleven townwide land trusts have achieved some of the same efficiencies by joining under the umbrella of a preexisting regional land trust, the Berkshire County Land Trust and Conservation Fund (BCLTCF). The resulting Berkshire County Land Trust Alliance publishes an excellent journal with general articles and specific reports on individual land trusts' successes. The alliance also sponsors conferences and training sessions. Finally, BCLTCF staff members help in negotiations with landowners, and BCLTCF serves as a backup enforcer of conservation easements held by alliance members. BCLTCF's director, George Wislocki, credits the town land trusts with using their local contacts to secure gifts of land and easements that would never have come to a countywide organization.

Making Use of a Decentralized Organization. In some places, local communities interested in promoting land conservation do not need to form independent nonprofit organizations at all. An existing national, statewide, or regional organization may have local representatives or chapters that can help with individual partnership projects. In Vermont, for example, The Nature Conservancy assists communities with important projects and the statewide Vermont Land Trust (VLT) establishes local committees that provide direction, presence, and assistance to local efforts. VLT provides substantial technical, legal, and stewardship expertise as well as fundraising and administrative coordination to a wide variety of local conservation efforts.

If a local project is sufficiently important to attract government support in the first place, chances are that a staffed organization in the state will be willing to help make the project succeed in exchange for some credit. It is important to remember that the lifeblood of land conservation organizations is success in preserving acreage, whether single-handedly or in cooperation with others. A little sharing of credit will pay off handsomely to the local group in terms of professional assistance from a larger entity. Every land conservationist has seen good local projects stall or fail for lack of knowledge or resources, when such projects might well have succeeded if their proponents had been able—or willing—to ask for outside assistance.

Making Do with Little

Even if a small land trust has a staff of its own, the inevitable endless demands of partnership work make it important to ensure maximum productivity of whatever staff exists. Robert Hutchinson, of ACT in Gainesville, and Keith Lewis, formerly the unpaid staff person of the Block Island Land Trust, exemplify many of the attributes of the ideal staff member for a small land trust.

Both of these individuals have become highly computer literate, so they do not require much secretarial or administrative support. In Bob Hutchinson's words: "Today, land conservation work doesn't mean tromping through woods looking for endangered plants as often as it means processing words at a terminal while the fax machine beside you is rapidly scrolling urgent messages onto the floor. The segregation of our population today between those who are making the machines work for them and those who hesitate to climb the steep learning curve is also happening in the land trust field."

At ACT, all of the different government agency forms the organization works with are stored in computers. A recent cooperative project involved one floppy disk making five trips from Gainesville to the state capital and back and an equal number of trips back and forth to the seller's attorney. Each time changes were made, they were highlighted so that the three parties could see what the issues were in minutes without any secretarial assistance.

Just as computers can help maximize the efficiency of hard-pressed land trust staffers, outside expertise can help small land trusts avoid costly duplication of effort and mistakes. ACT's Bob Hutchinson attributes the running start he and his land trust got in government partnership work to the formal training program of the Trust for Public Land. Keith Lewis worked closely with The Nature Conservancy and attended every conference and training session he could—from the annual rallies sponsored by the Land Trust Alliance to workshops of Rhode Island environmental groups. In part, of course, this book is an attempt to pass on the wisdom of forerunners in partnerships to those just beginning to work in the field. There are many other sources of expertise, starting with the books and organizations listed under Selected Readings and Selected Private Assistance Organizations at the back of this book.

Most important of all to the success of local partnership projects are the character and personality of the land trust staff members. Often, one person will need to be attorney, trail clearer, fund-raiser, politician, and diplomat. Of the qualities listed by ACT in its director's job description, including "community roots, ability to communicate effectively with a broad range of people, independence, judgment and ability to master the long-range and the mundane," the trait the current director considers most necessary for effective partnerships with government is ". . . an optimistic disposition, as evidenced by an ability to deal with bureaucrats in an unflaggingly good-humored manner."

CAPITALIZING ON LOCAL STRENGTHS

Although small land trusts embarking on land conservation partnerships with government may be handicapped in some ways—problems for which this book suggests some practical solutions—in other ways they are uniquely advantaged in such dealings. These advantages often make a local, private land trust a key partner in any public/private enterprise to protect land regardless of who initiates the project and which other partners are involved. For example, The Nature Conservancy's work in Connecticut, Maine, and many other states depends on the support of strong local land trusts; the Trust for Public Land's work in New York City and other urban areas is designed to empower and strengthen community open space groups; the surroundings of many national parks are being protected by local groups; and many of the successes of the North American Waterfowl Management Plan are attributable to in-state private efforts.

What is it that so often makes national conservation efforts dependent on local groups? The answer, of course, is that no piece of land in any community can be protected without local support. This principle, though a truism, deserves elaboration so that newly forming land trusts can learn from others how best to create and maintain that support and turn it into effective action with government agencies at all levels.

SERVING AS LOCAL FACILITATORS

At the same time that local land trusts need larger organizations to fill in gaps in expertise or resources, large public and private partners increasingly depend on community-based groups to make projects work. As land becomes scarcer and more expensive, the need to build local political support to save it becomes greater. Taxpayers' revolts and hard-hit local economies have put every land acquisition project under a local spotlight. Government land protection programs must usually be "sold" to local governments and community groups. Equally important is interpreting a government acquisition program for the landowners, who will typically feel more comfortable making a donation, or even a sale, through a familiar local person or entity.

Facilitating a Federal Program: Maine Coast Heritage Trust

Although the federal government is often perceived as a much more solid holder of conservation lands and easements than is a local land trust, a private group is often helpful in negotiating a deal. One land trust with a great deal of experience in facilitating protection of public land with private staff time and local expertise is the Maine Coast Heritage Trust (MCHT), a statewide land trust with a local office near Acadia. The partnership between MCHT and the National Park Service at Acadia National Park on the Maine coast dates back to 1970, when the trust was formed to help preserve privately owned coastal properties in the Acadian archipelago through conservation easements. Since then, MCHT has helped to negotiate more than 135 donations of easements to the National Park Service, permanently preserving more than 6,000 acres and approximately fifty entire islands. Acadia National Park now holds more easements than any other federal or state agency or local land trust in Maine.

MCHT's role in the easement process has always been that of a facilitator—seeking out new opportunities, following up on landowners' inquiries, offering technical advice, leading negotiations, and finally placing the easement with the most appropriate holder. Because of the National Park Service's criteria and its strength as a holder, Acadia National Park is often the preferred easement recipient.

Why the need for MCHT's role in the process? In the words of MCHT's Caroline Pryor: "There is real worth in having a neutral party negotiate the terms of protection; since MCHT is not going to hold the easement, we're not pressing any 'agenda.' We're not representing the park, nor are we working on behalf of the landowner; we try to weigh the interests of both and finally do what's best for the land. Landowners like the idea that the Park Service will probably be around longer than a local land trust. But they also appreciate assistance from a smaller, more local entity because dealing with 'the Feds' is still intimidating to some."

Facilitating a County Program: Big Sur Land Trust

The Big Sur Land Trust (BSLT) is a private land trust dedicated to the preservation of natural and cultural resources in Big Sur and the Monterey peninsula. To date, BSLT has facilitated seven of ten purchases by Monterey County of parcels along State Route 1 along the California coast. Like the Alachua Conservation Trust in Gainesville, Florida, the Big Sur Land Trust obtains options on the properties—which have totaled $3 million—and pays for appraisals and other costs of qualifying for funding. BSLT sees its role as "representing the landowners and guiding them through the qualification and purchase process with the county." In one case, a landowner who thought he would rather avoid the cost of an intermediary (BSLT, like the Alachua Conservation Trust, covers its costs through bargain sales) came back to the trust after trying to negotiate the deal himself, saying that 15 percent was a cheap price to pay for the trust's services.

The Big Sur Land Trust provides another illustration of private involvement helping the public sector spend its money better. Using a grant from the Packard Foundation, BSLT performed a comprehensive viewshed analysis to help target private efforts and public funds on the most significant coastal properties.

Facilitating a Local Program: Peconic Land Trust

Even a town-level government land acquisition program may need a private facilitator. When the town of East Hampton, on the eastern end of Long Island, took the bold step of passing a $5 million bond to preserve its remaining open space and farmland, it turned to a local land trust to implement the project. East Hampton contracted with the Peconic Land Trust to negotiate with owners of targeted acquisitions because the land trust already had both staff, with time to meet with landowners, and expertise to work out individual tax and financial packages.

On one farm, the landowner wanted more money for the property than the town was able to pay and had filed for subdivision approval. It would have been difficult for the same town government that wanted to buy the land to be responsible for approving or denying the request for the subdivision. As an intermediary with no conflict of interest, the Peconic Land Trust was able to forge a compromise, protecting the critical farmland at a price the town could justify while allowing the family to subdivide and retain a limited number of residential lots in another, less sensitive location to meet its long-term financial needs.

DEVELOPING COMMUNITY SUPPORT AND LEADERSHIP: VERMONT AND BLOCK ISLAND

Previous examples have detailed how important it often is to have a private, disinterested, but expert interpreter for government land acquisition programs. Before and after securing the cooperation of individual landowners, however, much work must usually be done in a local community to "sell" the government program to important constituencies, from the town government to the voters. More and more, applications for funding from state and federal sources require demonstrations of local support, such as votes for matching funds to support individual projects or written endorsements in local comprehensive plans.

But as Tim Traver from the Upper Valley Land Trust (UVLT) in Vermont points out, local support is not just a means to an end, a question on an application. It is also an end in itself. Part of UVLT's mission is to build local capacity to protect natural resources; so all the better if, as part of a successful project, a town creates a permanent land protection fund or develops an open space plan.

Traver points out that local support can be a thorny issue. People who have lived in a town for a long time, who have worked hard and saved carefully, may have deep feelings about a project in general and about a landowner at the receiving end of a grant in particular. They may feel that "Joe doesn't deserve the money" or "the farm next door is better." These feelings will not necessarily be expressed at the public meeting on the project, but they will be expressed at the coffee shop. Earning solid, visible support from the "old guard" in town is essential. The right person can stand up at the annual town meeting, at which you are asking the taxpayers to contribute tax dollars or accept a partial interest in land, and win your case for you.

On Block Island, Keith Lewis is a good example of a leader who has been able to build local support, even at the cost of higher taxes, for government land protection projects. Keith's success owes much to the trust he inspires locally. He was born on the island, attended school there, and expects to be buried there. People know all about him and his successes and failures. He keeps in touch at the local coffee shop and listens to people's gripes and suggestions about conservation on the island. He can then pass these on to more distant partners.

When the town-funded land trust that Keith spearheaded was getting under way, he and the newly formed board sent out a questionnaire to all island residents to get their views on what resources and parcels in town were most important to protect. From the start, Keith helped set the tone for an inclusionary process that depended on community support.

Another lesson Lewis teaches that local land trusts need to heed is the importance of building continuity and redundancy into the local support structure. Ongoing partnerships with government cannot survive if local volunteer support depends on only one or a very few individuals. Before resigning from the land trust board, Lewis made sure that other islanders were trained in the intricate process of applying for outside funds, negotiating deals, and stewarding the land.

ENLISTING LOCAL SUPPORT FOR FEDERAL HELP: CHICAGO'S OPENLANDS PROJECT

The value of local support does not end at the town council chamber's door, of course. The same people who vote for town leaders vote for congressional representatives too. When a government agency or a national conservation group needs help from Congress with a particular conservation project, individual congresspeople are more likely to respond if their local voting communities have been galvanized first. This is well illustrated by the work of Chicago's Openlands Project—a regional land trust—in creating the Illinois and Michigan Canal National Heritage Corridor.

When the Openlands Project formed in 1963, one of the fledgling conservation group's first goals was to establish the Illinois and Michigan Canal as a linear historical park and recreational trail. The task was daunting: Forty-two separate communities and nineteen Chicago neighborhoods lie along the canal. Clearly, a unifying agency was needed, but the logical one, the National Park Service, caused concern in the state and localities about loss of control. And although federal funds were clearly needed to make the linear park a reality, President Ronald Reagan and his new secretary of the interior, James Watt, were scaling back federal park protection drastically.

The key to moving the project forward was political. Charles Percy, then the senior senator from Illinois, had almost lost his most recent campaign for reelection because of criticism that he was not bringing enough federal attention and funding to the state. Eager to prove otherwise, he was receptive to the Openlands Project's proposal for some sort of federal protection for the Illinois and Michigan Canal. And while Percy was getting federal planning funds for the project, a local newspaper writer was successfully raising consciousness and support for the effort—something local land trusts with good media contacts can often help achieve.

To make federal assistance for land acquisition and development in the corridor a locally and nationally acceptable reality took all the negotiating skills and time of the local Openlands Project. Industry was initially fearful that federal involvement would mean that pollution control standards would be raised and their land would eventually be taken. Only by patiently working with industrial leaders on a vision of the corridor that kept the federal role limited and emphasized an economically beneficial renewal of the area was the Openlands Project able to win business support.

Finally, it was the group of industrial executives that the Openlands Project had enlisted who took the cause before Secretary Watt—and, to everyone's surprise, got his support. That support led in turn to Reagan's signature on a bill creating a national heritage corridor for the canal. Gradually, in the intervening years, that legislation has provided the framework for efforts at all levels of government to turn the canal from a "paper park" into a place where new nature preserves and bicycle paths and recognition in local planning and zoning are possible.

CREATING SUPPORT FOR FUNDING MEASURES: PENNSYLVANIA, CONNECTICUT, AND CAPE COD

Nowhere is public support more necessary than in the funding of land acquisition. In many instances, it is local land trusts, acting in coalitions or individually, that help to galvanize the required popular support, whether for statewide, county, or local bonds or for appropriations to buy land.

Fund-seeking coalitions involving local land trusts take many forms. Some are one-time efforts, such as the Chester County, Pennsylvania, Committee to Save Open Space, which formed to pass a $50 million bond to preserve agricultural lands and parkland. Representing a broad array of individuals, groups, and agencies, the committee received endorsements from the county's six land trusts and drew on the trusts' members to fund publicity and to provide volunteers for getting out the vote—which went in favor of the bond by 82 percent.

Other coalitions form to seek funding on a continuing basis. In Connecticut, for example, a group of more than 100 land trusts, conservation commissions, garden clubs, hunting and fishing groups, and statewide environmental organizations, as well as several hundred individuals, has formed with organizing help from The Nature Conservancy to lobby the legislature for overall funding for land protection and individual purchases. In Connecticut, where land acquisition money is bonded on a parcel-by-parcel basis, a dozen timely letters from a key legislator's constituents make all the difference—and land trusts have been very effective at generating them. Equally important, land trust members have developed a habit of writing to thank the governor and legislators for funding, a practice observers credit with helping to sustain a respectable level of land protection monies despite Connecticut's serious budget crisis.

An interesting example of a purely local effort to secure funds comes from a small town on Cape Cod, where a successful community-based fund drive went on to become the basis for a land trust. As part of its 300th birthday celebration in 1986, the town of Falmouth set a goal of protecting 300 acres of open space. A private organization called the "300 Committee" formed to make the goal a reality. In an interesting twist on the usual approach of campaigning for overall funding prior to identifying any particular purchases, the committee first raised private seed monies to fund appraisals and surveys and then optioned nine parcels, totaling 402 acres and $8.3 million. Only then did the volunteer committee take its message door-to-door. Approval by citizen vote at the town meeting was over-whelming.

Buoyed by success, a large membership, and offers of land donations, the 300 Committee decided to metamorphose into a full-fledged 501(c)(3) land trust, which continues to assist the town with acquisitions as well as holding land in its own right.

Promoting Local Stewardship: Maine, Rhode Island, and Tennessee

If being local and having strong roots in the community helps at the beginning of a project, it is indispensable at the end of most projects. A government agency or large conservation organization can sometimes complete a deal without the help of a local group but often needs local assistance if the deal requires long-term stewardship or monitoring. Groups that have performed similar management work or that are located near the site of the project have a tremendous advantage.

An example of this is the Maine Coast Heritage Trust's role in helping to improve the easement monitoring program at Acadia National Park. The National Park Service was accustomed to managing land it owned in fee but had not established consistent monitoring practices for its easements. MCHT, which pioneered the use of easements in Maine and has researched other agencies' monitoring methods, recommended specific steps for NPS to take in order to steward its easement holdings more effectively. As part of this process, MCHT assisted Acadia National Park in its first compre-hensive gathering of baseline aerial photos. MCHT photographed each of the 135 easement properties, labeled the photographs, and entered them into Acadia's files.

Although some land, once it is saved, can be left with little attention given to it, more often land requires active management to enhance its natural or recreational qualities. With government budgets stretched and priority usually given to high-use properties such as recreational beaches, local land trusts and their volunteers are needed more often to make open space projects work in the long run.

Thus, on Prudence Island in Rhode Island, it took the federal govern-ment, the state of Rhode Island, and The Nature Conservancy working together to preserve an important coastal addition to the Narragansett Bay

National Estuarine Research Reserve. It was the tiny Prudence Island Conservancy, however, that put in the grass parking lot to make the property accessible and that erected the memorial to honor the wishes of the land's seller, a condition of the purchase. Sometimes large bureaucracies, be they public or private, simply are not as effective as local groups in getting the seemingly small—but often vital—tasks done.

Increasingly, government agencies are seeking support from organized local conservation groups to help them plan for and manage new acquisitions in a time of straitened state finances. The commonwealth of Massachusetts and the Williamstown Rural Lands Foundation, a land trust in the Berkshire Hills, recently completed a joint management plan for an addition to the state's Mt. Greylock Reservation—the first time a nonprofit organization has been a partner in developing a plan for state land in Massachusetts. The Williamstown land trust has "adopted" the new parcel and will play an important role in its management.

Meanwhile, far to the south, the nonprofit Tennessee River Gorge Trust in Chattanooga is playing a similar role for Tennessee's recently acquired 450-acre Williams Island, which lies at the gateway to the dramatically scenic and ecologically and historically significant Tennessee River Gorge. Initially, the underfunded state park agency was reluctant to acquire such a large but inaccessible holding. Only by agreeing to take on the island's management via five-year leases—and raising private funds to fill a gap in state acquisition monies—did the Tennessee River Gorge Trust make the project a reality. Now the trust coordinates the agricultural use of the island as well as educational programs, archaeological studies, and nature walks on a trail that the trust built.

LESSONS FROM THE PAST

Not surprisingly, the lessons local land trusts point to differ little from those that have become well known from other partnership endeavors, but the size and constituency of a local land trust bring important variations to familiar themes.

WORKING WITH LOCAL LAND TRUSTS

Government agencies entering into partnerships with local land trusts must remember the lessons repeated in earlier chapters of this book. Small land trusts often face local challenges that larger organizations do not. Lessons that have particular applicability to local land trusts include the following:

- *Local land trusts live with landowners.* A small land trust's local reputation—and the reputation of the government agency that the land trust is working with—is only as good as the last deal. Dissatisfied landowners will make their sentiments known in the community. Government agencies must be particularly careful to fulfill their promises if the local land trust is to be an effective partner.
- *Share the benefits as well as the burdens.* Local land trusts are extremely dependent on public goodwill. If they are to obtain and maintain their desirable tax status as a public charity, they need to build membership in the local community. Partners must be sure to give adequate publicity to local land trusts' accomplishments.
- *Local land trusts may be particularly sensitive politically.* A corollary of the previous lesson is that local land trusts are more often politically dependent than their larger brethren. Even if they do not depend directly on the backing of their local government, they are more likely than outside partners to need to bend with local political winds. For example, it may be difficult for a state government agency to gauge how aggressive it can expect a local land trust to be in lobbying local government for matching funds.

PROFESSIONALISM AND FOLLOW-UP IN WORKING WITH GOVERNMENT

From the government partner's side, the main message is that to be effective, a local land trust must be reliable and professional. Often, given the complexity of public/private partnership projects, this means that a land trust should hire staff members or team up with a larger, staffed organization. If this is not possible, the land trust's volunteers must nevertheless be sure to do the following:

- *Start with simple projects.* In a land trust's first cooperative project, especially if it is working with an agency that is new to partnerships with nonprofit organizations, the simpler the project, the better. Government officials are typically risk averse, and the land trust should not get in over its head.

- *Tackle doable projects.* Land trusts must be careful not to request funds from government agencies for pie-in-the-sky projects or projects in which the landowner may never be willing to come to the table. Such projects waste agencies' time and tie up funds that might otherwise go to more practical projects. If possible, the land trust should secure the site by obtaining an option at an early stage of the project.
- *Abide by accepted ethical and professional norms.* The Land Trust Alliance's published standards and practices for land trusts are a good measure of whether a land trust is set up and managed according to rules that will be acceptable to government. Indeed, at least one government funding source, the Maryland Environmental Trust, requires that LTA's standards be met.
- *Keep good records.* Even if no other staff members are hired, it might be worthwhile to hire a part-time or short-term bookkeeper to deal with the complex accounting that projects require, especially if broad-based fund-raising or multiple projects are contemplated.
- *Keep agency officials informed at every step of the way.* Here is where the significant time commitment comes in. It is not enough to make an occasional telephone call; the land trust must have someone who can hand-deliver documents, go over surveys in person with agency officials, and the like. A land trust must also ensure that all of its representatives are "singing the same song" and do not make substantive changes at the last minute. Local projects can become bogged down or even fall through if the land trust does not meet with agency officials to iron out problems with surveys, appraisals, or title or if there is no one person coordinating a project.

PATIENCE AND INTERIM GOALS

It is often easy for staff members of a government agency or a large land conservation organization to be patient because they are working on many deals simultaneously. Patience may be harder to achieve for staffers and volunteers of a land trust, which may be focused on one particular deal. One suggested remedy is for the land trust to set interim goals for completion of different stages of the partnership project and, ideally, to celebrate and publicize its success as those goals are reached, keeping workers' morale from slumping as the months, and sometimes years, drag on. Thus, in a greenway project, the land trust may want to celebrate individual pieces as they are bought or trails as they are cleared. Perhaps a landowner will agree to a management agreement or a visit to the property even before it is bought so that the trust can secure some of the benefits of protection before the deal is closed.

PROMISE FOR THE FUTURE

With no end in sight to their explosive growth, there is every prospect that land trusts will become even more involved in the partnership game. Perhaps the most exciting potential of land trusts is their ability to tap an ever-expanding constituency for land preservation. This can be translated into effective government action through sponsoring local, state, and even federal funding initiatives; through revising local plans and regulations to make them more environment-friendly; and through reaching out to land-owners who prefer dealing with their peers—or who might never before have given conservation of their land much thought.

Like their larger national brethren, local land trusts are becoming more involved in the government planning process. There is irony in this because many land trusts originally were formed because of people's frustration with the planning and regulatory processes. Only acquisition of land seemed to promise its permanent protection. Now, more conservationists are facing the limits of acquisition—not every important land-based re-source can be protected through purchase, especially in hard economic times—and are becoming interested in working with other tools for broader-spectrum protection.

One land trust that has always emphasized planning is the Brandywine Conservancy in southeastern Pennsylvania. On a par with its direct land protection activities—a distinguished history of protecting private lands through easements—are the conservancy's efforts to promote better plan-ning and zoning in the towns and counties of its region. The conservancy contracts with local communities to complete open space plans that typ-ically include not only recommendations for cluster zoning and the like but also a landowner contact program, in which the conservancy contacts landowners on behalf of government. It is never enough to plan for open space in the abstract; communities must reach out to the affected land-owners, hear *their* plans, and try to work with them to protect what is most important about their land. The Brandywine Conservancy considers its stock in trade to be its good relationships with landowners and its understanding of their needs. These are qualities that a private land trust has a unique ability to bring to the government planning process.

In the Hudson River valley farming country of Dutchess County, New York, this process is being taken one step further. There, the Dutchess Land Conservancy has raised funds through the J. M. Kaplan Foundation to pay the landowner's cost of planning sensitive development. Thus, when the sale of a few discreetly placed lots will enable a farmer to keep his or her farm, the local conservancy will loan the money to cover the costs of the subdivision plan and approval to ensure that the development is as sensitive as possible to scenic and agricultural preservation issues. The no-interest loan is then repaid from the sale of the first lot, allowing the conservancy to work with more farmers. Although a stagnant real estate market has lessened current demand for these services, the conservancy is confident that they will be of great value in the future.

The foregoing examples are typical of a much larger movement. As discussed in chapter 11, the new generation of government funding programs for land protection not only has given private land trusts a role in land acquisition but also has strengthened land trusts' role in focusing attention on growth management and resource protection. Although land trusts still eschew much involvement in regulatory and political processes, they have become effective advocates for comprehensive statewide planning and environmentally sensitive local planning and zoning.

In the past decade, it has been fascinating to watch the developing sophistication, clout, and resourcefulness of local land trusts as they accomplish complex land conservation partnership projects. In the next decade, it will be interesting to see whether they, along with their larger counterparts, can affect larger landscapes through even closer and more wide-ranging partnerships with both the public sector and the landowning community.

ACKNOWLEDGMENTS

This chapter reflects the contributions of many individuals, all of whom I wish to thank for giving so generously of their time. Principal contributors were Robert Hutchinson of the Alachua Conservation Trust in Gainesville, Florida; Keith Lewis of Block Island, Rhode Island; Jill Riddell of the Openlands Project in Chicago, Illinois; and Tim Traver of the Upper Valley Land Trust in Vermont and New Hampshire. Additional contributors were Kathy Barton of the Land Trust

Alliance in Washington, DC; Story Clark of the Jackson Hole Land Trust; Michael Clarke of the Natural Lands Trust in Pennsylvania; Grant Dehart, formerly of the Maryland Environmental Trust; Graham Hawks of the Tennessee River Gorge Trust in Chattanooga, Tennessee; Caroline Norden and Bill MacDonald of the Maine Coast Heritage Trust; Randall Parsons of the Peconic Land Trust on Long Island; Rock Ringling of the Montana Land Alliance; Mark Robinson of the Compact of Cape Cod Conservation Trusts; Bill Sellers of the Brandywine Conservancy; Charlotte Sornborger of the Barrington Conservation Land Trust in Rhode Island; Brian Steen of the Big Sur Land Trust; and George Wislocki of the Berkshire Natural Resources Council.

PART IV

⚘

Financing Partnerships

The two chapters in this part address the crucial issue of how public/private partnerships for land conservation have been and can be financed. Earlier chapters have touched on the kinds of funding that have fueled the extraordinary number and variety of partnerships over the past two decades. If nonprofit organizations and public sector representatives are to make new partnerships work, however, they must fully understand the array of financial arrangements open to them and choose the method best suited to the job at hand, be it stretching payments for an expensive parcel over time or enacting a comprehensive program for land acquisition.

Chapter 10 describes a broad array of financing techniques, from conventional bonding to real estate transfer taxes to the use of mitigation banks, which are usable by different levels of government. Nonprofit organizations have important roles to play in making these various forms of funding work, whether by developing community support for required legislation, serving as necessary intermediaries in installment financing techniques such as lease purchases and certificates of participation, or administering trust or mitigation funds.

Knowledge of the full array of financing tools available is particularly important when public funds are scarce. The right technique can allow a government agency—and its nonprofit partners—to get a lot done with limited funding. Phyllis Myers illustrates this throughout chapter 10; examples include Florida's use of revenue anticipation notes to buy lands necessary to protect water-related resources; Arizona's use of a nonprofit broker to buy parkland worth five times the state's constitutional debt ceiling through the issuance of certificates of participation backed by park entrance fees; and Howard County, Maryland's, creative use of securitized installment sales to preserve farmland. Ms. Myers also addresses the timely issue of preserving supposedly dedicated funds from raiding for other public purposes, a threat that has become reality in several states.

Other funding techniques that may have particular utility in areas of continued growth within financially strapped states are those that put the burden on the developer or the buyers of new homes through various devices such as development exactions and benefit assessment districts. Also described are the increasing number of jurisdictions that, when land conservation is left out of the bonding or general funding budget, resort to special taxes on cigarettes or gasoline or, locally, to the property tax. The growing role of utilities and developers in providing needed open space is illustrated by a number of projects, deals that often were brokered by the nonprofit sector.

Chapter 11 has a narrower focus, providing a detailed analysis of a particularly interesting financing development of the past decade: state programs that directly fund land acquisition by nonprofit organizations. These programs take public/private partnership deals to their logical end: a formalized program of direct grants instead of a series of ad hoc arrangements. Direct grant programs grew out of both the promise and the problems of previous ad hoc deals. Public officials were surprised and excited by how much the private sector could help them accomplish but were worried, in some cases, about the lack of clear priority setting, confusion over cost reimbursement, and the small number of nonprofit groups typically involved. Nonprofit organizations were enthusiastic about the prospects of raising the visibility of—and levels of funding for—land conservation programs by formalizing partnerships. In many cases, they liked the idea of being able to purchase valuable lands in their own name, giving them access to land previously unavailable to them because the owners were wary of public ownership, or, in other cases, allowing the nonprofit organization to manage particularly sensitive tracts.

More than a dozen such direct funding programs currently exist, but there is considerable variation among them. Some states, such as New Jersey, allow nonprofit organizations to own the land they acquire with public funds, while others, such as Connecticut, require that title be held by the state or another public agency. Some states, such as California, make operating grants available to and foster the growth of nonprofit organizations; others, such as Iowa, take a more passive role, leaving the initiative up to the nonprofit group.

Chapter 11 profiles four such innovative state funding programs in detail: those of California, Iowa, Vermont, and Rhode Island. How the

Vermont program works on a day-to-day basis is described in chapter 8; chapter 11 compares Vermont's program with the others and analyzes all four programs' strengths and weaknesses. Direct public funding of land protection by the private sector raises many questions and issues. Chapter 11 examines the way state agencies have successfully used these programs to advance the public agenda by formalizing partnerships and makes comprehensive recommendations for how to duplicate and even improve on these programs' success.

10

Financing Open Space and Landscape Protection: A Sampler of State and Local Techniques

Phyllis Myers
for The Trust for Public Land

Public financing plays an important and changing role in the transactions of growing numbers of private land trusts. During the 1960s, 1970s, and early 1980s, a single source—the federal Land and Water Conservation Fund (LWCF)—accounted for most of the public funds used in land transactions involving private groups. Most of these transactions involved federal lands as well as federal funds. These early public/private financing partnerships were also generally limited to large national land conservation organizations (see part I of this book). By and large, the then-small local land trust movement focused its attention on acquiring gifts of land or easements from private landowners or on raising private funds.

NEW COMMITMENT BY STATE AND LOCAL GOVERNMENTS

In the early 1980s, this picture changed sharply as a result of the rapid expansion of the land trust movement and rising concern about the effects of untrammeled growth. Although more people were becoming aware of the degradation of special landscapes and loss of open space, habitat, and other critical resources, there were deep cuts in federal spending for the LWCF. Throughout the country, states and localities responded to citizen concern by increasing monetary support for protecting environmentally sensitive lands and developing collaborative projects with the growing number of private groups to help achieve these objectives. (See figures 1 and 2 for a graphic comparison of the dramatic decline in federal funding and the surge in state and local funding in the late 1980s.)

These developments have had a profound effect on the way national, state, and even local land conservation groups do business. Although much of their activity continues to involve private lands and private owners, transactions increasingly involve states and local governments as sources of funds or as entities to which lands are conveyed.

Recent state successes, some proposed by citizen initiative or approved in statewide referenda, include a one-tenth of a cent sales tax set-aside in Missouri passed in the 1980s that produces about $25 million annually for state parks (and an equal amount for soil conservation); a $776 million bond for parks, wildlife, and open space overwhelmingly approved by

FIGURE 1.

Annual appropriations of the federal Land and Water Conservation Fund for fiscal years 1965–1992 (not adjusted for inflation).

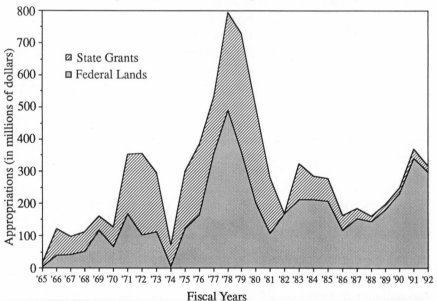

SOURCE: National Park Service

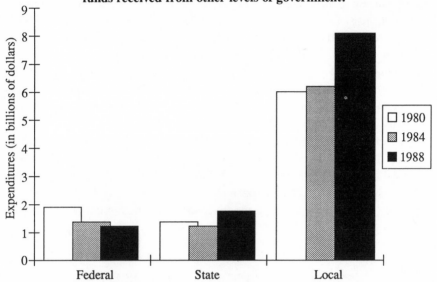

FIGURE 2.
Direct government spending on parks and recreation for fiscal years 1980, 1984, and 1988, in constant 1982 dollars. Funds are tracked according to the level of government that spends them; thus expenditures may include funds received from other levels of government.

SOURCE: U.S. Department of Commerce, Bureau of the Census, *Governmental Finance Series*, 1979–1980 (Table 10), 1983–1984 (Table 11), 1987–1988 (Table 10).

California voters in 1988; ten-year comprehensive land protection programs passed in 1989 in Wisconsin and Iowa, one for $250 million and the other for $300 million; a $35 million Legacy for the Future land acquisition bond approved in 1987 in Maine; and a Greenspace for Delaware Program established in 1990 that authorizes $7 million per year for ten years to "permanently protect the finest examples of Delaware's diverse natural heritage." In November 1990, despite a general retrenchment in voter approval of bond measures and the failure of environmental "megabonds" in California and New York, Nevadans approved a $47.5 million bond for restoring, preserving, and expanding parks, open space, and critical habitat, while citizens of Minnesota and Arizona voted for constitutional amendments to target lottery funds for land conservation and recreational programs.

Over the past decade, counties, cities, and towns have also approved funds for open space, sometimes in startling amounts: a $125 million bond issue in King County, Washington, proposed by a citizen initiative; $69 million in Suffolk County, New York, in 1986 and another $300 million in 1988, financed by a 0.25 percent sales tax; and a $95 million bond issue in Dade County, Florida, backed by a two-year tax on developed parcels. A 1990 survey identified at least twelve county land acquisition programs in Florida, most funded by voter-approved bonds backed by increased property taxes.[1] In the late 1980s, Rhode Island towns approved some $130 million worth of open space bonds. Small increases in sales taxes in Albuquerque, New Mexico, and Pitkin County, Colorado (which includes Aspen), have created sizable open space funds (for a state-by-state survey of recent financing initiatives see appendix A at the end of the book).

This surge in state and local conservation funding is more than a make-do reaction to federal cutbacks. It represents a shift in public attitudes about the impacts of unplanned development—degraded and polluted natural systems, diminished visual character, and costly and inadequate public services—and the important role that governments "close to the people" can play in guiding a more sensitive balance of conservation with needed growth.

ROLE OF NONPROFIT ORGANIZATIONS

Nonprofit organizations have played an important role in conceptualizing and building needed public support for these financing measures as well as in using them creatively for projects. This positive experience has served to stimulate state programs that not only increase conservation funding but also are specifically designed to nurture collaborative projects. (These innovative state programs are also discussed in chapter 11.)

Despite these successes, officials, conservationists, financial experts, legislators, and others have had only fragmented knowledge of the diverse public financing mechanisms being used creatively to foster land conservation. The importance of stretching financial resources to protect vital natural resources makes it essential, now more than ever, to collect and share this information so that both the public and private sectors can learn from innovators and develop creative financing methods of their own.

To meet this need, the following pages provide an overview of state and local financing techniques and specific examples of how they have been used in collaborative conservation projects. Intentionally illustrative rather than comprehensive, this overview includes traditional techniques for raising funds, such as bonding and general appropriations from the state legislature, as well as more recent innovations in structuring debt, earmarking special taxes, and establishing trust funds. Also included are examples of funds for land acquisition being made available as part of publicly regulated private investments or other private activities to meet infrastructure and development needs. The availability of these funds is a recognition of the public dimension in the activities involved. This chapter briefly describes how these measures work, assesses their benefits and drawbacks, and offers recommendations about improving their usefulness in financing partnerships for land conservation.

Because of the diversity of states and localities, techniques are not necessarily easily transferable from one part of the country to another or even within the same region. There are overarching generalities—all jurisdictions obligate for debt, for example—but variations in state constitutions, legislation, institutions, economic health, and a jurisdiction's borrowing history, as well as traditions and inclinations, influence the feasibility and desirability of options in a particular situation.

Although in the early 1990s the picture changed as state-level land conservation funding competed, with varying success, for a share of recession-squeezed budgets, the usefulness of the information in this chapter is not limited to good times. The forces fueling the ground swell for conserving America's distinctive landscapes and special resources—threats to vital natural systems, the degradation of America's cultural, historic, and scenic landscapes, and the high costs of inefficient growth—have not gone away. Like households, governments will be more prudent. But also like households, they face ongoing needs, many of which cannot be put off, and special opportunities. They will continue to spend. The country's long list of notable conservation accomplishments has always drawn its strength from creative responses to the times, today, as in the past, often fashioned by the private sector working with government.

LONG-TERM BONDS

Long-term loans secured by states and municipal governments to finance essential public improvements are usually arranged through the issuance of tax-exempt bonds. These involve a formal obligation to repay the amount borrowed, typically in equal payments over a specified period of years. The threshold for long-term debt is usually considered to be more than five years.

From the early 1980s on, state and local borrowing of capital to acquire parks, natural areas, and open space accelerated noticeably. States approved some $2 billion in bonds to protect open space and recreational and environmentally sensitive areas between 1985 and 1990. (This is an approximation because the official tracking systems for bond issues do not have a separate category for land conservation.) States that had regularly approved park and open space bonds for decades, such as California, New York, and New Jersey, enacted new issues. Other states that were less accustomed to this financing option—Maine, Massachusetts, Rhode Island, Wisconsin, and Nevada—also approved open space bonds. Both large statewide bond issues that finance many projects and small community issues for specific projects have made possible an extensive list of state and local transactions by private conservation groups.

Tax-exempt bonds issued for public purposes are divided into two major classifications: general obligation bonds and revenue bonds.

GENERAL OBLIGATION BONDS

General obligation bonds are backed by the "full faith and credit" of the issuing government, which is unconditionally obligated to raise taxes or to take whatever action is necessary to ensure repayment. These bonds are the least risky to investors and are the least expensive form of credit available to governments. They are the basic financing mechanism for constructing, acquiring, and maintaining public capital assets with a long term life.

General obligation bonds always require approval by the legislature or voters or both. Almost half of the states limit issuance of general obligation bonds through constitutional or statutory requirements such as voter referenda and caps on the amount issued. There may be a numerical maximum, or the limit may be set as a percentage of property values or the general fund or as a specified increase over some aspect of the prior year's spending. In some states, the process is centralized; in others (such as strong home rule states), it is not. A state agency, legislative committee, or other body may play a regulatory or oversight role.

Competition for general obligation bonds is keen among the many programs in need of financing, and strategies vary for securing funds for parks and recreation purposes. Sometimes, parks and recreation projects have been packaged in general capital funding measures passed by the state legislature and, where required, by voters. In other instances, open space programs have been funded by a separate bond or, to increase voter appeal, paired with related environmental programs—agricultural land preservation, soil conservation, tourism, or environmental measures (as in New York State's successful 1986 bond and narrowly defeated 1990 bond). Each situation demands a carefully developed strategy. In California, a sizable general obligation bond for parks and open space was successfully placed on the ballot in 1988 by citizen initiative, overcoming the absence of gubernatorial or legislative support. Passage of the measure was enhanced by the inclusion of specific local projects with strong grass-roots appeal.

In the early 1990s, conservationists are finding that all bond issues are being given greater scrutiny and that with land prices stable, the cost of debt service is more of an issue than it was when the rate of inflation was higher than the cost of borrowing. By the same token, falling land prices create one-time opportunities to acquire valuable resources and to leverage public money. Conservationists wishing to explore the feasibility of access to general obligation bonds should seek advice from independent underwriting experts as well as state bond authorities, legislators, and conservation leaders from other states, keeping in mind the different perspectives of private sector experts, who are accustomed to "making bond issues work," and public agency officials, whose responsibilities inherently lead to a conservative view of general obligation debt.

REVENUE BONDS

Revenue bonds provide a means of financing capital expenditures without pledging the full faith and credit of the issuing government or seeking approval of voters. Principal and interest are typically repaid with the stream of funds generated by the project—user fees, tolls, special taxes, rents, or other earmarked revenues—although they may also be financed by general appropriations. Revenue bonds are often issued by special districts or authorities set up to administer a particular function, such as utilities, which generate a flow of taxes or revenues from their users. (An example of a revenue bond for land acquisition paid by utility customers is presented later in this chapter.) Revenue bonds may be either taxable or, if they serve a general government purpose, tax-exempt.

The use of revenue bonds increased sharply in recent years—from one-third of all bonded indebtedness in 1970 to almost three-quarters in 1984. Reasons for the increase in use of revenue bonds include the growing needs of traditional beneficiaries of this form of debt, such as infrastructure; state and local financing of projects that have not traditionally been considered "public goods," such as hospitals and industrial parks; citizen-imposed restrictions on general tax increases; and greater reliance on user fees to pay for infrastructure.

Revenue bonds may have several important advantages from the point of view of conservation interests seeking funding. They are not affected by the ceilings that constrain general obligation debt. Also, voter or legislative approval is not necessarily required because government is not obligated to repay the debt if the revenue stream does not flow as predicted. They may be more costly to package than general obligation bonds, however. Although revenue bonds tend to carry a somewhat higher interest rate, the spread between the two bond types has narrowed in recent years—a market signal that the risk is not markedly different. In September 1991, according to *The Bond Buyer*, the average weekly yield was 6.95 percent for a selected group of general obligation bonds and 6.78 percent for a selected group of tax-exempt revenue bonds. Florida's Preservation 2000 Program, enacted in 1990, is financed by revenue bonds, backed by a projected increase in the revenues generated by the documentary tax. Approval by the state legislature sufficed for passage. Delaware's Greenspace Program is also funded by tax-exempt revenue bonds.

PRIVATE ACTIVITY BONDS

Another potentially useful municipal bond category involves so-called private activity bonds. Private activity bonds may be general obligation or revenue issues and may be taxable or tax-exempt. The definitions of private bond, eligible uses, and tax-exempt status are governed by IRS regulations, which were tightened in 1986 in response to the rapid expansion in these issues. Examples of activities often financed by private tax-exempt bonds include industrial park development, student loans, housing, sports complexes, pollution control, and sewage and waste disposal.[2]

Private activity bonds can be issued by nonprofit land conservation organizations to finance a specific transaction or to attain a more general line of credit for projects. This could enable nonprofit organizations to take on a more direct role in financing projects, much as nonprofit groups conducting other programs with broad public benefit have done, provided that the issue makes economic and strategic sense. In at least one instance, The Nature Conservancy decided that an issue merited this approach and issued a bond on behalf of a government agency.

Issuing Private Bonds to Preserve Wetlands: Mississippi River

In 1983, the state of Mississippi requested The Nature Conservancy's help in acquiring a 3,642-acre parcel of ecologically distinctive wetlands along the Mississippi River. Officials were reluctant to ask the legislature to float a bond because the state had recently concluded a large land purchase and the economy was weak. However, they anticipated that they could raise the funds within a few years through collections from increased hunting and fishing license fees and other sources. To keep eventual interest costs to the state as low as possible, TNC decided to explore the option of issuing tax-exempt private bonds. The IRS, in a July 1983 special revenue ruling, authorized a $2 million, five-year bond issue, saying that the obligations of a non-profit corporation would be considered issued on behalf of a governmental unit (and, therefore, tax-exempt) if the following five conditions were met:

1. The nonprofit corporation must engage in activities which are essentially public in nature.
2. The corporation must be one which is not organized for profit.
3. The corporate income must not inure to the benefit of any private individual.
4. The state or subdivision thereof must have a beneficial interest in the purchased property while the indebtedness remains outstanding, and it must obtain full legal title to the property upon retirement of such indebtedness.
5. The corporation must have been approved by the state or one of its political subdivisions, either of which must also approve the specific obligations issued by the corporation.

TNC satisfied the fourth condition of the revenue ruling by entering into a lease contract with the Mississippi Wildlife Heritage Commission, the state agency supporting the purchase. The fifth condition was satisfied by having the bonds issued by The Nature Conservancy of Mississippi, Inc., a wholly owned subsidiary of The Nature Conservancy. Also, the legislature passed a resolution approving the arrangement and eventual state ownership of the property.

TNC's bond was placed privately because it did not fit the standard categories of financial rating systems. However, the 8.25 percent interest rate it brought at a time of high interest rates reflected the bond's strength.

Because of the costs of packaging such a bond issue, amounts of less than $1 million generally are not cost-effective. Moreover, because of the nonprofit organization's obligation to the bondholders, a long-term, trusting relationship must exist between the nonprofit group and the government agency that will ultimately be repaying the debt.

SHORT-TERM DEBT INSTRUMENTS

States, localities, and other government units employ a variety of other tax-exempt—and some non–tax-exempt—debt instruments, such as revenue, bond, and tax anticipation warrants; promissory notes; drafts; and other variations. These debt instruments generally have a shorter term life than bonds. They are useful if a government unit faces limitations on bonding but has assurances of revenues or other income to cover the debt service of a loan until the funds are received. For example, special districts may be supported by tax revenues or user fees but may not have the authority to bond. This is the case with California's Midpeninsula Open Space District, which has regularly raised funds for its active land acquisition program with ten-year promissory notes that provide an unconditional promise to repay the borrowed sum. (See the section on special districts later in this chapter.)

Whether promissory notes or revenue anticipation notes make economic sense in a particular situation depends on the terms that can be negotiated, including interest rate and payout period, and on the project itself. In general, these instruments have a higher yield and a shorter term than bonds, making them attractive to the investor and more costly to the issuer. However, they may be the best alternative and a prudent mechanism in a particular situation.

ACQUIRING LAND WITH REVENUE ANTICIPATION NOTES: WEST PALM BEACH, FLORIDA

The South Florida Water Management District in West Palm Beach has used revenue anticipation notes to acquire fee title or other interests in lands necessary to protect and manage the state's water supply and conserve its water-related resources. Florida's five water management districts are financed by a percentage of the state documentary tax on real estate sales— 0.0506 percent per $100—which generates about $43 million annually. The South Florida Water Management District receives 30 percent of the funds, or $13 million, with more than half targeted to land acquisition. Since the district's receipt of transfer tax funds is delayed while the funds are collected by the state and reallocated, the district issues short-term anticipation notes to enable it to spend funds that are not yet in hand. The district has explored the possibility of issuing revenue anticipation notes for longer periods (three to five years) but lacks clear authority to do so.

LEASE PURCHASES AND CERTIFICATES OF PARTICIPATION

Bonding or short-term borrowing may not be feasible or attractive in some situations because of a declining economy, constitutional or statutory limitations, or an unenthusiastic legislature. A land acquisition project with considerable merit and support may present itself, however, the costs of which cannot be met out of current revenues. Jurisdictions faced with this dilemma have come up with a number of creative techniques.

The funding alternatives for land acquisition projects presented here are illustrative and are by no means a comprehensive list. In many respects, they are tailored to geography, jurisdiction, and project, making transferability to another situation a question that needs to be carefully examined. What the following examples show most importantly is that constraints to debt financing for a land conservation project that otherwise has support and makes economic and conservation sense can often be overcome.

LEASE PURCHASES

Lease purchase contracts can be used when a decision has been made to buy a property but up-front funds are not available. Under such an arrangement, acquisition can be paid for in periodic payments, or installments, that include principal, interest, and associated costs. The contract can grant possession or use for a specified or indeterminate period.

Lease purchase contracts do not necessarily bind a future government to a purchase, which often would not be legally feasible. Most governments can, however, enter into a conditional agreement that involves payment of principal and interest subject to annual appropriation. Insurance, reserves, and other measures to ensure repayment are sometimes needed to secure a viable interest rate.

In general, the economic effect of a lease purchase is similar to that of a bond, but the arrangement is structured so that it does not violate constitutional limitations on borrowing or affect the debt ceiling. A drawback is that the more complicated a transaction is, the higher are the transaction costs, unless these are offset in other ways.

Buying Parkland over Time Through a Lease: Lakewood, Colorado

The city of Lakewood, Colorado, in the foothills of the Rocky Mountains, had already committed its share of county open space funds when a valuable property within city limits became available. The bonding option was not available because of a weak economy and voter resistance to higher taxes for debt service. The Trust for Public Land arranged a lease purchase for a thirty-year period and assigned the lease to the city. The landowner receives an annual payment of $200,000 from Lakewood (for principal, interest, and project costs), paid out of its capital funds. The owner is exempted from paying property tax under Colorado law, since the property is leased to a government entity, and the city provides liability insurance. The lease is renewable year by year. The property was acquired at a present value of $2 million, which was three-quarters of a million dollars below its appraised value.

The risk that Lakewood will not ultimately purchase the property diminishes the longer the lease is extended, since the city would forego equity payments already made if it chose not to make additional payments. Moreover, the public becomes accustomed to owning the property. The city has reserved the option to buy the property earlier if it wishes.

CERTIFICATES OF PARTICIPATION

Certificates of participation, or COPs, are a variation on the leasing theme structured to enable a group of investors to buy proportionate shares in tax-exempt income from a lease pursuant to a lease purchase agreement. A relatively new financing mechanism, COPs are finding increasing acceptance and are now used in more than half of the states. Although they typically finance sizable purchases of equipment or buildings, they are also being applied creatively in open space financing to provide up-front cash, usually without a referendum or vote of the legislature (although at least one state, New York, requires one) and without affecting the debt ceiling.

The details of COPs vary. Typically, the arrangement involves a state or municipal agency, investors, and some type of intermediary, such as a nonprofit organization, a government office, or a "shell." The intermediary in a land transaction project acquires the land and leases it to government; collects lease payments structured to include principal, interest, and related costs over the life of the arrangement; and disburses these payments to the investors. The payments are tax-exempt because they serve a government purpose. The debt is not added to the jurisdiction's obligations because it is subject to annual appropriations. The cost of issuing COPs is generally higher than the cost of issuing general obligation or revenue bonds because investors do not have the full faith and credit guarantee or the assurance of tax revenues to retire the debt.

Buying Parkland over Time Through COPs: Arizona

Arizona's general obligation debt is constitutionally limited to $350,000, which effectively means that the state cannot issue bonds. In the past decade, Arizona has used lease purchases and COPs to finance a range of public improvements.

The state's first use of COPs to finance a state park occurred in 1987, when the land for Arizona's Kartchner Caverns State Park was purchased from a private owner. The Nature Conservancy negotiated the $1.62 million bargain sale and helped to build public and legislative support for the purchase, which was paid for by the issuance of COPs backed by revenues from statewide park entrance fees and other fees dedicated to park acquisition and development. The legislature approved the use of full faith and credit as an additional guarantee should user fees fall short of need, a move that enabled the state to secure a favorable interest rate. The offering was easily sold to an institutional investor. The COPs were repaid within two years. In 1990, Arizona issued certificates of participation for $3 million to acquire Tonto Bridge State Park, a natural bridge.

Although Arizona voters have since approved the use of lottery funds to establish the Arizona Heritage Fund, which will provide a more predictable flow of public funds for land conservation, Kenneth E. Travous, Arizona's state park director, believes that certificates of participation are still an excellent financing mechanism for raising the large sums sometimes needed to acquire sizable parks.

Repaying a Nonprofit Preacquisition Through COPs: Pacifica, California

The city of Pacifica, a coastal community fifteen miles south of San Francisco, wished to acquire a building owned by AT&T and to renovate it for community use. The Trust for Public Land, acting as an intermediary, arranged a bargain sale between AT&T and the city. Since California's tax-limiting Proposition 13 restricted bonding, and AT&T insisted on cash in advance in order to discount its price, the arrangement made use of the COP mechanism.

In the $3.1 million transaction (the amount included funds for renovating the building and waterfront improvements), TPL purchased the property from AT&T and sold it to the city, which conveyed the land to the redevelopment agency. The latter leased the property to the city for seven years and assigned its rights to collect lease payments to a bank, which acted as trustee. Certificates of participation in the city's lease payments were marketed to investors, providing the funds for TPL to pay AT&T and to finance other improvements. The city covenanted that it would take such actions as might be required to include the necessary annual appropriations in its budget to cover lease payments. The COPs are additionally secured by several other properties. The agreement was not backed by the city's full faith and credit or by tax revenues, but there was no difficulty in marketing the COPs.

SECURITIZED INSTALLMENT SALES

In many of the financing techniques discussed so far, the government borrows from investors. Another approach is to have the government borrow, in effect, from the landowner through an installment sale. Typically, this financing technique has been used on a case-by-case basis, using nonprofit organizations as intermediaries, as discussed in chapter 1. In the case of at least one land conservation program, however, the agricultural preservation program in Howard County, Maryland, the installment sale has been institutionalized in a way that holds lessons for other land preservation programs.

PAYING FOR FARMS IN INSTALLMENTS:
HOWARD COUNTY, MARYLAND

The population of once-rural Howard County, situated between Baltimore, Maryland, and Washington, DC, has tripled since 1970. In response, the county has taken strong steps to preserve its agricultural character. These include a pioneering program established in 1980 to purchase development rights from farmers, which is funded by a county real estate transfer tax, and a 5 percent state tax on sales of agricultural land being converted to urban use. Revenues generated by these taxes are shared with the state. Currently, the county keeps three-quarters of its tax and one-quarter of the state tax. However, in the late 1980s, the rising cost of land brought the program to a virtual halt.

In crafting a program to stretch limited county funds, an investment banker who advises the county developed a tax-exempt installment purchase program. Under this scheme, the county buys development rights from farmers with a promissory note rather than cash. This note represents an unconditional promise to fulfill the terms of the sale. Payment for most of the principal is deferred to the end of the thirty-year contract period. Meanwhile, the farmer receives semiannual interest-only payments at the market rate, which, importantly, are tax-exempt, and small principal payments every two years. Capital gains taxes are largely deferred until the final balloon payment, either in thirty years or, if the owner dies sooner, when the estate is probated. The agreements are "securitized," enabling the landowner to cash out of the program by selling his or her interest in the installment payments in the capital market as certificates of participation.[3]

The county's final balloon payment is secured by zero-coupon Treasury obligation bonds that will mature in thirty years. Since these are sold at steep discounts (10 cents on the dollar), the county has been able to buy bonds with a future value of about $24 million for approximately $2.4 million. The program has had great appeal to county farmers: by July 1990, the county had commitments to purchase development rights on more than 4,100 acres. It paid about $5,500 per acre, about one-third of the appraised value.

The transferability of the Howard County program to other jurisdictions depends on a number of technical factors and must be investigated case by case. Maryland's laws give Howard County considerable authority as a "charter county" to initiate and manage its debt. Some other counties in the state, however, are structured differently and would need enabling legislation to adopt this program, as would communities in New Jersey, where adoption of a similar plan is being considered. Such action would be needed in other states to overcome the general prohibition on binding government to future payments or to comply with specific requirements. Meanwhile, an independent review of the plan's federal tax benefits has concluded that they are on solid footing.[4]

Of course, any jurisdiction adopting such a program must have a steady source of income for interest payments. Howard County started the program with $9 million and receives approximately $2.9 million per year in transfer tax receipts. California's Marin Agricultural Land Trust, which administers a sizable allotment of state bond funds for agricultural land protection, is also considering the program.

PAY-AS-YOU-GO APPROACH

Although the headline-producing action in open space funding over the past decade has generally involved large-scale borrowing, the old-fashioned pay-as-you-go approach remains the choice of many states and localities. A 1985 survey of state park budgets found that appropriations from general funds were the single most important source, overall, for capital spending on parks.[5] Typically, the state legislature appropriates money from general funds or from dedicated funds, such as special taxes, lotteries, revenues, or fees from a designated program, or from other recurring or "windfall" pots of money.

An important advantage to the pay-as-you-go approach is that it saves financing costs and reflects the fiscal choices of the current electorate. It may be the only political strategy that the governor or mayor and electorate will support. The disadvantage is that project costs are not spread out over the useful life of the asset or among future as well as present beneficiaries. Paying for a large project could mean either raising taxes significantly— often an unpalatable choice—or doing without. Fewer projects may be initiated than could or should be, and in the case of land acquisition, critical resources may be irrevocably lost.

Advantages to general appropriations include the fact that park needs are considered during the regular government funding cycle. Visibility at this time could help conservationists gain needed friends in the political mainstream. An important disadvantage is the attendant uncertainty, which leads to "stop and go" financing that hampers implementation of a strong acquisition program and limits the state's capacity to respond to threats and opportunities. Additional drawbacks include the effort involved for conservation groups to mount repeated campaigns for appropriations and to energize constituencies for land conservation programs in order to compete with highly organized lobbies for education, highways, corrections, and other programs. Cutbacks in the federal Land and Water Conservation Fund eroded a program that successfully raised the priority of acquisition in state legislatures by offering matching funds. In recent years, however, the legislative scorecard for land conservation has improved as national, state, and local groups mount increasingly effective campaigns to raise annual or biennial appropriations.

A summary of the experience of selected states that rely significantly on appropriations for acquisition includes the following:

- The state of Washington appropriated $53 million for land acquisition and outdoor recreation programs in 1990 and another $60.4 million in 1991. Faced with competing demands for the general obligation bonds favored by environmentalists and concerned that the state was stretched beyond its bonding debt limits, the governor supported these large appropriations. Private groups have helped identify projects to be funded. Legislators also approved $100 million to buy school trust lands to protect old-growth forests from timber cutting.
- Alaska's legislature annually appropriates $1.5 million to $2.5 million for park capital needs, with about 5 to 10 percent targeted for land acquisition. The Nature Conservancy and the Trust for Public Land have played important roles in negotiating several key acquisitions using these funds.
- New Hampshire's $50 million, five-year Trust for New Hampshire Lands program has been funded by appropriations. Significantly, New Hampshire's conservationists are attempting to establish a modest trust fund to provide a continuing source of funds to monitor conservation easements. (Trust funds are discussed in more detail later in this chapter.)
- Delaware's Land and Water Conservation Trust Fund, established in 1986, provides matching grants for outdoor recreation and land protection. It was initially financed by three consecutive appropriations of $7 million for land acquisition. These funds, approved when the state

had a surplus, helped trigger the more ambitious Greenspace Program, enacted in 1990, which is financed by revenue bonds and a real estate transfer tax.

Many states, however, have had more difficulty in dipping into the state legislative well for adequate land acquisition funding—for example, Georgia, South Carolina, Ohio, Pennsylvania, North Dakota, Idaho, and Oklahoma. Reasons for the difficulties include lagging economies, weak constituencies for conservation, failure by conservation groups to develop a compelling vision, or strong ideological opposition to land acquisition. State legislatures also appropriate funds for local programs, either directly or through state grants to local governments. (See chapter 11 for a detailed discussion of state funding programs.)

SPECIAL TAXES

The uncertainties of appropriations, the effort and costs of mounting legislative campaigns, and the vulnerability of conservation funding in economic downturns have led to concerted efforts in a number of states to identify a specific ongoing revenue source to dedicate to land acquisition. Outstanding park systems in states such as California, New York, Florida, and Maryland, for example, have owed their accomplishments to significant regular infusions of funds from bonds and special taxes rather than general appropriations.

Inspired by such examples, voters and legislators in a number of other states approved set-asides, or special dedication of taxes on real estate transfers, retail sales, mineral and gas exploration, cigarettes, utilities, and tourism in recent years. They have approved use of lottery funds and special fees on sales of conservation or vanity license plates for land protection. Sometimes these measures were put in place by citizen initiatives that bypassed state legislators, who were cool to the tax measures.

Experts in public finance often oppose dedication of specific tax proceeds in "shoeboxes" of program support, arguing that this reduces needed flexibility to allocate funds in ways that reflect the electorate's current priorities and constraints, rather than the policy choices of earlier electorates. Nevertheless, earmarked funds have become increasingly popular as voters who resist general tax increases show their support for selected programs. "Green" measures have benefited from this trend.

Typically, advocates attempt not only to target the tax or fee but also to ensure, by statute or constitutional provision, that the revenues be used only for park, open space, and natural resource purposes. For example, a 1983 Missouri sales tax set-aside is dedicated to state parks (and soil conservation) by a constitutional amendment, as is an earlier sales tax set-aside in the state for fish and game lands. Montana's mineral severance tax is also constitutionally protected. The legal design of such restrictions and receptivity to them vary from state to state. The use of trust funds to protect revenues from diversion is discussed later in this chapter.

Ideally, the source of funds for a special tax should expand with a growing economy yet be reasonably buffered from a decline, should be equitable and efficient to collect, should demonstrate some connection with the spending objective, and should be politically acceptable. Passing a special tax is difficult and usually requires considerable effort to forge public and private coalitions. Partnerships formed to secure such funding often need to continue beyond the initial success to defend the arrangement from raiding by other interests.

REAL ESTATE TRANSFER TAXES

Real estate transfer taxes have been levied for land acquisition and conservation programs in at least nine states and localities. (See appendix A at the end of the book prepared by The Nature Conservancy.) This tax, which has the logic of tapping a percentage of funds generated by development, is relatively easy to collect and increases with the size of the property involved in the transaction. During the 1980s, it was a large source of revenue in "go-go" states such as Florida and Maryland and in booming summer communities such as Nantucket and Block Island, Rhode Island.

Maryland's Program Open Space, enacted in 1965, is the oldest state acquisition fund financed with real estate transfer tax revenues. Since its inception, the 0.5 percent tax has dedicated more than $529 million for state and local purchase of 139,000 acres and related improvements. Maryland's program softens the effects of the tax on first-time home buyers by exempting the initial $30,000 of the cost of a home. Advocates recently succeeded in lifting a cap on the amount of the tax's revenues that were available for Program Open Space, but legislators raided $81 million from the program in 1991 to reduce the state's overall budget deficit.

Passing a transfer tax is difficult because real estate and housing interests mount strong opposition campaigns. Another drawback is that revenues can drop sharply if the real estate market slows, as has happened in several states in recent years. For example, revenues in Delaware declined by 30 percent between 1989 and 1991.

Bonding for Open Space Through a Transfer Tax: Block Island, Rhode Island

Block Island is an 11-square-mile island off the coast of Rhode Island with a magnificent natural setting, distinctive cultural and historic buildings dating back to colonial days, and numerous rare species of birds and plants. In 1985, Block Island residents approved a referendum establishing a 2 percent transfer tax on real estate sales, with revenues to be used to acquire open land. The measure was preceded by a tough battle in the Rhode Island state legislature for enabling authority to levy the special tax. The revenues are administered by the Block Island Land Trust, a public land trust created by the enabling legislation. So far, the transfer tax, which was raised in 1989 to 3 percent, has generated about $1.47 million. The town voted to sell $2 million worth of bonds backed by the tax in order to preserve threatened parcels that would have been developed had the island had to wait for funds to accumulate.

Realtors supported the tax on Block Island because they saw a link between the island's natural beauty and their business profits. To help address the criticism that transfer taxes raise the cost of real estate and price out moderate-income home buyers, Block Island exempts the first $75,000 of the purchase price of a primary residence for first-time buyers. Unfortunately, the size of the transfer tax fund has not kept pace with demand for land protection funds. Still, the tax has meant a dependable source of conservation money and has leveraged millions of dollars in state matching funds to make it possible for Block Islanders to protect land with a high market value.

Sales Tax

Another productive special tax is a set-aside from the sales tax. It is easy to administer, and it can tap into tourism profits generated by open space amenities. However, revenue from this tax also declines if the economy slows. Another drawback is that the sales tax is often considered a regressive tax, falling disproportionately on lower-income people.

Protecting Habitat and Parkland Through a Sales Tax: Missouri

Missouri parks, wildlife habitat, fishing areas, and other natural lands are supported by two set-asides from a state sales tax. The first sales tax set-aside was enacted in 1976 after a vigorous campaign spearheaded by the Conservation Federation of Missouri, a powerful coalition of conservationists, hunters, and fishers. Voters approved a constitutional amendment to target a small percentage (one-eighth of a cent) of the sales tax in perpetuity for fish and game lands. In the fourteen years since, the tax has raised $514 million, with about $190 million spent to buy 291,000 acres.

Passing an additional sales tax set-aside for state parks in the early 1980s was more difficult. There was no sizable, politically effective constituency for parks as there was for fish and game lands. Good-government groups voiced some opposition to a new dedicated tax. However, the parks faced a fiscal crisis after the loss of federal funds from the Land and Water Conservation Fund. An effective coalition paired parks with soil conservation, another urgent, seriously underfunded state program. The grass-roots campaign succeeded—narrowly—in gaining voter approval in 1984 for a constitutional amendment to levy the new one-tenth of a cent tax for five years.

The campaign to extend the tax began soon after it was put in place. This time, the measure came before voters as a citizen initiative, since legislators failed to approve the necessary legislation. It was overwhelmingly approved by 70 percent of the voters for a ten-year period. In 1990, the tax raised $25 million for state parks.

CIGARETTE AND GASOLINE TAXES

Cigarette and gasoline taxes are other examples of special taxes being used for land conservation. A cigarette tax passed in 1979 helps support Texas's state and local parks, and Minnesota has financed acquisition of natural areas for twenty-three years with a portion of a cigarette tax. A small tobacco tax in California provides $15 million for land protection. Environmental critics dislike linkage with cigarettes, however, and the declining number of smokers jeopardizes the revenue potential of the tax.

Gas taxes are a logical source of funds for parks and outdoor land conservation. Protection of distinctive land and cultural resources contributes importantly to automobile-based tourism, a major source of jobs and revenues in most states. Favored by environmentalists, especially in view of broader energy conservation objectives, use of gas taxes for conservation purposes nevertheless often faces vigorous opposition. In November 1992, Oregon voters rejected a 2-cent gas tax increase dedicated to parks.

The greater flexibility in using Highway Trust Fund dollars for scenic easements, trails, and other transportation "enhancements" mandated by Congress in 1991 as part of an overhaul of federal transportation policy may stimulate more flexible use of state gas tax revenues.

TRUST FUNDS

Land conservation advocates often seek to establish trust funds to protect earmarked funds from being diverted and to build up a sizable sustainable principal that can spin off regular interest payments to pay for acquisition of critical lands. In this way, trust funds can finance a comprehensive program over a period of years and insulate spending from the vagaries of the economy. Spending from trust funds can also be counted as off-budget expenditures, lessening their impact on reported budget deficits.

Trust funds come in many sizes and varieties, with different statutory and constitutional protections for the corpus as well as varying provisions for withdrawals. Some trusts may simply consist of earmarked funds deposited in a separate account and withdrawn by legislative action. The strongest are enacted by constitutional amendments that specify what the funds can be used for. Changing these provisions would require passage of another constitutional amendment. Some funds are structured to provide for spending of some of the capital, usually after a specified amount has accumulated; others provide that only interest can be spent.

Of course, a source of funds is needed for the trust fund. It is often difficult to identify one that is economically productive and politically acceptable. Revenues that have been used include general appropriations (either one-time or ongoing), lotteries, mitigation funds, special taxes, and user fees. Trusts are difficult to establish and require considerable coalition and consensus building to move beyond the proposal stage.

Sometimes the perception that funds are completely protected may be misguided; advocates of the federal Land and Water Conservation Fund believed they had established an inviolate trust fund in 1965 and were disappointed by its evolution into a program dependent on annual appropriations. On the other hand, the federal Dingell-Johnson and Wallop-Breaux programs provide solid, ongoing support. These trust funds, nourished by excise taxes on hunting gear, sportfishing equipment, motorboat fuel, and the like, were put in place as a permanent, ongoing authorization and do not require congressional appropriations prior to disbursement.

State land acquisition trust funds that are protected by constitutional amendments include the Michigan Natural Resources Trust, funded by royalties and leases for extracting oil, gas, and natural resources from state-owned lands, and Minnesota's Environment and Natural Resource Trust Fund and Arizona's Heritage Fund, both paid for by state lottery proceeds.

THE MICHIGAN NATURAL RESOURCES TRUST

The Michigan Natural Resources Trust was established in 1985 following a constitutional amendment approved in a statewide referendum that requires that revenues for oil, gas, and other mineral leasing on state-owned lands be placed in a trust fund, with proceeds used for acquiring and protecting lands of scenic, recreational, and environmental importance.

The enabling legislation is very specific about the fund's creation and use. Each year, the amount available for project grants and program administration is derived by combining one-third of the annual leasing revenues with interest from the trust fund account. The latter, which will be capped at a total of $200 million, is generated by deposits of most of the remaining two-thirds of annual revenues.

In any year, not less than 75 percent of the trust fund's money must be used to acquire land and no more than 25 percent may be used to develop recreational facilities. A five-member board, consisting of the chair of the Natural Resources Commission (or his or her designee) and four governor-appointed citizens, oversees the trust fund.

Projects are selected in a competitive process, with nominations from the state's natural resource agency, local governments, and citizens, including conservation organizations. In the latter category, projects nominated by the Little Traverse Conservancy and The Nature Conservancy have been funded. In 1990, the trust provided $24,114,875 for grants, with more than $18 million targeted to land acquisition. The total trust fund account amounted to $62,581,060.

SPECIAL DISTRICTS

With open space and natural area protection increasingly viewed as basic community infrastructure, a variety of other mechanisms are evolving to provide streams of funds for open space financed by the people who benefit, be they residents or business interests. These mechanisms increase local choices about land protection.

Government's authority to raise funds can be exercised by so-called special districts. Also known as limited-purpose governments, special districts administer a specific function or functions within defined boundaries that often cut across the more familiar local, county, and even state political boundaries. Those that administer parks, recreation, utilities, and water reclamation can be of special importance to land conservationists because of their ability to raise funds through taxes, user fees, and bonds. (See also the section on utilities later in this chapter.)

Other advantages include special districts' ability to finance services and facilities by going to voters directly and without having to balance competing demands. Popular programs, such as parks and recreation, probably get more money through the special district mechanism than they would in a consolidated, centralized government. Parks and recreation districts are also well positioned to draw boundaries for effective management and recreation. They may introduce a new management objective, such as open space protection, in addition to the more traditional recreational amenities such as ballfields and small neighborhood parks.

Special districts are sometimes criticized for fostering fragmentation in provision of funding and services and for the relative obscurity in which districts and managers may conduct their activities. Despite such arguments, the number of special districts has doubled since 1962, as has the number of park and recreation districts. All told, there are about 1,000 parks and recreation districts, with about 200 in Illinois, including Chicago, which has one of the largest and oldest special districts for parks.

California's six open space districts have exercised unusual ingenuity in acquiring and managing open space, parks, habitat, agricultural lands, wetlands, and other special resources acquired as the edge of settlement moved outward. The first of these districts, the East Bay Regional Park District in the San Francisco Bay Area, dates back to a campaign during the Great Depression to protect forested watershed and hillside lands that water companies had declared surplus. The East Bay system today includes 70,000 acres of parks, open space, and natural areas.

The establishment of special districts in other parts of the Bay Area and in Sonoma and Monterey counties followed Proposition 13 restrictions in the early 1970s on communities' ability to raise taxes to acquire lands on the urban fringes and an expansive vision of open space needs. The districts are funded by small property tax surcharges, except for the Sonoma County district, which is supported by a 0.25 percent sales tax increment.

Funding an Open Space District Through Property Tax: San Francisco Bay Area

The Midpeninsula Regional Open Space District was established by voter initiative and has as its mission "to preserve a greenbelt of open space following the ridges and baylands of Santa Clara and San Mateo counties" in the San Francisco Bay Area. The district's strong acquisition program has preserved more than 34,000 acres of rolling terrain, streams, ponds, and forests in an area of beauty and intense development. It has worked closely with the nonprofit Peninsula Open Space Trust (POST), which has arranged easements or conveyed land to the open space district for management. In 1987, for example, the district acquired 112 acres of outstanding lands in the La Honda watershed through a below-market purchase brokered by POST.

The mainstay of the district's funding is a small share of the property tax—1.6 cents for each dollar collected. This source accounted for 62 percent of the district's total revenues in fiscal year 1989. Backed by this assured income, the district has entered the capital market regularly to raise up-front funds for its acquisition and stewardship activities. Since it cannot bond, it has issued revenue anticipation notes and tax-exempt COPs. Several of California's districts have bonding authority.

Benefit Assessment Districts

Benefit assessment districts are similar to special districts in that they create a financing mechanism to provide community services, facilities, or infrastructure within defined boundaries. Since benefit districts are not units of government, the process for creating them, though not inconsequential, is less onerous than that involved in creating a special district.

There are a number of variations on the theme. Typically, a levy is placed on individual parcels and the assessment is structured so that landowners pay in proportion to their benefit, which may mean a flat surtax per property or a percentage of value. Benefit districts have been created to finance parks, recreation, and open space as well as schools, roads, sewerage, and other traditional community infrastructure. Here again, California—faced with rapid development and restrictions on voters' ability to finance infrastructure through the ballot box—has been in the forefront in devising benefit district mechanisms.

Taxing New Development to Fund Open Space: Fairfield, California

Citizens of Fairfield, California, successfully challenged the city's annexation of three large new subdivisions outside of its jurisdictional boundaries on the grounds that the action would cause the "premature" conversion of open space and agricultural land to urban uses. Under the resulting legal settlement, the city created the Mello-Roos Community Facilities District, composed of the new communities, as a way of financing additional open space acquisition. Each developed parcel in the district pays a tax of $80.

Mello-Roos districts (named after the California legislators who sponsored the state enabling legislation) provide a way for residents in a new and growing community to assess themselves to pay for common facilities with a life of five or more years, such as schools, libraries, utility transmission lines, and parks and recreation facilities. This mechanism is structured to bypass Proposition 13 restrictions on local authority to bond and tax residents to pay for debt service. Home owners can deduct these payments from their federal income taxes.

The Fairfield agreement created the Solano County Farmlands and Open Space Foundation to direct the acquisition of open space with the proceeds of the parcel tax. Although the parcel tax has so far raised only about $300,000 because of the slowed real estate market, the foundation, by virtue of its authority in a developing county readily acknowledged to need open space protection, received an additional $7 million from state and private sources in loans, commitments, and grants.

Benefit assessments have been used elsewhere in the country, too. One interesting example is the preservation of a community golf course in a highly developed suburb of Newton, Massachusetts, funded in part through a benefit assessment on fifty-one surrounding parcels.[6]

UTILITIES

To carry out their mission, providers of essential public utilities—electrical power, gas, water, sewage treatment, and telephone and telecommunications services—often have extensive real estate holdings. The Los Angeles Department of Water and Power has jurisdiction over 365,230 acres, for example. In addition to acquiring land in fee or with easements, utilities manage, exchange, lease, and dispose of lands. They also have independent, if closely regulated, authority to receive and raise revenues. Their wide-ranging activities are financed by rate payers, primarily through user charges.

An advantage to working with utilities is their ability to finance activities, including land purchases, essential to their objectives by increasing user chargers. One caveat is that utilities are not unaffected by external events and the economic climate: California water utilities may be overextended as a result of a lengthy drought, for example, and the relocation of several large businesses from Providence, Rhode Island, has reduced utility companies' earnings in that city. Also, it should be noted that negotiations with utilities tend to be more structured and time-consuming than those with other land management agencies. It is essential to understand the rules that guide utility operations in order to work effectively with them.

Land conservation and recreational development by utilities can take several forms, including direct land acquisition, partnerships with open space protection entities, and provision of mitigation funds for land protection. Examples of these activities follow.

PRESERVING LAND THROUGH A UTILITY SURTAX: PROVIDENCE, RHODE ISLAND

In 1987, Rhode Island approved a surcharge of one-hundredth of a cent per 100 gallons of water to finance the acquisition of buffer zones around watershed areas to protect water quality. The program, said to be unique in the Northeast, was triggered by rapid development threatening the Scituate watershed, a large reservoir system near Providence that serves about two-thirds of the state.

The measure was developed by a Watershed Task Force made up of local communities and state agencies. Based on the finding that only one-quarter of critical watershed lands was protected, the task force recommended that the water companies buy more lands to protect present and future supplies of safe drinking water. The legislature agreed and authorized the state Water Resources Board to issue revenue bonds backed by a surcharge on water bills. The law required at least 55 percent of the funds to be used for land acquisition, with priority for surface land around water reservoirs, direct tributary streams, and wetlands.

So far, 2,000 acres have been acquired with funds collected under this program, most in the watershed near Providence. The revenue yield of the water surtax has been lower than anticipated, however, largely as a result of the recession and exemptions for elderly consumers and agriculture.

PARTNERSHIPS WITH UTILITIES FOR OUTDOOR RECREATION

Utilities have also entered into a number of collaborative cost-sharing arrangements with governments and private groups that offer benefits to all the parties. These arrangements serve the utilities' basic missions and also enhance recreational access and land stewardship.

- California's East Bay Regional Park District has collaborative arrangements to lease 25,000 acres from four water management districts in the region. It manages the lands to enhance the public's visual and recreational opportunities, including boating and fishing with restrictions that ensure protection of the water supply. The utilities continue to pay taxes on the lands, which comprise one-third of the park's extensive holdings.
- The Denver Urban Drainage and Flood Control District provides part of the funding to construct and maintain hiking and bicycle trails along Denver's Platte River Greenway. Since the district's mission is served by the increased physical access that the trails provide to the river and creek system for maintenance workers and vehicles, it funds gravel trails and takes responsibility for structural maintenance. Local governments pay for the increased costs of upgrading or maintaining trails for recreational purposes.
- The construction of a major regional pipeline by New Jersey's Columbia Gas Transmission Company is helping to create a 60-mile Cross-Jersey Trail and greenway tying together seventeen existing state and local parks, streambeds, railroad rights-of-way, and other recreational

corridors. The utility, working with a private consultant, developed a $3.5 million package to fund improvements in the two counties and nine municipalities that have parks affected by the pipeline.[7] The Conservation Fund's American Greenways Program is conducting a national survey to examine prospects for replicating this model.

- Seattle, Washington, negotiated a twenty-five-year permit with U.S. Sprint for installation of a fiber-optic line along 6.2 miles of the Burke-Gilman Trail. U.S. Sprint will pay Seattle $728,000 for the permit fee and construct a mile of trails, retaining walls, and other park improvements. Since communications companies seeking rights-of-way prefer dealing with one large landowner, they offer a promising source of funds for greenway projects that involve land owned by a state or local government, a railroad company (for rails-to-trails projects), or another single entity.[8]

USE OF MITIGATION FUNDS TO ACQUIRE LAND

Substantial funds for acquisition may also be made available in compensation or mitigation settlements.

- In 1980, Congress directed the federal Bonneville Power Authority to spend about $1 billion in mitigation funds in four states—Washington, Montana, Idaho, and Oregon—to mitigate for losses to fish and wildlife habitat inflicted in the course of constructing dams along the Columbia River. Although most of the funds have been used for hatchery improvements, the complex and controversial arrangement, still being negotiated, is likely to provide acquisition funds as well. Rate payers will finance the settlement. The Trust for Public Land has acquired a 2,800-acre parcel along the Columbia River, which it anticipates conveying to the power authority.
- Seattle's City Light Department will be spending about $17 million to acquire some 4,000 to 5,000 acres under an agreement worked out with representatives of Native American tribes, state officials, environmentalists, and others in connection with a relicensing application for a hydroelectric project on the Skagit River. The agreement follows more than a decade of controversy, studies, and negotiations. TPL is negotiating purchases of riparian resources within a wild and scenic river corridor, which the municipal utility will manage for preservation and wildlife values.

- In 1978, a court settlement created the Platte River Whooping Crane Maintenance Trust with $7.5 million in mitigation funds from a consortium of midwestern power companies. The trust is designed to offset the effects of the Grayrocks, Wyoming, dam and power plant by providing for downstream land acquisition to protect critical migratory bird habitat in Nebraska. The Nature Conservancy has helped the trust purchase more than 8,000 acres.

DEVELOPMENT EXACTIONS AND MITIGATION BANKS

Through regulation and negotiation with officials and communities, the private development process has become another important source of funds to pay for community infrastructure, including open space. Although the source of funds—developer contributions—is private, the process by which these funds are raised and allocated is often authorized by public action, either in specific legislation or in more general home rule authority. Surveys report that parks and open space are one of the community needs most frequently financed by these public/private partnerships.[9]

Although requirements that developers dedicate land or facilities for community development date back to the 1920s, the character, complexity, and volume of these exactions have expanded significantly in recent years. In addition to there being a longer list of requirements, more arrangements now allow developers to pay a sum of money (so-called impact fees) instead of dedicating land or facilities to the community or, in certain circumstances, to make compensatory arrangements for development impacts outside of the project site. The expansion in the use of impact fees is rooted in increased sophistication about the costs of growth, voter opposition to higher property taxes, and a mixture of motivations on the part of people who want to finance, restrict, or manage growth or mitigate damage caused by development.

Authority to levy or negotiate exactions is granted by the state legislature, either in specific legislation or in more general home rule legislation. According to a 1990 survey by the Government Finance Officers Association (GFOA), impact fee programs have been authorized in at least fifteen states, with most legislation enacted in the first five years of the survey. Several states have enacted legislation in recent years to ensure that fees are reasonable and are related to careful estimates of the impact of a development.

Impact fees can be sizable. In the GFOA survey, they accounted for 60 percent of the capital budgets of the California communities surveyed, 21 percent of Washington State's, and 8 percent of Florida's. One government study cites exaction payments of $5,625 in Boulder, Colorado, for a typical single-family house; $6,107 in the San Francisco Bay Area; and $2,929 in Anne Arundel County, Maryland.[10]

Respondents to the GFOA survey reported developer payments for parks and recreation ranging from $70 to $2,600, with $519 as the average. Representative park impact fees for single-family homes in Florida include $882 for Lee County and $422 for Hillsborough County. Martin County, Florida, requires residential developers to contribute to a beach acquisition fund based on a calculation of projected increased demand for beach access as a consequence of a new development.

In spite of growing popularity, exaction arrangements are controversial, with continuing debate about equity and the difficulty of calculating the added burden on capital facilities rightly attributed to new communities. Demonstrating this nexus between new development and the cost and type of exactions has become more demanding since the United States Supreme Court's 1987 *Nollan v. California Coastal Commission* decision, which nullified a California exaction. Exactions that are intended as mitigation, as is often the case with environmental exactions, raise complex scientific and philosophical questions, including how a good program can be administered without seeming to create a green light for environmental destruction. Nonprofit organizations operating in the public interest can play an important role in ensuring the integrity of the process.

IMPACT FEE POOLS

The most important opportunity from the perspective of nonprofit conservation groups involves the pooling of developer impact fees to provide a fund for off-site purchases of sizable tracts of open space and habitat. "We are seeing major park acquisitions through the impact fee," says Professor James Nicholson of the University of Florida Law School. Piecemeal preserves established on the site of a development were often too small to result in significant environmental benefit or to be managed efficiently.

Off-site purchases with pooled impact fees raise a number of questions, including where the new purchase should be located, what should be the criteria for selecting the site, and who should decide. A purchase in the same community is most likely to involve comparable resources and to benefit the community directly. But this may be impractical at times, and comparable resources may be located at more reasonable cost some distance away. Land trusts have helped agencies identify suitable sites and negotiate purchase options or other mechanisms to reserve the tracts until the impact fund is large enough to pay for acquisition.

MITIGATION BANKS

Mitigation banks provide a mechanism to deal with the difficulty of arranging a single land acquisition transaction that balances diminished and added resource values, and they provide a way to ensure that developer fees are used to acquire a high-quality resource. Under an agreed-on accounting system, both environmental damage of a development and environmental benefits of resource acquisition, restoration, or creation are quantified into a system of developer debits and credits. The fund created by developer payments is used to purchase tracts as these become available or to pay for a valuable land resource incrementally that may have been acquired through a nonprofit intermediary.

Mitigation banks have been established most often in California, Florida, Louisiana, and Oregon for projects involving wetlands. The concept is also being applied to uplands and state highway projects. State mitigation banks could be fostered by the 1991 federal highway reauthorization bill.

Mitigating Habitat Loss Through a Public/Private Partnership: Northeastern Florida

The Trust for Public Land and Florida's Game and Freshwater Fish Commission are collaborating in a statewide mitigation program, funded by developer fees, to deal with losses of upland habitat. Florida's growth management law calls for state review and approval of developments of regional impact. The commission, one of the review agencies, has authority to require that a developer protect additional lands to mitigate for the loss of upland habitat of threatened and endangered species.

Working with the commission under a memorandum of understanding, TPL has set up two mitigation land banks in northeastern Florida, the Duval Mitigation Land Bank and the Withlachoochee Mitigation Land Bank, near Tampa. Purchase of the sites, which provide habitat for endangered species, was financed with developer fees combined with TPL and commission funds.

Under the bank arrangement, the commission determines when off-site mitigation is acceptable, identifies suitable property, and negotiates developer payments, which are deposited into a trust fund administered by TPL. TPL periodically withdraws money from the fund and conveys land of equal value to the commission. Florida Defenders of the Environment receives a percentage of the fund, earmarked for management.

Nonprofit involvement achieves several important ends: First, the conduit arrangement allows fees to be reserved for environmental mitigation instead of being deposited in the state treasury. Second, the organizations provide expertise in acquisition and management without burdening the state.

Key elements in the success of a developer-funded mitigation program, says TPL official Don Morrow, are a strong public policy mandating resource preservation, an institutional framework in which mitigation requirements are enforced, and an acquisition entity.

Concerns raised about the banks include the limited reach of the state process for reviewing developments of regional impact, which comprise only 7 to 10 percent of development; the desire of localities to play a stronger role in deciding which mitigation lands are acquired; and the effects of a slowed real estate market, which has reduced developer payments.

A Mitigation Land Bank: Southern California

In an interesting variation on the mitigation theme, the Irvine Company, a large southern California developer, has created a land bank of 16,000 wilderness acres. The Nature Conservancy will manage the land for rare species and public recreation until it has been transferred over time to different public agencies in conjunction with Irvine's development of adjoining parcels. One of the selling points for the developer in preserving so much acreage is that its preservation will enhance the value of neighboring developed parcels.

As the foregoing review makes clear, land conservation organizations need to look afresh at the world of public finance. The topic can no longer be subsumed under a single question, "How much can states and localities expect from the federal Land and Water Conservation Fund this year?" Nor is it a dry subject explored in little-read texts whose publishing date barely matters. Responding to the public's well-founded concerns over environmental degradation, traditional and new public financing mechanisms are being inventively crafted to conserve important lands efficiently and with maximum leverage of private resources. These mechanisms display a great deal of variety as a result of legal, fiscal, political, and other variations among states and localities and different pressures, opportunities, and traditions.

Regardless of what happens in Washington, DC, and with the Land and Water Conservation Fund, private groups stretching limited state and local funds will continue to play a decisive role in determining how much land is saved and where. Given the urgency of land-saving efforts and the critical role of partnerships, land conservation groups are challenged to increase their understanding of public financing mechanisms and the implications for their particular state, to work more closely with public officials and one another, and to exercise leadership in building constituencies for increased funding.

ACKNOWLEDGMENTS

The author gratefully acknowledges the Trust for Public Land, which sponsored and assisted with the preparation of this chapter, and the Surdna Foundation, which made this research possible.

NOTES

1. Memorandum from Clay Henderson, Volusia County Council, Florida, to John Hart, Broward County commissioner, and others on local land acquisition efforts, November 20, 1990.
2. Dennis Zimmerman, "Tax-Exempt Bonds and Twenty Years of Tax Reform: Controlling Public Subsidy of Private Activities," November 23, 1987, Library of Congress 87–922E.
3. Sturdivant & Company, Inc., "Securitizable Tax-Exempt Installment Purchase Open Space Financing Program." For a copy, write to Daniel O'Connell at Sturdivant & Company, Inc., 14 E. 76th St., P.O. Box 57, Harvey Cedars, NJ 08008.
4. Memorandum by John M. Elias, Esq., in *Farmland Forum* 3, no. 2. (August 1990), published by the New Jersey Conservation Foundation.

and Water Conservation Fund, the logic of a direct grant program for private groups inspired a number of state programs.

In recent years, Rhode Island, Vermont, New Jersey, Iowa, Maryland, Wisconsin, Florida, and Delaware have established statutory programs that provide for grants to nonprofit organizations for planning, acquisition, and/or management projects. For the most part, these programs were created in states experiencing strong development pressures, but as the examples of Iowa and Wisconsin indicate, this is not necessarily the case. The common thread among the programs is a comprehensive vision of resources at risk, a protection strategy that includes increased funding, and a stronger role for land trusts and nonprofit organizations in implementation and advocacy.

These programs recognize nonprofit groups as partners with government in accomplishing the program's goals, eligible to propose projects and to seek funding. Such direct grant programs have several obvious advantages. From the perspective of land trusts, projects can be judged on their own merits without having to be reshaped to interest an eligible government applicant whose priorities may differ. From the perspective of public officials, the programs provide a systematized way of encouraging, reviewing, and focusing projects proposed by nonprofit groups. From a broader policy perspective, competitive grants, even in small amounts, have the power to stimulate fresh approaches and creative solutions by drawing on the energy, ideas, and knowledge of those close to the problem.

Even though these grant programs have been enacted with broad-based support, they are not without critics. Some have worried that private groups would divert scarce public funds from priority projects. There are concerns that private groups will misuse government funds, drive the government's conservation agenda, or mismanage lands acquired with public money. Others have suggested that government aid for private projects could weaken land trusts by lessening their independence or that it could dampen private giving or co-opt private groups by making them dependent on public funds.

This chapter, like the more extensive report it is drawn from,[2] was conceived to provide early feedback about how these fledgling state grant programs are working. It is intended to serve the growing number of people in the public and private sectors who are asking, from the critics' side, whether these programs are a sound and effective use of public dollars and, from the proponents' side, how future programs can most effectively operate. It attempts to answer the following questions:

- What are these programs accomplishing?
- How are the programs structured, and do these structures work?
- How do partnership projects influence government land conservation programs?
- How does participation in a government program affect the way land trusts do business?
- What is the effect of these programs on overall funding and public support for land conservation?
- What are the lessons from early experience in advocating and administering these programs?

What follows is more a survey and review of the workings of these programs than an in-depth analysis. Since most of the state programs discussed have been in place for only a short time, systematically collected data are limited, and many of the evaluations are necessarily anecdotal, drawn from the opinions and perspectives of people familiar with them. Many of the issues addressed will merit further investigation as these programs mature.

AN OVERVIEW OF FORMAL PARTNERSHIP ARRANGEMENTS

There are at least fourteen land conservation programs in thirteen states whose statutes lay out a significant collaborative role for nonprofit groups.[3] Ten programs provide for direct grants to nonprofit organizations for acquisition, planning, and/or stewardship projects, either in a special set-aside or in a category of funds that land trusts share with municipalities and other government entities.[4] They are the primary focus of this report. The other four have various formalized roles for nonprofit organizations but no direct provisions for grants. All but two were created in 1985 or later. Programs with direct grants to nonprofit organizations include the following (parentheses indicate larger state programs of which the nonprofit programs are a part):

- California: State Coastal Conservancy; Santa Monica Mountains Conservancy
- Connecticut: Recreation and Natural Heritage Trust
- Florida: Communities Trust

- Iowa: Resource Enhancement and Protection
- Maryland: Land Trust Grant Fund (Program Open Space/Maryland Environmental Trust)
- New Jersey: Nonprofit Grant Program (Green Acres)
- Rhode Island: Open Space and Recreation Grants
- Vermont: Housing and Conservation Trust Fund
- Wisconsin: Stewardship Program

Programs with other significant statutory roles for nonprofit organizations include the following:

- Delaware: Land Protection Program (Greenways)
- Maine: Land for Maine's Future
- Michigan: Natural Resources Trust
- New Hampshire: Land Conservation Investment Program

In all of these programs, collaborative arrangements are an integral part of the land conservation strategy. As the names indicate—Land for Maine's Future, Resource Enhancement and Protection, Land Conservation Investment Program, Housing and Conservation Trust Fund—each was developed to implement a conservation vision that is carefully tailored to the state and that calls for an invigorated commitment of state dollars.

The chief characteristics of these programs are outlined in concise form in table 2. For each state program, the table provides information about the number of nonprofit projects approved to date, public dollars allocated to these projects, acreage protected and method (in fee and less than fee), current funding status, and distinctive features, such as the type of resources protected by the program, the statewide coalition that helped build support for the measure, and linkages to broader growth management policies.

Much of the diversity evident in the grant programs reflects differences among the states in goals, laws and traditions, and strengths and capabilities in the public and private sectors. Vermont, for example, provides funds to nurture new land trusts, since one of the purposes of its Housing and Conservation Trust Fund is to develop a stronger local land trust community. Its program also relies heavily on conservation easements, reflecting a commitment to preserve not only pastoral scenery but also the farm economy. Vermont's program encourages but does not require matching funds, since advocates did not want to eliminate promising projects

TABLE 2.

An Overview of Accomplishments: State Land Conservation Programs with Formal Partnership Roles for Nonprofits

	California		Connecticut
PROGRAM	State Coastal Conservancy	Santa Monica Mountains Conservancy	Recreation and Natural Heritage Trust
DATE ESTABLISHED	1982[1]	1984[2]	1986
DIRECT FUNDING FOR LAND TRUSTS NONPROFIT GROUPS	Yes	Yes	Yes[3]
FUNDING			
Current funding status	Has $10.1 million in unspent funds from 1988 bond. $60 million recommended by governor for a two-year period in proposed 1992 bond	$48 million recommended by governor for 1992 bond	Zero funding for 1992. Governor recommended $5 million for FY 1993
Source of funds	Successive bonds in 1976, 1980, 1984, 1988. Also, miscellaneous sources such as environmental license plate fund and federal grants	Successive bonds in 1984 and 1988; miscellaneous sources including environmental license plate fund	Bonds
Authorized for entire program	$193 million ($184 million in bonds, $9 million in other)	$70.7 million	$52 million
Appropriated to date	$186 million	$70.7 million	$35.6 million
Nonprofit projects[4]	$39.8 million	$10 million	$16.4 million
LAND PROTECTED			
Total number of approved projects	800+ (187 grants with 75 nonprofit grantees)	210 (4 with nonprofit grantees)	71 (29 assisted by nonprofit groups)

Acreage protected in entire program	31,648 (4,114 with easements)	17,000 (1,000 with easements)	6,000 (143 with easements)
Acreage protected in nonprofit projects[5]	18,300 (14,236 in fee, 4,064 with easements)	211	1,720
Title holder of nonprofit projects	Nonprofit groups, state, counties, open space districts, SCC (for ten years)	Nonprofit groups, state, counties, SMMC (for ten years)	State
DISTINCTIVE FEATURES	• Entrepreneurial state agency • Provides start-up training for nonprofit groups • Nonregulatory companion to coastal regulatory program • Large number and diversity of nonprofit grantees (75 in all) • No specific nonprofit match required • Jurisdiction limited to coastal zone and San Francisco Bay Area • Has made pivotal grants to major land trusts in coastal region • Model is replicated in state and elsewhere	• Focused on rich riparian areas • Works closely with Mountains Conservancy Foundation to enhance public access and preserve historic sites • Jurisdiction limited to Santa Monica Mountains and rim of the valley zone	• Goal of preserving 10% of state • First open space acquisition program in the state • State lands are acquired at average of 63% of fair market value • Nonprofit group cooperates in purchase, does not hold land • Projects require approval of bond commission • Cooperators provide a minimum of 20% match • Department can contribute up to 20% of project cost for stewardship fund • Nine-member advisory board recommends acquisition priorities and program directions. Includes two state officials, two state legislators, and five representatives of land conservation organizations

Continued on next page

TABLE 2—*Continued*

	Delaware	Florida	Iowa	Maine
PROGRAM	Land Protection Program	Florida Communities Trust	Resource Enhancement and Protection	Land for Maine's Future
DATE ESTABLISHED	1990	1989	1989	1987
DIRECT FUNDING FOR LAND TRUSTS/NONPROFIT GROUPS	No	Yes (but not yet funded)	Yes	No
FUNDING				
Current funding status	Bond sale in fall 1991 funds greenways program and state land acquisition	Legislature authorized sale of bonds under Preservation 2000 program. New funding round anticipated for September 1992	Legislature approved $10.9 million for FY 1992 (reduced to $10.6 million by across-the-board cuts) and $9.9 million for FY 1993	Future funding uncertain following defeat of bonds in 1990 and 1991
Source of funds	Revenue bonds, real estate transfer tax for debt service	Preservation 2000 bonds, panther license plates	Lottery, general funds	Bond
Authorized for entire program	$7 million annually for ten years	$30 million annually for ten years, subject to annual appropriation	$30 million annually for ten years	$35 million
Appropriated to date	$14 million	$30 million	$45.6 million	$28 million
Nonprofit projects			$1.2 million	
LAND PROTECTED				
Total number of approved projects	7 greenway planning grants (2 assisted by nonprofit groups); 5 development grants to counties, municipalities, and the state	21 (5 assisted by nonprofit groups)	Approximately 140 (10 with nonprofit groups)	28

Acreage protected in entire program	1,500	11,316	18,700	47,745
Acreage protected in nonprofit projects			1,784	
Title holder of nonprofit projects		Trustees of Internal Improvement Trust Fund	State	
DISTINCTIVE FEATURES	• Statutory language encourages cooperation with nonprofit groups • Holds quarterly meeting with nonprofit groups and others to encourage involvement in projects • Statewide open space council with citizen members approves acquisition proposals within designated state resource areas. $300,000 for planning grants for state resource areas available only to counties	• Program helps implement local comprehensive plans under state's growth management law • Current funding source (Preservation 2000 bonds) restricts funds to local government applicants • Created as nonregulatory state agency with governing body consisting of two state officials and three appointed members, including an elected local official, a nonprofit representative, and a developer	• Comprehensive conservation program in place after three-year, twenty-six-member coalition effort • Department of Natural Resources reimburses counties for taxes forgone on land acquired under private/public program • Strong citizen conservation education component	• Eleven-member board, with six private members, five public officials • Statute encourages projects with cooperating entities • Publishes a monthly newsletter

Continued on next page

TABLE 2—Continued

	Maryland	Michigan	New Hampshire	New Jersey
PROGRAM	Land Trust Grant Fund (Program Open Space)[6]	Natural Resources Trust	Land Conservation Investment Program	Nonprofit Grant Program (Green Acres)[7]
DATE ESTABLISHED	1990	1985	1987	1989
DIRECT FUNDING FOR LAND TRUSTS/NONPROFIT GROUPS	Yes	No	No	Yes
FUNDING				
Current funding status	Funding for FY 1992 reduced to balance budget. Governor proposed an additional $500,000 for FY 1993	$20.7 million for 1992 grants	Sunset in June 1993	One-time appropriation
Source of funds	Real estate transfer tax	Royalties and leases for oil, gas, and mineral resources	General funds and bonds	Bonds
Authorized for entire program	$500,000 (FY 1992)	Perpetual source of funds	$48.5 million	$10 million
Appropriated to date	$413,000	$216 million	$48.5 million	$10 million
Nonprofit projects	$413,000			$10 million
LAND PROTECTED				
Total number of approved projects	6 (with nonprofit groups)	517 acquisition grants between 1978 and 1991 ($185 million)	333	27 (with nonprofit groups)
Acreage protected in entire program	459	Over 101,000	96,640 (54,321 in fee, 42,319 with easements)	About 4,300 (in nonprofit program)

	Maryland	New Hampshire
Acreage protected in nonprofit projects	459	About 4,300
Title holder of nonprofit projects	State/local government or land trusts	Nonprofit applicant. May be conveyed to municipal, state, or qualified nonprofit group
DISTINCTIVE FEATURES	• Administered by Maryland Environmental Trust (MET), a state land trust • Applicant must contribute at least 15% match unless land is reconveyed to local or state government • All grants are reimbursable loans • MET also provides limited administrative funds for new land trusts • Trust fund is constitutionally protected • Citizens nominate acquisition projects • In 1991, 60 out of 124 nominations came from citizens • Trust must allocate 75% of expenditures for land acquisition • Five-member board includes four citizen members	• Goal is to protect over 100,000 acres with a $50 million commitment for five years • Program was created after a campaign by fifty private groups • Much of protected land remains privately owned, on tax rolls • Unique partnership of state entity (LCIP) with private Trust for New Hampshire Lands (TNHL), which raised over $3.3 million to staff the state program • LCIP board has fifteen members, including four legislators, five public members, and six nonvoting state officials. TNHL nominates three citizen members • $500,000 cap on grants • Nonprofit groups hold land. No funds for stewardship • All grants are approved by the governor and legislature • Review board consists of agency staff • Nonprofit group donates conservation/historic preservation restriction on lands acquired with grant

Continued on next page

TABLE 2—*Continued*

	Rhode Island	Vermont	Wisconsin
Program	Open Space and Recreation Grants	Housing and Conservation Trust Fund	Stewardship Program
Date Established	1986, 1987, 1989	1987	1989
Direct Funding for Land Trusts/Nonprofit Groups	Yes	Yes	Yes
Funding			
Current funding status	Governor placed moratorium in 1991 on sale of additional bonds, but approved projects will be funded	Legislature in FY 1993 approved $13.1 million, including $11.65 million in capital bonds and $1.45 million in transfer tax for $13.1 million total, almost double previous year	Bonding authority ongoing through life of program. $23.1 million for FY 1992
Source of funds	Bonds	Bonds, real estate transfer tax, appropriations	Bonds
Authorized for entire program	$122 million	$41.2 million	$250 million in ten-year period
Appropriated to date	$104 million	$41.2 million ($16.2 for land conservation)	$46.2 million
Nonprofit projects	$2.3 million to private land trusts, $3.6 million to municipal land trusts	$32.5 million ($15 million for land conservation)	Approximately $1 million
Land Protected			
Total number of approved projects	77 (14 with private and municipal land trusts)[8]	102 land conservation projects (73 with nonprofit groups)	600+ (8 with nonprofit groups)

Acreage protected in entire program	2,342	37,947 (20,868 in fee, 17,079 with easements)	Approximately 40,000 (includes ± 100 with easements)
Acreage protected in nonprofit projects	216 by private land trusts, 390 by municipal land trusts	25,293 (17,079 with easements)	About 700
Title holder of nonprofit projects	Private and municipal land trusts	Nonprofit groups and sometimes state agency	Nonprofit groups
DISTINCTIVE FEATURES	• $129 million in local open space bonds approved to match state bonds • Match ranges from 20% to 50% • Projects reviewed by commission with seven citizens, three officials • Two municipal land trusts raise funds by a transfer tax • State holds conservation easements on all towns and nonprofit projects	• Unique coalition of affordable housing and environmental advocates • Strong legislative advocacy by coalition • Board: five citizen members, four state officials • Fund administered by quasi-public agency • Committed to protect working farms (not just open space)	• Largest conservation program in state's history • Ten-year program • 50% match for nonprofit group participation • Grants are reviewed by state department of natural resources • Comprehensive program to fund trails, habitat restoration, urban green space, and local and state park development as well as acquisition

SOURCE: Phyllis Myers, *Lessons from the States:: Strengthening Land Conservation Programs through Grants to Nonprofit Land Trusts* (Washington, DC: Land Trust Alliance, 1992).

1 The State Coastal Conservancy was established 1976; the nonprofit program was approved by the legislature in 1982.

2 The Santa Monica Mountains Conservancy was established in 1980; the nonprofit program was approved by the legislature in 1984.

3 Nonprofit groups may receive funds as designated "primary managers" of specific sites. They may be reimbursed as cooperating organizations for acquiring a site that the state agrees to purchase later.

4 Approved and in various states of completion.

5 Approved and in various states of completion.

6 Both Maryland's and New Jersey's direct grants programs were enacted as part of two longstanding conservation/recreation programs, Program Open Space and Green Acres. Because these programs have been in existence for decades, statistics about their overall accomplishments are not detailed in the matrix.

7 See note 6.

8 These projects are in the local open space and recreation grant program only; they do not include state projects funded by the bonds.

from economically distressed regions, where attracting private funds would be very difficult. In Iowa, in contrast, the match is a requirement, since a primary motivation for involving private groups is their ability to raise private funds. No program is quite like another: Each is tailored to special circumstances.

The state programs identified in the reconnaissance for this chapter include four—those of New Hampshire, Michigan, Maine, and Delaware—that involve nonprofit organizations in important statutory ways in an invigorated conservation program, although they do not provide direct grants for projects, and nonprofit groups do not take title to the parcels involved. In New Hampshire, the private Trust for New Hampshire Lands helps the state develop and review acquisition proposals and negotiates state-approved purchases. The organization has raised several million dollars from the private sector for its activities. In Michigan, nonprofit groups as well as officials propose conservation projects to a state board that is charged with administering a mitigation fund generated by revenues from oil and gas exploration on state lands. The direct role of nonprofit organizations ends at this point, however. The Land for Maine's Future program has a broad participatory process that involves land trusts and other nonprofit groups in nominating and packaging projects. The review board includes citizen members, some of whom have ties to land protection groups, and procedures encourage partnership projects.

Delaware's Land Protection Program is also guided by statutory language that encourages collaboration with nonprofit groups as one way of implementing its objectives. Nonprofit groups work with counties on planning projects in designated state resource areas and meet regularly with agency staff members to discuss available funding, acquisition priorities, and the like.

Although examining such indirect programs in detail is outside the scope of this chapter, these programs illustrate important variations on the theme, which officials and private groups may wish to explore as they craft their own programs.

THE PROGRAMS' STRUCTURES: TWO MODELS EMERGE

In considering a state grant program, a primary question of state officials, legislators, and nonprofit organizations is "How should it be structured?"

This chapter summarizes four of the best-developed state programs—those of California, Rhode Island, Vermont, and Iowa—and then highlights and compares the principal aspects of their operation. The four programs illustrate two models that reflect somewhat different philosophies about partnerships, differences that in turn lead to contrasting operations.

FOUR REPRESENTATIVE PROGRAMS

To look at the experience of direct grants closely, four programs were selected as case studies. An effort was made to select programs that had been in existence for some time and had a record to show, that are geographically diverse, and that vary in the amount and type of nonprofit activity. Distinctive features, such as land protection innovations and program structures, also were taken into account.

California State Coastal Conservancy

The California State Coastal Conservancy's nonprofit program is almost a decade old, making it the "granddaddy" of the programs examined here. The State Coastal Conservancy was established in 1976 as a companion nonregulatory agency to the California Coastal Commission, which was created by a statewide citizen initiative calling for strong measures to save California's coastline. The conservancy, a small entrepreneurial state agency, was given broad authority to resolve contentious disputes arising over development of the state's magnificent 1,100-mile stretch of coastal lands. Almost from the organization's inception, conservancy officials found nonprofit organizations to be valuable partners, and in 1982 its granting authority was formally expanded to include grants to nonprofit groups to undertake projects in all of its program areas, including acquisition, resource restoration, and coastal access.

Grants to nonprofit organizations now account for about one-third of the conservancy's annual budget of approximately $25 million, which is derived primarily from successive statewide bonds. Nonprofit groups have been involved in acquiring more than 18,000 acres (4,064 with easements), an amount representing more than half of the land that all conservancy grants have helped purchase. Through early 1992, almost $40 million had been granted to nonprofit projects. The conservancy's model—its regional focus, broad and flexible powers, nonbureaucratic mode of operation, and direct funding and fostering of nonprofit organizations, which now number more than sixty in the coastal region alone—has inspired replication efforts within California and elsewhere.

Rhode Island's Open Space and Recreation Grant Program

In a remarkable outpouring of support, Rhode Islanders voted in the late 1980s for a series of bonds to protect open space and recreational lands. In all, the 1986, 1987, and 1989 bonds authorized $122 million in state funds for protecting open space, coastal, natural, and recreational areas and for developing recreational facilities. State funds were matched by local bonds approved by virtually all of the towns. Two of the three state bonds provided a percentage of funds that nonprofit organizations could access directly; a small amount of funding was made available to nonprofit groups from the other bond through administrative action.

Although the land trust community was small at the time the bonds were proposed, the availability of a percentage of bond funds for private projects helped to motivate grass-roots political action and stimulated the formation of more land trusts.

Rhode Island's program is administered within the state's Department of Environmental Management. Land trust projects are reviewed by an independent commission appointed by the governor, which recommends projects for funding to the department's director. (This commission reviews municipal projects as well.) Through early 1992, private land trusts had received eight grants totaling $2.3 million and municipal land trusts had received six grants for $3.6 million, enabling them to acquire 600 acres of wetlands, open space, and habitat. Although a severe economic crisis in the state halted sale of the final $20 million worth of state open space bonds in 1991, the bond initiatives have left a strong legacy of partnerships and protected lands. (Examples of this legacy may be found in chapter 7.)

Vermont Housing and Conservation Trust Fund

The Vermont Housing and Conservation Trust Fund was established in 1987 with the assistance of an unusual alliance of housing and environmental groups. The innovative program was crafted to deal with the adverse effects of rapidly escalating land prices on both environmental quality and housing affordability.

Like the California State Coastal Conservancy, this program created a small but powerful new entity—the Vermont Housing and Conservation

Board—with broad powers to act quickly, flexibly, and non-bureaucratically. Through April 1992, approximately $41 million had been appropriated to the trust fund, of which about $16.2 million went for land conservation projects involving outstanding natural, scenic, recreational, agricultural, and historic resources. About three-quarters of these projects were initiated with nonprofit organizations. The Housing and Conservation Board operates statewide. (Details on the day-to-day workings of the Vermont program can be found in chapter 8.)

The alliance of housing and land conservation interests has served as a model for other efforts, although Vermont remains unique in the steadfastness of the coalition and in the single board allocating grants for the program's dual objectives. The program, which also provides technical assistance and capacity grants to nonprofit organizations, is financed by a combination of real estate transfer taxes and capital bonds. The trust fund received a sizable increase in funding for 1993. This is attributable to the governor's strong support and the effectiveness of the coalition in making the case for the program's contribution to the state's tourism, agricultural, and housing industries and its ability to respond to the acquisition opportunities of the recession.

Iowa's Resource Enhancement and Protection Program

Iowa's Resource Enhancement and Protection program (REAP), a public/private cost-sharing program approved in 1989, was shaped over a three-year period by a twenty-six-member coalition of environmental, farm, and outdoor recreation groups. Unlike the other programs, which were formed in response to rapid development, REAP had its origins in the public's growing awareness of the state's lackluster record in protecting public lands and the need to halt the severe loss of critical topsoil, wetlands, and other resources vital to the state's economy.

REAP, designed as a comprehensive $30 million per year, ten-year program, sets forth protection of the state's natural resource heritage as official state policy. It funds state acquisition of sensitive and distinctive natural, historic, scenic, and recreational resources; improved management of public and private agricultural lands; and extensive education and outreach activities to build public awareness about environmental issues.

Nonprofit organizations are eligible to apply directly for funds for land acquisition projects under a small (2.9 percent of the total appropriation) public/private cost-sharing program. Title to all property passes to the state. The program is administered by Iowa's Department of Natural Resources, and projects are approved by an independent policy commission of private citizens appointed by the governor.

Through early 1992, this program had funded ten projects, for $1.2 million, proposed by nonprofit organizations to acquire 1,784 acres of land for the state. Appropriations for REAP so far have totaled $45.6 million. Budget deficits caused the 1992 appropriation to fall to $10.6 million, far less than advocates hoped, but a victory under the circumstances. At this writing, however, the legislature has approved $9.9 million for fiscal year 1993. The program's survival in spite of the state's economic plight is attributed to the quality of its projects, its broad outreach to many state constituencies, and continued strong advocacy by the coalition that founded it.

THE TWO BASIC MODELS: PROACTIVE AND REACTIVE

The four programs illustrate two quite different approaches to structuring collaborative grants programs:

- The proactive model, represented by the California State Coastal Conservancy and the Vermont Housing and Conservation Trust Fund, in which the program is overseen by a specially tailored institution responsive to both officials and private groups that actively fosters partnerships and cooperative projects and assists nonprofit groups as a central part of its mission.
- The reactive model, represented by the Rhode Island and Iowa programs, in which the nonprofit program is fit into the traditional land management agency. The program responds to projects proposed by nonprofit organizations but does not have a commitment to seek them out.

The Proactive Model

In California and Vermont, a new, small institution was created with a broad mandate to oversee a nonbureaucratic grant program and to foster innovative partnerships between government and private groups. This model most closely resembles the institution recommended by the President's Commission on Americans Outdoors to foster innovation in land conservation.

In Vermont, the Vermont Housing and Conservation Board is organized as a quasi-public agency. Staff members, who work in a renovated stable in downtown Montpelier, Vermont, are selected without regard to formal civil service criteria. In California, the State Coastal Conservancy is a state agency that consciously cultivates a style and culture close to those of the private groups with which it works. Although this practice is hard to define, the result is evident to the nonprofit groups. The conservancy is "like us," says Audrey Rust of the Peninsula Open Space Trust; "they want to get things done." Both agencies are placed outside the confines of the traditional bureaucratic structure and given leeway to organize activities and to cut across agency boundaries to accomplish their missions. For example, the conservancy and trust fund boards are authorized to approve acquisitions, unlike traditional park departments in those states, which must seek line item approval by the legislature for each project.

Both programs operate with a minimum of formal guidelines and rules. Review boards meet monthly to consider applications on a rolling basis. Since staff members work with nonprofit applicants as they develop proposals, the programs operate less as competitive systems than as ones designed to result in a flow of good, collaborative projects to the board. In both, nonprofit organizations are seen as important elements in the programs' delivery systems.

The Reactive Model

The Rhode Island and Iowa programs illustrate how a grant program can be established with more limited institutional change—in these instances, in the existing state land management agency. To inject fresh perspectives, a review board representing citizens and officials examines projects submitted by nonprofit organizations. Staff members with special affinity for these programs may be assigned to them to act as a focal point for interacting with the nonprofit community. The review board makes recommendations to the director in Rhode Island and to the agency's policy commission in Iowa.

In this model, although the land acquisition process is modified up front to accommodate the objectives of the new programs, many of the agencies' conventional procedures remain in place. Detailed regulations guide the programs. Staff members are helpful and want their programs to work, but nurturing the nonprofit community is not a direct mandate of the legislation they implement. Review boards meet less often, and their decisions are recommendations subject to higher levels of approval. Non-profit projects are restricted to a small component of the programs (although the groups may play a larger role in influencing other aspects of the programs).

COMPARISON OF OPERATIONS

The difference in philosophy underlying these two models helps explain differences in structure and procedures that might otherwise seem idiosyncratic. In analyzing the differences among programs, it is helpful to consider the advice of J. Glenn Eugster, chief of state wetlands programs for the U.S. Environmental Protection Agency: "A lot of details are important in implementing a partnership program. The key question is not how [can we] avoid failure but how can we *enable* nonprofits and give them the opportunity to succeed?"

Scope of Nonprofit Involvement

The programs differ in the scope of the role they give to nonprofit organizations. In the proactive California and Vermont programs, nonprofit organizations are eligible to apply for project funds in all program categories (as are public agencies), and the amount or percentage that may go to nonprofit groups is not restricted by statute or regulation. In the Iowa program, nonprofit organizations apply for funding under a small set-aside component specified in the legislation and regulations. The Rhode Island program was funded by three bonds. The first bond provided freer access to funds for nonprofit groups, but successive bonds confined direct access to a smaller portion of funds.

Match Requirements

The California and Vermont programs have flexible match requirements. Officials want to decide on a case-by-case basis how much is needed to make a good project succeed. This would not rule out a vital project proposed by a nonprofit group that could not attract substantial funds from other public or private sources, for example. In the Rhode Island and Iowa programs, the match is specified by statute: at least 25 percent in Iowa and 20 to 50 percent in Rhode Island, depending on the bond.

Composition of the Review Board

In all four cases, the review boards contain a mix of citizen representatives and agency officials. The citizen members equal or outnumber agency officials in each case. The boards' composition is as follows:

- California Conservancy's board has four citizen members appointed by the governor and legislature, three officials (including the head of the California Coastal Commission), and six legislators who are non-voting representatives. The chair is selected by the head of the resources agency.
- Vermont's board has five citizen members appointed by the governor and four ex officio agency officials.
- In Rhode Island, citizen members dominate, with seven citizen members appointed by the governor and three ex officio agency officials.
- Iowa's six-member board, appointed by the director of the Department of Natural Resources, is evenly balanced between agency and citizen members.

Vermont and Iowa restrict the governor's choice of citizen members somewhat: in Vermont, the governor must appoint a farmer and a representative of low-income persons; in Iowa, the governor must select public members from a list provided by nonprofit organizations.

Although the effects of fine variations in representation may or may not be pivotal, depending on the circumstances, strong representation by non-government members who understand the nonprofit community and officials who know agency priorities is obviously essential. In addition, legislators on the California State Coastal Conservancy's board are helpful in moving the agency's agenda in Sacramento, advises executive officer Peter Grenell.

Role of the Review Board

Although the composition of the review boards is similar among all four programs, their roles differ. In the proactive Vermont and California programs, the review board has the authority to approve and fund projects, including acquisitions. In Rhode Island and Iowa, the board makes a recommendation to the agency director or the governor-appointed policy commission, respectively. This difference in authority may account for the broad representation on the California State Coastal Conservancy's board and its links to the governor, legislature, and head of the resources agency.

Role of the Program's Staff

Program staff members play a critical role in preparing projects and backup materials for board review and in determining when projects are ready to be submitted to the board. However, the extent of involvement is greater in Vermont and California than in the other two states. "This is to quite an extent a staff-driven activity," says State Coastal Conservancy board member Margaret Azevedo. "The board adopts criteria for project selection. The staff selects and works up the project, and then justifies these to the board." In Iowa and Rhode Island, program staff members describe their role in the process as more at arm's length.

Method of Application

Three of the four programs (all but the California State Coastal Conservancy) have formal grant applications. These request environmental, resource, and cost information and specific elements emphasized in a particular program (the match in Iowa and Rhode Island; the relationship to affordable housing and state and local land plans in Vermont). After several years of experience, California's program dropped formal applications and program criteria, arguing that these encourage groups to "write to the test" and diminish creativity.

Project Criteria and Rating

All of the states but California use a numerical scale to evaluate applications. In Vermont, although the board develops a quantitative score that addresses statutory requirements, its decisions depend on a consensus about how a project meets the board's policies. In addition, the board recently adopted a policy for rating agricultural projects that reflects increased interest by farmers in conservation easement programs and by state officials in ensuring that state funds are used to protect the highest-quality farms.

The California Coastal Conservancy does not quantify its review or publish criteria for funding. "We want to be positioned to respond flexibly," says executive officer Grenell. Staff narratives summarize proposed projects and make recommendations for board action.

The states vary in the amount of scrutiny or weight they give to the capability of nonprofit organizations in rating a project. In Iowa, since the state takes title to the properties, the capability of the proposing nonprofit group is not scored. In California and Vermont, the board looks closely at how solid nonprofit groups are and whether they are capable of doing what they propose. In contrast, in Rhode Island, although land trusts take title to lands funded by the state, the formal system is primarily resource driven. Land trusts' capabilities are assessed on secondary scoring criteria.

Project Approval

Iowa most actively uses its scoring system to define winners. REAP's board awards funds to the ranked list of projects until funds are exhausted. Given the large number of eligible projects and limited dollars—in February 1991, requests were received for nineteen projects, totaling $2,363,555, and only $273,000 was available—REAP has been able to fund only a few of those proposed in each round.

The other three programs have funded a substantial majority of projects submitted by land trust applicants. Rhode Island received thirty-five applications from municipal and nonprofit land trusts, for total funding of $10,592,350. It approved twenty-five grants, or about 75 percent of those submitted.

Until the recent budget crunch, both Vermont and California had an even higher approval rate—about 90 percent of projects submitted to their boards were approved. This reflects strong staff input in deciding when projects are ready for board review and in synchronizing requests with available funds.

In recent months, the pressure on limited funds has changed the ratio between applicants and awards somewhat and led to actions in both states to scrutinize priorities. In Vermont, landowners interested in selling development rights increased by more than 400 percent. Out of seventy-nine applications, the board in April 1992 anticipated funding only eleven to fourteen applications. In California, uncertainty over projects for bond funding in 1992 has stimulated board/staff discussions about developing more stringent criteria for focusing funds.

Time from Application to Approval

In all four programs under discussion, the time from application to approval varies greatly from project to project. For example, a decision by the California State Coastal Conservancy to fund a multimillion-dollar Solano County ranch purchase took only four months from the time the land went on the market. But projects can take a long time if conditions or a management plan are being "massaged." In Iowa and Rhode Island, there are more bureaucratic hurdles to leap after the board's approval, and the actual payment process reportedly takes much longer.

Who Holds the Land

In each program, title to nonprofit projects is held somewhat differently. The Vermont and California programs, again, are most flexible. In California, nonprofit organizations may hold title temporarily or permanently, and land may be transferred to state, local, or regional entities. In Vermont, the state land management agency or nonprofit groups take title (in either fee or less than fee), although the latter is more typical. Iowa and Rhode Island come out differently on the title question: In Iowa, properties are transferred to the state after the nonprofit organizations negotiate the transactions. In Rhode Island, nonprofit groups hold title to the land or interests they acquire.

These four programs exemplify two approaches to managing a nonprofit grant program; the main difference is in the degree of experimentation with nonprofit partners that the program will encourage. Any state considering adopting a state grant program involving nonprofit organizations needs to look at the full menu of choices for structuring a program and adapt the models to fit its circumstances.

In general, some type of proactive model seems desirable in order to reap the advantages of working with nonprofit groups. Rather than create a new institution, it may be possible in some states to adapt an existing agency that has been shaped to work with nonprofit organizations (the Maryland Environmental Trust is a case in point) and that has an institutional culture that accepts risk in order to gain the benefits of flexibility, creativity, and innovation.

One issue to watch in proactive, innovative approaches is that they may, over time, lose some of the political luster that comes with being on the cutting edge. Another issue is that their quick response, freedom of action, and flexibility can raise questions about the cohesiveness of the overall program, especially when public funds are in short supply. Also, states establishing new programs in the 1990s may find it difficult to create a new agency, even a small one, in the face of severe budget cuts.

The primary advantage of the reactive model is that it requires minimal change in administrative structures and procedures. It is thus less likely to be seen as a threat to vested interests and can be strengthened incrementally. It can, however, lead to a program that is more rigid, more bureaucratic, and less integrated with the entrepreneurial spirit of the nonprofit community. Moreover, the program is less institutionalized and thus may be more vulnerable to being shut down.

ACCOMPLISHMENTS AND BENEFITS OF DIRECT GRANT PROGRAMS

What have programs that provide direct grants to land trusts accomplished? Compared with more traditional programs, what special advantages do they bring? The principal accomplishments and benefits cited by those close to these programs include the following:

- *Significant acreage saved.* The quality and quantity of protected land are increased, often without burdening the state.
- *The land trust dividend.* Benefits include completion of projects that would not have been possible without nonprofit organizations' innovation and their leveraging of government money.
- *Increased constituency funding for land conservation.* Effective political support is generated by nonprofit organizations to sustain ongoing land conservation programs in the state.
- *Enhancement of growth management.* The programs enhance growth management sometimes by serving as an implementation tool of growth management plans and sometimes by promoting awareness of the need, and building support, for growth management measures.
- *Strengthening of nonprofit organizations.* The size and/or strength and capabilities of the land trust community are increased.
- *Greater openness of public land programs.* The programs enhance receptivity of state officials to partnerships for land conservation apart from the activities that are mandated in the grant program.

Most direct grant programs are quite new, and the findings reported here are based to a great extent on the opinions of the people who know them best—the program administrators and land trust personnel involved in their implementation. Although this assessment also relies on available documentation, the four highlighted programs vary in the amount of organized data available, and none has yet been able to give priority to in-depth analysis.

SIGNIFICANT ACREAGE SAVED

Although acquisition is not necessarily the sole goal of collaborative programs, it is an important one and is arguably the fundamental reason for the involvement of land trusts. Altogether, land trusts have directly saved some 46,000 acres under these four programs, 24,450 acres in fee and 21,143 acres in easements. Public funds for these nonprofit projects total $58 million—with the lion's share, $54.8 million, spent in California and Vermont. Although in some cases their involvement has been significantly limited by the amount of money available to them, nonprofit organizations have also had a wider influence by working indirectly on some projects.

California State Coastal Conservancy projects proposed and implemented by nonprofit organizations have resulted in the acquisition of some 18,300 acres of farmland, wetlands, and other sensitive coastal lands (more than 14,000 acres in fee and the remainder in conservation easements). This accounts for nearly 60 percent of all acreage protected by the conservancy. Approximately $25 million has been awarded to nonprofit organizations for these acquisitions.

Land trusts have been awarded an additional $13 million in grants for other purposes, including consolidation of small undeveloped coastal lots, restoration of wetlands and streambeds, construction of campgrounds and trails, and enhanced coastal access. Land trusts are also involved in preacquisition projects, in which they acquire land that they sell to the conservancy, and they receive some funds as reimbursable loans.

Vermont's Housing and Conservation Trust Fund, established in 1987, has resulted in the protection of some 38,000 acres of farmland and natural and recreational lands protected by nonprofit groups—almost 17,000 of these with conservation easements, reflecting the program's emphasis on helping farmers continue in business and keeping land on the tax rolls. Nonprofit acquisitions account for nearly 75 percent of all acreage acquired and 80 percent of funds expended for this purpose.

Trust fund dollars also have been used to buy some 12,000 acres of outstanding wildlife habitat and recreational and natural areas for addition to state lands with the assistance of The Nature Conservancy. In the nine years before the trust fund was established, only four parcels had been purchased by the state, for a total of $500,000.

In Iowa, REAP's nonprofit projects so far account for the addition of some 1,784 acres to state-owned lands, about 9.5 percent of the acreage acquired by the entire program to date. Only 2.9 percent of REAP funds is designated for nonprofit organizations in this program.

Rhode Island has provided $2,289,066 for the purchase of 216 acres by private land trusts and $3,642,444 for the acquisition of 390 acres by municipal land trusts, for a total of $5,931,510 in grants to both types of trusts. These represent 15 percent of the total funds allocated to local open space and recreational programs.

THE LAND TRUST DIVIDEND

Nonprofit organizations bring benefits to these programs in a number of ways. Says Rob Woolmington, a Bennington, Vermont, land use lawyer who chairs the Vermont Housing and Conservation Board: "This is an extremely efficient way to acquire land. . . . Moreover, we've made projects happen which neither party could pull off alone." Gus Seelig, executive director of the Vermont Housing and Conservation Trust Fund, comments: "Nonprofits have a spirit and commitment that would be difficult to sustain in a public agency. The contribution of private groups varies. Some raise a good deal of money privately; others bring local involvement, sustained interest, stewardship capability, and access to landowners that the state does not have." According to program administrators, the four overarching benefits of nonprofit organizations are that they make projects happen that could not have happened otherwise, leverage public funds, bring innovative approaches into the programs, and develop community support for acquisitions.

Making Projects Happen

In each state, advocates say that the collaborative program has "made projects happen" because private groups were able to strike a better deal than the state could have, have raised private funds to match public money, have had the patience and commitment to "massage" a complex project or build community support for it, or have brought an important parcel to the attention of an appropriate agency. "Without nonprofits, a great many State Coastal Conservancy projects would not have been done," says the conservancy's executive officer Peter Grenell. "They are the implementers, extending the ability of government to act."

Land trusts' ability to bring money to the projects allows the state programs to help fund projects that would otherwise be beyond these programs' budgets. In Iowa, for example, nonprofit groups' ability to raise a substantial cash match enabled the state to acquire several high-priority wetlands parcels in a scenic second-home region where high land values otherwise would have precluded the state purchase. In Vermont, the Vermont Land Trust has so far facilitated the purchase of five farms in a regional effort to protect the picturesque and productive Mettowee Valley. The Vermont Land Trust leveraged dollars from the Vermont Housing and Conservation Board with matching funds from a foundation and through community fund-raising.

Land trusts also package complex or unusual projects. In several projects in California—Nipomo Dunes, Sinkyone Wilderness, and Cowell Range—The Nature Conservancy, the Trust for Public Land, and the Peninsula Open Space Trust pulled together multiparty, multiuse, multimillion-dollar projects with key funding provided by the California State Coastal Conservancy. In Rhode Island, The Nature Conservancy completed a complex three-way land transaction with a land swap for a Kansas farm in the middle (see chapter 1 for details), and the Trust for Public Land helped the town of Narragansett package state and local funds and negotiated with the landowner to acquire one of the town's last remaining large undeveloped parcels. "We would never have been able to pull this off without TPL," says a town official.

Leveraging Public Funds

The state programs are also credited for their effectiveness in leveraging other public and private funds:

- Private groups provided about $600,000 in cash and land as the required match for the $1.2 million spent so far under REAP's public/private cost-share program, covering one-third of project costs.

- In Rhode Island, land trust projects provide from one-fifth to one-half of project costs, depending on the particular bond funding the project. The match source may be local government or private funds.
- In the Coastal Conservancy program, on average, other sources provide 75 percent of project funds, although the nonprofit contribution varies widely. Most of the additional project funds are provided by other state agencies.
- In the Vermont program, other sources also provide 75 percent of project costs, with Trust Fund dollars supplemented with other state funds, bargain sales, and donations in land conservation projects.

Providing Innovation

Nonprofit organizations have also sparked innovation. Although this is not easy to measure or even define, projects provide ample examples of land trusts pioneering new approaches to land protection.

In 1984, the California State Coastal Conservancy gave a $1 million demonstration grant to the Marin Agricultural Land Trust (MALT) to test the group's belief that farmers would agree to conservation easements if they received some payment for them. Until that time, most conservation easements had been donated by well-to-do landowners. MALT purchased 2,820 acres of farmland easements, permanently protecting the lands at one-quarter of the appraised value and, moreover, retaining them as working farms. MALT, now one of the nation's foremost agricultural land trusts, administers a $15 million county easement program financed by a state bond.

Land trusts under the Vermont and California programs have also experimented with transfers of development rights and limited development. Through the Mountains Restoration Trust, established by the California State Coastal Conservancy, development rights were extinguished in small California coastal lots and sold to other sites where development was deemed to be more compatible with coastal plans. Farmland projects by land trusts in Vermont have combined protection of a parcel's most productive soils with housing development on the less valuable section. Although the record of success in such projects is mixed, the experimentation is viewed as central to these state programs' mission.

Moreover, in working with diverse agencies and private landowners, nonprofit organizations play a critical role—one whose importance has not

been sufficiently recognized—in helping to overcome fragmented ownership of sensitive watersheds, habitat, and other sizable resource lands and to
put in place connectors or corridors between parcels already protected by
public or private means. Elkhorn Slough and Sinkyone Wilderness in California, the East Creek Preserve in Vermont, the North-South Trail in Rhode
Island, and the Loess Hills Prairie in Iowa are examples of such efforts
involving nonprofit groups in stitching together complex ecosystem protection projects and increasing public appreciation and use.

INCREASED FUNDING FOR LAND CONSERVATION

The political appeal of direct grant programs has been evident in successful
statewide campaigns to increase funding for land conservation and, more
recently, in stiff competition for revenues in states gripped by falling revenues and rising entitlements. In one striking example, in 1988, Californians
approved a $776 million parks, wildlife, and recreation bond in an outcome
widely attributed to the support generated by the state's numerous nonprofit
organizations. Nonprofit groups campaigned vigorously for the measure,
which funded the acquisition of specific parcels in which these groups were
interested. Although most grant programs are not quite so specific as
California's in naming specific projects, the prospect of assistance unquestionably activated letter-writing campaigns, editorials in community newsletters, and doorbell ringing to get out the vote in referenda.

The case study programs also—with the exception of hard-hit Rhode
Island—demonstrated the value of strong constituencies when recession
decimated state revenues in 1991. The Vermont and Iowa coalitions
successfully made the case for retaining their new programs in order to
capitalize on the opportunities to acquire significant land resources in the
softened real estate market and to sustain their contributions to the state
economy. Following the 1990 defeat of California's environmental mega-
bond proposal, Governor Pete Wilson recommended a more modest environmental bond for 1992, which included $60 million for the California
State Coastal Conservancy. The Rhode Island program is on temporary hold
due to the severity of the fiscal crisis there.

ENHANCEMENT OF GROWTH MANAGEMENT

These state programs fund land trusts, which typically work parcel by
parcel to implement projects that advance the priorities of a broad regional

or statewide land conservation agenda. All four programs share the general objective of protecting sensitive lands from inappropriate development, and two—the Vermont and California programs—were enacted at a time when comprehensive growth management mandates had just been or were about to be enacted. In both California and Vermont, the direct grant programs were mechanisms to help implement those new growth management laws. In Rhode Island and Iowa, meanwhile, the programs have fostered public discussion and advocacy of stronger measures to foster resource-sensitive development as well as to protect land through purchase. In fact, Rhode Island succeeded, in 1990 and 1991, in reforming state planning mandates and enacting legislation permitting communities to zone for environmental protection.

Serving as an Implementation Mechanism

Among the four case studies, linkage between nonprofit activity and growth management measures is historically strongest in California. The direct grant program of the California State Coastal Conservancy was enacted specifically to help implement the conservancy's mission as a nonregulatory companion to the state's coastal regulatory agency. With the assistance of the conservancy, land trusts have helped to resolve a number of projects that were at variance with statewide or local coastal planning goals by working out solutions such as transfers of development rights from sensitive coastal lots, conservation easements with farmers owning key agricultural parcels in coastal areas, acquisition with either nonprofit or public stewardship, and land exchanges.

Vermont's growth management law was enacted one year after the Vermont Housing and Conservation Trust Fund was passed. Still, the report of the governor's commission that recommended passage of Vermont's Act 200, which mandates statewide and local planning, saw the trust fund as an important mechanism to implement its goals.[5] Not incidentally, the trust fund received the largest appropriation in the year the state legislature enacted Act 200. In a 1990 policy paper discussing its policies vis-à-vis Act 200, the trust fund's board explained how its actions are "consistent," "coordinated," and "compatible" with the goals of the state's land-planning act. These actions include explicit attention to how proposed projects relate to local and regional plans and support for a strong "infrastructure" of nonprofit groups.[6]

At the same time, the profiled programs have not necessarily hitched their wagons to the growth management vision, in part to preserve their authority to act independently of possibly controversial planning and regulatory measures. The prudence of some distancing seems borne out by experience. In California, the State Coastal Conservancy has continued functioning and has even expanded its authority despite the coastal regulatory system's weakening by gubernatorial opposition in the 1980s. In Vermont, the trust fund's independent authority enables it to act despite the fact that town planning to implement Act 200 planning mandates has lagged.

Fostering Advocacy for Growth Management

Involvement of private nonprofit organizations in government conservation programs seems to enhance land trusts' awareness of the need for broader measures to manage growth more effectively and to tap powers of local and state government over land use. Although many land trust representatives are wary of taking prominent roles in land use planning debates— concerned that involvement in local controversy may erode their ability to work with all landowners and interests in the community—many are becoming involved in such activities that reinforce or complement their organization's goals.[7]

This hypothesis is supported by the initiatives in all four program sites. Representatives of a number of land trusts fostered by the California State Coastal Conservancy, for example, have become influential voices for more sound growth policies in their communities. In one instance, the Marin Agricultural Land Trust came into being in a struggle against a county land use plan deemed threatening to the county's rural character; the organization has gone on to influence a host of county land planning decisions aimed at reinforcing and strengthening regional agriculture.

In Rhode Island, land trusts were effective members of the coalitions that helped enact a statewide growth management law in 1990 and, the year after, legislation giving towns the authority to enact zoning measures for environmental protection. Land trust representatives in Rhode Island help towns map conservation lands for mandated local plans and educate citizens about the importance of zoning and planning.

Given the conservatism of a state like Iowa, such measures as zoning, planning, and growth management are not an explicit element in the REAP program. Yet the dialogue it fosters in each of the state's ninety-nine counties on environmental education, soil conservation, habitat enrichment, land conservation, and other resource-based economic and environmental activities is clearly pivotal not only in building immediate constituencies for REAP but also, over the long term, in promoting awareness of the need for an improved decision-making process about land uses.

STRENGTHENING OF NONPROFIT GROUPS

How have these state programs affected the nonprofit land conservation community? Both officials and land trust representatives credit the state programs with stimulating a significant increase in the number of land conservation groups in at least three case study sites—California, Vermont, and Rhode Island. Those interviewed also cite other effects on the land trust movement, most quite positive and a few that will bear watching over time.

Increased Numbers of Land Trusts

In California, the handful of land trusts along the coast in the early 1980s, when the State Coastal Conservancy began working with nonprofit organizations, has grown to some sixty groups. Some organizations that were then small—the Marin Agricultural Land Trust, the Peninsula Open Space Trust, and the Sonoma Land Trust, for example—now have six-figure operating budgets, multimillion-dollar landholdings, and regional operations. Their leaders credit conservancy grants with providing pivotal funding at early points in the organizations' histories.

Vermont has about sixteen land trusts, a number that is considered large given the state's size and population. The largest of these, the Vermont Land Trust, has grown since its establishment in 1987 into an organization with an operating budget of nearly $1 million and eighteen paid staff members. About one-fifth of the conservation projects completed by VLT—and half of the acreage involved—was funded with Vermont Housing and Conservation Trust Fund dollars.

Rhode Island's open space bonds have "unquestionably" stimulated the growth of land trusts, says the Department of Environmental Management's Judith Benedict, noting that there were only a few land trusts when the first bond was approved and now there are about fifteen. Rhode Island's program has affected the structure of land trusts as well as their number: requirements for a local match and the small set-aside for private land trusts have led to the creation of both municipal and private land trusts.

Municipal land trusts raise money through the public tax system (for example, through surcharges on real estate transfers) and are eligible to apply for grants as local governments.

Because the REAP program is so new, it is too early to discuss its effect on the growth of nonprofit land trusts in Iowa. Some new ones are being assisted by the Iowa Natural Heritage Foundation, the large statewide land trust/environmental advocacy organization that played a seminal role in developing REAP. The other nonprofit groups participating in REAP's cost-sharing program so far are established outdoor sports and hunting groups that raise money to acquire and manage wildlife habitat.

Nationwide surveys conducted by the Land Trust Alliance support the contention that land trust numbers have grown rapidly in these three states. From 1985 to 1991, Vermont, Rhode Island, and California ranked first, third, and fourth, respectively, in terms of their percentage of increase in numbers of land trusts. Certainly state grants for land trusts are not the only impetus to land trust growth. However, officials and land trust representatives in the case study states feel strongly that the grant programs have had a catalytic effect.

Observers give several reasons for the programs' influence in enlarging the land trust community: they widen the circles of people who understand what land trusts do; they provide funds for important projects, sometimes ones that help set an organization's course for the future (for example, the State Coastal Conservancy grant to the Marin Agricultural Land Trust in the early 1980s that helped the trust purchase development rights from farmers at market prices rather than be limited to charitable donations); and they confer a stamp of public approval on land trust activities. The availability of grants for projects is a stimulus for organizational action: simply by offering an incentive to work on an application—to view possible sites, confer with neighbors and officials, consider financing options, and so forth—the programs move groups and projects along.

Moreover, two state programs, Vermont's and California's, provide active assistance and support. The Vermont Housing and Conservation Trust Fund's capacity grants help nonprofit organizations (both land conservation and housing groups) to hone their project management skills. About $600,000 is set aside annually for this purpose. The California State Coastal Conservancy funds training workshops for land trust boards and publishes a widely distributed how-to publication, *The Nonprofit Primer,* to provide basic guidance to new groups about setting up and managing land trusts.

Increased Effectiveness of Land Trusts

Do larger numbers make for a stronger, more effective land trust community? Does the acceptance of public funds jeopardize land trusts' credibility and independence in the eyes of their members and donors? Does it diminish land trusts' flexibility and creativity?

The overarching answer seems to be that the larger numbers have brought increased effectiveness. Land trusts have matured in their expertise in implementing specific projects and have demonstrated their influence in achieving and retaining supportive public policies. Land trust representatives say that they are learning to work together on topics of mutual concern and learning to sort out roles and activities with less competitiveness. Some individuals and groups have become community and statewide leaders.

Some members of private groups have feared that accepting public funds would adversely affect an organization's ability to raise money privately because donors would think that their funds were no longer needed or would criticize land trusts for consorting with a public agency. This has not turned out to be a problem, at least in these case study programs. To the contrary, private sector leaders say that their work in publicly assisted projects boosts private fund-raising for their programs as a whole.

Audrey Rust of the Peninsula Open Space Trust in California reports that donors are attracted by the group's efforts to find suitable public agencies to manage projects and to improve public management. By funding four large farm preservation projects, the Vermont Housing and Conservation Trust Fund has enhanced the credibility and visibility of the Upper Valley Land Trust, according to UVLT's executive director Timothy Traver. James B. Wooley, Jr., of Pheasants Forever, reports that Iowa's REAP program "helps us achieve something that we can point to, which helps us go for higher levels of private funding, which generates more private involvement in conservation. It's a win-win situation."

At the same time, land trust officials stress the importance of diversifying funding, so that the trusts are not dependent on one public or private source, and of not expanding unduly in response to a big project. The effects of "stop and go" funding have been an issue in Vermont because budget reductions could threaten the program's ability to provide capacity grants to assist land trusts. Officials and land trust personnel talk about regionalizing and clustering small groups in order to use limited funds most effectively. (Some examples of how this has been done around the country can be found in chapter 9.) In Rhode Island, a private foundation and The Nature Conservancy have taken the initiative to act as a support system for land trusts in the wake of that state's bond moratorium.

INCREASED OPENNESS OF PUBLIC LAND PROGRAMS

These programs also have had a profound effect on state land protection methods. This is most evident in California, where the conservancy model has become a generic term for a public agency partnership with private groups that responds to the complex challenges of protecting critical land resources, be they multiple landowners, diverse uses, limited public funds, or the need for leadership and grass-roots support.

The success of the model has led not only to its being replicated in two other state conservancies in California but also to changes in other agencies that have adopted partnerships as a working style. The Wildlife Conservation Board, the acquisition arm of the state's Fish and Game Department, recently established a grant program to regularize its dealings with private groups. State park officials have come to see multitiered partnerships in large projects as the wave of the future.

The ripple effects can be seen in the other case study programs as well. The Vermont Housing and Conservation Board has become the funding source for purchasing state lands, often using private partners and virtually replacing a cumbersome state process. In Rhode Island, despite the shutdown, at least for the time being, of the state's bond program, the close relations between its Department of Environmental Management and private groups have already resulted in new partnership initiatives for greenways and trails. Although REAP is new, Iowa officials speak highly of its mandates for working with private groups and involving the public in regular statewide assessments of the program.

The nonprofit grant programs profiled in the case studies have made substantial and important contributions to land protection in their states. The people interviewed for this report—program administrators, personnel of nonprofit groups involved in the program, and legislators alike—were in surprising agreement that the programs are accomplishing important objectives and have a number of benefits and advantages.

This is not to say that the programs are trouble free or that there are no issues of concern (see the following section). Nor are these programs a panacea for solving all of a state's land conservation needs. Grant Dehart, former director of the Maryland Environmental Trust, says: "We should not be complacent. Maryland has lost about 145,000 acres of farmland and natural areas in the last five years, while all the state and private programs combined saved some 250,000 acres in 25 years." But the formalized role for nonprofit organizations is allowing them to make greater contributions to these public programs and is building stronger and more broadly supported conservation efforts while strengthening the nonprofit communities in the states—potentially laying the groundwork for even more effective partnerships in the future.

ISSUES AND SOLUTIONS

That the direct grant programs are successful does not mean that they are trouble free. This section addresses several important issues that seem to come up repeatedly in discussions with program administrators, land trusts, and/or legislators and compares ways in which the case study programs deal with them. Although officials and land trusts have grappled with some of the complex issues posed by collaborative partnerships in case-by-case preacquisition projects, the issues are somewhat different when the partnership is ongoing and is codified by statute. This discussion provides some guidance and ideas for dealing with these issues in crafting new programs. Of course, each program needs to take into account a state's particular legal, political, statutory, and constitutional circumstances.

The principal issues addressed here are the following:

- *Safeguarding the public interest.* How can the program ensure that grants go to responsible nonprofit organizations operating in the public interest?
- *Land trusts' capacity to do the job.* How do program administrators know whether the land trust has the capacity to carry out the transaction?
- *Use of public funds.* How can the state be sure that grants to nonprofit groups are spent for the intended purposes?
- *Compensation.* How much should the grant be for? What costs should it cover?
- *Stewardship by nonprofit groups.* If the land trust takes title to the property or conservation easement, how does the state ensure that the property will be protected over time and used for the intended purposes?

- *Stewardship by the state.* Alternatively, if the state holds the title, what assurances does the nonprofit group have that the property will be protected over time and used for the intended purposes?
- *Setting of the agenda.* When private groups become partners with government in implementing land conservation projects, how does this influence the program's overall design and goals?

SAFEGUARDING OF THE PUBLIC INTEREST

The case study programs use two approaches in an effort to ensure that a particular nonprofit organization is operating in the public interest and should be granted public funds:

1. *The programs generally require tax-exempt certification by the IRS.* In all the case study states except Iowa, the private organizations must be incorporated as nonprofit organizations and certified under the Internal Revenue Code as tax-exempt 501(c)(3) organizations with land conservation as a principal purpose. (In Vermont, the public purpose can also be affordable housing.) At a minimum, this process provides federal certification of charitable status and ensures that private funds raised by land trusts will be tax-exempt to the land trust and tax deductible for the donor.

   Iowa's public/private program under REAP does not require private applicants to have 501(c)(3) status. Since all land is turned over to the state, program administrators consider that this issue is not relevant and want to ensure wide access to the program.

2. *Program administrators rely on the group's reputation and their personal knowledge of it.* Government officials say that a private group's accomplishments and reputation in the community are the most important basis for judgments about the extent to which it serves the public interest. In Vermont and Rhode Island, questions about how groups are assessed are invariably answered with a reference to the small size of the state and the fact that everyone knows everyone else.

   The response of California State Coastal Conservancy officials, who deal with a larger geographic area, is nevertheless similar: "Staff know everything that's going on up and down the coast." If the group is new, board members will expect staff members to be thoroughly briefed about who the group represents, who its officers are, what it has done, and the like. Longtime conservancy board member Margaret Azevedo explains: "We look very closely at how solid nonprofits are and whether they're capable of doing what they say. There are many we know because we've worked with them. For others, we ask such questions as "How representative is this group? Can they work well with others? How effective are they in raising private money?" The single most important factor, says Azevedo, is the people who run the organization. "These shouldn't just be people who are wealthy or have well-known names. We want people who get the job done—who can get people with names to work with them."

LAND TRUSTS' CAPACITY TO DO THE JOB

A land trust may have good intentions, be recognized by the IRS, and be working hard for the public benefit—but that does not necessarily mean it has the capacity to undertake a particular transaction, especially if it is a complicated one. The case study programs use two approaches to try to ensure that land trusts do have this capacity.

First, the programs rely substantially on the organization's track record, with varying attention to documentation. Although the four profiled programs call for financial statements and other documentation of past activity, here too government officials emphasize that track record, reputation in the community, and working relationships are the most important factors in assessing land trusts' capacity to do the job. Among the four states, Vermont is most specific about requiring financial records of the applicant nonprofit group, including detailed budgets and IRS forms. (Two newer programs, Maryland's and Wisconsin's, provide for a first-stage review of nonprofit groups to qualify them to participate.) Land trusts are evaluated with respect to their skill and professionalism as well as their commitment to follow through to ensure that complicated projects are completed.

The trick is to keep the goals of partnerships in mind as paperwork requirements are laid down. "Government should not try to be land trusts, and land trusts should not try to be government," says William O'Connor, who helped craft Wisconsin's program. "We should not ask land trusts to put on a shoe that doesn't fit."

Although public officials and legislators are understandably concerned about the abilities of nonprofit organizations, experience shows that private land trusts can bring capabilities to certain tasks that are equal to or sometimes superior to those of government bodies. In Rhode Island, for example, one state official commented about the striking difference in the way towns and land trusts fill out their applications for state funds: "Towns don't have staff or time. They dump their applications and appraisals in the mail, and that's it. Land trusts drop them off in person, quickly answer our questions, and keep calling to check on their applications."

A second approach is to bolster land trusts' capabilities by offering technical assistance. Both Vermont and California provide technical assistance to help land trusts strengthen their project development and management capabilities.

The private conservation community is itself concerned about maintaining its credibility and retaining the capacity of its members to do the job regardless of whether public dollars are involved. In the case study states, The Nature Conservancy, the Trust for Public Land, the American Farmland Trust, the Audubon Society of Rhode Island, and the Iowa Natural Heritage Foundation provide some technical assistance and joint venturing for smaller or less experienced organizations. Throughout the country, the Trust for Public Land, the Land Trust Alliance, and a variety of statewide land trusts provide training on a wide range of land transaction and organizational management topics. The Land Trust Alliance provides a central source of information and referral to assistance on transactions for land trusts and has established standards and practices that LTA believes are essential for the responsible operation of a land trust.

Nevertheless, problems do arise when groups try to take on too much or grow too quickly. Also, says Grenell, some groups are ineffective because they are inflexible; they want to do things only in their way.

USE OF PUBLIC FUNDS

Perhaps one reason why program administrators seem comfortable in making judgments about land trusts' capacity is that they are careful when it comes to handing over the money. They use two safeguards:

- *Acquisition funds are released only when the transaction is ready to close.* In all four cases, grant funds to purchase a property or interests in a property are released only when the deal is ready to be closed. In this way, public oversight over the arrangement continues as requirements for appraisals, management plans, and other conditions are fulfilled. The California and Vermont programs have the flexibility to provide funds on a case-by-case basis if essential to reserve a site

while a decision to buy is deliberated. If a project is not consummated, the land trust may request that funds be applied to a different project, although such a step must be renegotiated and separately approved.
- *Nonacquisition funds are released in stages.* When the California State Coastal Conservancy and the Vermont Housing and Conservation Trust Fund award grants to nonprofit groups for purposes other than land acquisition—for example, for assessment of project feasibility, planning and resource management, or public access improvements—funds are given out in stages matched to tasks and deliverables.

COMPENSATION TO NONPROFIT GROUPS

Probably the most sensitive issue concerns the price that government pays for land acquired with the assistance of nonprofit groups and the way in which land trusts will be compensated for their related transaction costs. There are direct expenses (for surveys, appraisals, legal closing fees, maps, photographs, and other baseline documentation and, perhaps, property taxes) and indirect expenses (for staff, salaries, office costs, and the like). Some officials expect land trusts to raise these funds privately, and though many are able to do so, such funds can be difficult to raise, and land trusts often fall short. Their transactional expenses have to be met somehow.

In preacquisition projects in the past, states often have paid fair market value based on appraisals, and land trusts have tried to recoup their expenses by negotiating a price lower than fair market value with the seller. Land trusts have worked out arrangements in which the landowner receives noncash benefits that help make up for the reduced sale price—for example, with a bargain sale or a tax-deferred land exchange. Landowners may be interested in assurances about land protection or continued limited access to the property that land trusts can work out.

This general approach continues in the direct grant programs, with savings over the fair market value often used to make up a required match. Often, however, the new programs specifically provide for reimbursement of expenses. There is likely to be a system for close scrutiny of appraisals and land trust expenses in order to ensure an arrangement that is fair to land trusts and that is an appropriate use of public funds.

Specifically, the case study programs use the following approaches:

- Vermont and California are flexible about reimbursing land trusts for a broad package of transactional expenses, including property taxes, interest on loans, and administration. Says executive officer Peter Grenell, the California State Coastal Conservancy has "no problems" with the nonprofit group's recouping expenses from a "win-win" project. The conservancy will not fund membership campaigns and other institution-building activities, however. The Vermont Housing and Conservation Trust Fund's board insists on being privy to the details of a prospective sale (going into executive session if the deal is still being negotiated) but takes a flexible view of reimbursable expenses, including project development and staff time "up to a point." But costs are watched carefully: "We have a good sense of what these should be," says the board's chairman, Rob Woolmington.

- In Rhode Island, the board approves an amount equal to the appraised market value minus the percentage for the required private match, and it pays a percentage of appraisal and survey costs. If the land trust that takes title to the property can negotiate an acquisition price at less than fair market value, it is able to recoup more of its transactional expenses. If it cannot (for example, as in the Barrington Land Conservation Trust's recent acquisition of Johannis Farm in Rhode Island), it has to raise additional private funds.
- In Iowa, the state approves an amount equal to the land trust's purchase cost. It reimburses nonprofit groups for surveying, appraisal, and legal fees and some interim ownership costs, such as the cost of fencing. The land trust must cover its own staff and overhead costs.

STEWARDSHIP BY NONPROFIT GROUPS

The states have diverse ways of protecting their investment in projects involving private conservation groups. These are crafted to respond to each state's special legal situation as well as its program goals and method of financing and may vary depending on whether the land trust owns the property or holds a conservation easement on it. The case study programs use the following approaches:

- *Public ownership.* Iowa requires that all properties be owned by the state, eliminating all such concerns. The other states see nonprofit ownership as an advantage, and it is either one option or the sole option for land trust projects.
- *Reversionary interest.* Under California law, the State Coastal Conservancy holds a reversionary interest in property and conservation ease-

ments purchased with the assistance of conservancy funds. Ownership automatically and immediately transfers to the state if the land trust dissolves or if there is a violation of the agreement, unless the conservancy works out another arrangement meeting the legal specifications.

- *Conservation easement overlays.* In Rhode Island, the state holds a conservation easement on each property owned in fee by a nonprofit organization whose purchase has been financed with state funds. This does not give the state the right to take the property, as a reversionary interest does, but does give it an ongoing role and responsibility in safeguarding the property's management and use.

- *Coholding.* When the transaction involves a conservation easement held by a nonprofit group, the Vermont Housing and Conservation Board becomes a coholder with the private group. (The state's department of agriculture is also a party if the transaction involves development rights to farms.) Although both entities have the right to enforce the easement, the document's legal language specifies that one, in this case the private group, has primary responsibility.

- *Right of first refusal.* In Vermont, the Vermont Housing and Conservation Board reserves a right of first refusal to purchase the property should it be put up for sale.

- *Backup interests.* In Rhode Island, for easements purchased with open space bonds and held by nonprofit organizations, the state has the right to enforce the easement if the private group, which has primary monitoring responsibility, is not exercising stewardship responsibilities under the approved management plan.

- *Management plans.* In Vermont and Rhode Island, nonprofit groups manage conservation easements or fee title property in accordance with an approved management plan that becomes part of the legal paperwork closing the deal. In California too, nonprofit applicants are often required to develop a management plan, which is approved by the board. Separate grants to prepare the management plan may be available. Although no funds are available for stewardship per se, the conservancy may give grants to improve access, restore wetlands, and the like.

These approaches, however, are largely fail-safe mechanisms and do not obviate the need for sound stewardship programs. Both public agencies, which rarely want to exercise a reversionary interest if they have one, and land trusts need to focus more attention on the issue of stewardship, which takes on increased importance as more land is protected. "Land trusts have been busy creating organizations and doing the 'deal.' What comes after is just beginning to be addressed," says Darby Bradley, president of the Vermont Land Trust, which has launched a large private fund-raising campaign to strengthen its easement stewardship program.

STEWARDSHIP BY THE STATE

Just as state officials and legislators must answer to the public; land trusts must answer to their members and contributors. When a nonprofit project is transferred to the state, what ownership arrangement recognizes the investment that the land trust has made in the project and its concern that the land be protected in perpetuity? This somewhat sensitive subject is treated differently among states. Iowa does not accept restrictions on lands to which it takes title, but nonprofit groups retain the right of first refusal on properties they have helped the state acquire if the state decides to sell. State management of natural areas in Vermont and Rhode Island acquired with the assistance of nonprofit groups may be guided by legal arrangements to ensure retention of natural values. In Vermont, for example, the Vermont Housing and Conservation Trust Fund and the nonprofit grantee may cohold conservation easements or have other contractual understandings on lands purchased with trust fund dollars and transferred to the state's land management agency. The California State Coastal Conservancy frequently funds enhancement plans, which lay out a management path for a parcel that will be transferred to a government agency. The agency and nonprofit group are usually part of the team preparing the plan.

SETTING OF THE AGENDA

Inherent in programs involving closer collaboration between officials and nonprofit groups is the question of who sets the agenda. One hears officials welcome nonprofit collaboration but define this narrowly as assistance with carefully defined tasks, in implementing plans and projects determined by professionals. One also hears nonprofit personnel say simply: "We have to change the public agenda so that it is our agenda."

Such attitudes fall short of those needed to realize the full potential of partnerships. Certainly, some effective land conservation groups will seek opportunities to express their views about program directions and priorities. Although many land trusts focus on specific parcels, others have become involved in conserving land because of a commitment to strengthening resource protection. And officials legally responsible for administering programs will understandably want to make certain that they are making the final decision. They are wary of groups that may try to end-run their decisions by going to the state legislature or the press.

Clearly, a delicate balance needs to be maintained between public policy and specific land protection policies advanced by nonprofit groups. This is usually addressed in the statute that establishes the program but needs attention throughout the process of implementation—in rule making, in maintaining working relationships, and so on. Attention must be given to both reality and perception, within and outside of the agency.

Those involved in partnership programs emphasize the importance of close communication in a range of activities beyond specific collaborative projects—from needs assessments and strategic planning to informal discussions—so that private groups and officials will be attuned to changing opportunities and perspectives. Officials of the Sempervirens Fund, which has helped to purchase redwoods for California state parks for years, have met frequently with park staff members to exchange information about land the government is interested in and opportunities that the private group may be more attuned to. Harriet Burgess of the American Land Conservancy emphasizes that effective land trusts are attuned to the priorities of different agencies as they assess parcels that come on the market. "We don't just go shopping for land in a vacuum."

To maximize the benefits of collaboration, both public officials and private groups need to be venturesome about roles and risks while being sensitive to the special and differing constraints under which the two parties work.

At the same time, some turf issues raised by these shifting arrangements are not easily resolved. The legislative committee in Vermont that formerly approved additions to Vermont's public lands has remained a critic of the Vermont Housing and Conservation Trust Fund. And one official in a state that had just adopted a collaborative conservation program said pointedly, "This idea did not originate in this department."

In most instances, as officials and private groups work together more closely, they develop more understanding of the advantages of collaboration and the niche each occupies. "We are not responsible for the entire system," says Nan Jenks-Jay, president of the Williamstown Rural Lands Foundation in Massachusetts, "and we don't want to be."

*   *   *

This discussion has highlighted lessons and issues gleaned from case studies of pioneering state programs designed to foster successful land conservation partnerships between private groups and government agencies. Substantial progress has been made in dealing with partnership issues experienced in ad hoc preacquisition activities (discussed in chapter 1), but the difficulties certainly are not all resolved. True, the formalizing of partnerships has meant more continuity and less confusion over how nonprofit projects will be handled, including the setting of priorities and compensation for nonprofit groups. But uncertainties and tensions remain, and some new issues have arisen, such as the importance of adequate staff in both the public and private sectors to carry out partnership responsibilities and the effects of irregular funding. The big difference is that these issues are now discussed in the context of how to improve partnerships rather than in the context of whether to have partnerships at all.

ADVOCATING, DESIGNING, AND IMPLEMENTING A DIRECT GRANT PROGRAM

Programs to systematize and fund public/private partnerships for land conservation are likely to increase in number at all levels of government. Throughout the country, citizens and officials seek ways to retain and revitalize attractive natural settings, critical biological and productive resources, and close-in recreational amenities. To translate their visions into actions, especially at a time when there are pressing needs for housing, jobs, and community services, closer partnerships between government agencies and local and regional land trusts are inevitable.

This section draws lessons from the four state programs described earlier in order to help those interested in establishing a direct grant program to organize a campaign, design a program appropriate for their circumstances, and begin to implement a program that is on the road to long-term success.

RECOMMENDATIONS FOR SUCCESSFUL ADVOCACY

Advocates for new programs have an excellent source of lessons and ideas in the successful advocacy described in the case studies. Despite the diversity of the four programs analyzed, their successful enactment resulted from a strikingly similar set of circumstances. The consistent elements include a persuasive vision, a recognition of urgency, compelling examples of successful partnerships, a "homegrown" hero, and a broad-based, effective alliance.

Two additional elements that might be considered essential—an already strong land trust community and top-down leadership from the governor or a key legislator—are, of course, helpful but were not present in all cases.

A Persuasive Vision

Each of these programs was impelled by an invigorated commitment to conserve a state's special land heritage.

• In Rhode Island, there was a rallying cry for open space as subdivisions replaced fields and wetlands and blocked familiar vistas of the sea.

• In Vermont, citizens were moved by the desire to preserve the working farms and moderately priced housing that not only defined Vermont's physical beauty but also sustained its residents. This populist program drew additional support from business interests, who recognized the close link between the pastoral scenery and the vacation economy.

• California's nonprofit program was shaped by a conviction that creative citizen groups could help save the new coastal regulatory regime by developing win/win alternatives to development as usual along the coast.

• In Iowa, devastating statistics about the loss of wetlands and topsoil and an exodus of young people led to a comprehensive program, initiated by citizens' groups, to build a strong, environmentally informed statewide constituency for improved protection and management of the state's natural heritage. Iowa's participation in the North American Waterfowl Management Plan gave additional impetus to REAP, which funds wetlands acquisition.

Recognition of Urgency

In California, Vermont, and Rhode Island, rapid development and escalating prices underscored conservationists' warnings that time was short.

• Projections of population growth and development pressures led Californians—in retrospect, without exaggeration—to fear the effects of these factors on coastal preservation in the absence of firm measures to regulate and manage growth.

• In just the two years before the Vermont Housing and Conservation Trust Fund was enacted, housing prices increased by 48 percent, and 10 percent of the state's dairy farms were lost.

• Rhode Island's small size and fragile resources heightened its sense of vulnerability.

• In Iowa, a flow of information from respected public and private sources about resource losses, the low percentage of land in public ownership, and the lackluster state economy created its own sense of urgency.

Compelling Examples

In each state, examples of land conservation achieved efficiently or creatively by land trusts and other nonprofit organizations were used to illustrate the benefits of collaboration. Examples include the following:

• The pioneering limited development projects spearheaded by the Vermont Land Trust, in which small-scale development on less environmentally sensitive portions of a parcel of land helped finance protection of the remainder of the property.

• The intricate transactions orchestrated by The Nature Conservancy and the Block Island Conservancy in Rhode Island to protect coastal bluffs and farms on Block Island and increase public enjoyment of the island's spectacular resources.

• The patient efforts of the Marin Agricultural Land Trust and the Sonoma Land Trust in northern California to develop voluntary agreements with farmers, through the use of conservation easements, that would retain agriculture and restrict future development of productive lands.

• The accomplishments of the private Iowa Natural Heritage Foundation and hunting and fishing groups in identifying, protecting, and restoring sensitive wetlands and other resources by raising private funds.

• Such projects were demonstrably different from state projects.

A Homegrown Hero

In each state, observers can point to one person without whom the program would not have come into being:

• Joseph Petrillo, an attorney who crafted the California State Coastal Conservancy in a distinctive can-do mold, drawing on examples of urban development corporations and citizen empowerment.

• Robert L. Bendick, Jr., then director of Rhode Island's Department of Environmental Management, who played a pivotal role in forging the coalitions of officials, philanthropists, businesses, and private groups that supported the state's successive bonds.

• Mark C. Ackelson, associate director of the Iowa Natural Heritage Foundation, who worked for three years with a cohesive coalition of conservation constituencies to hammer out a consensus program that could be approved by the legislature.

• Richard Carbin, then president of the Vermont Land Trust, whose vision of community provided the philosophical underpinnings of the Vermont Housing and Conservation Trust Fund.

It is notable that all of these heroes were at one time or another government employees, and two of them conceptualized the partnership programs within the ranks of government. These people knew how government works but were frustrated by its limitations.

A Broad-based, Effective Alliance

In each state, a broad-based coalition of interests skillfully advanced the land protection initiative. The dominant character of the coalitions was shaped by state and local groups, sometimes with assistance by professional lobbyists and national conservation organizations. The bipartisan coalitions moved beyond environmentalists and growth management advocates to appeal to business and industry, hunting and fishing groups, historic preservation organizations, and others. Leaders kept the coalitions focused on overriding goals, setting aside often substantial differences. In Iowa and Vermont, coalition members virtually made a blood pact not to deviate from their consensus agreement. In each state, somewhat different groupings emerged:

• In California, movie stars and developers joined environmental activists concerned about pollution and toxins as well as land use.
• In Vermont, advocates for affordable housing and farm and land conservation found common cause.
• In Iowa, environmentalists, county officials, farmers, and hunting and fishing groups combined their efforts.
• In Rhode Island, political, environmental, philanthropic, labor, and business leaders allied behind the state's $65 million bond in 1987.

The states in which these programs were adopted varied widely in environmental consciousness, from California, which had a large infrastructure of environmental advocacy groups with a dizzying array of agendas, to Iowa, where a single large environmental advocacy organization was in place. The absence of organized groups does not necessarily mean that strong statewide support for an environmental initiative does not exist. There have been surprising successes in building alliances in states that have not had an earlier record of significant environmental collaboration or advocacy.

STEPS FOR DESIGN AND IMPLEMENTATION

A series of recommendations follow to guide those considering how to craft programs for their state or region. Although the recommendations are most appropriate to state direct grant programs, they have relevance to other forms of partnerships and to federal and local land conservation partnerships as well.

Advocacy

• *Develop a comprehensive conservation initiative tailored to the state's assets, opportunities, and concerns.* It is essential to go beyond the constraints of the day to develop a compelling vision that energizes the electorate and to articulate how private groups will work as partners with the government in achieving it.

• *Build coalitions that are as inclusive as possible, going beyond the traditional conservation community.* Skill, patience, commitment, and discipline are required to identify the players, to develop a legislative program and strategy, and to hold the coalition together. Successful coalitions report that professional strategists and at least a part-time staff can make a critical difference. Participants in coalitions have numerous lessons on coalition building: "Involve a broad constituency to counter the power of special interests." "Include people with access to different legislators so you'll get good feedback about what is needed to shape a winning bill." "It doesn't hurt to have access to the governor, but you can manage without it." "Don't be diverted." Although land trust leaders talk about flexibility in other aspects of partnerships, regarding coalition they consistently advise: "Strike a deal and stick with it." "Speak to the legislature with one voice."

• *Identify good examples of partnerships to educate officials and the broader public about their potential.* Despite the common use of the term, partnerships can sometimes be threatening or difficult to understand. "People need to understand that these arrangements may be unconventional, but they are not crazy or illegal," says Robert L. Bendick, Jr., former director of the Rhode Island Department of Environmental Management and now deputy commissioner of New York State's Department of Environmental Conservation. Legislators, bond counsels, agency lawyers, and governors' aides—in addition to land managers—must be in this communications loop because they often play crucial roles in determining whether a program moves on a fast or slow track or, indeed, whether it moves at all. Compelling examples of what land trusts have accomplished, ideally in the state or from states to which citizens easily relate, are essential. In fact, these partnership programs can help counter traditional arguments against accelerated government land conservation. The acquisition projects funded by the programs discussed in this chapter involve willing sellers who receive fair compensation for their land, often in negotiated agreements in which the imprint of private expertise is clear.

• *Arrange, if possible, for the coalition's activities to be advised by professional legislative strategists and assisted by a secretariat.* While retaining a strong hold on the grass roots, successful coalitions have found political astuteness a necessary ingredient of success. Some campaigns go on for years, so the advice of professionals about changing winds and emerging opportunities can determine an initiative's fate. Also, a small clerical fund can help keep the coalition informed and allied. Members can either share costs or contribute in-kind assistance.

Structure

• *Design institutional mechanisms that are responsive, flexible, and entrepreneurial and that incorporate the perspectives of both the public and private sectors. If possible, create a new entity whose mission is to encourage partnerships.* Examples include the California State Coastal Conservancy and the Vermont Housing and Conservation Board. Other institutional innovations along these lines, not discussed in detail in this chapter, include the Maryland Environmental Trust and the Trust for New Hampshire Lands. Such arrangements have successful partnerships as their overriding mission. They are structured to encourage, support, and build partnerships and to make them work efficiently and effectively. They also can increase the visibility of the program with the governor, the legislature, and the public and institutionalize the changes. The down side could be a certain isolation from workaday government and opposition from vested interests. At a minimum, however, program staffing should have as a priority the special needs of entrepreneurial programs.

• *Balance accountability and protections for public investments with flexibility to permit experimentation in roles and responsibilities.* Experience also suggests that both public and private monies have been well spent in partnership programs, with good lands acquired or protected and few scandals or problems, all things considered. The program's structure and guidelines should not try to dot every *i* and cross every *t* lest they drain the juices that lubricate creative partnerships. "The most important thing is flexibility," says William O'Connor, a Wisconsin attorney who has played a pivotal role in shaping that state's new stewardship program. Partnership must allow for testing of new relationships, evaluation, and midcourse corrections when some innovations do not work as well as was hoped.

• *Evaluate funding sources realistically, in terms of the conservation vision and the political/economic climate.* The reconnaissance of state programs for this chapter did not uncover any magic bullet for a sustained funding source, save the power of coalitions. The medley of funding sources includes general obligation and revenue bonds, dedicated taxes and fees (such as sales taxes, real estate transfer taxes, mineral severance fees, and vanity license plates), lottery funds, and general appropriations. Likely to be increasingly important in the tightening economy are such innovations as mitigation banks of various types, utility funds, special tax districts, and reimbursable loans.

In determining a funding source, consideration must be given to requirements for referenda and legislative approval and the importance of the governor's support (or at least his or her neutrality). The source of funds may have implications for the potential to involve nonprofit organizations, depending on the state, statutory language, and legal interpretation. The use of bond funds for certain private group activities, for example, has been successfully challenged in several states. Since it will undoubtedly be more difficult in many states to enact grant programs in the early 1990s than it was in the late 1980s, advocates should probably be conservative in drafting a funding strategy.

• *Land conservation partnerships should educate citizens and communities about the importance of balanced growth and measures to achieve this goal.* A nonprofit grant program may be a component of a growth management program, or it may be parallel or complementary to it. The case studies in this chapter illustrate all of these approaches and the increasingly active interest that land trust representatives are taking in educating citizens and officials about why these measures are important. Although land trusts typically have worked quietly in their communities on a parcel-by-parcel basis, involvement with public programs—such as applying for and receiving grants and engaging in advocacy for land-planning measures—helps land trusts' separate efforts add up to a sum that is larger than its components. Of course, land trusts need to evaluate how such activities may affect their ability to work effectively in their communities.

• *For the most part, there are no clear ideal structural approaches. Programs should be structured to fit the needs and circumstances of the state.* Issues that need to be addressed include the following:

Changes to the process. What is the existing decision-making process for land acquisition? What needs to be fixed, and what are the implications for a new process?

Scope and type of nonprofit involvement. Will public/private collaboration be one component of a larger, comprehensive program of resource protection, heritage conservation, and outdoor recreation, or will nonprofit organizations be able to participate in all parts of the program? How will participation of nonprofit groups be encouraged? Will they have direct or indirect access to funds? Will their requests be competitive with those of local governments and other agencies, or will they be funded by a special set-aside?

Geographic emphasis. Will grants be targeted to a specific geographic region, or will they be awarded throughout the state?

Nonprofit role in agenda setting. Will there be a strong centralized set of statewide policies and priorities, or will land trusts be encouraged to be entrepreneurial and respond to opportunities?

Composition and role of review board. What type of review board should be established to select and approve projects? Who will sit on the board, what will its powers be, and how will it respond to various interests— private groups, traditional land management agencies, the governor, state legislators, and the broader public?

Conservation techniques. Which land protection tools will be used? Will the program depend primarily on fee title acquisition or conservation easements or on some combination of the two?

Flexibility versus structure. Is the atmosphere conducive to a certain amount of risk taking and experimental activity or to structure and control? Can there be a little of both?

Compensation. Will nonprofit organizations be reimbursed for transaction-related expenses? Will grantees be expected to pass on bargain sale savings to the state and be separately reimbursed for transactional expenses? Which expenses will be covered?

Support. Will the program nurture nonprofit groups and strengthen their ability to initiate and manage projects? Will it provide training and technical assistance to land trust boards and staff? Will it have a grant program to help new land trusts get started?

Ownership. Who will hold title to nonprofit projects? Is there interest in expanding public ownership or rather in crafting a program that will minimize the public costs of land management? Can this be determined on a case-by-case basis? Observes David King, executive director of Rhode Island's Champlin Foundations, "It isn't important who manages the land, so long as there are proper restrictions on it."

Safeguards for long-term protection. What legal safeguards will ensure adequate long-term protection of state investments in properties if these are to be owned and/or managed by nonprofit organizations (in addition to localities, which more typically receive state funds for purchasing land)? What measures will safeguard nonprofit interests in land that private groups have helped the state acquire?

Initial Implementation

• *Once a program is enacted, public officials should move quickly to build a compelling track record of projects.* Special care needs to be taken in selecting initial projects because these will set the tone for the program and could make a significant difference in its continued support. Experience in Vermont and Iowa demonstrates this pointedly. Vermont was positioned to receive a large infusion of funds from a state surplus because of the wide appeal and success of its early actions. Because of the Iowa program's accomplishments, it was able to withstand a near-fatal blow when the economy slipped downward soon after the program was enacted. More recently, the Maryland Environmental Trust was able to disburse $413,000 in reimbursable loans for six compelling nonprofit projects within months after the program was granted legislative approval. The trust's quick action demonstrated the resource needs, the readiness of private groups to organize projects that leverage public funds, and ways in which the projects reinforce other state programs.

• *Land trusts should make sure there is a steady flow of good projects to the nonprofit program and should build a mechanism for networking with other private conservation groups to coordinate their activities and brain-storm their larger common agenda.* This may be a formal or an informal coalition, organized on the basis of resources or location. Although there is inevitably competition as well as collaboration, established organizations should consider ways to assist new groups and to enlarge their thinking about the planning and growth management context in which collaborative state programs operate.

• *Land trusts need to understand and, to a certain level, accept that publicly funded partnerships will probably involve additional accountability requirements.* Fears that land trusts would be co-opted by working with government or that they would face unworkable constraints have not been borne out in practice. Issues do arise that need attention, however, such as reimbursement of transactional expenses and issues not dealt with in this chapter, such as confidentiality of transactions, notification of owners, and the currency of appraisals. Participation in public programs does put a bigger burden on private groups for record-keeping, audits, and financial management, although such requirements are incumbent on all land trusts dealing in the public interest and especially those that are tackling bigger projects. But agencies must be sensitive—they should not try to fit non-profit organizations into government shoes.

• *Partnerships, though essential to meet today's land conservation challenges, are not necessarily for every deal.* The fact that partnerships work well does not mean that they work for every transaction. There will be reasons why a particular land trust's negotiation should be worked out without the baggage that comes with a publicly funded program. To retain their independence and flexibility, land trusts need to diversify funding sources and not expand unduly in response to a particular government program. Similarly, public officials should be free to move ahead without private involvement. Healthy partnerships thrive on the growing opportunities for mutual advantage and need not be forced.

Regardless of how partnerships are structured, they rest ultimately on trust, says Cynthia Pappas, a realtor on Block Island, Rhode Island, who is active in the municipal land trust there. A distinct impression is that in public programs and land trusts alike, these pioneering grant programs have attracted unusually good people who are committed to making them work.

As these programs mature, retaining this attraction will be a challenge, particularly in the climate of the 1990s. Legislators and the public are likely to demand more assurances about how scarce public dollars are being spent and to expect more than before that private groups and officials demonstrate what they have accomplished and what has and has not worked. The atmosphere that once welcomed experimentation may become more risk averse.

We can expect these early models of government and private action to evolve—they are changing even as this book is being written—with circumstances and with additional experience. More models will emerge. It is hoped that this chapter will contribute to continued experimentation and commitment to partnerships.

ACKNOWLEDGMENTS

The author is grateful to Jean Hocker, President and Executive Director of the Land Trust Alliance, and Kathy Barton, Associate Director, for their interest and guidance throughout this project and to the H. John Heinz III Charitable Trust, the Henry M. Jackson Foundation, and the David and Lucille Packard Foundation for their generous assistance. An advisory group of experts from the public and private sector provided incisive comments on the draft manuscript: Mark Ackelson, Iowa Natural Heritage Foundation; Carol Baudler, The Nature Conservancy; Robert Bendick, New York State Department of Environmental Conservation; Elizabeth Byers, Trust for Public Land; Grant Dehart, Maryland Environmental Trust; Glenn Eugster, U.S. Environmental Protection Agency; Peter Grenell, California State Coastal Conservancy; Sarah Thorne, Trust for New Hampshire Lands; William O'Connor, Wheeler, Van Sickle, & Anderson; Gus Seelig, Vermont Housing and Conservation Board; and William C. Walters, National Park Service.

NOTES

1. The President's Commission on Americans Outdoors, *Americans Outdoors: The Legacy, The Challenge* (Washington, DC: Island Press, 1987), pp. 248–50.
2. This chapter is a condensation and adaptation of a report titled "Lessons from the States: Strengthening Land Conservation Programs through Grants to Nonprofit Land Trusts," written by Phyllis Myers for the Land Trust Alliance, copyright 1992. Copies of the complete, 71-page report, which contains more detailed case studies of the California, Rhode Island, Vermont, and Iowa grant programs, may be obtained by writing to the Land Trust Alliance, Publications Department, 900 17th St., NW, Suite 410, Washington, DC 20006–2501.
3. See table 2. Two new partnership programs not included in the table were

enacted in late 1991: the Riparian Habitat Conservation Program of the Wild-life Conservation Board, a grant program in California, and the Hudson River Valley Communities Council and Conservancy in New York State.

4. Different provisions in enabling legislation and funding mechanisms can affect how and whether nonprofit organizations gain access to program funds. In Florida, the Communities Trust Program provides for participation by non-profit groups as well as local agencies. The Preservation 2000 bonds that currently provide funding for the Communities Trust Program, however, re-strict eligibility to government agencies.

5. *Report of the Governor's Commission on Vermont's Future: Guidelines for Growth,* January 1988, p. 29.

6. Vermont Housing and Conservation Board, "Interim State Agency Plan," December 26, 1990. It is interesting to note, however, that VHCB also empha-sizes its statutory authority to act swiftly in response to "unpredictable circum-stances or special opportunities," apparently to stake out a separate if parallel path to allow for timely action that is not delayed while longer-term, more comprehensive planning measures are put in place.

7. For a discussion of land trusts and land use planning, see *Exchange: The Journal of the Land Trust Alliance* 9, no. 4 (Fall 1990).

Appendix A

State Funding for Land Protection
as of November 1992*

ALABAMA

Trust Fund
- Establishes Alabama Forever Wild Land trust
- Twenty-year program with annual cap of $15 million
- Revenue source: percentage interest of offshore natural gas lease trust fund
- Natural areas, parks, and recreation areas

ALASKA

1992: $50 million to state from Exxon [criminal penalties portion of $1 billion settlement for *Exxon Valdez* oil spill]; no requirement that it be spent on land acquisition, but it is expected to be

ARIZONA

Lottery
- Arizona Heritage Fund ballot initiative passed November 1990
- $20 million/year of lottery proceeds into Fund annually; can be carried to next fiscal year
- Parks, wildlife, natural areas, endangered species

Entrance Fees
- $1 million/year
- Recreation sites (60 percent), historical sites (20 percent), natural areas (20 percent)

ARKANSAS

Real Estate Transfer Tax
- Transfer tax increase, passed 1987
- $4 million/year

* Data compiled by The Nature Conservancy.

- Natural area acquisition and stewardship, historical sites, state parks (agencies make applications to a council on a competitive basis)

CALIFORNIA

Bonds

- $776 million in bonds passed June 1988; $200 million to natural areas
- Endangered species habitat, open space, parkland, wetlands

Trust Fund

- $30 million/year for thirty years to be transferred from existing environmental funds and general fund into Habitat Conservation Fund; $20 million/year for state-listed endangered species and communities protection
- Passed on June 1990 ballot

Direct Appropriation

- $7.15 million appropriated for TNC-related acquisition projects as of September 1989
- $8.6 million for fiscal year 1990–1991 secured in Governor's budget

Cigarette Tax

- Passed an increase November 1988
- $650 million/year, of which
- $32 million/year goes to the Public Resources Accounts—half for parks and half for habitat
- $14 million/year (in addition to a variety of other existing funds) goes into Inland Wetlands Conservation Program, beginning in January 1991; program funding to total $60 million over thirty years

Vanity License Plate Fees

- Environmental protection program from personalized license plate fees since 1971
- $28 million/year to rare and endangered species habitat protection, environmental education and protection

COLORADO

Lottery

- One-half of lottery proceeds is authorized to go to state parks; however, only one-tenth is being appropriated to that purpose ($3 million/year)
- GO Colorado ballot measure to recapture lottery proceeds (up to $35 million per year by 1998)

CONNECTICUT

Bonds

- 1986–1992: $56 million total authorized by legislature for Recreation and Natural Heritage Trust; $32 million has been approved by bond commission

- Approximately 15 percent for natural areas
- Heritage Lands, open space, recreation projects

DELAWARE

Bonds

- $70 million over ten years, passed June 1990
- Companion Land Protection Act identifies priority areas for protection
- Debt service on bonds to be provided by any increase in baseline revenues from the real estate transfer tax

FLORIDA

Bonds

- $300 million passed 1986, 1987
- $3 billion over ten years; $300 million/year, passed 1990
- Documentary stamp tax provides debt service (increase passed 1991)
- CARL program (Conservation and Recreation Lands) acquisition and Save Our Rivers program
- Rivers, wildlife lands, natural areas, wetlands, coastal lands

  Counties/Cities:
  (information in parentheses is the debt service mechanism)
- Boca Raton: $12 million bond issue (.250 millage ad valorem property tax) for environmentally sensitive lands
- Brevard County: $55 million bond issue (.250 millage ad valorem property tax) for environmentally endangered lands
- Flagler County: $7.8 million bond issue (.330 millage ad valorem property tax) for recreation and water recharge
- Hillsborough County: $100 million bond issue (.250 millage ad valorem property tax) for environmentally unique and irreplaceable lands
- Indian River: $26 million bond issue (.500 millage ad valorem property tax) for environmentally sensitive lands
- Manatee County: $25 million bond issue (raised locally) for conservation lands
- Marion County: $20 million bond issue (.500 ad valorem property tax) for environmentally sensitive lands, recreation areas, and water recharge areas
- Martin County: $20 million bond issue (.625 ad valorem property tax) for open space, parks, and contingency
- Palm Beach County: $100 million bond issue (.250 millage ad valorem property tax) for native ecosystems
- Volusia County: $20 million bond issue (.250 millage ad valorem property tax) for parks, recreation, water recharge areas, and endangered lands

Documentary Stamp Tax
- Transfer tax increase, passed 1982, 1991
- $20 million to $40 million/year
- Rivers, wildlife lands, natural areas, wetlands

Ad Valorem Tax
Counties:
- Broward $75 million (.250 millage ad valorem property tax) for parks and open spaces
- Dade $90 million (two-year .750 millage ad valorem property tax) for acquisition and restoration of environmentally sensitive lands
- Lee $2.5 million annual appropriation (ad valorem property tax) for endangered uplands
- Seminole $20 million (.250 ad valorem property tax) for parks, recreation, water recharge areas, and endangered lands

Resort Tax and State Park Surcharge
Monroe County: $1 million annual appropriation for areas of critical concern— half for Key West, half for county

Local Sales Tax
Pinellas County: $68 million—$5 million for a specific rails-to-trails site— ($.01 local sales tax) for environmentally unique land and recreation sites

Vanity License Plates

GEORGIA

Bonds
- $20 million/year, passed 1992
- Funding source: Increased fees on hunting and fishing licenses and outdoor boat motors
- Natural areas and wildlife management areas

HAWAII

Revolving Fund (formerly Special Fund)
- Natural area reserve (NAR) fund established in 1987
- 1992: Legislature changed special fund to revolving fund
- Identification, establishment, and management of NARs, acquisition, Heritage Program, matching funds for natural area partnership program

Direct Appropriation (to NAR fund)
- $750,000 in 1987–1988; one-to-two (public/private) match for Heritage Program
- $.25 million in 1988–1989

- $2 million in 1989–1990
- $2 million in 1990–1991
- $2.6 million in 1991–1992 [$2.3 million, NAR system; $250,000, NAP; $50,000, Forest Stewardship]
- $2.69 million in 1992–93 [$600,000, NA partnership; $2.041 million, NAR system; $50,000, Forest stewardship]

IDAHO

ILLINOIS

Bonds

- Passed $25 million Build Illinois program in 1985
- $7.5 million to natural areas over four years; 6,000 acres purchased

Real Estate Transfer Tax

- Transfer tax increase, passed 1989
- Heritage lands, stewardship, open space
- Estimated $12 million/year after three-year phase-in period
- One-third dedicated to natural areas, two-thirds to grants to local government; one-to-one match required

Direct Appropriation

- 1986: Authorized $5 million stewardship trust fund; one-to-one match from private contributions required
- State has appropriated $1.1 million to date
- TNC is raising private match; $467,000 raised to date

INDIANA

Vanity License Plate Fees

- Indiana Heritage Trust Fund 1992
- Revenue source: $25 fee charged for an environmental license plate
- Approximate annual revenue: $2 million
- Natural areas, wildlife habitat, historical areas, parks and recreation areas

Direct Appropriation

- $10 million over five years, passed 1984; one-to-one match required
- Heritage land

IOWA

Direct Appropriation/Lottery

- Resources Enhancement and Preservation (REAP) program, passed July 1989

- $30 million/year for ten years ($20 million/year standing appropriation, $10 million/year in lottery proceeds): approximately 5 percent of total monies goes to critical areas acquisition; actual appropriations have been less
- 1990: $8 million
- 1991: $11 million
- 1992: $7 million (as of June 3, 1992, subject to change by governor or special session of legislature but will probably be in the $5 to $10 million range)
- Open space, county conservation, city parks, state land management, conservation education

Lottery

- $.5 million/year in lottery proceeds; one-to-one match required since 1986 for natural areas

KANSAS

KENTUCKY

Direct Appropriation

- $600,000 for Nature Preserves Commission appropriated in 1990
- $200,000 for Nature Preserves Commission appropriated in 1992
- $300,000 authorized for 1993 for land acquisition in Kentucky River Palisades

LOUISIANA

Bonds

- 1990: $20 million from sale of bonds to Wildlife and Natural Heritage Trust–type projects
- Bond sale proceeds probably will be spent before ever being "placed" in trust

Trust Fund

- Wildlife Habitat and Natural Heritage Trust Fund established in 1988
- Wetlands, heritage sites
- Not officially funded

MAINE

Bonds

- Passed $35 million on 1987 ballot [$12 million remains to be spent]
- Optional match; increases priority
- Open space, wildlife, parks, natural areas, endangered species habitat, exemplary natural communities

MARYLAND

Bonds

- 1992: Program Open Space (POS) authorized $10.5 million for fiscal year 1993, not appropriated

Real Estate Transfer Tax

- Transfer tax improvements passed 1987, 1989, 1990 ($39 million cap on POS until 1990)
- 1990: Consolidated Land Preservation Act passed; remove POS cap incrementally beginning in 1991. After five years, 100 percent of transfer tax will be dedicated to natural area acquisition
- Currently $1 million out of POS for natural areas; after five years, $2 million
- Parks, local parks, heritage lands

Vanity License Plates

MASSACHUSETTS

Bonds

- Passed $500 million in December 1987; roughly $250 million for land acquisition, $250 million for capital improvements to facilities
- $10 million for endangered species
- Open space, parks, agricultural lands, rivers, beaches, endangered species habitat

MICHIGAN

Trust Fund, Oil and Gas Lease Revenue

- Natural Resources Trust Fund enacted in 1976
- Funded by interest and earnings from oil and gas leases on state lands ($200 million cap)
- 1984: Constitutional dedication of $20 million of these funds annually to Michigan Strategic Fund (state venture capital); sunset in 1994
- Heritage lands, game habitat, rare and endangered species, recreation land, access

MINNESOTA

Bonds

- 1986: Enacted Reinvest in Minnesota (RIM)
  - $16 million total; $2.5 million for critical habitat; one-to-one match required
- 1987: Passed added funds—$3.5 million acquisition, $2 million match required

- 1990: Environment and Natural Resource Acquisition and Enhancement Act
  - RIM: $3.75 million; acquisition and enhancement: $1.7 million
- Agricultural lands, wetlands, scientific and natural areas, fish and wildlife habitat
- 1991: $12 million to wetlands preservation and restoration
  - RIM: $4.9 million for fish and wildlife habitat acquisition, agricultural lands; $145,000 for forest acquisition
- 1992: RIM: $2.6 million for fish and wildlife habitat acquisition, agricultural lands, scientific natural areas; $600,000 for park acquisition; $385,000 for forest acquisition

Trust Fund/Lottery

- Environment and Natural Resources Trust passed by ballot November 1988 (constitutional amendment); funded with lottery proceeds
- Constitutional amendment to protect permanently the dedication of lottery proceeds to trust passed by ballot November 1990
- Eventually to reach $1 billion corpus
- Agricultural lands, wetlands, scientific and natural areas

MISSISSIPPI

MISSOURI

Sales Tax

- One-eighth of 1 percent of the general sales tax goes to the Department of Conservation
- Hunting and fishing sites, wetlands
- One-tenth of 1 percent of the general sales tax goes to the Department of Natural Resources
- Split fifty-fifty between soil conservation and state parks (includes natural areas)
- Approximately $44 million/year total (depends on the economy)
- Ten-year sunset (1998)

MONTANA

Coal Severance Tax

- Coal severance tax passed in 1975; portion went into parks acquisition trust fund (capped in 1986)

NEBRASKA

Lottery

- Nebraska Environmental Trust Fund Act dedicates 25 percent of annual lottery proceeds for environment

- $6 million to $7 million/year
- Critical habitat areas (wetlands), acquisition and easements of areas critical to rare or endangered species

Direct Appropriation

- Fiscal years 1990–1992: appropriation of $500,000 for Sandhills Lakes; river and stream access

Cigarette Tax

- $1 million/year
- Parks

State Habitat Stamp

- $500,000 to $700,000 annually for state wildlife management areas

NEVADA

Bonds

- Nevada Parks and Wildlife Bond Act referendum passed by ballot November 1990
- $47.2 million for recreation, parks, and protection of wetlands

NEW HAMPSHIRE

Direct Appropriation

- $20 million appropriated in 1987
- $18 million appropriated in 1989
- Open space, forests, natural areas

NEW JERSEY

Bonds

- Green Acres bonds: $60 million in 1961; $80 million in 1971; $200 million in 1974; $100 million in 1978; $300 million in 1989; Green Trust—$52 million in 1983; $35 million (localities only) in 1987; state acquisition monies through direct appropriation
- Shore protection, open space, parks, forests, natural areas
- Green Acres, Clean Water, Farmland & Historic Preservation Bond Act passed by ballot November 1992
- $345 million for open space acquisition and matching grants for nonprofit organizations

NEW MEXICO

Bonds

- $400,000 passed by legislation and ballot in 1988, combined with severance tax

- Threatened and endangered species, natural areas

Severance Tax

- 1988: $500,000 in severance tax proceeds, passed by legislature and ballot in 1988, combined with bonds
- 1992: $200,000 in severance taxes
- Threatened and endangered species, natural areas

NEW YORK

Bonds

- $75 million, passed in 1960
- $25 million, passed in 1962
- $175 million, passed in 1972
- $250 million, passed in 1986
- Broad criteria, natural areas
  Counties/Cities:
- East Hampton: $5 million, passed in 1989
- Nassau County: $3.5 million, passed in 1988
- Southampton: $8 million, passed in 1986
- Southold: $2 million, passed in 1987
- Suffolk County:
  - 1986: $90 million total; $30 million for heritage sites
  - 1987: Voters approved a referendum authorizing an extension of an existing ¼-cent county sales tax, dedicating the sales tax revenues to the county's open space/aquifer protection program
  - 1988: Voters approved an amendment to this program authorizing Suffolk County to issue $300 million in bonds for land acquisition. A portion of the ¼-cent sales tax provides the revenue stream for debt service

NORTH CAROLINA

Trust Fund

- Recreation and Natural Heritage Trust Fund (RNHTF)
- Heritage, wildlife lands

Direct Appropriation
1987–1988: $275,000

Vanity License Plate Fees

- 1989: Increase of $10 to RNHTF [estimated $1.5 million/year]
- 1990: $1.5 million to RNHTF
- 1991: $1.7 million to RNHTF

Real Estate Transfer Fee

- Passed an increase in 1991; estimated yield $1.5 to $2 million/year for RNHTF

NORTH DAKOTA

OHIO

OKLAHOMA

OREGON

PENNSYLVANIA

Bonds

- Chester County: $50 million, passed in 1989
- Open space, natural areas, county parks

Direct Appropriation

- $6 million for counties/municipalities program, funded in 1988 for two years
- $3 million for counties/municipalities program, funded in 1990 for one year
- Open space, natural areas, county parks

RHODE ISLAND

Bonds

- $8 million, passed in 1986
- $65 million, passed by legislature and ballot in 1987
- $74.5 million, passed by legislature and ballot in 1989; approximately $25 million for open space, natural areas, parks
- Parks, open space, natural areas

Real Estate Transfer Tax (Block Island)

- Transfer tax established 1986
- $300,000 to $500,000/year
- Open space, agricultural, and shorefront land; access, recreation, conservation

SOUTH CAROLINA

Real Estate Transfer Tax

- Transfer tax increase enacted 1986 ($1.10 per $500)
- $2.2 million/year goes into Heritage Trust Fund
- Heritage lands, wildlife habitat

Income Tax Checkoff for Wildlife

- $200,000/year goes into Heritage Trust Fund

SOUTH DAKOTA

TENNESSEE

Real Estate Transfer Tax

- Transfer tax increase enacted 1986
- $2.5 million to $3 million/year
- Wetlands
- Transfer tax increase passed 1991
- $4 million/year
- State parks and natural area acquisition; local parks acquisition and improvements; programs to control agricultural water pollution

TEXAS

Cigarette Tax

- 2-cent tax on each pack of cigarettes since 1979
- Proceeds into Local Parks, Recreation, and Open Space Fund
- 40 percent for park acquisition (approximately $15 million), 60 percent to park development and operations (approximately $22.5 million)

UTAH

VERMONT

Direct Appropriation

- 1988: $450,000 to Kingsland Bay Project, $920,000 to Victory Bog

Trust Fund/Direct Appropriation

- 1987: Appropriated $3 million to Housing and Conservation Trust Fund
- 1988: Appropriated $20 million to Housing and Conservation Trust Fund
- 50 percent for open space, agricultural lands, historic sites, natural areas; 50 percent for housing

Trust Fund/Real Estate Transfer Tax

- 1988: Transfer tax increase passed (0.25 percent)
- $3 million into Housing and Conservation Trust Fund
- (1992: transfer tax still in effect, raising $1 million to $2 million/year)

Trust Fund/Bonds

- 1990: Passed authorization of $7.25 million in new bonding for Housing and Conservation Trust Fund in June 1990; with $3 million rescission to balance general fund budget, net gain of $4.25 million
- Fund will have approximately $10 million to spend in fiscal year 1991, split evenly between housing and conservation

- 1992: passed authorization for $11.65 million in new bonding for Housing and Conservation Trust Fund.

VIRGINIA

Direct Appropriation/Lottery

- Appropriated $1.5 million of lottery monies from general fund in 1988, 1989; one-to-three private/public match

Bonds

- 1992: $95 million
- parks, recreational areas, natural areas, including approximately $11.5 million for heritage sites

Specialty Plates

- Revenue source: $25 charged per year for environmental license plate (effective December 1)
- $15 from each sale will go to Chesapeake Bay Restoration Fund

WASHINGTON

Real Estate Transfer Tax

- Transfer tax enacted 1987 (0.05 percent); sunset in 1989
- $18 million total over two years
- Heritage lands, four conservation areas

Direct Appropriation

- 1987: Appropriated $4 million for heritage sites; three-to-one public/private match required
- 1989: Appropriated $1.5 million (natural areas acquisition) subject to 50 percent TNC match, $60,000 (needs assessment for bond act for land acquisition), $70 million (school trust lands dedication)
- 1990: Appropriated $53 million in 1990 for Washington Wildlife and Recreation Program, $80 million for school trust land transfer to state conservation areas, and $35,000 for study of stewardship needs on state lands
- 1991: Appropriated $60 million for Washington Wildlife and Recreation Coalition, $6 million for heritage sites, $20 million for critical wildlife sites including some heritage sites, $160,000 for Heritage staff positions
- 1992: State lands stewardship bill passed, with new account created for potential new tax funds for managing important sites

WEST VIRGINIA

WISCONSIN

Bonds

- $.5 million/year passed 1986; one-to-one match required (heritage sites only)
- $250 million over ten years passed July 1989
- Heritage lands, parks, open space, rivers

WYOMING

Appendix B

Selected Private Assistance Organizations

The following is a selected list of nonprofit organizations involved in one or more aspects of land conservation.

NATIONAL LAND PRESERVATION ORGANIZATIONS

American Farmland Trust
1920 N St., NW, Suite 400
Washington, DC 20036

The Conservation Fund
1800 N. Kent St.
Arlington, VA 22209

Ducks Unlimited
One Waterfowl Way
Long Grove, IL 60047

National Audubon Society
950 3rd Ave.
New York, NY 10022

National Trust for Historic Preservation
1705 Massachusetts Ave., NW
Washington, DC 20036

The Nature Conservancy
1815 N. Lynn St.
Arlington, VA 22209

Trust for Public Land
116 New Montgomery St.
San Francisco, CA 94105

NATIONAL TECHNICAL ASSISTANCE ORGANIZATIONS AND RESOURCES

The American Forestry Association
P.O. Box 2000
Washington, DC 20013

American Planning Association
Publications Office
1313 E. 60th St.
Chicago, IL 60637

American Rivers
801 Pennsylvania Ave., SE, Suite 303
Washington, DC 20003

Land Trust Alliance
900 17th St., NW, Suite 410
Washington, DC 20006

National Association of Conservation Districts
509 Capital Ct., NE
Washington, DC 20002

Rails-to-Trails Conservancy
1400 16th St., NW
Washington, DC 20036

River Network
P.O. Box 8787
Portland, OR 97207

World Wildlife Fund
(now incorporates The Conservation
   Foundation)
1250 24th St., NW
Washington, DC 20037

For a complete list of environmental organizations, see "The Conservation Direc-tory," published by the National Wildlife Federation, 1400 16th St., NW, Wash-ington, DC 20036. For a good selective list of land conservation groups and agencies, see Samuel N. Stokes et al., *Saving America's Countryside: A Guide to Rural Conservation* (Baltimore, MD: Johns Hopkins University Press, 1989).

Glossary

agricultural preservation restriction: The term generally used for conservation easements or conservation restrictions (see definition) used to protect farmland. This more descriptive, separate term has developed because of specific programs set up to protect farmland through the so-called "purchase of development rights" from farmers.

assignment: A transfer by legal document of certain legal rights to another entity. Thus if a nonprofit organization holds an option to purchase a property, it may, if permitted under the terms of the purchase option or operable law, "assign" those rights to a government agency.

balloon payment: A large, final payment on a promissory note after one or a series of smaller payments. Typically, such an arrangement allows a land purchaser to buy and enjoy the use of the land for a long period at reasonable cost and then to either refinance or resell the land to pay off the balloon on his or her mortgage. As described in chapter 10, Howard County, Maryland, has adopted this technique to preserve farmland. Balloon payments to farmers are timed to coincide with the maturing of thirty-year bonds.

*bargain sale: A sale for less than fair market value. The term is usually used in the context of the federal tax code, under which a bargain sale, if supported by an appraisal accepted by the IRS, qualifies the seller for a charitable deduction equal to the difference between the appraisal and the actual sale price paid by a qualified nonprofit organization or public agency.

*basis: A term used in tax accounting to describe that portion of the taxpayer's investment in property which is not subject to taxation upon resale. Typically, a taxpayer's basis in property is the original cost of the property plus any eligible expenses, for example, capital improvements.

benefit assessment district: A geographically based method of allocating the cost of a public improvement—such as a school, a sewer, or a park—among those who benefit from the improvement. The homeowners or landowners or other

---

* The terms marked by asterisks are terms of art used in the U.S. Internal Revenue Code. For more precise definitions, readers are urged to consult the code itself.

beneficiaries within the area that are defined as receiving the benefit are each assessed a share of the cost of the improvement according to a formula designed to reflect their proportional benefit.

bridge financing: A loan designed to fill a short-term gap in funding. While traditionally the term describes a short-term loan prior to a longer-term one, an example of bridge financing can be when a nonprofit organization purchases land for a government agency pending that agency's ability to finance the purchase itself.

capital bonds: Bonds used for capital improvement projects, such as highways, school buildings, or land acquisition, rather than for operating costs or other frequently recurring costs.

challenge grant: A grant of funds designed to encourage additional fund-raising by the organization receiving the grant.

coholder; coholding: A term often used in the context of conservation easements (see definition). A conservation easement must be "held" by an agency or organization that is given the right to enforce the restrictions set forth in the conservation easement. This right can be, and often is, shared by two or more agencies or organizations with the expectation that in the future one of them may be in a stronger legal, financial, or political position to pursue such enforcement. In order to avoid interorganizational confusion, is it usually advisable to specify the order in which the holders may assert their enforcement rights. The coholders who are not first in line are said to have "backup" enforcement rights.

condemnation: The legal acquisition of property by government. While the forfeit of their property is involuntary, just compensation must be paid to the private owners.

conservation buyer: The name often given to a private individual brought into a land conservation partnership who wishes to purchase and own a portion of the land but is willing to comply with conservation restrictions on that land. When such private ownership is compatible with the goal of the conservation project, conservation buyers can play an important funding and management role. Conservation buyers are brought into projects through so-called "conservation brokerage."

conservation easement: See easement.

COPs, or certificates of participation: A financing mechanism in which investors put up the cash to pay for the purchase of a capital improvement—a building or, increasingly, a park—by an intermediary. Investors are paid back over time from the rents the government pays the intermediary through a lease-purchase agreement (see definition). The payments are usually tax-exempt to the investors, and the government benefits from the use of the asset without having to increase its general debt, since the payments under the lease are subject to general appropriation.

development exaction and impact fees: Arrangements through which land developers are required to compensate for any consequences of their development or pay for amenities to enhance their development. In the land conservation area, such arrangements can range from a mandatory dedication of open space on the site of the development to the payment of fees, which are often pooled to purchase sizable tracts of parkland, beach, or other recreational space.

development rights value: The value of the right to develop a piece of property for its most financially lucrative purpose or "highest and best" use as permitted under current planning and zoning regulations. Thus in the context of a program that purchases development rights, for example, an agricultural preservation program, the payment to the farmer for giving up his or her development rights is determined by the difference between the development value of the land minus the residual value of uses, such as farming, permitted under the agricultural preservation restriction.

documentary tax: The tax imposed on land transactions collected at the registry of deeds, or other record office, when the documents are entered into permanent record books. The payment of the required tax is often represented by so-called documentary stamps affixed to the deed. Since real estate sales reflect development pressures, a number of jurisdictions have dedicated a portion of this tax to land conservation.

easement; conservation easement; conservation restriction: In this book, the term "easement" is almost always used in the context of a "conservation easement." Yet there are many different types of easements. The most familiar are the power line or right-of-way easements, under which a power company acquires the right to cross a landowner's property with transmission equipment or a property owner is given the right to cross a neighboring property to gain access to a road. Conservation easements are perhaps better termed conservation "restrictions," their legal name in some states, since conservation easements place restrictions on land rather than confer affirmative rights. Each conservation easement document pertaining to a particular piece of land states what those restrictions are. The document may prohibit all or only some building and may include restrictions on alterations of vegetation and water courses, and other stipulations designed to preserve the property's natural values. In order for a conservation easement to be recognized under federal and, typically, state law, it must give the right to enforce its restrictions to a qualified entity, often a government agency or a private charitable conservation organization. The easement may also give the right to use or manage the property to that third party. Although in most states conservation easements are now of perpetual duration, the easement document or state law may provide for its modification. Only some donated (or bargain-sold) conservation easements are eligible for treatment as tax deductible gifts under the federal tax code. See Selected Readings for more information on conservation easements.

eminent domain: A legal term for condemnation.

fee; fee interest; fee title: The legal terms used to describe the underlying ownership interest in property, as distinguished from partial or "less than fee" interests in property such as a leasehold, a conservation easement, or water or mineral rights.

full faith and credit: See general obligation bonds.

general obligation bonds: Bonds backed by the "full faith and credit" or general taxing authority and other financial resources of the issuing government, as opposed to revenue bonds, which are typically backed only by a defined revenue stream, such as toll receipts for highway construction.

greenbelt: Usually an area of protected open space around a city or town, or one that separates one built-up area from another.

greenway: An increasingly popular term used to describe linked, open, usually linear spaces that generally consist of a trail corridor or a river protection zone.

impact fees: See development exaction.

installment sales: The sale of land or other property for which payment is made over a period of months or years instead of in a lump sum. The payment terms are often set out in a "promissory note" and payment of the note is "secured" by a mortgage on the land. The failure of the buyer to make one or more installment payments can cause the seller to "foreclose" on the mortgage and take the land back.

lease purchase: A mechanism for buying land in which the would-be buyer leases the land and also enters into an agreement to purchase it. If the purchase goes forward under the agreement, usually all or a portion of the lease payments are credited to the ultimate purchase price. This arrangement is similar to an installment sale, but the main difference is that under a lease purchase the buyer doesn't have an ownership interest until he or she makes the last lease payment.

leverage: A term used to describe the positive effect of putting up a portion of a parcel's purchase price, or of negotiating a land gift, in attracting other funds or gifts to a land acquisition project or campaign.

memorandum of understanding: A written agreement setting forth the specific terms to which the memorandum's signatories accede. Unless it is drawn up as and meets the legal requirements of a contract, such an agreement is not specifically enforceable by the partners, but it conveys a moral obligation and clarifies the partners' respective responsibilities and expectations.

mitigation banks, funds, payments: Mitigation banks for land conservation can be either banks of money or banks of land. Where money is involved, the mitigation bank or fund is customarily made up of monetary exactions ("mitigation payments") imposed on developers or, in some cases, polluters, to compensate for their actions. The monies are often used to buy land to offset the development or pollution of land or land-related natural resources. A mitigation land bank involves a third party that purchases, assembles, and then "banks" extensive tracts of land to offset development. Resale by the intermediary of all or a portion of the land to the designated government authority can be made as money in the mitigation fund accumulates. The involvement of a third party facilitates the preservation of significant land unconstrained by the balance in the mitigation fund at any particular time.

municipal land trust: A land trust created under the authority of a town government that is therefore entitled to the benefits and restricted by limitations of government agencies. For example, a municipal land trust might be eligible for grants from government agencies that would not be available to a private land trust, but it also might be subject to financial limitations in terms of borrowing money against future income.

Natural Heritage Program or Inventory: A nationwide, computerized system of inventorying a state's rare plants, animals, and plant communities originally developed by The Nature Conservancy. Such systems track the status of threatened habitats and help in setting acquisition priorities for both public and private entities.

option: A legal agreement in which a seller of land gives a potential buyer the exclusive right to buy land at a set price for a set period of time.

option consideration: The amount of money a land buyer pays a land seller for an option. Option consideration is often nonrefundable should the buyer fail to buy the land, but is deducted from the agreed purchase price if the buyer does go forward with the purchase.

option exercise: A land buyer "exercises" his or her option to buy land when he or she provides written notification of intent to consummate the purchase. The exercise of an option converts it into a purchase and sale contract binding on both parties.

preacquisition: The purchasing of land by one entity in anticipation of its resale to another entity. As detailed extensively in this book, government agencies that wish to purchase land may not be able to do so directly in many cases, and therefore may ask a private organization to "preacquire" the land for them.

*private activity bond: A bond issued for a public purpose by a nongovernment entity, which is hence given favorable treatment under the Internal Revenue Code.

purchase money mortgage: An arrangement through which a land seller receives only a portion of the sale price in cash and accepts a promissory note for the balance that stipulates a schedule of payments for the buyer. The seller secures payment on the note by retaining a mortgage on the land.

reserved rights: In conveying property to another party, one party may reserve specific rights in the deed of transfer. In a private transaction, for example, a landowner might reserve the right to fish on his former property, or in a transfer from a nonprofit organization to a government agency, the nonprofit might reserve the right to manage the property's rare plant and animal species. Landowners seeking tax advantages from gifts or bargain sales of land should note that reservations of rights generally disqualify them from receiving favorable tax treatment.

revenue bonds: See general obligation bonds.

reversionary interest: An interest in land retained, usually by a clause in the deed, when the land is transferred to another owner. The reverter clause stipulates terms under which the land reverts to a named entity, usually a previous landowner. Such a reverter usually is triggered by the current landowner's failure to comply with a condition of the deed, such as a restriction against building on the land. Reverters may be "automatic" or "nonautomatic," the latter referring to a case in which the holder of the reverter may decline to take the property back.

revolving loan fund: A land acquisition fund that provides loans to buy land with the understanding that the loan will be repaid from a government grant, a private fund-raising effort, or a combination of the two. The loaned money can then "revolve" into a new project. Both nonprofit organizations and public agencies administer such loan funds.

right of first refusal: A legal agreement to notify a person or organization of a landowner's intention to sell property. That person or organization is then given a certain period of time (usually thirty to ninety days) to indicate whether they wish to buy the property under the terms specified. The holder of a right of first refusal is often required to match an outside offer, but there are some rights of first refusal that stipulate other ways of arriving at a purchase price, for example, through an appraisal process.

shared equity agreement: An arrangement in which a land trust or an affordable housing organization co-owns a parcel of land (often a farm) or a house with the landowner or homeowner. This mechanism allows the nonprofit organization to assist the landowner in preserving the farm or purchasing the low-cost house. The terms of the agreement typically specify that the nonprofit organization can buy out the landowner should he or she ever decide to sell, and thereby can ensure that a farm is sold to another farmer or that a house is sold to another low-income person or family. In addition, since the nonprofit organization owns a (variable) percentage of the fee, it shares in any appreciation of the property and thus can help keep the property's price affordable.

simultaneous closings: A misnomer, since it is physically impossible to "close" or consummate the sale of a piece of property more than once at the exact same time. A more descriptive term is "back-to-back" closings to describe what actually takes place in a so-called simultaneous closing: Party A sells parcel X to party B, who turns around and sells the same parcel X to party C. Party B is often a nonprofit organization and party C is usually a government agency. The "closing" with party B takes place in order to accomplish some objective that party A and party C could not accomplish by closing directly with each other, for example, a placement of restrictions enforceable by B in the deed to C, or a loan or gift of money from B that B wishes to memoralize by being in the chain of title.

transfer of development rights (TDRs) or transfer of development credits: Such schemes, which have many different variations and names, generally involve channeling future development from one place to another. This is done by designating a transferor zone, or a geographical area that should remain an open space, a farmland, an historic district, or the like; and a transferee zone, or an area that can support a higher density of development. Landowners in the transferor or preservation zone are compensated for restrictions on developing their land by receiving rights or credits that then can be sold to landowners in the transferee or development zone, allowing them to make use of the higher density allowance.

transfer tax: A tax on the transfer of land, and an increasingly popular mechanism for financing land conservation. Such a tax may be separate from and in addition to the documentary tax.

zero-coupon bonds: Bonds that do not pay regular interest, the lump sum of which is payable at the redemption of the bond.

*501 (c)(3) organization: An organization qualifying, under section 501 (c)(3) of the Internal Revenue Code, as a publicly supported charity, donations to which are eligible for the highest levels of tax deduction available.

NOTE: A particularly good glossary of land conservation terminology is found in Michael A. Mantell, Stephen F. Harper, and Luther Propst, *Creating Successful Communities: A Guidebook to Growth Management Strategies* (Washington, DC: Island Press, 1990).

Selected Readings

The following is a brief and somewhat idiosyncratic list of books having to do with land conservation. A few books that discuss regulatory approaches are included, but for a much more detailed bibliography covering the entire field of land planning, growth management, and resource conservation (including historical preservation), see Stokes et al., cited in this section.

Arthur Anderson & Company. *Charitable Giving: A Tax Guide for Individual Donors*. (Order from Arthur, Anderson & Company, One International Pl., Boston, MA 02110. Attn.: Anne Marie Rogers.)

Brenneman, Russell L., and Sarah M. Bates, eds. *Land-Saving Action: A Written Symposium by Twenty-Nine Experts on Private Land Conservation in the 1980s*. Washington, DC: Island Press, 1984.

Brown, Warren L., and Michael Auer. *New Tools for Land Protection: An Introductory Handbook*. Washington, DC: U.S. Department of the Interior, Office of the Assistant Secretary for Fish and Wildlife and Parks, 1982.

Burlington Community Land Trust and Vermont Land Trust. *A Citizen's Guide to Conserving Land and Creating Affordable Housing*. Burlington, VT: Burlington Community Land Trust, 1990. (Order from Burlington Community Land Trust, P.O. Box 523, Burlington, VT 05402.)

Coyle, Kevin J., and Christopher N. Brown. *Handbook of State River Conservation Programs*. Washington, DC: U.S. Department of the Interior, National Park Service, July, 1992 (draft).

Diehl, Janet, and Thomas S. Barrett. *The Conservation Easement Handbook: Managing Land Conservation and Historic Preservation Easement Programs*. Trust for Public Land and Land Trust Exchange, 1988. (Order from Land Trust Alliance, 900 17th St., NW, Suite 410, Washington, DC 20006.)

Hoose, Phillip M. *Building an Ark: Tools for the Preservation of Natural Diversity Through Land Protection*. Washington, DC: Island Press, 1981 (currently out of print).

Institute for Community Economics. *The Community Land Trust Handbook*. Emmaus, PA: Rodale Press, 1982. (Order from Institute for Community Economics, 151 Montague City Rd., Greenfield, MA 01301.)

Johnson, Andrew L., and Michael G. Clarke. *A Handbook for the Landowner: The Use and Protection of Privately Held Natural Lands*. Philadelphia, PA: Natural Lands Trust, 1982. (Order from Natural Land Trust, 1616 Walnut St., Suite 812, Philadelphia, PA 19103.)

Kusler, Jon A. *Regulating Sensitive Lands*. Washington, DC: Environmental Law Institute, 1980.

Land Conservation Law Institute. *The Back Forty: The Newsletter of Land Conservation Law*. Published ten times a year. (For subscription information, write to Land Trust Alliance, 900 17th St., NW, Suite 410, Washington, DC 20006.)

Land Trust Alliance. *Exchange: The Journal of the Land Trust Alliance*. Published four times a year. (For subscription information, write to Land Trust Alliance, 900 17th St., NW, Suite 410, Washington, DC 20006.)

Land Trust Alliance. *Starting a Land Trust: A Guide to Forming a Land Conservation Organization in Your Community*. Washington, DC: Land Trust Alliance, 1990. (Order from Land Trust Alliance, 900 17th St., NW, Suite 410, Washington, DC 20006.)

Lemire, Robert A. *Creative Land Development: Bridge to the Future*. Lincoln, MA: Massachusetts Audubon Society, 1986. (Order from Massachusetts Audubon Society, South Great Rd., Lincoln, MA 01773.)

Libby, James M., Jr. "Vermont Housing and Conservation Trust Fund: A Unique Approach to Developing Affordable Housing." *Clearinghouse Review* (February 1990): 1275–1284. (Published by the National Clearinghouse for Legal Services.)

Little, Charles E. *Greenways for America*. Baltimore, MD: Johns Hopkins University Press, 1990.

Mantell, Michael A., ed. *Managing National Park System Resources: A Handbook on Legal Duties, Opportunities, and Tools*. Washington, DC: The Conservation Foundation (now World Wildlife Fund), 1990.

Mantell, Michael A., Stephen F. Harper, and Luther Propst. *Creating Successful Communities: A Guidebook to Growth Management Strategies*. Washington, DC: Island Press, 1990.

Montana Land Reliance and Land Trust Exchange. *Private Options: Tools and Concepts for Land Conservation*. Washington, DC: Island Press, 1982.

The President's Commission on Americans Outdoors. *Americans Outdoors: The Legacy, The Challenge*. Washington, DC: Island Press, 1987.

Schnidman, Frank, Michael Smiley, and Eric G. Woodbury. *Retention of Land for Agriculture: Policy, Practice and Potential in New England*. Cambridge, MA: Lincoln Institute of Land Policy, 1990.

Simon, David, ed. *Our Common Lands: Defending the National Parks*. Washington, DC: Island Press, 1988.

Small, Stephen J. *Preserving Family Lands: A Landowner's Introduction to Tax Issues and Other Considerations*. Boston, MA: Powers & Hall Professional Corporation, 1988. (Order from Powers & Hall Professional Corporation, 100 Franklin St., Boston, MA 02110.)

Stokes, Samuel N., A. Elizabeth Watson, and contributing authors Genevieve P. Keller and J. Timothy Keller for the National Trust for Historic Preservation. *Saving America's Countryside: A Guide to Rural Conservation*. Baltimore, MD: Johns Hopkins University Press, 1989.

U.S. Department of the Interior, National Park Service. "Easements." Chap. 8 in *Planning Process Guidelines*. National Park Service Document no. NPS-2. Washington, DC: U.S. Department of the Interior, 1986.

Ward, Wesley T., ed. *Land Conservation Methods and Their Tax Advantages: A Guide for Massachusetts Landowners*. Essex, MA: Essex County Greenbelt Association and Trustees of Reservations, 1987. (Order from Essex County Greenbelt Association, 82 Eastern Ave., Essex, MA 01929.)

Yaro, Robert D., Randall G. Arendt, Harry L. Dodson, Elizabeth A. Brabec. *Dealing with Change in the Connecticut River Valley: A Design Manual for Conservation and Development*. Cambridge, MA: Lincoln Institute of Land Policy, 1990.

Acknowledgments

I would like to extend my sincere gratitude to all those who encouraged and helped me with this book. First of all, thank you to the authors, who gave freely of their time, with no remuneration, in order to share their experience with others. Next I wish to thank The Nature Conservancy, both the institution for supporting my work on the book and especially the individuals there who believed in me and the project: Dennis Wolkoff, Philip Tabas, Bruce Runnels, Mike Dennis, and Bill Weeks. Many other Nature Conservancy staff all over the country helped with facts and case histories and have my deep appreciation for interrupting their hectic land-saving work.

There are also many people in other institutions who assisted along the way. While many of those are acknowledged at the end of chapter 9, I would like to single out Jean Hocker and Kathy Barton of the Land Trust Alliance, who, busy as they are, were never too busy to help; and Edo Potter, Keith Lewis, and Bob Bendick, visionary individuals who were my original inspiration and models for conservation partnerships. I extend my thanks also to the Lincoln Institute of Land Policy, which sponsored this book, and especially to Ben Chinitz, who saw merit in the project at the outset; to Deanne Moroni and her support staff for seemingly endless word-processing; to Alice Ingerson for help with publication; and to Marie Foss and Mary Beth Martin for keeping up my spirits.

Finally, I became interested in conservation because of my parents, and I most want to thank my mother, whose tireless and devoted help with my children made this book and my other conservation work possible.

Index

Acadia National Park, 107, 115, 207, 212
Ace Basin, South Carolina, 34, 88–89,
    95–100
Ackelson, Mark C., 305
Adirondack Forest Preserve, 161, 169
Adirondack Mountain Club, 119
Adirondack Park, 149, 161–62, 164
Advance funding, 18–19
Agricultural land, *see* Farmland
Agricultural preservation restrictions, 47
Agricultural Resources Conservation
    Program, 102
Alabama, 10
Alabama Forever Wild Land Trust, 10
Alachua Conservation Trust (ACT), 20,
    197–98, 201, 204, 205
Alaska, 239
Albuquerque, New Mexico, 64, 226
Allegheny Highlands Trial, 132–33
American Battlefield Protection Plan, 114
American Farmland Trust, 43–60, 296
    farmers remaining on conserved land,
        46
    founding of, 44
    the future, lessons for the, 56–58
    mission of, 44
    partnerships in practice, 46–58
    role of government in preserving
        farmland, 44–45
    role of private partners in preserving
        farmland, 45–46
    sustainable agriculture and, 6, 56–58,
        59
    Tenth Annual Report, 56
American Land Conservancy, 301
American Rivers, Inc., 143
America's Industrial Heritage Project, 120
Appalachian Trail, 113–14, 117–18

Appalachian Trail Conference, 118
Archaeological Conservancy, 108, 109,
    112
Arizona, 10, 225, 235–36
Arizona Heritage Fund, 235, 245
Army Corps of Engineers, 95, 142
Assembling of parcels, 64
Association of State Floodplain Managers,
    143
AT&T, 236
Auctions, 20–21, 80–81
Audubon Society of Rhode Island, 296
Austin, Texas, 80
Azevedo, Margaret, 278, 295

Balcones canyon lands, Texas, 41
Baltimore, Maryland, 80
Banking of land, 80
Bargain sales, 24, 180, 181, 182, 235,
    236
Barrington Land Conservation Trust, 200–
    201, 298
Bear River Project, Wyoming, 137, 138
Bendick, Robert L., Jr., 11, 149–71, 304–
    305, 307
Benedict, Judith, 289
Benefit assessment districts, 247–48
Bergen County, New Jersey, 79–80
Berkshire County Land Trust and
    Conservation Fund (BCLTCF), 203
Biesecker Tallgrass Prairie Preserve, 29
Big Sur Land Trust (BSLT), 207–208
Bioreserve Program, *see* Nature
    Conservancy, Bioreserve Program
Blaine, Edie, 159
Block Island, Rhode Island, 157–60,
    163–67, 209, 241, 242
Block Island Conservancy, 158, 165, 304

Block Island Land Trust, 204, 242
Blue Sky Ranch, California, 68
Bonds, long-term, 62, 64, 154, 208, 211,
    224, 225–26, 228–32, 286
  general obligation, 228–29
  private activity, 230–32
  revenue, 229–30
Bonneville Power Authority, 251
Boston, Massachusetts, 72
Boston Redevelopment Authority, 72
Boston Urban Gardens, 72
Boy Scouts of America, 95
Bradley, Darby, 300
Brandywine Conservancy, 216–17
Brevard County, Florida, 68–69
Brookside Farm, Vermont, 181–82
Brown, Chris, 84
Brown, Warren, 84, 104–28
Bureau of Land Management, 90, 106
Bureau of Land Reclamation, 84
Burgess, Harriet, 301

Cache/Lower White Rivers Joint Venture,
    91
Cache River, Illinois, 33–34, 88, 92, 93–
    95
California, 48, 88, 108, 228, 243
  benefit districts, 248
  bond acts, 224–25, 229, 286
  East Bay Regional Park District, 250
  special districts, 246–47
California Coastal Commission, 34, 113
California Midpeninsula Open Space
    District, 232, 247
California State Coastal Conservancy, 9,
    258, 262–63, 271–72, 274–312
    passim
California Wildlife Conservation Board,
    66, 68
Canada, 85–86, 92, 103
Canadian Wildlife Service, 86
Capacity grants, 185–86, 187
Cape May, New Jersey, 33–34
Capital gains taxes, 25–26
Carbin, Richard, 305
Case, Leland and Joan, 73

Central Maryland Heritage League, 200
Central Vermont Community Land Trust
    (CVCLT), 177, 178
Certificates of participation (COPs), 234–
    36
Chaco Culture National Historic Park,
    111–12
Chafee, John H., 11, 158
Champlin Foundations, 155, 157, 159,
    166
Charitable donations of land, 107–109
  tax deductions for, 24, 192
Cheehaw-Combahee Reserve, 100
Chester County, Pennsylvania, Committee
    to Save Open Space, 211
Chevron Corporation, 137
Chicago, Illinois, Openlands Project, 209–
    11
Cibola National Forest, 64
Cigarette taxes, 243
Citizens of Fairfield, 248
Citizens to Save the Cache River
    (CCSCR), 93–94
Civilian Conservation Corps, 171
Clarity to avoid misunderstandings, 36,
    141
Clark, Story, 199
Cleveland, Ohio, 66–67
Clinton Community Gardens, 75–76
Colorado, 10–11
Columbia Gas Transmission Company,
    250–51
Communication between partners, 36,
    165–66, 193–94
Compact of Cape Cod Conservation
    Trusts, 202–203
Conanicut Island Trust, 156
Conflict resolution by nonprofits, 26–27
Connecticut, 211
Connecticut Department of Environmental
    Protection, 65
Connecticut Recreation and Natural
    Heritage Trust, 262–63
Consensus for action, building, 9, 163–64
Conservation easements, 66–67, 90–91,
    153, 159, 161, 168, 285

encouraging donations of, 182–83
farmland preservation and, 45–49, 51, 54
Farrell Farm, Vermont, 176
land trusts as facilitators of, 206–207
National Park Service and, 114, 115, 117, 119, 124–25
Smith Farm, Vermont, 177
Webster property, 47–48, 49
Conservation Foundation, 159
Conservation Fund, 108, 111, 112, 159, 251
Consumnes River valley, California, 89–90
Contributions, *see* Charitable donations of land
CSX Corporation, 133
Cuyahoga Valley National Recreation Area, 116
Cypress Creek National Wildlife Refuge, 94

Dade County, Florida, 226
Davis, George, 162
Dedication programs, 39
Dehart, Grant, 292–93
Delaware, 225, 242, 251
Greenspace Program, 230
Delaware Land and Water Conservation Trust Fund, 239–40
Delaware Land Protection Program, 264–65, 270
Denver Urban Drainage and Flood Control District, 250
Department of Agriculture, U.S., 84, 189
Forest Service, *see* Forest Service, USDA
Department of Defense, U.S., 34, 84
Department of Energy, U.S., 68
Department of Interior, U.S., 23, 114, 122
Development impact fees, 252–55
Development rights, 48, 158, 161, 162
Farrell Farm, Vermont, 175, 176
purchase of, 48, 168, 178
sale of, 53, 181
transfer of, 51–52, 112

valuation of, 189–90
Dingell-Johnson trust fund, 245
Direct government funding of nonprofit land protection, 258–312
accomplishments and benefits of, 281–93
advocating, designing, and implementing a successful program, 302–12
issues and solutions, 293–302
overview, 261–70
structure of programs, 270–81
comparison of programs, 276–81
proactive model, 274–75
reactive model, 275–76
Donations of land, *see* Charitable donations of land
Donnolley, Gaylord and Dorothy, 96
Douglas Manor Environmental Association, 70
Dow Chemical Company, 89
Ducks Unlimited, 4, 21–22, 88–96 *passim*, 100, 102–103
Dutchess Land Conservancy, 217
Dutch Harbor, Rhode Island, 154–57

Easements, *see* Conservation easements
East Hampton, Long Island, 30–31, 208
Economic reasons for partnerships, 28–30
Education, partnerships for, 92–93, 132, 308
El Centro Español, 76
Eminent domain, 26, 153, 160
Enchanted Forest, Florida, 20–21
Endangered Species Act, 41
Endicott, Eve, 195–217
Environmental protection, land conservation as, 169
Environmental Protection Agency (EPA), 142
Estate taxes, 181
Euclid Beach Amusement Park, 67–68
Eugster, J. Glenn, 276

Fairfield, California, 248
Fairfield County, Connecticut, 64–65
Falmouth, Massachusetts, 211–12

Farmland, 168
American Farmland Trust's preservation efforts, *see* American Farmland Trust
importance of protecting wide expanses of, 43–44
in Vermont, *see* Vermont Housing and Conservation Board
see also individual properties
Farms for the Future, 193
Farrell Farm, Vermont, 175–77, 179
Federal agency partnerships, 83–145
Federal Emergency Management Agency, 142
Federal Land Bank, 54
Fee title acquisitions, 90–91, 115, 117, 124, 159, 182
Financing partnerships, 59, 67–68, 219–312
benefit assessment districts, 247–48
bonds for, *see* Bonds, long-term
bridge financing, 59–60, 67
with certificates of participation, 234–36
decline in federal funding, 224
development impact fees, 253–54
direct funding, *see* Direct government funding of nonprofit land protection
foundation grants, 200
fund raising, 83, 137, 184
government loan funds, 200–201
installment sales, 21–22, 236–38
with lease purchase contracts, 68–69, 233–34
leveraging of funds, 181–84, 190–92, 284–85
loan funds, government, 200–201
local funds, 225–26
local support for, 211–12
with lottery funds, 235, 240, 245
mitigation banks, 254–55
mitigation funds, 68, 72, 81–82, 251–52
pay-as-you-go approach to, 238–40
private philanthropy, 107–109
with promissory notes, 232
with revenue anticipation notes, 232–33
revolving funds, 199–200
role of nonprofits in, 226–27
special districts, 246–48
state funds, 224–25, 315–30
taxes, *see* Taxes
trust funds, 244–45
utilities, 249–52
First Florida Bank, 77
Fish and Wildlife Service, U.S., 4, 27, 35, 83, 85, 86, 106, 107–108, 142
North American Waterfowl Management Plan, *see* North American Waterfowl Management Plan
Florida, 10, 26, 241, 251
Alachua Conservation Trust, 20, 197–98, 201, 204, 205
Preservation 2000 Program, 230
Florida Communities Trust, 264–65
Florida Department of Natural Resources, 76
Florida Department of Transportation, 81–82
Florida Game and Freshwater Fish Commission, 254
Food, Agriculture, Conservation and Trade Act (Farm Bill), 102
Forest Legacy Program, 193
Forest Service, USDA, 4, 84, 106, 198, 199
Foundation grants, 200
Franklin D. Roosevelt National Historic Site, 119
Franklin Land Trust, 47, 49
Fund raising, 83, 137, 184

Gainesville, Florida, 197–98
Gallatin National Forest, Montana, 199–200
Garden of Union, Brooklyn, 76
Gardens, urban community, 62–82
Garthright House, 117
Gasoline taxes, 243–44
Gateway National Recreation Area, 79

General Motors, 23

General obligation bonds, 28–29

Georgia, 10, 240

Glossary, 331–37

Goethal's Bridge Pond, 66

Government:

direct funding of nonprofits, *see* Direct government funding of nonprofit land protection

federal agency partnership, 83–145

future of partnerships with government, 10–11

issues arising from partnership with government, 7–9

reasons it needs nonprofits, *see* Nonprofit organizations, reasons government turns to

reasons nonprofits need, *see* Nonprofit organizations, reasons they need government

role in preserving farmland, 44–45

Government Finance Officers Association (GFOA), 252, 253

Grand Junction, Colorado, 68

Grand Teton National Park, 107, 115

Grand Traverse Regional Conservancy, 203

Gray, Jack, 159

Graziano, Angela, 85–103

Great Rivers of America posters, 136–37

Green Acres Farm, Vermont, 182–83

Green Guerillas, 75

Green Mountain Club (GMC), 186, 202

Greenspace for Delaware Program, 225

Greenways Commission, 51

Grenell, Peter, 277, 279, 284, 296, 298

Handley Ranch, 53–56

Hardwick Farm, Vermont, 180–81

Hatchet Ranch, Wyoming, 198–99

Highway Trust Fund, 244

Hither Woods Site Park, Long Island, 30–31

Hodgkiss Farm, Rhode Island, 154–57, 163, 169

Housatonic Valley Association, 117, 118

Housing, state partnerships to provide, *see* Vermont Housing and Conservation Board

Housing Conservation Coordinators, 75

Housing Vermont, Inc., 176

Howard County, Maryland, 236–38

Hudson Greenway Council, 167

Hudson River Waterfront Conservancy, 81

Huntington Farm, Vermont, 184

Huntsville Land Trust, 70

Hutchinson, Robert, 204, 205

Hyde Park, New York, 118–19

Idaho, 240, 251

Illinois, 39

Illinois and Michigan Canal National Heritage Corridor, 210

Illinois Department of Conservation, 94

Illinois Department of Corrections, 95

Illinois Department of Energy and Natural Resources, 57, 58

Illinois Sustainable Agriculture Society (ISAS), 56–58, 60

Impact fees, development, 252–54

Independent party, nonprofits' role as, 61, 63, 65–66

Indiana, 28–29

Installment sales, 21–22, 236–38

Internal Revenue Service (IRS), 294

private activity bonds and, 230, 231

see also Taxes

International Association of Fish and Wildlife Agencies, 102

Iowa, 225, 259

Iowa Natural Heritage Foundation, 290, 296, 304

Iowa Resource Enhancement and Protection program (REAP), 264–65, 273–312 *passim*

Irvine Company, 255

Jackson Hole Land Trust (JHLT), 115, 198–99

Jamaica Bay, 79

Jenks-Jay, Nan, 301

Jewett Pond, Vermont, 183

Kaplan Foundation, J. M., 217
Kennebunk Plains, Maine, 31–32
Kies, Bill, 50, 52, 53
King, David, 310
Knight Island, 179–80

Lake Champlain Islands Trust, 179–80
Lakewood, Colorado, 234
Lancaster Farmland Trust, 60
Land and Water Conservation Fund, 11,
        106, 158, 170, 223, 224, 244–45,
        256, 258–59
    decline in funding for, 224, 239, 243
Land for Maine's Future, 32, 264–65,
        270
Landowners:
    dealing with needs of, lessons from the
        past on, 39–40
    local land trusts and, 214
    ownership and financial problems,
        nonprofits' role in handling, 66
    reasons for dealing with nonprofits, 22–
        27
Land Trust Alliance, 119, 143, 195, 205,
        215, 290
Land trusts, 69–72, 113, 123, 127, 151,
        310–11
    the capacity to do the job, ensuring,
        295–96
    increased number and effectiveness of,
        289–92
    local, partnerships of, *see* Local
        partnerships with government
    see also names of individual land trusts
Lapham, David and Elise, 158
Lease purchase contracts, 68–69, 233–34
Legacy for the Future, 225
Leveraging of funds for financing, 181–
        84, 190–92, 284–85
Lewis, Keith, 159, 165, 204, 209
Lewis, Rob, 158, 165
License plate fees, 240
Limerock Preserve, Rhode Island, 25
Little Compton, Rhode Island, 166
Little Traverse Company, 245
Loan funds, government, 200–201

Local partnerships with government, 195–
        217, 284
    capitalizing on local strengths, 205–13
    creating support for funding
        measures, 211–12
    developing community support and
        leadership, 206, 208–209
    enlisting community support for
        federal help, 209–11
    local facilitators, 206–208
    promoting local stewardship, 212–13
    efficient use of staff, 201–205
    financing, *see* Financing partnerships
    the future, 216–18
    helping to assemble capital for land
        purchases, 199–201
    lessons from the past, 213–16
    overcoming limitations of size, 196–205
    overview, 195–96
    protecting expensive land, 196–99
Lottery funds, 235, 245
Loudon County, Virginia, 133–34
Louis Harris and Associates, 12
Lowell National Historic Park, 126
Lyons Falls Pulp and Paper Company, 161,
        162, 164, 168

McManaman Farm, Vermont, 178–79,
        190
Maine, 48, 225, 228
Maine Coast Heritage Trust (MCHT), 22,
        115, 151, 202, 206–207
Management and operations, partnerships
        for, 118–19, 170–71, 193
    by nonprofits with direct government
        funding, 298–300
    role of local land trusts, 212–13
Manassas National Battlefield Park,
        114
Manhattan, New York City, 71–72
Marin Agricultural Land Trust (MALT),
        60, 238, 285, 288, 289, 290, 304
Mary Flagler Cary Charitable Trust, 72
Maryland, 48, 241, 251
Maryland Department of Agriculture, 51,
        52, 53

Maryland Department of Natural
Resources, 51
Maryland Environmental Trust (MET), 39,
200, 215, 293, 310
Maryland Land Trust Grant Fund, 266–67
Massachusetts, 48, 168, 213, 228
Massachusetts Department of Food and
Agriculture, 47, 48
Massengale, Tom, 85–103
Mather, Stephen, 108
Mellon Foundation, Richard King, 107–
108
Mello-Roos Community Facilities District,
248
Melrose estate, Natchez, 20, 109–10
Mendham Township, New Jersey, 69
Metropolitan Life Insurance Company, 77
Metropolitan Recreation Corridor Planning
Project, 143
Mexico, 86, 92
Michigan, 270
Michigan Natural Resources Trust, 245
Midpeninsula Open Space District, 232,
247
Minnesota, 225
Minnesota Environmental and Natural
Resource Trust Fund, 245
Mississippi Wildlife Heritage Committee,
231
Missouri, 88, 224, 241, 243
Mitigation banks, 254–55
Mitigation funds, 68, 72, 81–82, 251–52
Monitoring and evaluation:
of partners, 187–88
partnership approach to, 91–92
Montana, 241, 251
Montana Land Alliance, 200
Montana Land Reliance, 202
Montgomery County, Maryland, 51, 52, 53
Morrow, Don, 255
Mountains Restoration Trust, 113, 285
Mount Gilboa, Massachusetts, 64
Mt. Greylock Reservation, 213
Multiple-objective projects, 49–52
Murtha, John, 120
Myers, Phyllis, 223–312

Natchez National Historic Park, 109–10
National Audubon Society, 92
National Fish and Wildlife Agencies, 102
National Fish and Wildlife Foundation, 11,
89, 102
National Park Service, 4, 20, 83–84, 104–
28
Bureau of Outdoor Recreation, 129
the future, 126–28
Heritage Conservation and Recreation
Service, 129
lessons from the past, 121–26
the need for partnerships, 105–107
partnerships for acquisition, 107–14
buying time, 109–10
flexibility, 110–14
private philanthropy, 107–109
partnerships in park management and
operations, 118–19
partnerships with park neighbors to
protect adjacent lands, 114–18
regional partnerships, 119–21
Rivers, Trails, and Conservation
Assistance Program, 85, 129,
130–45
the future, 142–45
lessons from the past, 140–42
projects of, 131–40
technical assistance to state and local
governments outside national
parks, 129–45, 170
National Register of Historic Places, 52
National Trust for Historic Preservation,
76
National Wildlife Federation, 92
Natural Lands Trust, 117
Natural Resources Trust, Michigan, 266–
67
Nature Conservancy:
state partnerships
conveyance of land acquisitions to
states, 151, 152, 156, 184
Nature Conservancy (TNC), 4, 17–42, 83,
88–89, 90, 92, 94, 96, 100, 150,
197, 211, 245, 252, 255, 292,
296, 304

Nature Conservancy (TNC) (*Continued*)
  Bioreserve Program, 6, 35, 40–42,
    160, 167
  bond issues by, 230–32
  breadth of experience in partnerships,
    17
  economic reasons for partnerships, 28–
    30
  lessons from the past, 35–40
    communication and clarity, 36
    landowners' needs, 39–40
    permanence of protection, 38–39
    publicity, 37–38
    reliability, 36–37
  mutual conservation interests with the
    government, 27–28
  packaging of projects by, 30–32
  patchworks, 32–35
  preacquisition, reasons for, 18–26
    advance funding, 19
    auctions, 20–21
    conflict resolution, 26–27
    flexibility, 20–22
    installment sales, 21–22
    landowners' reasons, *see*
      Landowners, reasons for dealing
      with nonprofit organizations
    optioning a property, 19–20
    speed, 18
    surplus land, 22
  Ruby Valley Ranch and, 54–56, 60
  state Natural Heritage Programs, 28
  state partnerships, 152, 155–62, 165,
    166, 167, 179–86, 188, 204, 205–
    206, 212, 235, 239, 283, 284
Nebraska, 10
Nebraska Environmental Trust Fund, 11
Negotiations, nonprofits' role in, 65
Neighborhood parks, preservation of, 62–
  82
Nevada, 225, 228
Nevada Department of Wildlife, 27
New Hampshire, 48, 239
New Hampshire Land Conservation
  Investment Program, 266–67
New Jersey, 48, 228, 250–51, 259

New Jersey Audubon Society, 33
New Jersey Conservation Foundation,
  33
New Jersey Green Acres, Clean Water,
  Farmland, and Historic
  Preservation Bond Act, 11
New Jersey Nonprofit Grant Program,
  266–67
New York, 48, 225, 228, 229
New York City, 78, 206
  Operation Greenthumb, 75–76
New York City Audubon Society, 79
New York Land Program, 78
New York State Department of
  Environmental Conservation
  (DEC), 66, 161–62
New York State Garden and Parks
  Preservation, 76
Nonprofit organizations:
  bond issues by, 230–32
  direct government funding of, *see*
    Direct government funding of
    nonprofit land protection
  farmland preservation, *see* Farmland
    preservation
  future of partnerships with government,
    10–11
  issues arising from partnerships with
    government, 7–9
  preacquisition by, *see* Nature
    Conservancy, preacquisition,
    reasons for
  reasons government turns to, 4–6
    agility, 4–5
    "atmosphere of possibility," 5
    personnel, 5–6
    see also individual nonprofit
      organizations
  reasons they need government, 6–7
    landscape-scale preservation, 6
    more expensive land, 6
    move from pragmatic to
      programmatic protection, 6–7
    renewed interest in planning, 6–7
    see also individual nonprofit
      organizations

role in financing partnerships, 226–27
urban and suburban gardens and parks, preserving, 62–82
see also individual organizations
Noonan, Patrick F., 56
North American Waterfowl Management Plan (NAWMP), 9, 11, 34, 83, 85–103, 206, 303
  achievements of, 86
  board membership, 86–87
  the future, 102–103
  lessons from the past, 100–101
  objectives of, 86
  origins of, 85–86
  partnerships, 87–100
    cost-sharing, 87–88
    for education, 92–93
    functions of, 87–88
    with individuals, 91
    model projects, 93–100
    multiple strengths of, 89–91
    in research and monitoring, 91–92
North American Wetlands Conservation Act, 88, 102
North American Wetlands Conservation Council, 88, 100
North Carolina, 48
North Chickamauga Creek Greenway, 141
North Dakota, 240
Norwich Conservation Commission, 176

O'Connor, William, 295, 308
Ohio, 240
Ohio & Erie Canal Corridor Coalition (OECCC), 116
Oklahoma, 240
Old Mission Conservancy, 203
Olin Foundation, Spencer T. and Ann W., 94
Openlands Project, 209–11
Optioning a property, 19–20, 63–64
Oregon, 10, 244, 251

Pacifica, California, 236
Pacific Gas and Electric, 34
Packaging of individual projects, 30–32
Packard Foundation, 207

Pappas, Cynthia, 311
Partners for Wildlife, 91
Partners in Conservation Program, 29
Patchworks, 32–35
Patience Island, 151–52, 164
Patten Corporation, 161, 162
Pay-as-you-go approach to financing, 238–40
Peconic Land Trust, 208
Peninsula Open Space Trust (POST), 247, 284, 289
Pennsylvania, 48, 120, 240
Pennsylvania Game Commission, 21
Percy, Charles, 210
Permanence of protection, 38–39
Petersburg Battlefield, 112
Petrified Forest National Park, 108–109
Petrillo, Joseph, 304
Pheasants Forever, 291
Pioneer Valley, Massachusetts, 46–47, 59
Pitkin County, Colorado, 226
Platte River Whooping Crane Maintenance Trust, 252
Poconos Wetlands, 21
Poole, William, 61–82
Poor Mountain, 29–30
Potomac-Heritage Trail, 134
Prairie Habitat Joint Venture, 90
Preacquisition, 48–49
  financial participation by local land trust partners in, 48–49
  by Nature Conservancy, *see* Nature Conservancy, preacquisition, reasons for
  written agreement for, 48
President's Commission on American Outdoors, 62
Priorities, setting, 188–89
Private activity bonds, 230–32
Promissory notes, 232
Promotional aids, 136–37
Providence, Rhode Island, 249–50
Prudence Island, 212–13
Prudence Island Conservancy, 213
Prudential Insurance Company, 23, 72
Pryor, Caroline, 207

Publicity and public announcements, 37–38, 132, 165–66
Purchase of development rights (PDR), 48, 168, 178

Quill Lakes, Saskatchewan, 90–91

Rails-to-Trails Conservancy, 143
Real estate transfer taxes, 241–42
Redwood National Park, 107, 108
Regional Affordable Housing Corporation, 188
Regional partnerships, 119–21
Reliability of partners, 36–37
Remainder interest, 177–78
Research, 91–92
Resolution Trust Company, 42
Revenue anticipation notes, 232–33
Revenue bonds, 229–30
Revolving funds, 199–200
Rhode Island, 154, 200–201, 212, 226, 228, 259
Rhode Island Agricultural Lands Preservation Commission, 156, 157
Rhode Island Audubon Society, 155, 158
Rhode Island Department of Environmental Management, 155, 158, 166, 272, 292
Rhode Island Open Space and Recreation Grants, 268–69, 272, 274–312 *passim*
Richmond National Battlefield Park, 116–17, 123
River Network, Inc., 143
Riverside, California, 65
Rockefeller, John D., Jr., 107
Ruby Valley Ranch, Nebraska, 53, 58–59, 60
Rust, Audrey, 275, 291
Ruth Mott Fund, 57

Sacramento River, California, 35
Salem Maritime National Historic Site, 120–21
Sales taxes, 224, 226, 241, 242–43
Salmon Creek, Washington, 63–64

San Bruno Mountain, California, 65–66
San Francisco Bay Area, 82, 247
Santa Barbara County, California, 34
Santa Monica Mountains Conservancy, 262–63
Santa Monica Mountains National Recreation Area, 112–13
Saskachewan Wildlife Federation, 90, 91
Save the Redwoods League, 107, 108
Scenic Hudson, Inc., 119
Schaefer, William Donald, 51
Seattle, Washington, 74, 251
Seattle Yacht Club, 74
Seelig, Gus, 283
Sempervirens Fund, 301
Sequoia National Park, 108
Service Corps of Retired Executive (SCORE), 184
Shared equity agreements, 53
Shared Housing for Rural Elders (SHARE), 177, 178
Shumann Foundation, John and Florence, 80
Smith, Walter, Vermont farm of, 177–78
Snohomish-Arlington Centennial Trail, 139–40
Society for the Preservation of New England Antiquities, 154–55
Society for the Protection of New Hampshire Forests, 135, 151
Soil Conservation Service, 95, 142, 189
Solano County Farmlands and Open Space Foundation, 248
Somerset County Rails-to-Trails Association, 133
Sonoma Land Trust, 289, 304
South Carolina, 240
South Carolina Development Board, 99
South Carolina Waterfowl Association, 99
South Carolina Wildlife and Marine Resources Department, 96
South Florida Water Management District, 232–33
Special districts, 246–48
Splitting of parcels, 64
Staffing, 5–6, 201–205
Stanley Works tool company, 117

State financing of conservation efforts, *see* Bonds, long-term; Financing partnerships, state funds

State partnerships, 4, 147–94
consensus for action, building, 163–64
creating relationships with the private sector, 164
direct funding of nonprofits, *see* Direct government funding of nonprofit land protection
financing, *see* Financing partnerships
to preserve land and provide housing, *see* Vermont Housing and Conservation Board
to preserve open space, 149–71
evolution of state/private partnerships, 150–53
the future, 168–71
lessons from the past, 163–67
in practice, 153–62
see also individual states
Statutory funding of nonprofits, *see* Direct government funding of nonprofit land protection
Stewardship, *see* Management and operations, partnerships for
Stillwater National Wildlife Refuge, 26–27
Streeter, Robert G., 88
Stronghold, Inc., 50
Suffolk County, New York, 226
Sugarloaf Citizens Association, 50
Sugarloaf Farm, Maryland, 49–53, 58–59
Surplus land, ability to sell, 22
Sustainable agriculture, 6, 56–58, 59
Swapping of property, 25

Tampa, Florida, 76–77, 81–82
Tampa/Hillsborough County Historic Preservation Board, 76
Taxes, 192
advantages to landowner of dealing with nonprofits, 22–26, 192
bargain sales and, *see* Bargain sales
capital gains, 25–26
corporate dissolution for saving of, 66
estate, 181

remuneration of owners of farmland through, 45, 59
sales, 224, 226, 242–43
special, to finance partnerships, 240–44
utility surtaxes, 249–50
Technical papers, 137–38
Telegraph Hill, San Francisco, 67
Tennessee River Gorge, 213
Tennessee River Gorge Trust, 213
Tennessee Valley Authority, 142
Thompson, Edward, Jr., 43–60
"300 Committee," 211–12
Toxic cleanup funds, 68
Training of partners, 188
Transfer of development credit (TRC) system, 113
Transfer of development rights (TDR), 51–52, 112
Transportation policy, 169
Traver, Tim, 208–209, 291
Travous, Kenneth E., 235–36
Tripartite Agreement, 86
Trustees of Reservations, 47, 151
Trust for Appalachian Trail Lands, 113–14, 117
Trust for New Hampshire Land, 239, 270
Trust for Public Land (TPL), 4, 20, 61–82, 110, 113, 140, 150, 197, 206, 251, 254–55, 284, 296
founding of, 61
funding of, 61
the future, 79–82
lessons from the past, 77–79
local land trusts in public/private partnerships, 69–72
model projects, 72–77
National Land Counselor Program, 69
neighborhood parks and urban community gardens, preservation of, 62–82
private partnerships, local governments' need for, 62–69
assembling a critical mass, 64–65
assembling and splitting of parcels, 64
cost sharing among multiple agencies, 64

Trust for Public Land (TPL) (*Continued*)
  creating a possible atmosphere, 65
  easements, 66–67
  financial and legal needs of
      landowners, 66
  financing, 67
  help with negotiation, 65
  independent party, 65–66
  lease purchase agreements, 68–69
  leveraging of corporate and
      foundation funds, 67–68
  limited development, 69
  mitigation funds, 68
  option pending a bond act, 63–64
  options to bring out votes, 64
  tax savings through corporate
      dissolution, 66
  timing of transactions, 63
  toxic cleanup funds, 68
  role as independent third party, 61, 63,
      65–66, 69, 77
  state partnerships and, 151, 165, 167,
      205, 236, 239
  watershed protection, 6
Trust funds, 244–45
Tucson, Arizona, 73–74
Tudor City, New York City, 70
Turf issues, 7–8
Turner, Ted, 23
Twaits, Alan, 50, 52, 53
Twin Pines Housing Trust, 176–77

Uniform Relocation Assistance and Real
      Property Acquisition Act, 111
Union Camp Corporation, 23
Updike, Jerry, 85–103
Upper Valley Land Trust (UVLT), 175,
      176, 177, 181–82, 184, 188, 202,
      208–209, 291
Urban community gardens, 62–82
U.S. Sprint, 251
Utilities, 249–52

Vanderbilt Mansion National Historic Site,
      119
Vermont, 259

Act 200, 287, 288
Vermont Conservation Lands, Inc., 193
Vermont Department of Agriculture, 184,
      188, 189
Vermont Department of Fish and Wildlife,
      183
Vermont Department of Forests, Parks,
      and Recreation, 179, 180
Vermont Division for Historic
      Preservation, 178, 179
Vermont Housing and Conservation Board
      (VHCB), 173–94, 202, 272–75,
      284, 299
  funding of, 174
  the future, 192–94
  guiding principles of, 173–74
  lessons from the past, 188–92
  partnerships, 175–88
    to build organizations, 185–88
    to leverage funds, 181–84, 190–91
    to preserve land and promote
        affordable housing, 175–78
    to preserve other resources, 178–79
    to promote speed and flexibility, 179–
        81
    to share and expand protected
        ownership, 184–85
  staff of, 174
Vermont Housing and Conservation
      Coalition, 172, 192
Vermont Housing and Conservation Trust
      Fund, 268–69, 272–312 *passim*
Vermont Land Trust, 151, 177, 178, 179,
      180–81, 188, 193, 204, 300, 305
Vicksburg National Military Park, 111
Virginia, 10, 29–30
  Coast Reserve's barrier islands, 417
Virginia Park and Recreational Facilities
      Bond Act, 11
Virgin Islands National Park, 107

Wallace Genetic Foundation, 52
Wallop-Breaux trust fund, 245
Walters, William C., 130
Washington, 10, 48, 239, 251
Washington, D.C., 80

Washington Wildlife and Recreation
  Coalition, 10
Waterfowl, *see* North American Waterfowl
  Management Plan
Water Quality Incentive Program, 102
Watt, James, 210
Webster, Paul, 47–48
Weir Farm, 64–65
West Palm Beach, Florida, 232–33
West Side Community Garden, Inc., 71–
  72
Westvaco, 98–99
Wetlands, 85, 231–32
  on Handley Ranch, 53, 54, 55
  see also North American Waterfowl
    Management Plan
Wildcat Brook, New Hampshire, 135–
  36
Wildlands Conservancy, 21, 22
Wildlife Conservation Board, 292
Wildlife Habitat Canada, 90

Williams Island, 213
Williamstown Rural Lands Foundation,
  213, 301
Wilson, Pete, 286
Winakee Land Trust, 119
Wisconsin, 29, 225, 228, 251
Wisconsin Stewardship Program, 29, 268–
  69
Wislocki, George, 203
Wood-Pawcatuck River system, Rhode
  Island, 134–35
Wooley, James B., Jr., 291
Woolmington, Rob, 283
Working Land Fund, 184

Xerox Corporation, 134

Yale University School of Forestry and
  Environmental Studies, 80

Zoning, 44, 45, 150

About the Contributors

Robert L. Bendick, Jr., has headed the natural resources programs within the New York State Department of Environmental Conservation since June 1990. Prior to coming to New York, he was director of Rhode Island's comprehensive environmental agency for eight years, during which time he participated in many land conservation partnerships. He twice chaired the Committee on the Environment of the New England Governor's Conference. He is currently chairman of the Northern Forest Lands Council, studying strategies for protecting the northern forests of New York and New England.

Christopher N. Brown has spent fifteen years in the conservation field, holding positions in the public and private, nonprofit sectors, as well as being active as a volunteer. He is currently deputy chief of the Recreation Resources Assistance Division in the National Park Service, where he has responsibility for programs in Rivers, Trails, and Conservation Assistance, Federal Surplus Property, State Comprehensive Outdoor Recreation Planning, and Recreation Planning Assistance to Military Bases. Mr. Brown is the former chief planner for the Appalachian Trail for the National Park Service and was conservation director, vice-president, and executive director of American Rivers, Inc., the nation's leading river conservation organization.

Warren Lee Brown is a program analyst in the National Park Service's Division of Park Planning and Protection in Washington, DC, where he coordinates policy reviews of general management plans, boundary studies, and studies of potential new parks in the NPS's Southeast and Southwest regions. He wrote the National Park Service's guidelines for easements and instructions for land protection plans. He now reviews these plans for parks throughout the country that contain non-federal lands within their authorized boundaries. His work on federal land acquisition policy issues began in 1978 and includes publications such as *Case Studies in Protecting Parks*. Prior to joining the National Park Service, he was a project associate at the Environmental Law Institute and a legislative assistant to Senator

Charles McC. Mathias, Jr., of Maryland and worked in local government on land use and environmental issues. He graduated from the University of Chicago and received a master's degree in city planning from Harvard University.

Pamela M. Dennis was a grants administrator for the Vermont Housing and Conservation Board from 1989 to 1991, during which time she was responsible for the evaluation of natural area and public outdoor recreation projects. Prior to her employment by the VHCB, she earned a master's degree in environmental law from the Vermont Law School and a bachelor of science degree from Davidson College.

Eve Endicott is a former vice president of The Nature Conservancy, where she worked for fourteen years protecting land in the Northeast. A 1970 graduate of Radcliffe College and a 1973 graduate of the Yale Law School, she practiced real estate law in Boston prior to joining the The Nature Conservancy. A fellowship from the Lincoln Institute of Land Policy enabled her to undertake the editing of this book.

Angela V. Graziano is currently communication specialist for the U.S. Fish and Wildlife Service's North American Waterfowl and Wetlands Office. Prior to coming to USFWS, Angela worked for the Department of the Interior's Minerals Management Service, during which time she conducted a regional public affairs program. Additionally, she has written for the Office of the Secretary of the Interior, developing a series of communications products for the outdoor recreation initiative. Her works have been published in various literary magazines and newspapers. She received a B.A. in English and journalism from Radford University.

Phyllis Myers is president of State Resource Strategies, which assists government and private groups in developing and implementing collaborative conservation strategies that respond to the special pressures and opportunities of the 1990s. A senior associate in The Conservation Foundation's Land and Wildlife Program for fifteen years, she was a principal author of The Conservation Foundation's seminal study, *National Parks for a New Generation*, and directed the first study of state parks in twenty-five years, authoring *State Parks in a New Era*, a four-volume series on finance, stewardship, tourism, and partnerships. She has written and spoken frequently on land conservation, historical preservation, state and local conservation funding, and growth management. She has a B.A. in history and economics from New York University and a master's degree in urban and regional planning from George Washington University.

William Poole is a San Francisco–based free-lance journalist and commercial writer who writes frequently about America's public lands. His work has appeared in *Geo, Woman's Day, Motorland, California Living, San Francisco Focus, In Health, Image*, the *San Francisco Examiner*, the *San Francisco Chronicle*, and other magazines and newspapers. His chapter for this book was completed with the close cooperation and review of Trust for Public Land staffers nationwide.

Edward Thompson, Jr., served as general counsel of the American Farmland Trust from 1981 until his appointment in 1992 as its director of public policy. He has been the architect of AFT conservation real estate transactions and a legal advisor to the land trust movement for many years. Prior to joining AFT, he was director of the Agricultural Lands Project of the National Association of Counties and worked on wetlands issues as a staff attorney for the Environmental Defense Fund. He currently serves as chairman of the Montgomery County (Maryland) Agricultural Preservation Advisory Board. He graduated from Cornell University in 1971 and received his law degree in 1974 from George Washington University Law School.

Also Available from Island Press

Balancing on the Brink of Extinction: The Endangered Species Act and Lessons for the Future
Edited by Kathryn A. Kohm

Better Trout Habitat: A Guide to Stream Restoration and Management
By Christopher J. Hunter

Beyond 40 Percent: Record-Setting Recycling and Composting Programs
By The Institute for Local Self-Reliance

The New Complete Guide to Environmental Careers
By The Environmental Careers Organization

Crossing the Next Meridian: Land, Water, and the Future of the West
By Charles F. Wilkinson

Death in the Marsh
By Tom Harris

The Energy-Environment Connection
Edited by Jack M. Hollander

Farming in Nature's Image
By Judith Soule and Jon Piper

Ghost Bears: Exploring the Biodiversity Crisis
By R. Edward Grumbine

The Global Citizen
By Donella Meadows

Green at Work: Making Your Business Career Work for the Environment
By Susan Cohn

Healthy Homes, Healthy Kids
By Joyce Schoemaker and Charity Vitale

Holistic Resource Management
By Allan Savory

The Island Press Bibliography of Environmental Literature
By The Yale School of Forestry and Environmental Studies

Landscape Linkages and Biodiversity
By the Defenders of Wildlife

Last Animals at the Zoo: How Mass Extinction Can Be Stopped
By Colin Tudge

Learning to Listen to the Land
Edited by Bill Willers

The Living Ocean: Understanding and Protecting Marine Biodiversity
By Boyce Thorne-Miller and John G. Catena

Nature Tourism: Managing for the Environment
Edited by Tensie Whelan

Not by Timber Alone
By Theodore Panayotou and Peter S. Ashton

Our Country, The Planet: Forging a Partnership for Survival
By Shridath Ramphal

Overtapped Oasis: Reform or Revolution for Western Water
By Marc Reisner and Sarah Bates

Population, Technology, and Lifestyle: The Transition to Sustainability
Edited by Robert Goodland, Herman E. Daly, and Salah El Serafy

Rain Forest in Your Kitchen: The Hidden Connection Between Extinction and Your Supermarket
By Martin Teitel

The Snake River: Window to the West
By Tim Palmer

Spirit of Place
By Frederick Turner

Taking Out the Trash: A No-Nonsense Guide to Recycling
By Jennifer Carless

Turning the Tide: Saving the Chesapeake Bay
By Tom Horton and William M. Eichbaum

Visions upon the Land: Man and Nature on the Western Range
By Karl Hess, Jr.

The Wilderness Condition
Edited by Max Oelschlaeger

Wildlife and Habitats in Managed Landscapes
Edited by Jon E. Rodiek and Eric G. Bolen

For a complete catalog of Island Press publications, please write
Island Press, Box 7, Covelo, CA 95428, or call 1-800-828-1302.